Third Edition

AMERICAN MADE

SHAPERS OF THE AMERICAN ECONOMY

Third Edition

AMERICAN MADE

SHAPERS OF THE AMERICAN ECONOMY

Harold C. Livesay
Texas A&M University

PEARSON

Boston   Columbus   Indianapolis   New York   San Francisco   Upper Saddle River
Amsterdam   Cape Town   Dubai   London   Madrid   Milan   Munich   Paris
Montreal   Toronto   Delhi   Mexico City   Sao Paulo   Sydney   Hong Kong
Seoul   Singapore   Taipei   Tokyo

Editor-in-Chief: Dickson Musslewhite
Publisher: Charlyce Jones Owen
Editorial Assistant: Maureen Diana
Senior Marketing Manager: Maureen Prado Roberts
Marketing Assistant: Samantha Bennett
Production Manager: Fran Russello
Creative Art Director: Jayne Conte
Cover Designer: Suzanne Behnke
Cover Photo: ©Roger Bamber/Alamy
Manager, Visual Research and Permissions: Beth Brenzel
Composition and Full-Service Project Management: George Jacob/
    Integra Software Services. Ltd.
Printer and Binder: Courier Companies, Inc.

For permission to use copyrighted material, grateful acknowledgment is made to the copyright holders on p. 241, which are hereby made part of this copyright page.

Library of Congress Cataloging-in-Publication Data
Livesay, Harold C.
American Made : Shapers of the American Economy / Harold C. Livesay.—3rd ed.
    p. cm.
Includes index.
ISBN-13: 978-0-205-20229-4
ISBN-10: 0-205-20229-2
1. Businesspeople—United States—Biography.   2. Entrepreneurship—United States—History.
3. Business enterprises—United States—History.   I. Title.
HC102.5.A2L58 2012
338.092'273—dc22

                                                                    2011009244

1 2 3 4 5 6 7 8 9 10—V313—15 14 13 12 11

ISBN 10:   0-205-20229-2
ISBN 13: 978-0-205-20229-4

Dedication

To My Father, Who Told Me

*Horace Heidt's Pot of Gold may call and give you a thousand
dollars, but if I were you, I wouldn't count on it.
(I didn't, Pop, and you were right: Horace didn't call.)*
Compound interest works better anyway.

To My Mother, Who Warned

*When you get right down to it, life is just a question of
"Root hawg, or die!"
(Don't worry, Mother, I'm steady rootin'.)*
But now I'm groovin' too.

To My Grandmother, Who Demanded

*Enough of this dithering. What is to be done?
(Get tenure, Mom, and try to stay human.)*
I got the first one; the second's a lifetime project.

To My Grandfather, Who Said

*Son, one of the nice things about getting old is that
you can remember things any way you want, so you
might as well remember them happy.
(I'm looking forward to it, Mr. Brown.
I'll try not to start too soon.)*
It's all good, Pop.

ACKNOWLEDGMENTS

Without the encouragement of Marian Ferguson at Little, Brown, this project might have remained an idea. After an odyssey through the wondrous world of publishing, the revision project landed first on the desk of Priscilla McGeehon of Pearson Longman, who made the second edition happen. The current revision enjoyed the blessing of Charlyce Jones-Owen at Pearson.

Without Professor Alfred D. Chandler, Jr., my mentor and friend, I wouldn't be writing history in any case. My late colleague Professor Charles B. Forcey took the time and care to read the original manuscript with scrupulous attention to every line. Professor Thomas R. Dunlap, a friend for twenty-five years, did the same for the revision. I hope the extent to which I have heeded their advice expresses my respect and gratitude for their efforts.

I have over the years benefited from the kindness and generosity of more people than I could possibly list here, but among those I remember Samuel Haber, David Healey, Stephen Salsbury, Harold Woodman, Stanley Engerman, Robert Forster, and Kenneth Lockridge with particular gratitude.

In a life that brought more good fortune than any one person can deserve, I had the wondrous luck to do my graduate work in the unique program at Johns Hopkins, where I met Glenn Porter, Bob Shorthouse, Alan Tully, Peter Wallenstein, and Mary Yeager, friends of a lifetme.

Portions of the research for this book received the generous support of the American Philosophical Society, the Carnegie Endowment for International Peace, and the National Endowment for the Humanities. They provided crucial help and I am pleased to acknowledge their support.

CONTENTS

PREFACE TO THE THIRD EDITION

I came to history as a fascination early, as a profession late (first university job at 36). Perhaps for this reason I have always seen myself as a participant in and a witness of history, as well as a student, analyst, and teacher of it. To me, raised on tales of railroads, farm life, carriages stuck in mud, the wonders of the Model-T Ford, the terrors of Ohio River floods, the past seemed ever visible in the present. This perception made life more explicable and more fun, and still does, because all the things that humankind makes, uses, and discards, even the newest ones, encode tales of the past, clues to the present, and omens of the future.

I realized in the late 1970s that the notion of an independent, self-sufficient American economy ("autarky") masked an irreversible process in which markets and the agencies that competed for them intertwined globally. By the 1980s, one could see at every turn in the streets and stores proof that in the economy at least, Americans' destiny depended on decisions made abroad, by SONY and Toyota and their compatriots in the 1980s, later joined by producers in China and other "Asian Tigers." In an effort to grasp this transformation better, besides burrowing through the books, articles, and archival materials from which historians traditionally mine the past, I set out to see as much of the world as I could.

Hampered by a superficial knowledge of non-European cultures and no knowledge whatever of non-European languages, I thought, nevertheless, that open eyes could see a lot, and so it proved. Watching steam locomotives shift freight cars in China, or Mongolian herders arrive at Ulaan Bataar convenience stores on horseback and ride away with plastic bags looped to their saddles, I saw tradition and innovation mix and match in myriad ways.

At Toyota's factories, I saw that the storied "kan-ban" system kept track of just-in-time inventory for mass production by using not computers, but colored ping-pong balls to control the flow of components from supplier to assembler. I didn't need to understand *kabuki* to see that this method rooted in simple logic, not some uniquely Japanese cultural trait. The myth that the Japanese could not create but only imitate evaporated with exposure to Japanese textiles, ceramics, or for that matter, fireworks displays.

Long before cell phones became commonplace in the United States, virtually every Shanghai subway passenger had one. I didn't need to know any Chinese to see at once that this new technology would enable China to leap over one of the long-cited obstacles to its economic modernization: the lack of a communications network and the millions of tons of steel, copper, and aluminum it would take to create one. For years I had heard ignorant people—some of them supposedly experts—dismiss Red China as an economic rival on the grounds that communism had extinguished entrepreneurial drive and capacity. In the early 1990s, the first Beijing street corner I encountered, teeming with furious entrepreneurial energy, exposed this condescension as an ignorant assessment of the present, and a dangerous miscalculation of the future.

Despite these enlightening encounters and the benefits I (and hopefully others) have derived from them, from time to time colleagues have warned me to banish or, more accurately, seem to banish myself from my pages, but I have resisted. My grandfather remembered the Wright brothers' first flight and lived to see Neil Armstrong walk on the moon. His memories enriched his life and the lives of those who knew him. I have tried to do the same, and the many letters (and lately emails) received from students and faculty members since *American Made* first appeared have persuaded me to persist. I too have now lived long enough to see a lot, to remember an America without computers, in which ordinary people rarely ate out, retail discounting was against the law, few people went to the dentist except to have teeth pulled and replaced with false ones, rap meant something the cops pinned on you, and web referred to spiders' work. I have seen all that change, mostly for the better. I have seen hopes rise and fall, and rise again. Watching the demise of corporate giants once thought omnipotent and immortal, I have learned that historians have good reasons for rarely saying "never" or "always."

I have lived through at least three wars (or more, depending on the definition) and learned that war rarely produces the desired outcome for anyone, winners or losers. I remember drinking fountains labeled "whites only," and I have lived to see the first African American president of the United States. I have watched many things we thought "uniquely American" proliferate as others embraced them and mastered them, for better or worse.

In the pages that follow, then, readers will find me as participant, witness, analyst, and perhaps if all goes well, as teacher. I hope readers will find it all, as I do, part of Life's Great Pageant.

WHAT'S NEW IN THE THIRD EDITION

As this book analyzes several American businesses and their managers and includes a number of multinational enterprises that operate today (e.g., Ford Motor, Dell Computer, McDonalds, Walmart), the revision embodies significant changes based on extensive research in the United States and abroad. These changes update the work with regard to developments since the previous revision (2005).

Chapter 1: Updates the discussion of the contents of the chapters to follow.

Chapter 2: Discusses changes in the automobile industry in the past 20 years. Draws parallels between U.S. and Japanese manufacturing.

Chapter 3: Expands discussion of the role of agriculture to show its continuing and currently increasing relevance.

Chapter 4: Discusses the relevance of Carnegie management methods to steel and other industries outside the United States.

Chapter 5: Contextualizes Edison's methods and impact in the light of modern inventor/entrepreneurs such as Edwin Land, Sergey Brin, and others.

Chapters 6 and 9: Revises the story of the Ford Motor Company in the context of the changing global automotive industry, as well as the company's decline and resurgence between 2000 and 2010.

Chapter 7: Updates the history of Du Pont to reflect recent changes.

Chapter 8: Contrasts the continuing viability of Alfred Sloan's principles of management in the United States and abroad even as his erstwhile company, General Motors, declined into bankruptcy.

Chapter 10: Adds a discussion of Steve Jobs and relates Jobs's career to that of Edwin Land.

Chapter 11: New in the 2005 edition, the revision now brings the Dell, McDonald's, and Walmart stories up to date (as of 2010).

Chapter 12: New conclusion melding new and previous summaries.

Also updated **Index** and **Note on Sources**.

Chapter 1

Introduction

I n 1978, for the original version of this book, I wrote in and of an America that manufacturing had made, literally and figuratively. I wrote in Vermont, in a converted one-room schoolhouse overlooking a dairy farm. The hayfields, the cows gleaning them, the barns, and the machinery fitted together like tiles in the mosaic of agricultural self-sufficiency that underlay American prosperity since the first few starving years in the colonies. Nestled in a stunning mountain valley deep in rural New England, this farm nevertheless exemplified the importance of science, technology, and manufacturing to every facet of American society. Its very existence depended upon science, embodied in breeding and inoculating the cows, fine-tuning their feed mixes, and testing the milk, as well as upon an arsenal of equipment: tractors, manure spreaders, hay balers, feed mixers, conveyor belts, milking machines, storage facilities, testing equipment, and on and on.

The farmers themselves, though dimly aware of a time gone by when such equipment didn't exist, could no more imagine doing without it than they could imagine their windows without glass, or their lives without an automobile. In 1978, these Vermont farmers, like virtually all Americans then and since, lived and expected to live in a world of high consumption, mechanized comfort, and entertainment, sustained by access to a factory-made cornucopia of things readily found at stores and in catalogues, at an intersection of good quality and low prices.

The notion of consumption as a routine part of daily life has so deeply interwoven the American fabric that those who do not or cannot engage in it—the homeless, the mentally ill—find themselves consigned to the margins of American society. Charity shops such as those of the Salvation Army or Goodwill Industries serve many purposes, not least of them enabling economic (and thus social) participation by providing jobs for some people who otherwise would have none and selling goods to some customers who otherwise could not afford them.

Since colonial days, the core American religions have defined prosperity as proof, rather than a contradiction, of worthy life. "As soon as ever a man begins to look toward God and the way of his Grace," said the Reverend John Cotton, a pillar of early New England Puritanism, "he will not rest 'til he finds out some warrantable calling and employment." His grandson, Cotton Mather, declared, "Would a man *Rise* by his Business? I say, then let Him Rise to his Business. . . . Let your *Business* ingross the most of your time." The Quaker William Penn urged diligence as "the Way to Wealth." *"The diligent Hand makes Rich,"* he declared; moreover, diligence coupled to frugality offered a "better way to be rich," for it led to a more peaceful life, with "less Toil and Temptation."

In 1978, Americans prided themselves, as Americans had since the late nineteenth century, that these "things," as well as the people who invented them, the factories that produced them, and the outlets that sold them all bore the label "Made in the U.S.A." By then, however, plenty of evidence existed for those who could see that beneath that perception, reality had changed. Japanese and German cars proliferated even as American cameras, for example, gradually disappeared. Gloomy pundits loosed a spate of books and articles predicting dire consequences looming in the Japanese economic ascendancy, a threat now largely forgotten or, more accurately, now perceived in a different quarter: China.

As an optimist, I found it hard to take these forebodings seriously; as a historian of American business, I thought them flawed by an ignorance of the past (a chronic problem with pundits, especially in the field of business analysis). It, therefore, appealed to me to write a book that focused on the construction of the American industrial economy and some of those who built it. From the array of possibilities, I chose manufacturers for reasons both personal and professional. Born into a family of factory and railroad workers, I had my share of pride in American creativity and productivity (and had swallowed a dose of the macho nonsense with which society coated blue-collar tedium as a sweetener). In addition, I shared with Andrew Carnegie a preference for people who "made things" such as steel over those who generated "bits of paper."

Professionally, I favored manufacturers because the centrality of factory-made goods to American life formed the core around which ancillaries such as finance, transportation, and distribution arrayed themselves. In addition, most Americans had long accepted the notion that science and technology, especially the homegrown variety, had facilitated the country's rise as an industrial powerhouse. I knew, however, from both personal business experience and research in business history that whatever scientists and engineers might dream up mattered little until manufacturers turned it into a product that people bought.

Above all, from any viewpoint, the American reality stemmed from the ability, past and present, to mass-produce and mass distribute. In 1978, most of the production had taken place and took place still in the United States itself, so I felt comfortable writing a book about some American businessmen, their impact on the country, and the country's influence upon them. From the host of actors who had played the businessman's role in America's past, I chose a particular cast that shared a common trait: they manufactured things, and the things they made, or the way they made them, became part of the kit of tools used, first to carve American civilization out of the continent's wilderness, and then to construct the world's most powerful economy.

One could easily and literally see that business had shaped America's past and present. In the seventeenth and eighteenth centuries, churches and steeples had dominated the city skylines; in the nineteenth century, the horizon had silhouetted mills and smokestacks; in the twentieth century, corporate skyscrapers reigned. This visible progression of business dominance, although not uniquely American, surely enveloped American society more completely, and sooner, than elsewhere. In American cities, business shouldered aside the past to make room for its symbols of present power, spiking itself deep in the earth and high in the sky from coast to coast. With the John Hancock Building in Boston, the World Trade Center in New York, the Sears Building in Chicago, and the Transamerica Tower in San Francisco, businesses nationwide memorialized their own achievements and the values of a society that found such power congenial and reassuring. The fact that to less fortunate folks elsewhere, or to those who might follow a different creed, these symbols might evoke fear or hatred, few Americans knew, and fewer still cared until September 11, 2001, when the World Trade Center towers collapsed into blazing funeral pyres.

In other societies, business, retarded by the state of economic development, or constrained by different sorts of ideals, often projected a lower profile. Cities served as pedestals for monuments to the past—the Acropolis in Athens, Palatine Hill and St. Peter's in Rome, the Sacré Coeur and the Louvre in Paris—or furnished settings for symbols of cultural imperatives—the Holmenkollen ski jump in Oslo, Tivoli Park in Copenhagen, Big Ben in London, and the "Blue Mosque" in Istanbul. Vivid examples of alternatives mark cities such as Paris and Copenhagen. In these capitals of countries where businesses have long thrived, the citizens allowed the building of one skyscraper within the city limits and decided to have no more. The history of manufacturing thus offers an unpromising starting point from which to study societies such as these.

In the history of America, however, manufacturers had played a dynamic role in propelling the country from colonial dependency to world power, a role with which Americans still struggled in 1978 after thirty years of the Cold War and in the wake of the Vietnam tragedy. Other factors had facilitated the passage to prosperity, of course. The country's original economic viability had grown from the capacity of its land, the benevolence of its climate, and the industry of its farmers. (In the long run, ironically enough, clinging to vestigial prosperity may depend primarily on the same factors. A lush country such as New Zealand, with millions of sheep and cows but few factories, offers a hopeful prospect.) Other people, people who grew nothing and produced nothing, had contributed by assembling the capital needed by those who did. But, more than anything else, twentieth-century America had ridden to prosperity on a human-made river of goods.

Thus, I thought, the goods makers deserved attention, not just as builders of prosperity, but also as architects of the society as a whole. Conversely, their society had molded them as well, providing much of their mental equipment, shaping their aspirations, and inculcating some sense of moral propriety and political pragmatism. That the culture was American made a difference. Every society confronts the problem of coming to terms with its physical environment and presumably does so with a core of universal instincts among its members, but the responses vary from the furiously energetic to the fatalistically passive, a variety too great to explain solely by differences in climate and natural resources. Sweden, cold and resource poor, has made itself rich; Indonesia, warm and resource rich, remains poor. Even among societies that embrace the creed of industrialization, dissimilar answers emerge to such fundamental questions as who raises capital, how, and for what, as well as who decides what to produce, in what quantity, and how to price it.

American manufacturers' behavior formed a vital component of the country's particular response to humankind's fundamental dilemma: in the pure state of nature, every human awakens every day cold, hungry, and uncertain of living to see another dawn. The human race tightropes across the span between cradle and grave with necessities few and simply stated: something to eat, some way to keep warm, something to believe in. These requirements, so simply put, have proven achingly difficult for most societies to fulfill, but mass production, for those that have achieved it, holds the wolf, if not the demons, at bay, at least for a time. In the nineteenth century, American manufacturers made mass production the core of the business system; in the twentieth century, they forged an economy of unprecedented potency, as well as an enduring national way of life.

That said, the choices for the original version of this book came readily enough: Eli Whitney, for the cotton gin and interchangeable parts that unleashed torrents of change; Cyrus Hall McCormick, who mechanized American cereal agriculture and developed a dealer network that truly opened millions of acres in the West, thus loosing the titanic potential of free-soil agriculture; Andrew Carnegie, a legendary success story who learned cost-based management on the railroad and used it to build the largest steel company in the world; Thomas Edison, for all his wizardry, but also as the prototype of market-focused professional innovators who deride "inventions" as gadgets or as hobbies unless they sell; the Henry Fords, I and II, and Alfred P. Sloan, who by revolutionizing product development, manufacture, assembly, and marketing drove the automobile industry into its role as the central dynamic force in twentieth-century America and in much of the world by the twenty-first; Pierre du Pont, who created the archetypical management bureaucracy around the principles of cost accounting, "return on investment," and market forecasting; and Edwin Land, a scientist turned entrepreneur, whose Polaroid camera showed the potential for science-based products, driven not by the science, but by an accurate market perception.

Well and good in 1978, but almost three decades later, the world had changed in ways that touched virtually every American. Strikingly, many of the alterations involved interactions with the two most menacing opponents during the Cold War—China and Russia. "O.K.," observed the *New York Times* in 2005, "Japan Isn't Taking Over the World. But China . . . " Think tanks, economists, and essayists issued forebodings of the twenty-first century as "the Chinese Century" in the wake of the American twentieth. Indeed, the shelves of virtually every American retail outlet groaned with once-banned Chinese goods, harbingers, perhaps, of the arrival of a new order of business. Certainly China's relationship to America had mutated out of all recognition compared to the first decades after the Communists took power. In the 1950s, 1960s, and 1970s, some fools, seeing in China an ongoing "yellow peril," anticipated Chinese paratroopers dropping from the sky onto the streets of San Francisco, or troops wading ashore on the beaches of Los Angeles, never mind the lack of planes or ships to haul them across the Pacific. Instead, Communist China proved itself a paper tiger, doomed to economic failure by a regime that thought it could forge industrial might from iron smelted in backyard blast furnaces.

Within that Maoist straitjacket had lurked an enormous force ready to burst forth: the profound Chinese entrepreneurial energy and ability, on display not only in the Chinese diaspora that had built businesses on every continent, but also in the streets of Beijing itself, where virtually every corner sported enterprisers ready to cut hair, make clothes, mend bicycles, cobble shoes, and serve lunch. This entrepreneurial vigor, coupled to the savings of thrifty Chinese peasants and the vast capital amassed by Chinese people abroad, held the potential for an economic transformation. It should, therefore, have come as no surprise that when the wallop landed, it came not from Communist but from newly capitalist China, transformed as if by alchemy, or some particularly Chinese elixir, from a paper tiger into a ferocious dragon inhaling coal and iron ore and petroleum, exhaling a river of goods, and belching a miasma of pollution into the gasping streets of Beijing, Shanghai, and Guangzhou.

In the streets of Chinese cities, the once grey-clad ranks now rippled with the color and shimmer of what had become some of the best-dressed people in the twenty-first-century world. In grim contrast, through those same streets, the ever more polluted winds of change blew millions of discarded plastic bags that swirled in a calypso of modernity's promise and peril until they drifted like a never-melting snow against fences and buildings.

In the face of these changes, American dread of the communist "Red Menace" in Asia had yielded to worry about the potential impact on the price of gasoline at home if the ratio of motor vehicles to population in China (1 vehicle for every 650 people in 2005) rose to match that in the United States (5 for every 6). Dread of Chinese troops landing on California beaches had given way to anticipation of well-heeled Chinese tourists swarming the beaches of Maui. The delight in low prices attached to Chinese goods in American stores trumped the fear that American factory jobs had vanished forever into the Far Eastern mists.

Meanwhile, the American dream of reaching the vast Chinese market (embodied in the "China Clipper" ships of the early nineteenth century) had found fruition at last for a few American companies, both old (General Motors, Ford, Boeing) and new (Dell Computer, McDonald's, Walmart). Indeed, the Beijing McDonald's, opened in 1991, together with the Moscow branch (1990) had quickly become the most famous McDonald's outlets in the world, bizarrely ballyhooed by gleeful xenophobes as proof positive of America superiority.

The 1989 fall of the Soviet Union, once the heart of Ronald Reagan's "Evil Empire," produced a different outcome in Russia, a country that had effectively outlawed capitalism for seven decades with the upshot that only outlaws and foreigners knew how to work it. The startling results clearly appeared in Moscow's Red Square (around the corner from McDonald's), where the tomb of Lenin, architect of the 1917 Russian Revolution, gazes across the cobblestones at such upscale emporia as Gucci and Louis Vuitton, caterers to capitalism's glitterati, a sight no doubt sufficient to spin Lenin in his grave. The sprawling GUM building, long a cocoon of drab offices for

Soviet apparatchiks, metamorphosed into a sparkling galleria of Western shops, many of them trendy numbers such as Harvey Nichols, Burberry, and Hugo Boss, as well as more middling brands such as Levis and The Gap. These rugged capitalist paladins did as much as any nuclear arsenal or military alliance to unhorse Soviet communism (and could easily do the same if unleashed in Castro's Cuba, an unlikely scenario given that in my lifetime, self-styled "conservatives" have lauded capitalism but thought it frail, while "liberals" have felt the reverse).

Meanwhile, away from the fleshpots of Moscow and St. Petersburg, abandoned factories rotted amid clusters of idle freight cars rusting on idle tracks along six thousand miles of the Trans-Siberian Railway, casualties of the abrupt shift to capitalism, a system that few Russians understood and fewer still welcomed. Past these relics of Soviet futility rattled trainloads of Korean and Polish pipeline materials destined to carry Russian natural gas to the more agile economies of Western Europe. Russian timber, coal, and petroleum rumbled eastward to more muscular markets, especially those of China, whose booming border cities cast an ominous glow across the Amur River onto the darkling, emptying spaces of Siberia. By 2005, the United States itself had, of course, witnessed massive changes in its economic landscape. Huge businesses once deemed immortal, omnipotent, and unassailable by economists such as John Kenneth Galbraith had shown the folly of these analyses by staggering toward, and sometimes over, the brink of bankruptcy. The once-mighty American steel industry had crumpled, its titan, U.S. Steel, reduced to a fragment of the firm J.P. Morgan had built around Carnegie Steel; Bethlehem Steel, long number two, had vanished in insolvency. The American automobile industry, long the envy of much of the world, staggered under assaults from foreign competitors that it seemed powerless to resist.

By 2005, America no longer had a domestic consumer electronics industry, or a high-tech camera industry. Indeed, so deeply had the American economy intertwined with the rest of the world's that a vow to buy only goods manufactured entirely of American components amounted to a decision to buy nothing at all. On the other hand, some American firms held their own against all comers in fields such as computers and their implementation, and they had used this expertise to catalyze the reshaping of the American economy into one more balanced among agriculture, manufacturing, and service industries.

Any revision of *American Made* had to acknowledge this evolution and relate it to the theme of the original edition, a task less difficult than one might imagine, for America remained a country of high-consumption lifestyles shaped by manufacturing. Many of the factories that sustained it, however, lay elsewhere, often in erstwhile enemies such as Germany, Japan, China, and Vietnam, a shift symbolized by Walmart's abandonment of its once trumpeted slogan "We Buy American So You Can Too" in favor of an unstated policy "we buy Chinese (or Indian, or Bangladeshi, or Vietnamese) so you can buy cheap." Americans had in general accepted this proposition, despite job loss through buying abroad and "offshoring" work once done in American factories. Manufacturing, wherever it took place, thus remained crucial to American life, although factory jobs may not have.

The rise of the "service" economy had not negated but rather had perpetuated the importance of manufacturing to maintaining Americans in the style to which the past had accustomed them. Whatever elusive definition of "services" one employs, the underlying reality involves manufacturing in multiple roles. The U.S. government, for example, includes in its definition of "Service Producing Industries" the following: "transportation, communications, electric, gas, and sanitary services; wholesale trade; retail trade; finance, insurance, and real estate," and then adds the deliciously nebulous "and services." Whatever. Scratch any of these and find a mountain of machinery and machine-produced goods, for even providers of such "invisible" services as insurance require multiple factory products ranging from computers to toilet paper; no self-respecting real estate agent could function without an array of electronic gear and a motor vehicle.

To illustrate the relationship of recent change to the historical evolution of American business, I chose to add a chapter discussing three American firms: McDonald's, Walmart, and Dell Computer. These three had much in common: founded in the second half of the twentieth century in the United States and driven by the ambitions of an American entrepreneur, they grew from small beginnings, not in New York or Los Angeles or Silicon Valley, but in San Bernardino, California; Rogers, Arkansas; and Austin, Texas, respectively. From a drive-in hamburger stand, from a hick-town dime store, from a college dormitory room, by 2005, they had grown into giant corporations that ranked among the world's largest. Each had found in "globalization" (the increasing tendency for commerce to cross national and regional boundaries) an opportunity for expanded profit and a means to maintain a nonunion labor force.

Like the individuals and companies in the original *American Made,* each of these firms brought a lasting innovation to American business: McDonald's the mechanization and standardization of the fast-food industry, Walmart the concept of discount prices every day, Dell the direct sales method that eliminated intervening layers of distribution and allowed true "build-to-order" manufacturing. That these innovations seemed a natural part of daily American life testified to how deeply they had rooted in our consciousness. Their very rise to prominence exhibited both continuity with the lessons of the past, as described in the original *American Made*, and the impact of the three following decades, which these firms themselves played a role in shaping. Consider that in 1978 Ray Kroc's McDonald's had more than 4,000 "stores" in 40-odd countries but had only scratched the surface of its overseas potential; Sam Walton's Walmart had $1 billion in sales but operated in only 10 states and almost exclusively in small towns in the American South; Michael Dell, age 13, had yet to own a computer, much less build one.

Despite ups and downs at home and abroad in the 1980s and 1990s, McDonald's by 2005 had sold hundreds of billions of burgers and had expanded to operate 30,000 restaurants in 119 countries (including 1,100 "MacDos" in France, reputedly the home of gourmet food and mistrust of all things American). Its $19 billion in sales made it "only" #314 on the *Fortune* list, but its 438,000 employees (and their "McJobs") ranked #8. By technical definition a "service" company, the offspring of machinery salesman Ray Kroc in fact prospered as a global chain of factories churning out an irresistible fusillade of meat, grease, starch, and sugar in the guise of burgers, fries, and shakes, later leavened with a smidgen of more salubrious fare such as salads. McDonald's bought as well as sold in many countries, using New Zealand cheese, Uruguayan beef, and Russian pies collected through what the company called "a truly global purchasing structure" and dispatched hither and yon.

Walmart in 2005 ranked #1 on the *Fortune* global list in sales ($288 billion) and employees (1.7 million). I chose to include Walmart because it exemplified the twenty-first-century American economy in which mass distribution of factory goods, regardless of source, sustained the lifestyle. Moreover, although it exemplified a "service industry" (retail trade) business, not a manufacturing firm, Walmart operations nevertheless depended in multiple ways upon manufacturing in suppliers of the things it sold, its massive fleet of trucks, its network of warehouses, and the equipment that shifted stuff goods in and out of them.

Though a purveyor of mostly low-tech goods such as underwear, bleach, and toothpaste, the company relied on sophisticated optical and computer technologies for barcode scanning as well as data transmission and processing to achieve inventory control and track sales trends. Thus equipped, Walmart relentlessly and efficiently pursued its discount-price, low-wage, and antiunion strategy. It rode the wave of America's growing, shifting population far beyond the company's southern small-town origins into mushrooming suburbs and exurbs coast-to-coast and beyond, to Alaska and Hawaii. By 2005, it had 3,600 stores of various kinds in the United States.

Although Walmart touted itself as quintessentially American (as did many of its critics, but for different reasons), the company, like Dell and McDonald's, reflected the globalization of American business as both sellers and buyers in markets abroad. In 1991, Walmart opened two stores in Mexico City, the first outside the United States. By 2005, it had 1,600 in eight countries plus Puerto Rico. A massive purchaser abroad, its 2004 buying in China ($18 billion) and India ($1.5 billion) made it a major factor in both economies. Walmart itself said, "We source from the global market . . . from many regions such as Africa, Asia, Europe, and Latin America," a statement easily confirmed by a label-checking stroll through any Walmart store.

By 2005, according to *Fortune* magazine, Dell Computer had emerged, "by nearly every unit of measure" as "irrefutably the No. 1 company . . . in the computer hardware business . . . in the U.S." Its $49 billion in sales made Dell #84 on the 2005 *Fortune* list of the world's 500 largest corporations. Begun in Michael Dell's dorm room at the University of Texas with parts bought in Austin stores such as Radio Shack, Dell Computer in 2005 offered a prime example of an American manufacturing firm thriving in the globalizing economy by providing a deft combination of goods (computers, printers, televisions, etc.) and services (direct sales, maintenance, repair, software installation). Dell by then bought components globally, manufactured computer systems in six countries, and sold its products and services literally around the world.

Fortified with companies such as these, flourishing even as other firms such as Howard Johnson's Restaurants, Montgomery Ward, and Wang Computer had gasped their last, the American business system remained one of the best ever at supplying goods and services, necessary and otherwise. That is not to call it perfect; two of its major flaws—environmental damage and the persistence of a poverty-ridden underclass—festered stubbornly. But the very fact that these and other failings of our pluralist society sprang from economic causes reveals how deeply the business strand interweaves with the social fabric.

Businesspeople, never a race apart, did not operate in a vacuum. On the contrary, constraints obtruded at every turn—their own conception of what was legitimate and possible for them personally; their education; their estimate of public reaction to their activities; their desire to perpetuate their families' control of the business they built; the limitations and possibilities presented by existing laws; the prospect of government help; the fear of government interference; the obligation to answer to stockholders; and above all, the vagaries of a fluctuating, unpredictable, uncontrollable market, lately intensified by the globalization of that market. All these factors applied as much in 2005 as they had in 1905, as much to Michael Dell as to Thomas Edison.

The complexities of the American market largely resulted from the very prosperity of the country itself. Americans in growing numbers found they could afford things they wanted, not just things they needed. The luxury of indulging laziness or aesthetic tastes, of satisfying a craving for convenience or dissipation, hitherto the realm of the rich, over time came within reach of much of the American population. So much disposable current income, coupled to the American penchant for expecting even better times ahead, constituted an enormous potential market that businesspeople found ways to stimulate into immediate demand. Through advertisements and credit sales, they convinced the public to define yesterday's luxuries—color television sets, microwave ovens—as today's necessities, that the many could live now as only the rich had lived in the past, and that they had a right to do just that.

In a country dedicated to progress, largely defined in material terms, the proliferation of goods seemed moral, and those who made it possible seemed great benefactors. In 1888, Charles Elliott Perkins, president of the Chicago, Burlington, and Quincy Railroad asked:

> Have not . . . great manufacturers, great inventors, done more for the world than preachers and philanthropists? . . . Can [anyone] doubt that cheapening the cost of necessities and conveniences . . . is the most powerful agent of civilization and progress?

And answered:

> History and experience demonstrate. . . . [m]aterial progress must come first and . . . upon it is founded all other progress.

To a remarkable degree, Perkins's fellow citizens agreed with him and always had, contributing to the creation of a market in which Adam Smith's well-informed buyers and sellers jostled with unscrupulous producers and uncritical customers. In the "Great Barbecue" that ensued, most people got what they needed, many what they wanted, and a few what they deserved. The wicked often prospered, virtue sometimes found scant reward, and the innocent frequently suffered. Through it all, prosperity remained the goal of Americans from the top of society to the bottom. When asked, "What is it labor wants?" Samuel Gompers, first president of the American Federation of Labor, philosophical and organizational father of modern American organized labor, answered with a word no capitalist, however greedy, could have improved upon: "More," said Gompers, "more, more, more."

Businessmen's conduct, past and present, laudable or otherwise, has always reflected a complex interaction between themselves and their culture, not simply their own will, exercised unrestrained in pursuit of power and profit. For example, industrialization American style involved a disregard of life and limb that killed and maimed thousands of workers. But that fact says something not only about those who presided over the carnage, but also about a society that lionized the "Captains of Industry," financed them, and worked for them, while rationalizing casualties as "the price of progress" and smoke as "the smell of money." Industrialization drove some people to despair, some to rebellion, and some back to the old country, but most Americans tolerated it in hope of a better life for their children, if not for themselves. Although the worst abuses lasted a short time compared to the grim centuries of most human experience, they eventually ignited a reaction strong enough to propel labor unions such as the American Federation of Labor and government agencies such as the Food and Drug Administration, institutionalized evidence of public outrage, into the economic system to counterbalance corporate power.

In recent decades, critics of business have taken different, but equally revealing, tacks. Business, they say, has destroyed consumer sovereignty with an advertising blitzkrieg, enabling it to fob off on the mesmerized public a massive array of trashy, tasteless products that exhibit the short life expectancy and disgusting sameness of maggots on a cadaver. Dinner at McDonald's, eaten while squirming around in polyester pants from Walmart, followed by an evening watching television while the kids revel in computer-game mayhem on their Dell, can heighten anyone's receptivity to this critique. Undeniably American business will serve up pretty much anything that people will buy, and it certainly spends lots of money trying to make sure they buy plenty, but the power to produce goods (even shoddy goods) and mold opinion (even by willful deceit) adds up to something less than the power to dictate to the market.

In fact, the market has done much of the dictating throughout American history. It has provided a commercial polling place where sellers campaigned and buyers voted. Consumers rejected the Edsel and Apple's Lisa, denounced Windows Vista, but embraced the Mustang and the Macintosh and flocked to Windows 7. Just as in the political arena, the commercial hustings accommodated knaves as well as knights, the tawdry and the sublime, the garish and the comely; for free enterprise, like democracy, counted on the wisdom of the people to sort things out eventually. The Americans themselves have always cherished their rights at both polls, including the right to be lazy and ill informed and to go for tinsel instead of substance if they so chose.

That imperfections resulted no one could deny, but Americans generally have judged the market mechanism as Winston Churchill judged democracy, "the worst alternative, except for all the others," and they often bristle at paternalistic tampering with it. Informing the public is one thing—no one wants to buy children's pajamas fireproofed with carcinogens. Telling buyers what to do with the information is something else again. American consumers sometimes reject legislative intrusion in the market as an unwarranted restriction on individual liberty—witness the stubborn resistance to mandatory motorcycle helmet laws. As long as these attitudes persist, the market—the sum of individual consumer preferences, not some mystical "force of history"—will, for better or worse, prescribe what is produced, including, no doubt, massive doses of drivel, dross, and nitrate-laden frankfurters.

On the other hand, by 2005, technology had empowered the market as never before. The growing millions of Internet shoppers, armed with Dell and other computers and roaming the electronic marketplace, heralded a new age of informed consumer sovereignty, dictating higher standards of price and quality, and providing an expanded customer base for nimble website practitioners such as Amazon.com. (Indeed, in 2005, *The Economist*, arbiter of global trends, declared in "Crowned at Last: A Survey of Consumer Power," that "the digital marketplace has made . . . the customer . . . king.")

Technology also bolstered critics of business behavior and mass taste (both critiques surely valuable and legitimate). Popular demand and business's eagerness to supply it have long offended detractors such as turn of the (twentieth) century sociologist/economist Thorstein Veblen, who coined the term "conspicuous consumption"; economist John Kenneth Galbraith, whose 1958 book denounced *The Affluent Society*; and consumer advocate Ralph Nader, whose publication of *Unsafe at Any Speed* in 1965 doomed the Chevrolet Corvair to extinction and catalyzed the automobile safety revolution. That critical tradition lived on, bolstered, like consumer knowledge, by the Internet where in 2005 one found watchdog websites such as <McSpotlight.org>, <walmartwatch.com>, and <computergripes.com/dell>, attacking issues of environmental abuse, quality, nutrition, labor practices in the United States, exploitation of sweatshop labor abroad, and the like. These assaults reflected the continued interplay of cultural and economic imperatives in the marketplace, a process that far outran, in terms of material wealth, the palmiest expectations of its advance men, Adam Smith and Alexander Hamilton.

However much critics of the American economic system might demonstrate that wealth does not necessarily bring happiness, American businessmen through most of the country's history operated in a culture where the opposite assumption prevailed. ("First feed the face," snarled lyricist Berthold Brecht, "then let the talk begin.") Most Americans welcomed industrialization because it lessened their dependence on the mischievous, unpredictable Europeans; boosted farm productivity; exploited natural resources other than land; and generated wealth even faster than agriculture. Machines, moreover, had a quality that promised to provide jobs and goods in mind-boggling quantities: machines can reproduce themselves; the land cannot.

As masters of the new mechanized systems of production, manufacturers found themselves appointed chief caretakers of the American dream of universal prosperity and happiness. In this position, they were admired, excused, encouraged, and given free rein as long as times remained good or hopes high. In bad times, when despair prevailed, they found themselves accused, reviled, restricted, and regulated. As long as "all was well, because all got better" (in the smug words of Andrew Carnegie), their most casually uttered absurdities carried the weight of divine writs; when things fell to pieces, their best-informed opinions were derided as self-serving chicanery, or as the rankest nonsense. And since the very system they commanded further subdivided an already complex society into groups that perceived their self-interests as conflicting, the business elite, past and present, has often found itself damned on one side and praised on the other.

Like their predecessors in the first edition of this book, Ray Kroc, Sam Walton, and Michael Dell provided "more" and thus won the admiration and gratitude of multitudes of their fellow citizens despite controversial policies that critics claimed exploited labor and consumer gullibility. Like their predecessors, each played a central role in a crucial segment of the American economy. Each made lasting contributions to the American business system, contributions that live on regardless of the fate of their particular enterprises. Their efforts helped shape the most potent economy in history, an economy that could, at full stretch, feed and equip half the world or more.

I considered other manufacturers (Francis Cabot Lowell and Clarence Birdseye, to name two) but discarded them on the grounds of lesser historical importance, a judgment based on my reading of history and informed by my own experiences in business. I also excluded other possible categories, such as financiers (J. P. Morgan and John D. Rockefeller the most tempting) and leaders of organized labor (John L. Lewis and Walter Reuther deserve any economic historian's attention), because although I can conceive of the Carnegies without the Morgans and the Fords without the Reuthers, the reverse seems to me inconceivable. For the second edition, I debated including other service industry entrepreneurs such as Ted Turner of TBS and CNN (a fabulous character as well as a business visionary), or Jeff Bezos of Amazon.com in whose company I saw the future of retailing, but I decided against them based on the greater market penetration and popular recognition of McDonald's, Walmart, and Dell.

I've made only passing references to the role of organized labor and of government in the development of American economic society, not because I think their roles unimportant—they deserve equal time—but because big labor and big government as we know them emerged as a response to big business far more than the other way around, and I want to deal first with first causes.

Making such choices, and standing or falling by them, epitomizes the historian's craft, but the fact that I wound up with an all-white, all-male cast (and would have even if I had expanded the book's scope to include the most influential figures in realms of finance, labor, and government) reflects a salient aspect of American business history itself. In the creative and performing arts, as well as sports, women and minorities—for example, Liz Claiborne, Oprah Winfrey, Louis Armstrong, Jackie Robinson, Michael Jordan, Bill Cosby, Dr. J, Dr. Dre, Diana Ross, to name only a few—have had a transforming impact, but the cast of characters in this book reflects both my own judgment and the historical reality that when one speaks of the definers of American mass production and distribution, one perforce speaks of business*men*, and white businessmen at that. This fact may constitute a damning indictment of the system. Surely it speaks to tragedies rooted deeply in the American past, but hopefully not emblematic of the future.

All the men in the chapters that follow wielded great power, but their power stemmed from their understanding of the market and their mastery of the machine, not from the traditional preindustrial sources: land, politics, the military, mercantile trade, or hereditary privilege. None of them ever held a political office of consequence, and the few who tried cut ridiculous figures in the attempt. Most of them, however, knew presidents (and sometimes kings) intimately, often advised or controlled politicians, and some of them ruled companies with incomes and output greater than that of many countries of their times. None distinguished himself in military service, but several owed their fortunes at least partially to armed forces patronage; many dealt in products that had significant military applications, and most of them commanded echelons of managers and armies of workers bigger and more sophisticated than their military counterparts.

Only one of these could claim to be a successful merchant, and all of them engaged in activities that displaced the traditional merchant's dominant role in the economy, often destroying it altogether. Many of them, however, survived and prospered through access to mercantile capital and reliance on mercantile expertise to supply raw materials and distribute products.

In background and training, these men shared no membership in an elitist caste. Indeed, their very diversity reflected the complexity and fluidity of American society. Some were born poor (though none destitute), some rich, most neither. Some were immigrants, or the children of immigrants; some came from families long established in America. Some grew up on farms, others in cities. Some had no formal education worthy of the name; others graduated from distinguished universities. All, regardless of their families' material wealth or lack of it, had considerable cultural capital, including at least basic numeracy and English literacy, as well as a familiarity with Anglo-American traditions of law, business, and social behavior.

Some could rightly call themselves inventors or master craftsmen; some scarcely knew one end of a wrench from the other. Some built systems to manage their enterprises; others ruled personally and autocratically and belligerently resisted bureaucratization that might dampen their authority. Some worked all their lives and died in harness; some retired to opulence or philanthropy. Many traveled abroad and became internationalists; some never left the American shore; a few evinced unsavory traits of nativism, parochialism, and bigotry. Some mastered the art of being family men; some made a mess of the whole thing. A few embraced religion; most did not. Some gloried in the public's attention; others feared or despised it and retreated into reclusiveness. Some had personalities as unremarkable as dirt; others carried idiosyncrasies to the point of lunacy and used their wealth to trumpet their eccentricities across the land.

Living in America, they existed in a culture that not only tolerated such diversity but also propagated it. Inculcated with the sense that what mattered to their society was not who or what they were, but what they could do, they perceived opportunities and seized them. They, and others like them, left an indelible mark on America and cast an image that the rest of the world, whether friendly, envious, or hostile, could not ignore. "If they could," wrote one observer, "half the people in the world would start walking to America tomorrow." For some of these pilgrims, the lure might be American democracy and its tradition of individual liberties, but for most, the magnet would be what it always was: America, the land of opportunity, toward which a good part of the world *did* (and does) start walking at one time or another. These men—"the Vital Few," "the Potentates," "the Robber Barons," "the Entrepreneurs," "Movers and Shakers," "Masters of Enterprise," or whatever collective title one gives them—built and ran the dynamos that energized the American magnet.

This summary, which concluded the second edition of *American Made* in 2005, remains valid five years later. Events since then, however, have supplied a fresh perspective from which to evaluate the long story of American business and the men who built it. McDonald's, Walmart, and Dell have all survived as powerful firms— Walmart and McDonald's topping their respective fields globally, Dell as #2 behind Hewlett-Packard. Their continued success reflects an ability to adapt their strategies to swiftly changing economic environments. All three have shown, for example, the capacity to translate criticism into market opportunity and have learned to thrive and expand in a globalizing market in which they find suppliers as well as customers.

In the five years since the second edition of *American Made*, tumultuous events have raised vexing questions about the economy of the future. The meteoric rise of China to the status of superpower has made understanding such stellar international performers as McDonald's more crucial than ever to the future of American business in the inevitably globalizing future. The global recession in the second half of the twenty-first-century's first decade has exposed the double-edged nature of technology's impact on employment, amid predictions that many of the jobs lost will never return.

The passage of time has, however, also brought more information and better tools with which to analyze it. The relentless spread of the Internet, driving toward near-universal access, has revolutionized commerce at every level, business to business, business to customer, and indeed among customers themselves. Amazon.com has built a nationwide business through Internet sales alone and seems on the path to reincarnating Sears, Roebuck, using the Internet to interact with customers as Sears once used the U.S. mail and the telephone. Potential customers have access to market information as never before, and the Internet makes coast-to-coast shopping by price comparison the task of a few moments. Auction sites such as eBay often convert the classical supply and demand ideal of a "market-clearing price" from a purely theoretical concept to a reality. News of product defects, deceptive business practices, or inadequate technical support spreads like wildfire through blogs and Internet news sources. So universally have customers learned to invoke the Internet as a shopping aid that no major retail firm can ignore it as a marketing tool any more than as a means of internal management. This electronic imperative applies not only to McDonald's, Walmart, and Dell, but to older firms as well.

Among *American Made*'s cast of characters, only Michael Dell was still alive at the time of the writing of this edition, but with the exception of Eli Whitney, all the others founded firms that in one form or another live on, offering lessons of their own. Collectively, their stories show a truth often ignored by popular commentators on the U.S. economy: government has always played a crucial role in the history of American business specifically and an indispensable role in the American economy generally. Capitalism depends on a willingness to invest; the willingness to invest depends on confidence in a future return; confidence in the future depends on stability; stability depends on confidence in the government. The failure of the Articles of Confederation government to provide the stable economic environment on which capitalism depends set the stage for the Constitutional Convention of 1787 and the property-oriented document it produced. "Property" itself (real, personal, or intellectual), one of the foundations of capitalism, in fact has no meaning except as the government defines it, as anyone who has ever bought a house, made a will, or filed for a patent knows. These and other realities of American society have meant that government's participation has expanded over time and into the twenty-first century, despite a series of presidential administrations and political commentators who denounced it and demanded its diminution.

Indeed, China's arrival as an economic power and the apparent certainty of its future growth demonstrates that there exists no inherent contradiction between capitalism and pervasive government involvement in an economy. On the contrary, one key to China's future growth lies in the regime's resolve to perpetuate its hegemony by empowering its domestic markets to complement overseas demand. On the other hand, predictions of Chinese dominance may prove premature unless the government finds ways to deal with workers demanding more, popular discontent driven by uneven progress, ethnic strife, and industrial pollution. These problems have confronted all industrial societies' governments, that of the United States included. Recent violent eruptions among the Uighurs and Tibetans, as well as a series of strikes in Chinese manufacturing plants, suggest that China will prove no exception.

As prosperity spreads, evidence proliferates that "American excess" such as conspicuous consumption has little to do with nationality or specifically American culture, and a lot to do with the ability of once-poor societies to afford extravagance. The Japanese import ice from Greenland glaciers for their upscale hotels; *nouveau riche* Russians have made Moscow a major market for Maseratis; Chinese flock to the world's largest casino in Macao, not Las Vegas; Indian plutocrats compete with million-dollar weddings for their daughters.

At a more modest level, increased disposable income in remote districts in Brazil has induced Nestle to launch a "supermarket barge" on an Amazon tributary. This floating emporium will offer discount versions of 300 of its branded goods, including chocolate, yogurt, ice cream, and juice. With 3,950 products in formats designed for low-income shoppers, Nestle hopes to compete, Walmart style, with rival giant Unilever for this and other markets that it foresees as a billion people emerge from poverty.

In Brazil and elsewhere around the world, more and more people validate one early Ford executive's observation that "Everybody wants to go from A to B sitting down." (No doubt he would find great satisfaction watching Ford Focuses zipping through the streets of St. Petersburg and passing by the boatload through the Three Gorges Dam locks on the way to the Chinese car market, soon to be the largest in the world.) Firms domestic and foreign grapple for a foothold in the largest untapped car market in the world, India.

Watching these events unfold abroad, seeing some firms succeed while others fail, underlines the enduring and universal validity of such techniques as cost-based management, inventory control, market forecasting, and the application of return on investment as the ultimate measure of success or failure. For example, Andrew Carnegie and Henry Ford obsessed as much about inventory and its costs as Walmart does, although Carnegie and Ford had less effective tools with which to control them. Eiji Toyoda, past president of Toyota Motor, told a group of American journalists that "Henry Ford, not a Toyoda, invented the kan-ban [just-in-time] system."

In recent years, studies of business have posited analytical methods that offer fresh perceptions of business past and present. For example, Harvard scholar Clayton Christensen's concept of *disruptive technology* (a new technology or a new combination of technologies that unexpectedly overwhelms an established one, often with dramatic market consequences for both new and existing businesses) applies as much to the creations of Eli Whitney, Cyrus McCormick, and Edwin Land as it does to the commercial jet aircraft, the integrated circuit, and the photocopy machine. Moreover, the ability of their founders to see the potential of such market-breaking and market-making technologies and manage them effectively does much to explain the success of Carnegie Steel and Ford Motor Company, just as it does that of Apple Computer and Amazon.com.

In the pages that follow, I have tried to meld these stories of the recent and more distant past into a coherent analysis of some key businesses and the men who built them. Today, as in 2005 and 1978, it remains true that America made these men, and they in turn did much to make America. Today, however, we can see that their impact lives on, not only here in America, but in distant lands as well.

Chapter 2

The Artist of His Country

ELI WHITNEY

Eli Whitney in 1821, weary and prosperous

ong ago, in a previous incarnation, I made my living as a yardmaster for the Pennsylvania Railroad, known in days of yore as "The Standard Railroad of the World." My domain sometimes included yards that delivered parts to automobile assembly plants of the then unchallenged automotive "Big Three": General Motors in Wilmington, Delaware; Ford in Chester, Pennsylvania; and Chrysler in Newark, Delaware. Fifty years later, all these once mighty have fallen so far as to expose as rubbish once-popular notions of corporate omnipotence and immortality, as well as polemics that argue government should and could let failing businesses fail.

All the plants my train crews serviced have closed, as have the railroad yards that served them. General Motors and Chrysler survive only by virtue of federal government intervention, deemed essential as popular belief in "Big Three" long-term infallibility crumbled into a desperate assessment of them as "too big to let fail." The Pennsylvania Railroad itself, bankrupted by its 1968 merger with the New York Central, survived first as "Conrail," a creature of the federal government, and now in myriad bits and pieces scattered among the rail duopoly of CSX and Norfolk Southern, as well as a shifting array of short lines. By any standard, federal government intervention in the American market economy has grown since *American Made* first appeared in 1978; by 2010 it had reached new highs and seems unlikely to recede in the years ahead as American business confronts global competitors that enjoy the benefits of government support as well as low-cost labor.

All these changes lay far in the future as my experience with the car plants introduced me to the practicalities (and occasional absurdities) of interchangeable parts, a notion that, before then, had existed for me largely as an abstraction. Like most Americans, I had accepted as an obvious truth the statement that our prosperity rested on mass production, and that mass production meant assembly of interchangeable parts.

Like many Americans, I thought, based on nothing more than a blinding combination of ignorance and national pride, that as a people we had mastered these concepts better than any other people had or ever would.

Behind the simply stated interdependence of interchangeable parts and mass production, there lurked a complex and frantic world, as I soon learned from the bedlamites who inhabited a crucial part of it, my opposite numbers in the transportation offices of the car companies. I discovered that the assembly line itself, "a system designed," as novelist Herman Wouk said of the U.S. Navy, "by geniuses, to be operated by idiots," is child's play next to the web of transportation and communications that keeps it supplied. The jungle of apparatus that carries the parts to the line; props them in place; welds, glues, or bolts them together; and shuttles the whole contraption through the plant pales in cost and complexity compared to the machines spawning streams of identical parts in dozens of plants far removed from the assembly process itself.

The corporations that build and run these empires of supply, manufacture, and assembly wield enormous power, creating incomes through jobs and investments and supplying the market with swarms of products. The General Motors "economy" alone, even in its current depleted state, outsells and outspends many of the countries of the world. Power so great radiated apparent invulnerability, and indeed, an installation such as Ford's River Rouge, where boatloads of iron ore, coal, limestone, and sand came in one end and trainloads of cars came out the other, seemed a juggernaut with an unstoppable momentum of its own. In fact, the powerful engine created by mass assembly of interchangeable parts is finely tuned, delicate, and easily bogged down by anything that interrupts the flow of information or material.

Parts for today's assembly schedule may sit in the plant, but tomorrow's ride the rails, the roads, and the airways somewhere between manufacturing and assembly points, while next week's may yet await fabrication. It won't do, moreover, for *most* of the bits and pieces to arrive on schedule; they *all* have to get there or everything stops. Consequently, a huge assembly plant's multimillion-dollar machinery and thousands of workers can be idled for the lack of a sack of hardware worth a few dollars.

I first encountered this reality on a July afternoon in a Delaware railroad yard. Squinting through the glare and the fog, I saw a motorized combat team from the nearby Chrysler plant assault a boxcar with a cutting torch, dragging the oxygen and acetylene hoses across the tracks to get at their quarry. By the time I got to the scene, they had fired up and begun slicing a hole in the side of a boxcar. "We need some bolts," said the foreman, by way of what he thought sufficient explanation. "If we don't get them, the line will stop in an hour."

"What about using the door?" I asked him.

"We think they're in this end and we don't have time to unload the whole car."

"What if they aren't in this end?"

"We've got a lot of gas. We'll cut 'til we find 'em."

"What about the car?"

"The hell with the car. The company'll pay for it."

"I'll call the cops. You guys can't come on railroad property unless you sign a damages release, and you sure as hell can't cut cars open regardless."

"Call the cops. Call anybody you want. By the time they get here we'll be long gone, and even if we aren't, the company'll pay the fine. It costs $40,000 an hour [in 1959 dollars, equivalent to $300,000 in 2010] to stop that line. You think the company gives a damn about a two-bit fine from a hick-town judge? We're gonna get them bolts, whatever you do about it."

What I did about it was get the railroad crew to kick a boxcar full of fenders down the track, trisecting the hoses, suffocating the torch, and sure enough stopping the line, about $80,000 worth. I hadn't thought it possible, but they really did need those bolts.

Over the years, I witnessed similar scenes many times, when a shortage of tires, batteries, nuts, bolts, washers, or cotter pins loomed. On paper, such crises couldn't happen. The system translated dealers' orders into parts requisitions, shipping manifests, and assembly schedules that crisscrossed the communications network in precise columns of Telex printouts. On paper, everything arrived on time. On the ground, however, things sometimes went haywire. Strikes, snowstorms, train wrecks, loading mistakes, sabotage, locomotive breakdowns, misdirected shipments, and a plethora of other mishaps betrayed the corporations' inability, for all their power, to make steel, rubber, and plastic march with the precision of their printed surrogates.

As I learned its fragilities, the system impressed me more, not less. Most of the time things went exactly as planned. And one thing never failed: when the parts got there, they fitted. Getting them there absorbed most of my energies, but the precision and symmetry of them excited my imagination, for that made all the rest possible and necessary. For the first time, the schoolboy textbook phrase "Eli Whitney invented interchangeable parts" transmitted a fascination commensurate with the achievement. I felt pretty close to old Eli sometimes.

Later on, when I got to college, I found out I had been even closer than I knew—just about four engineering generations away, in fact. The assembly plants I strolled through were updated variations of Henry Ford's original; Ford was the "most distinguished disciple" of Henry M. Leland, who applied the concept of interchangeable parts to the manufacture of automobiles. Leland learned the concept and the precision machine work that effected it while working in the Springfield Armory and the Colt Arms works. At Springfield and Colt, Leland apprenticed with craftsmen who had known Eli Whitney: Simeon North, Roswell Lee, John H. Hall, and other pioneers who had struggled to transform interchangeability from engineering theory into manufacturing practice.

Among these pathfinders, Whitney ranks first, but not because he originated interchangeability, perfected it, or applied it successfully to mass production; he did none of these. He did perceive identical parts as a precondition to volume production, particularly in the circumstances of the early United States. He applied his energy and genius to the problem and influenced his contemporaries and successors who addressed the same challenge. Whitney built the first arch in the engineering bridge that spanned the gulf between the ancient world's handicraft methods of production and the modern world's mass manufacturing, a bridge across which his countrymen and the rest of the so-called developed world marched to prosperity.

Whitney was a practical man, a prototype of the pragmatic American. Like many of his contemporaries, he lived by and for his ambitions, aspiring to wealth and social position. These goals and the possibility of fulfilling them drove him forward in his work, not the kind of intellectual curiosity that led Ben Franklin to fly kites among the lightning bolts. A manufacturer before he became an inventor, Whitney yoked the two roles firmly together throughout his life, inventing things to make and sell in markets that existed right then, not squandering his creativity on gadgets that might find a use some day. These qualities, the hallmarks of the entrepreneurial personality, Whitney demonstrated while still a boy, growing up in rural New England.

Whitney was born on December 8, 1765, the year the British Parliament passed the Stamp Act and Patrick Henry's denunciation of it culminated in his cry "If this be treason make the most of it." Whitney grew up on his father's farm in Westborough, Massachusetts, about 40 miles west of Boston. The town, now spelled Westboro, lies near Route 128, the belt highway that encircled Boston and along which the American computer industry first blossomed, but in Whitney's day, the lack of waterways connecting it to any urban center kept Westborough, like other landlocked American towns, a provincial outback, culturally and economically.

The Whitney farm generated little cash but provided a comfortable living for the family. But, like so many children growing up in long-settled New England, Eli knew that redividing the home place among the children would reduce them and their parents from comfort to subsistence. Even before Whitney's birth, New England farmers had encountered this bedeviling phenomenon of rural life. Successful farming required big families, but as the population expanded, land got scarce. Lacking alternatives, Americans would doubtless have adapted their aspirations to the realities of scarcity, delaying marriage as the Irish did or controlling the birth rate as the French peasantry did. In America, the open lands of the frontier offered an alternative, one that a nation of farmers could exploit. For the young people of New England, as elsewhere in America, it came down to a choice: move, or abandon the ideals of independence and prosperity that had shaped the American cultural milieu from the outset. Land shortage thus drove people from New England as surely as from Olde England. As much pushed by the harsh realities behind them as pulled by roseate visions of what lay ahead, they spilled through the mountain gaps and filled up the land along the rivers and lakes of western New York and beyond.

Preserving American materialistic ideals thus meant that American parents raised their children to leave home. This environment reinforced the attitude of independence and individualism, even among the young, and impressed European visitors such as Alexis de Tocqueville. It also injected a dynamic concept into the emerging American culture, the idea that freedom to move inherently preserved individual liberty. This notion pops up again and again in American history: as part of the enthusiasm that greeted the coming of canals, steamboats, and railroads; in the American obsession with everyone's freedom machine, the automobile; in the spirit that ennobled hoboes as "knights of the road"; and in folklore that enshrines the train whistle as an anthem of free spirits:

> *I can settle down and be doin' just fine,*
> *'Til I hear an old freight blowin' down the line*

Or as a canticle of escape:

> *Far from Folsom prison, that's where I long to stay;*
> *So I let that lonesome whistle blow my blues away.*

Whitney himself, ambitious and restless in the dead end of Westborough, ultimately joined the ranks of his peregrinating countrymen; indeed, he spent much of his life hustling from one place to another, searching for an alternative career because he detested farming, with its drudgery, isolation, and uncertainties. Whatever joy, nobility, and hope his peers found in tilling the soil and coaxing things to grow from it eluded young Eli. Like many other Americans who turned to the worlds of commerce and machinery, Whitney derived part of his impetus from the barbarities of bucolic life.

Fortunately for young Whitney, his father's farm included a workshop among its paraphernalia. There, where his father made wheels and implements for the farm, Whitney discovered a fascination with tools, particularly those that themselves shaped other tools. He also exhibited a gift not only for the manual arts required by home manufacture (then, literally, a business of "making by hand"), but also for the logic of machines that replaced human energy and physical movements. In addition, he saw how to harness these skills to produce a marketable product, and he knew a market when he saw one.

The American Revolution broke out when Whitney was 10 years old. Boston, Concord, and Lexington lay not far off; neighbors and, before the war ended, boys

Eli's age marched away to join the ranks, but neither the political nor the military excitement infected him. The market opportunity presented by the wartime interruption to commerce did, however, stir him. With British trade stopped for the duration, hardware soon became scarce. Eli, age 14, talked his father into installing a forge in the workshop. There he made nails and knife blades that sold well enough to justify hiring an additional worker.

After the war, the British dumped shiploads of nails into American ports at prices no farm forge could equal. Undaunted, Eli shifted to the manufacture of hatpins and walking sticks, a move that sounds simple in the telling, but that demonstrated a combination of initiative, confidence, and flexibility rare at any time among people of any age, but extraordinary in an 18-year-old boy in the bushes of the Massachusetts outback.

As a young man, Whitney thus met and mastered one of the harshest realities of the American marketplace: under the continuous pummeling of world events, internal migration, population growth, and technological change, the market often shifted unexpectedly. Entrepreneurs who developed a skill and equipped a shop to turn out a specific product often found, as Whitney did, that the market disappeared or became too competitive. The ability to assess such a change as temporary or permanent and to react by shutting down, replacing obsolete equipment, or shifting to a new product often determined success or failure, and determines it still. Whitney, shifting his tiny shop from nails to hatpins, exhibited the same supple survival instincts that Andrew Carnegie showed a century later, turning his giant Homestead steel works from railroad rails to structural iron beams as railroad construction dwindled and urban building boomed.

People like Whitney and Carnegie have continued to appear (as witness Steve Jobs), constantly retooling industry to meet the fickle market, supplying much of the drive that has powered American economic growth. America has had no monopoly on such flexible minds, but its society seemed to produce a disproportionate number of them, a fact thought to reveal something distinctive about the society itself. Here, as elsewhere, the dominant human tendency is inertial, a craving for stability and continuity. But American society, born free of traditional European class rigidity; kept kinetic by social mobility real and imagined, up and down; held in flux by immigration from without and migration within; its religious traditions seamlessly melded with its secular faith in materialism; and dedicated to progress, nationally and individually, has remained incessantly in motion.

Americans soothed the anxieties inherent in constant movement by convincing themselves that the special circumstances here made change the keystone of stability. Dedicated to progress, they equated movement with change, and change with improvement. Clinging to the political ideals on which the country was founded, they justified alterations in law and society as necessary to preserve the original ideals themselves. In such an atmosphere, adaptability became a virtue, and a flexible mind a mind to admire.

Movement thus encouraged movers, and the ambitious found that the rough, shifting surface of American society offered hand- and footholds not found on the smooth, unmoving class barriers of Europe. The treacherous climb could be made. Strivers persevered, spurred on by the knowledge that at the top awaited wealth and power. Success also brought admiration and acclaim from the public and acceptance into elite circles, a plum withheld by the oligarchs of Prussia, France, and England, who despised businessmen and their posterity as vulgar unless they repudiated their professions and laundered their money through propitious marriage or generations of country living.

In addition to offering great rewards for success, American society encouraged ambition by attaching little stigma to failure, even to bankruptcy. Failing once or a dozen times meant little if one had the grit to keep trying, another notion embedded in generations of American consciousness by Edward Hickson's "If at first you don't succeed, Try, try again," in *McGuffey's Reader;* by the "I think I can; I think I can" of *The Little Engine That Could;* and by the metronomic chirps of encouragement pulsing through the characters and skits of *Sesame Street* and *Mr. Rogers' Neighborhood.*

Eli Whitney had plenty of ambition. By age 18, he had considered alternative outlets for it, dismissed the farm and shop as too limiting, and decided to go off to college. That the college option even existed for a young man like Whitney in the 1780s starkly differentiated American society from its counterparts in Europe. He had no money, a rudimentary education, and had never left his home district. He was, in fact, a rube—a clever, ambitious rube, but a rube nonetheless. In America, he could surmount all these obstacles and matriculate at Yale. In England, someone in Whitney's situation in life might as well have aspired to the archbishopric at Canterbury as to the baccalaureate at Oxford or Cambridge.

A systematic man, Whitney tackled the obstacles between Westborough and Yale one by one, but it took him six years, from 1783 to 1789, to surmount them all. By teaching school in nearby towns (his father, aware of Eli's meager qualifications, expected the worst, but Eli told him that with three weeks' head start he could keep ahead of his pupils all year, a truth learned by many a novice professor), he financed summer study at Leicester Academy. There, Whitney polished his mathematics and English grammar and grappled with the intricacies of Latin and Greek. There also, for the first of many times, he became a beneficiary of the Yale old-boy network, for the master at Leicester, Ebenezer Crafts, a Yale alumnus and booster, persuaded Whitney to go to Yale rather than Harvard and helped him get in when the time came.

Whitney's diligence, together with failing health brought on by his frenetic life as a teacher-scholar, finally overcame his father's skepticism and won a promise of $1,000 in support.

In March 1789, as the first Federal Congress convened in New York City, Eli set out for New Haven, stopping for a month in Durham, Connecticut, to study mathematics with the Reverend Elizur Goodrich, professor of divinity and mathematics at Yale, and a close friend of the college's president, Ezra Stiles. When Whitney presented himself to Stiles for his entrance examination in April 1789, he came well prepared and highly recommended. The examination itself involved a five-hour oral ordeal that few of today's university faculty, let alone students, would approach with much confidence, involving as it did parsing and translating Latin and Greek, in addition to demonstrating a knowledge of the fine points of English grammar and of mathematics.

Once admitted, Whitney flung himself into his studies. Poor, and old for a freshman, Whitney had no time to waste and faced a curriculum arduous in schedule, if not in content. The school day began at five in the morning and proceeded through alternating study and class periods, with the last recitation at seven o'clock in the evening. Somehow Whitney found time to earn a little pocket money and to socialize. He fraternized successfully with his classmates, most of them from families far wealthier and more prominent than his own. His popularity paid dividends in 1791 with his election to Phi Beta Kappa, then a tribute to social, rather than scholastic, agility.

Acceptance by his peers meant a lot to Whitney, for like many subsequent graduates, he viewed Yale more as a charm school than a vocational school. He went there determined to acquire the genteel manners, dress, speech, correspondence, and general knowledge that would gain him entry to polite society. In short, he went to college to become a gentleman, accepted by other gentlemen. That Whitney could aspire to such a goal reflected another unique facet of his society. Only in America could a man not born a gentleman become one. Years later, his letters to a nephew at Yale, urging the merits of gentility, revealed the lifelong satisfaction he derived from his collegiate accomplishments, and the efforts put forth to achieve them.

He reached graduation in 1792, however, without any specific vocational objective in mind despite his father's urging that he look to the future, and carefully. "As to your profession," the elder Whitney wrote, "my advice is to look forward and count the Cost before you plan . . . and Consider your Surcomstances for I shall not be able to help you much after you are through college."

From time to time Eli, like many an undergraduate down to the present day, pondered a career at law, then as now one of America's great growth industries. Ultimately, he decided against it. (He eventually got an education in law, nevertheless, the hard way, as a litigant.) The other professions for which Yale prepared its sons— the ministry, politics, mercantile trade, and teaching—didn't interest him either. As an undergraduate, he expressed disillusionment, writing home that he found "a great many Hypocrites" among the clergy. This comment alarmed his father who, steeped in orthodox New England religiosity, urged his son to "avoid infidelity and atheism. . . . We must not . . . excuse ourselves and have no religion at all because others make a bad Use of it." The advice went unheeded; throughout his life, and after his death, the more pious among Whitney's friends and relatives feared for his salvation.

Politics he found distasteful as well, avoiding it always and keeping his opinions on the subject to himself. He had neither the capital nor the connections to secure a partnership in a mercantile house, and he certainly hadn't gone to Yale to become a counting-house clerk. School teaching he had had a bellyful of already. The profession for which, as a mechanic with a college education, he would have qualified a generation later, engineering, did not yet exist.

In the end, Whitney—poor, urbane, polished, a bit cynical ("You know I always considered this a dam'd kind of world," he wrote a friend), and, at 28, approaching middle age—had to accept a post as tutor to the children of a South Carolina planter. A tutor, Whitney lamented, amounted only to a jumped-up school-teacher; worse, he feared for his life in the unhealthy climate of the South. His first tutor and one of his classmates had died in Georgia. "Perhaps I shall lose my health and perhaps my life," he wrote his brother Josiah. On the other hand, the job paid well, 80 guineas a year, of which, he told his father, "I hope to save fifty Guineas pr. Year." President Stiles, who found the job for him, "thought it a good offer on the whole." Swallowing his fears and disappointments, Whitney presented himself to

Phineas Miller, a Yale alumnus, "a Gentleman from Connecticut, a man of reputation and abilities," and the representative of Whitney's prospective employer.

Miller himself had originally gone south in similar fashion. In 1785, General Nathaniel Greene, hero of the Revolution, had asked Stiles to recommend a tutor for the Greene children. Stiles proposed Miller. A year later, Greene died and Miller became estate manager—and a whole lot more, as we shall see presently—to Greene's widow. The similarity of Miller's background to his own, and the fact that Miller "really treated [him] like a Gentleman," reassured Whitney. He accepted Miller's invitation to accompany him and Mrs. Greene on the voyage from New York to Savannah, whence he could easily reach his destination. The voyage, and his new friends, carried him to latitudes, both human and geographic, beyond anything he had experienced or anticipated.

In Catherine Greene, Whitney discovered a woman like none he had ever known. Born and raised in the merry and cultured society of Rhode Island, Catherine moved easily in the world of silk and brocade, among men and women who sat for Gilbert Stuart portraits and talked of the latest fashions in literature, dance, and science. Catherine saw no sin in pleasure. She wrung the utmost from life and chided the sober Whitney, offering to teach him "how to enjoy the few fleeting years which any can calculate upon."

In this formidable woman, however, a facade of fluff and hedonism masked a soul of grit and sand. Married to Nathaniel Greene, Washington's most trusted lieutenant and commander of the southern armies in the Revolution, she had accompanied her husband throughout the Revolutionary War. One of her experiences qualified her for membership in an exclusive and cherished circle: she had wintered with Washington at Valley Forge. Catherine's admirers included virtually everyone worth knowing in the Revolutionary generation: Washington, Jefferson, Lafayette, von Steuben, Kosciuszko, Hamilton, and Burr. Though recently widowed when Whitney met her, Catherine had rebounded quickly. She exuded charm, *joie de vivre*, and sexuality. Smitten at once, Whitney remained enchanted until Catherine's death in 1812. An inconvenient circumstance, however, stymied his affection from progressing beyond friendship. Catherine, as Whitney soon discovered, had promoted his friend Miller from estate manager to consort. Whitney's background had ill prepared him for association with a gentleman who cohabited with a lady not his wife, but Catherine's charm, Miller's friendship, and the couple's eventual marriage (in 1796) overcame his instinctive reactions.

Whitney found the South itself a revelation when he arrived in late 1792. Still reeling from the neglect and devastation of the Revolutionary years, the South foundered, mired in economic stagnation, groping for a crop that could restore prosperity. Tobacco had exhausted much of the soil; the market for rice and indigo had collapsed. The land that later billowed with white oceans of cotton remained yet an inland thicket, patrolled by bears and wildcats. Most of the inhabitants squatted along the coast and the shallow rivers and inlets, swatting mosquitoes, hacking at underbrush, and scratching out a bare subsistence. The slave population, once looked upon as a valuable resource, hung ever more heavily on the feeble neck of the economy. Violence, so rarely seen in Whitney's New England past, seemed a way of life. Casual tavern conversations ignited at the drop of an ill-chosen word into eye-gouging, ear-ripping brawls. Surveying all this, Whitney wrote, "I find myself in a new natural world and as for the moral world I believe it does not exist so far south."

Paradoxically, this feral environment supported many devotees of manners, grace, and good living. The lands along the Savannah River, where Catherine's plantation, Mulberry Grove, lay, enjoyed a climate so gentle and a soil so rich that no one's best efforts could ruin them entirely. "Oranges, Pomegranates, Figgs, Olives all grow within ten rods of the place where I now sit," Whitney wrote home. Like the Garden of Eden, Georgia boasted "several fruits which grow spontaneously in the fields . . . the figg tree putteth forth its figgs, the pomegranate its blossoms, the Indian corn its tassel and we have peas and Salad all winter."

When Whitney arrived at Mulberry Grove, once the residence of the royal lieutenant governor, he found it a shambles. The state of Georgia had confiscated the farm and given it as a prize of war to General Greene. Greene needed all the help he could get because he had passed out personal notes to the contractors who fed his army. After the war, the Confederation government, less grateful than Georgia's, had repudiated these obligations, stranding Greene in a morass of debt from which he never managed to extricate himself.

Whitney recognized the plantation itself and the trees from which it took its name as monuments to the long romance with the silkworm carried on by North Americans. Mulberry trees lined the streets of Whitney's New Haven, and Ezra Stiles's diary recorded "The Spirit for *raising Silk worms* [which] is great in this town . . . & other places in Connecticut." Stiles himself spread the silk fever, distributing "Mulberry Seeds . . . in this State, some up Mohawk R[iver], & Vermont Towns on L[ake] Champlain." Mulberry Streets in a hundred towns attest to the pervasiveness of America's recurring flirtation with the silkworm and its gossamer product. (In retrospect, the obsession with this will-o'-the-wisp seems silly, unless one realizes that the silkworm, contentedly munching mulberry leaves at one end and extruding a ready-to-weave filament at the other, accomplishes within its little body a task that humankind requires flocks of sheep, fields of cotton, and stacks of machinery to duplicate. Unfortunately, the silkworm, an oriental delicacy like barbequed sea horse, never did well in America.)

Greene had labored to get Mulberry Grove on its feet as a rice plantation by repairing dikes and fields ravaged by wartime floods. This Herculean chore ("The cultivation of rice requires much more labor than I had imagined," Whitney observed) Miller had assumed on Greene's death. What end might have resulted no one can know, but the state of the rice market boded ill. Fate, and Whitney's genius, intervened to rescue Miller from the paddies.

After a brief stay at Mulberry Grove, Whitney reluctantly crossed the river to assume his tutorial duties. He soon returned, however, claiming he'd received less than half the promised salary. Now at loose ends, he succumbed readily to Catherine's invitation to stay on at Mulberry Grove. His mechanical skills made him an asset around the plantation, and his social graces made him an ornament to Catherine's parlor. "He can do anything," she boasted to her friends. Catherine's salon drew the local gentry like moths to a candle. There Whitney "heard much said of extreme difficulty of ginning Cotton, that is, separating it from its seed. . . . A number of very respectable Gentlemen at Mrs. Greene's . . . agreed that if a machine could be invented [to] clean the Cotton with expedition, it would be a great thing both to the country and to the inventor."

A great thing indeed! If ever in history a chain of potentially explosive economic power awaited only the insertion of a single missing link, the time was 1792, and Whitney stood squarely at the gap. A world sweltering and chafing in wool and linen offered a global market of incomprehensible dimensions. English craftsmen had successfully mechanized every step of cotton manufacture. The fields, climate, and slave-labor force of southern America could grow the raw material in vast quantities. Only the problem of removing the seeds, which clung to the fibers like burrs to a woolen sock, remained. Picking the seeds out by hand required so much labor that the expense precluded profit. The alluring prospects of the cotton market nevertheless prompted some planters to put in a crop in 1792, hoping that by the time it matured, some genius would have figured out a way to remove the seeds.

This optimism proved premature, but not by much. Whitney put his mind to the problem, conceived a solution in early 1793, and soon produced a working model, for which he declined an offer of a hundred guineas. A simple machine, the first cotton gin, so simple that Georgia schoolboys described its essentials in a phrase, "wire teeth which worked thro' slats, and a brush." But it held enormous promise. Whitney, who had earlier described "the world" as "a Lottery in which many draw Blanks, one of which may fall to [me]," could now boast to his father, "'Tis generally said by those who know anything about it that I shall make a Fortune out of it. . . . I am now so sure of success," he added, "that ten thousand dollars, if I saw the money counted out to me, would not tempt me to give up my right and relinquish the object."

Encouraged by the enthusiasm of those who saw his first model, Whitney built a larger one and tested it, with dynamic results:

> With [this machine] one man will clean ten times as much cotton as . . . any other way before known and . . . clean it much better. . . . This machine can be turned by water . . . or a horse, with the greatest ease, and one man and a horse will do more than fifty men with the old [method].

The machine, he added, "makes the labor fifty times less, *without throwing any class of People out of business*" (italics added). Whitney thus articulated one of the principles that led people to seize upon industrialization as the remedy to misery and poverty. If the machine could render impossible tasks easy, put more people to work, lighten their labor, and generate wealth for everybody without injuring anyone, who could resist its appeal?

Thus was Prometheus unbound. This little machine—inspired, according to legend, by Whitney's observing a cat reach through a fence, snatch at a chicken, and come away with only a paw full of feathers, and by Catherine Greene's handing Whitney a hearth brush, saying, "La, Mr. Whitney, here's what you need," to remove the clean cotton from the gin's teeth—this machine unleashed a cataclysmic force. The southern cotton crop, insignificant when Whitney invented the gin, exceeded 200 million pounds annually by the time he died in 1825.

The total effects, however, defy the power of numbers to convey. A southern judge remarked, in 1806, that before Whitney's machine, "The whole interior of the Southern states was languishing," and people fleeing the South. Thanks to the gin, "Individuals . . . depressed with poverty, and sunk with idleness, have suddenly risen to wealth and *respectability* [italics added]. Our debts have been paid off, our capitals increased; and our lands are treble in value." Cotton cleared the southern wilderness, enriched northern merchants and ship owners, financed industrialization, and built the factories that absorbed much of the surplus population of England and Ireland. But it had a savage, dark side as well. Cotton reinvigorated slavery, hitherto expiring from its own weakness and wickedness; it laid its curse on Americans white and black, culminating in the mayhem of the Civil War, which killed more Americans than all the country's other wars combined. Cotton built the mill towns, squalid and stinking, that horrified Karl Marx and galvanized his speculations into a creed that shook the world.

But all that, good and bad, lay far beyond Whitney's ken in 1793. He had his invention, a truly new way of surmounting an obstacle and thus an innovation indeed, but nothing else had changed. Even the most dramatic movements in history begin with a small step in a world that remains, for the moment, unchanged. Whitney, rejoicing in his little model there on the banks of the Savannah, had visions of wealth and glory dancing in his head. But, as many another inventor has found, the exact route from inspiration to riches proved obscure and strewn with obstacles. Whitney had no capital, no business organization, no factory, no plan to sell or distribute the machines, and no precedents he could follow.

Meanwhile, Catherine's pride in her protégé's skill had led her to show off the machine to her friends; any of them might copy it, and Whitney had no patent to stop them. A patent he needed, and soon; furthermore, he had to build lots of machines, and quickly; otherwise, the whole chance must go a-glimmering. None of this could he accomplish down there in the "chigger and pellagra latitudes," as satirist Henry Mencken later derided them. The South, the "Sahara" of the beaux arts, was barren of the industrial arts as well. As Whitney realized, the southern swamps and thickets abounded with men clever enough to make individual copies of so simple a machine, but lacked everything—labor, raw materials, machinery—needed for a factory to produce it in volume.

Whitney concluded he must go north to get a patent and set up manufacture. In New England, he knew where to find all he needed. Forming a partnership with Miller, who advanced the necessary capital, Whitney sailed back to New York on June 1, 1793. Detouring to the national capital, Philadelphia, where he filed his patent application, he then moved on to New Haven to set up shop. The way he equipped his establishment demonstrated an embryonic grasp of modern manufacturing arrangements. He might simply have hired enough skilled workers to build gins one at a time by hand, but such workers commanded high wages, an omnipresent incentive that encouraged generations of American manufacturers to mechanize. Moreover, hand production would have moved slowly, far too slowly to match demand.

To accelerate the process Whitney needed tools, machine tools that could produce components in volume. Such devices he could not buy in the United States; he had to make them himself. Drawing on his experience in his father's workshop and as a manufacturer of nails and hatpins, Whitney built a lathe, a wire-drawing block, and a machine to cut the wire teeth for the gin. A forerunner of later tools, the tooth-cutting machine produced parts of uniform sizes. "It feeds itself," Whitney bragged, "and goes remarkably easy."

Making the machines to make the parts to make the gins took time—so much time that not until May 1794 could Whitney set out for Georgia with six gins. Before sailing, he returned to Philadelphia to complete the patent formalities. (This included depositing a model of his invention, as the patent law then required. The model collection burned in a Patent Office fire in 1836, a loss as grievous to historians of technology as Henry VIII's confiscation of the monasteries was to medievalists.) Whitney carried a letter of introduction from his old tutor Elizur Goodrich to Oliver Wolcott, comptroller of the treasury, citizen of Connecticut, and Yale graduate, 1778. This connection with Goodrich ultimately proved more valuable than the cotton gin patent that he secured on March 14, 1794. Whitney, wrote Goodrich,

> sustained a very fair reputation in the academic studies and is perhaps inferior to none in accordance with the mechanic powers, and those of the branches of natural philosophy which are applicable to the manufacturers and commerce of our country. He happily unites talents to reduce it to practice; a circumstance which is rarely found in our young men of collegiate education.

Buoyed by this praise and by the enthusiasm of Secretary of State Thomas Jefferson, who wanted a small gin for his plantation at Monticello, Whitney sailed south with high hopes. He wrote his father that he had

> accomplished everything agreeable to my wishes. I had the satisfaction to hear . . . a number of the first men in America [say] that my machine is the most perfect & most valuable invention that has ever appeared in this country . . . and I shall probably gain some honor as well as profit by the Invention. . . . One of the most Respectable Gentlemen in N. Haven [said] that he would rather be the author of the Invention than the prime minister of England.

When Whitney arrived in Georgia, he discovered that Miller had already worked out a marketing scheme and begun talking up the gin to the countryside. Miller planned to sell not the gin itself but its services. He offered to clean any quantity of cotton that planters might bring and to return one pound of clean cotton for every five pounds presented. This plan meant that Miller and Whitney would acquire two-fifths of a pound of clean cotton for every one pound returned to the planter, and demonstrated the timeless principle that people attack new problems with old ideas, the only ideas that they have. Miller's plan resembled the traditional arrangement between the owners of gristmills and their farmer customers. In theory at least, it solved two perplexing problems that confronted businessmen all over America.

Few planters had the ready cash to purchase a gin outright, and Miller, grappling with the debts that beset the Greene estate, had no mind to sell on credit. In addition, the United States at this time had no currency worthy of the name or rather labored under a blizzard of currencies of dubious worth. Business got transacted with a bewildering array of state banknotes, personal notes, commercial paper, and foreign currencies. Most of these "monies" had uncertain value, particularly in places as far removed from their origins as New Haven was from Georgia. Even small change was hard to come by. In port cities, merchants accepted exotic coins such as Russian kopeks and Portuguese escudos brought back by sailors, much as postage stamps and packets of chewing gum circulate as currency in Mongolia today.

Under the conditions that prevailed, then, selling for "cash" could prove even riskier than selling on credit. Cotton, on the other hand, was as good as gold; white gold, they called it. Throughout the period before the Civil War, businessmen readily accepted cotton in payment and often preferred it to cash or promissory notes. Cotton sold in England in exchange for English merchants' drafts, which, if issued by a reputable house, had a more certain value than any of the money or near money available in the United States. Cotton could also be held as a speculation, waiting for a rise in the market.

If Miller's scheme had worked, he and Whitney would have become wealthy men indeed, for they would have acquired title to one-third of the South's cotton crop. Miller apparently intended to gin the entire cotton output of the South. Unfortunately, cotton agriculture expanded far more swiftly than Whitney's production of gins. The planters would not, or could not, wait and found many reasons not to. Once Catherine Greene let the secret out of the bag, it ran free. Within a year, 300 unauthorized copies or "improvements" of Whitney's gin churned merrily away in southern towns and in plantation sheds. Even the news that Whitney had secured a patent on his machine failed to deter imitators. A patent supposedly converted an idea into a property and vested it with the same rights as any other kind of property, including protection against trespass and thievery. Most Americans—squatters on the frontier an exception—accepted such restrictions when applied to real, tangible property. After all, most of them had, or aspired to have, property of their own to protect. But restricting the use of an idea to its originator smacked of "monopoly," a battle cry that has always gotten the American blood up, whether raised against the British East India Company, the English king, Eli Whitney, the Second Bank of the United States, or Standard Oil. This howl the planters soon raised, adding to it a charge repeated with increasing frequency as the friction between North and South intensified: northern capitalists, in this case Whitney and Miller, had fastened themselves parasitically on the body of the South, sucking its blood and growing wealthy upon the sweat and capital of southerners.

Behind this bluster, some of it no doubt fueled by genuine resentment, lay cold calculation. Whether the infant federal government could, or would, enforce its patent law remained to be seen. Even if it did, it might take a long time to bring offenders to heel. In the meantime, miscreants might gin up so much money that the penalties, however stiff, might pale in comparison to the profits accumulated.

Whitney returned north to speed up production, the first line of defense against interlopers. "Do not let a deficiency of money, do not let anything hinder the speedy construction of the gins," Miller wrote to Whitney; "the people of the country are almost running mad for them." Meanwhile, Miller initiated a series of lawsuits designed to hold imitators at bay. He soon discovered that a lawsuit, as Ambrose Bierce later remarked, worked as "a machine that you go into as a pig and come out as a sausage." Throughout the rest of Miller's life (he died in 1802) and most of the rest of Whitney's, the partners found themselves embroiled in an endless series of lawsuits that consumed time, money, and energy, and for a long time brought scant reward.

Some defendants argued that they didn't use the gin, in one case shouting to make their disclaimers heard above the roar of gins thundering away next door to the courtroom. Others claimed that they did not use Whitney's gin at all, but rather an improved model of their own making, or one purchased legitimately from some other manufacturer. A few squeezed through a loophole in the wording of the patent law. Even after Congress filled this cavity in 1800, the two Yankee capitalists found it difficult to convince southern juries to bring judgments against their neighbors. Eventually the tide turned, and, state by state, Whitney managed to win vindication and some recompense. He always claimed, however, that the sums received fell short of the money he expended in production, legal fees, and traveling back and forth to attend court.

Most of Whitney's biographers have lamented his misfortune. Having created a machine that unlocked the enormous potential for wealth that lay in unused southern fields and idle southern slaves, Whitney himself received very little in return. The story of the cotton gin, however, typifies the difficulties confronted by inventors, even those who have a viable solution to a genuine problem, as Whitney did, and not a solution looking for a problem, as so many others have peddled in vain. Because so many wanted the gin instantly, Whitney faced a terrifying question that has baffled many an innovator: what to do if throngs of customers want one now? As Whitney learned, between invention and product, between creator and customer, lies a long, hard road requiring answers to questions of how, where, and by whom to produce it, market it, and maintain it. To these problems, he had no adequate solutions.

From the point of view of the growth of the national economy, however, Whitney's personal adversity may have served well. Enforced patents did create monopolies; monopolies slowed the diffusion of technology and delayed the economic benefits of inventions. The fact that patent laws functioned poorly in the early years of the United States meant that technology spread quickly. Theoretically, patent laws encouraged creativity by converting ideas into property and thus protecting inventors' prospects, but whether they worked that way in practice seems doubtful. Inventors could, as Whitney and others later proved, prosper mightily without the benefits of patent protection. On the whole, the feebleness of the laws probably served the country's best interests, at least in its early years, just as the destruction of the Second National Bank probably facilitated development of the frontier, whether or not Andrew Jackson intended that outcome.

The gin's impact did not fall only upon the fields and factories of the United States and the "dark Satanic Mills" of Britain. Cotton manufacture soon outstripped wool and silk in the textile industries of France and Belgium. In Japan, the Toyoda family created a firm to manufacture cotton textile machinery and brought American William A. Francis, formerly an engineer at machine tool pioneer Pratt and Whitney, to introduce the "American system" to the production of cotton looms. From the expertise and profits of the loom company there eventually emerged Toyota Motor Company.

Long before the final resolution of the cotton gin lawsuits, however, Whitney had diverted much of his energy to another area. Watching the southern markets slip away, despairing of legal redress, bogged down in debt deepened by a fire in his factory, Whitney sought another outlet for his talent as a manufacturer. In the late 1790s, however, the market for manufactured goods in the United States offered scant prospects for people of Whitney's abilities. British manufacturers controlled much of it, and at prices that no Americans could match.

Whitney's unhappy experience with the cotton gin had taught him several valuable lessons. First, the mere fact that one owned a patent guaranteed nothing. The only safeguard lay in producing in such quantity and at such a price that no competitor could succeed, even if he ignored the patent laws. Second, a manufacturer faced an uphill struggle finding the capital he needed. The most obvious sources, banks and wealthy merchants (the latter invariably controlled the former), underwrote agriculture and mercantile trade, with which they had done business for centuries. They proved reluctant, however, to finance manufacturing, which they regarded as an unfamiliar risk. Attuned to the seasons and to the timing of transatlantic voyages, they rarely granted credit for longer than 60 days to anyone. "But that," remarked Whitney, "is not a credit which, in the present state of the business, can be of much service to me."

A manufacturer, as Whitney had learned the hard way, required considerable time to tool up for production. His creditors had to have a patience that banks and merchants lacked. Not until the War of 1812 blocked the usual outlets for their capital, and a Boston merchant, Francis Cabot Lowell, convinced his colleagues that the potential profits justified the wait and the risk, did merchants in significant numbers make their resources available to manufacturers. Thereafter, much of American industrialization resulted from partnerships between merchant capitalists and mechanics. But in 1797, when Whitney decided to look for a new venture, that happy partnership lay in the future.

Whitney understood Adam Smith's maxim that the size of the market determined the division of labor. Given a large enough market, he thought he knew both theoretically and practically how to achieve the necessary division of labor by substituting machines for skilled hands. Such a method of production would, coincidentally, bypass what Alexander Hamilton had called in 1791 "the greatest obstacle to success," the shortage of skilled labor in the United States, and would bear out Hamilton's prediction that the solution lay "in the genius of people of this country, a peculiar aptitude for mechanical improvements." Despite Hamilton's optimism, few of Whitney's contemporaries could boast his qualifications to set up a mechanized factory. But before Whitney and his country could profit from his unusual talents, he had to find an appropriate market and adequate capital. He found both in the same spot, the federal government.

In the early 1790s, the deteriorating political situation in Europe increasingly alarmed the American Congress. One way or another, the United States might find itself embroiled in a war with England, France, or both. The country had no armaments with which to fight such a war and no way to make them. In an effort to achieve self-sufficiency in weapons, Congress set up the Springfield (Massachusetts) Armory in 1794 and later added an establishment at Harper's Ferry (then Virginia, now West Virginia). Congress soon realized, however, that the two government armories together could not do the job, or at any rate could not do it soon enough. In 1797, after three years of effort, the Springfield Armory had turned out a thousand muskets; Harper's Ferry had yet to produce any. Congress began debating the advisability of buying arms from private contractors.

Whitney at once perceived this as the opportunity he needed. He wrote to his old friend and fellow Yale alumnus Oliver Wolcott, now secretary of the treasury,

> By the Debates of Congress I observe that they [may make] some appro-priations for procuring Arms etc for the U.S. . . . . I have a number of work-men & apprentices whom I have instructed in working Wood & Metals and whom I wish to keep employed. These circumstances induced me to address you. . . . I should like to undertake to Manufacture ten or Fifteen Thousand Stand of Arms.

By any standards then known—Springfield Armory's output, for example—such a quantity of weapons constituted an enormous order for a single contractor to fill. Whitney made it plain that he intended to mechanize the process:

> I am persuaded that Machinery moved by water adapted to this Business would greatly diminish the labor and facilitate the Manufacture of this Article. Machines for forging, rolling, floating, boreing, Grinding, Polishing etc may all be made use of to advantage. . . . There is a good fall of Water in the Vicinity of this Town which I can procure and could have works erected in a short time. It would not answer however to go to the expense of erecting works for this purpose unless I could contract to make a considerable number.

There, in his last sentence, Whitney expressed the manufacturer's dilemma in early American capitalism. Investors would put up the money for expensive machinery only if they believed the goods produced would recapture the costs with something to spare. The best bet, a product for which a volume market existed, would enable the manufacturer to spread his capital costs over many units of production. If machine production offered significant savings over hand labor, as in the pin factory that inspired Adam Smith to rhapsodize on the wealth potential of mechanization and division of labor, so much the better.

Unfortunately, in 1798 America, few such markets beckoned. British producers dominated most of those that did—hardware and textiles, for instance. They had something Americans lacked: cheap labor and plenty of it. Eventually, the combina-tion of population growth, protective tariffs, decreasing transportation costs across the Atlantic, and technological progress created markets for American-made goods and lured American capital. But as Whitney surveyed his shop, his "workmen & appren-tices," and his own talents, all idled by the collapse of his cotton gin expectations, he faced bleak prospects until the federal government's determination to create an American arms industry came to the rescue.

The government presented Whitney with a volume market and a noncompetitive one at that. The determination to create a domestic arms industry excluded British manufacturers by definition, and no American ones existed outside of government arsenals. The federal government would accept a price that assured a profit and would advance the necessary capital. If he could secure such a contract, Whitney thought, his compound miseries would vanish at a stroke. He had in mind a more ambitious and detailed plan of manufacture than he vouchsafed to Wolcott (having learned the hard way with the cotton gin, he kept his best ideas to himself). With this scheme, he expected (mistakenly, as it turned out) to expedite production, cut costs, and get rich quickly. His optimism arose not from Hamiltonian visions of American industrial glory, nor from interest and skill in arms making (he knew nothing about it, in fact), but from the opportunity to use his assets to fulfill his personal ambitions.

Wolcott may have had his doubts about Whitney's grandiose proposal, but his letter arrived just as Congress appropriated $800,000 for the purchase of arms, without having any clear idea of where to get them. Contractors Wolcott had to find, and his general faith in Whitney as a fellow Yale alumnus, a fellow gentleman, and a craftsman of some reputation led him to endorse Whitney's proposal. "Knowing your skill in Mechanick," Wolcott wrote to Whitney, "I had before spoken of you to the Secretary of War as a person whose services might possibly be rendered highly useful."

On June 14, 1798, Whitney signed a contract with the U.S. government to supply 10,000 muskets and their accouterments within 28 months, the first 4,000 due before September 30, 1799. The government advanced Whitney $5,000 to begin setting up his works and promised another $5,000 when needed. The federal purveyor of supplies thought Whitney's offer too good to believe. He wrote Wolcott prophetically, "I have my doubts about this matter and suspect that Mr. Whitney cannot perform as to time." But war with France seemed an imminent possibility, and Whitney seemed the best bet, so Wolcott brushed these objections aside.

With a contract for $134,000 and an advance of $5,000 in his pocket, Whitney returned to New Haven rescued from the brink of disaster. "Bankruptcy & ruin," he wrote a friend, "were . . . staring me in the face & disappointment Trip'd me up every step I attempted to take. I was miserable . . . Loaded with a Debt of 3 or 4000 Dollars, without resources and without any business that would ever furnish me a support."

The longed-for security remained elusive, despite the government's largesse. Difficulties beset Whitney at every turn. He had to find workers ("I have not only the arms, but the armorers to make," he wrote Wolcott); floods, a severe winter, and a shortage of materials plagued him. By the spring of 1799, he had run out of money and was running out of time. Onto these concerns piled the exhaustion brought on by the need to do everything and to act everywhere at once. Purchasing agent, construction supervisor, employment officer, machine designer and fabricator: all these and other roles Whitney fulfilled himself. He concluded he must ask Wolcott for further help. "Cannot some arrangement be made by which I may obtain such indulgences as will enable me to pursue the business . . . and relieve me from the extreme anxiety which now . . . overpowers my ardor and dampens my resolution?" he wrote in June 1799. He reiterated his faith in his plan of manufacture, again without elaborating on the details.

Fortunately for Whitney, the government inspector on the site, Captain Decius Wadsworth, a classmate of Phineas Miller at Yale, expressed similar views in the report he submitted to Wolcott. Encouraged by Wadsworth's report, and determined to carry through the "wish of the Government to diffuse such a degree of skill in the manufacture of Musquets as will exempt this country from arranging further importations," Wolcott took Whitney off the hook:

> If you feel entire confidence in your project and will furnish me with additional security for a further advance, money shall be granted to enable you to make a fair trial. I should consider a *real improvement* in machinery for manufacturing arms as a great acquisition to the United States. For present purposes & to give you time to look out for good security, I enclose you a [letter] of credit . . . for 1500 Dols.

Wolcott did not entirely suppress his doubts, however. Pointing out that the government could have acquired muskets in the old way, he added, "My mind is inclined to skepticism with respect to all theories which have not been sanctioned by experience."

Alarmed by this shot across his bows, Whitney abandoned secrecy and for the first time gave the secretary a detailed account of the method he had in mind:

> My general plan does not consist in one great complicated machine, wherever one small part being out of order or not answering to the purpose expected, the whole must stop & be considered useless. . . . One of my primary objects is to form the tools so that the tools themselves shall fashion the work and give to every part its just proportion—which when once accomplished will give expedition, uniformity, and exactness to the whole.
>
> If each . . . workman must form . . . every part according to his own fancy & regulate the size & proportion by his own Eye or even by a measure, I should have as many varieties as I have . . . part[s]. . . . By long practice . . . mere Mechanics who have no correct taste acquire the art of giving a particular uniformity . . . to particular substances. But very few really good experienced workmen in this branch of business are to be had in this country. In order to supply ourselves in the course of the next few years with any considerable number of really good muskets, such means must be devised as will preclude the necessity of every workman's being bred to the business. An accurate Eye, close attention and much time are necessary to form things rightly.
>
> In short, the tools which I contemplate are similar to an engraving on copper plate from which may be taken a great number of impressions perceptibly alike.

There, in this brief statement made in 1799, Whitney summarized the prerequisites to mass production: the subdivision of the final product into component parts, shaped by machine to a standard size and thus interchangeable, with the work to be done by unskilled or semiskilled labor. (In fact, Whitney, like Henry Ford a century later, preferred unskilled workers as machine operators because, having nothing to unlearn, they could absorb his teachings more readily.) In practice, he never succeeded completely in mechanizing production or in making all parts of the weapon interchangeable. The fault lay not with Whitney's perception of the task at hand, but rather with the lack of proper tools to do it. In Whitney's lifetime, his mechanized production theory ran ahead of machine tool practice. The gap closed quickly, however, as shown by the fact that his son, executing a contract for 1,000 of Samuel Colt's six-shooters in 1847, tooled up and finished production in six months.

Whitney himself surmounted the prevailing state of the art and fulfilled his contracts by resorting to hand labor, achieving uniformity, or something close to it, in the firing mechanisms by having the workers measure their product against standard patterns and gauges. He did, however, mechanize many steps of the process, inventing some of the necessary machines and borrowing others. He achieved a greater degree of interchangeability than any manufacturer before him. He kept neither the results nor the methods secret. He never bothered to patent any of his machines, and he communicated freely with other arms manufacturers, such as Colonel Roswell Lee, a former employee of Whitney and Miller, and longtime superintendent of the Springfield Armories. From the Whitney works, from the Springfield Armory, from the factory of Simeon North, and from other New England armories came a whole generation of craftsmen like Henry Leland, whose skill at designing machine tools and production methods made interchangeable parts a widespread reality in America.

By the 1850s, the engineering generation that followed Whitney's had a large enough market, created by the growth of population and transportation, to justify this new "American system of production" (as British observers titled it) in many fields of manufacture. Interchangeability had swiftly diffused from the arms industry into consumer products such as locks, clocks and watches, sewing machines, farm machinery, and pianos. A British industrial commission, making an American tour of inspection in 1851, found that U.S. manufacturers "call in the aid of machinery in almost every department of industry. Wherever it can . . . substitute for manual labor, it is universally and willingly resorted to."

The British visitors, accustomed to the hostility between English industrialists and their workers, remarked on a startling commonality of purpose between American employers and employees. No outbreaks of Luddite machine-wrecking impeded mechanization in the United States. To the contrary, they discovered an "extreme desire, manifested by masters and workmen, to adopt all labour-saving devices" because all parties thought mechanization in "their mutual interest." American workmen, on whom "traditional methods had little hold . . . as compared with the English artisan," not only accepted improvements introduced by the boss, but also were themselves "continually devising some new thing to assist . . . in [the] work" and demanding to be "posted up" on new developments.

In such a propitious atmosphere, machine tools had become amazingly sophisticated. At the Springfield Armory, the Englishmen found machines "in which a succession of tools were brought to bear on the work one after another (with the 'most rigid accuracy')" and "edging machines" that traced "irregular figures and impart[ed] an exact outline" from a model to the part. The process virtually eliminated handwork (two and a half minutes, as opposed to twenty-nine minutes' machine work on each musket) and produced "parts . . . so exactly alike that any . . . part will . . . fit any musket."

American factories also produced high volume at low cost. In Whitney's hometown of New Haven, English engineer Joseph Whitworth inspected a padlock factory that turned out 2,000 a day, "of a superior quality to those of the same class ordinarily imported from England and not more expensive. . . . Special machines were applied to every part, and the parts . . . can be interchanged." Whitworth also visited a New Haven factory that produced 600 clocks a day with similar methods and successfully exported them to England and the European continent.

The Englishmen reported their findings with foreboding. By making manufacturing the province of "large factories with machinery applied to almost every process, the extreme subdivision of labor, and all reduced to an almost perfect system of manufacture," the Americans demonstrated an "ingenuity, combined with undaunted energy, which we would do well to imitate if we mean to hold our present position in the Great Markets of the world." (Ironically, similar warnings issued from Americans who toured Japanese factories in the 1970s.) Even by 1851, some harbingers of future American potency had appeared in Britain itself. From 1847 on, some British manufacturers imported American machine tools and, in a move that particularly shocked Britons, the famous Enfield Arsenal re-equipped itself with machine tools imported from Windsor "in the wilds of Vermont."

Oliver Wolcott, by answering Whitney's supplications for money to keep going, proved a crucial catalyst for the evolution of American manufacturing supremacy and made the federal government a partner in forging what proved free enterprise's most potent tool. But Whitney's tribulations did not end with Wolcott's gesture in July 1799. In fact, it took him 10 years to fulfill the original contract, what with delays caused by trips to southern courts, fires at the factory, and harassment from government officials. But things improved steadily thereafter, and Whitney gradually achieved the recognition and wealth he had so long sought. In September 1799, 10 of the leading citizens of New Haven, most of them Yale graduates, signed a bond that secured a further $10,000 advance from the government. In January 1801, Whitney went to the new capital, Washington, D.C., and put on a triumphant demonstration of interchangeability. Disassembling several firing mechanisms into their constituent bits, and mixing the parts, Whitney invited the dignitaries present to pick the parts at random and reassemble them. The reassembled mechanisms all fitted on the musket that Whitney had brought along. Among the impressed spectators was the president-elect, Thomas Jefferson, who had granted Whitney his original patent on the cotton gin. Jefferson's interest in and support for interchangeability had been piqued in the 1780s when, on a visit to France, he had witnessed a similar demonstration by a French locksmith. At the time, Jefferson had vainly tried to persuade the Frenchman to immigrate to the United States.

After this demonstration, the government indulged Whitney with all the patience and money he required. The public acclaimed him as "The Artist of His Country." With his methods perfected, the muskets rolled out and the money rolled in through a succession of contracts with federal and state governments. With the advice of his old friend Oliver Wolcott, retired from government service into a private banking and brokerage firm, Whitney invested his profits wisely and achieved financial security.

In 1817, he married, subsequently fathering three children, including a son, Eli Whitney Jr., who eventually succeeded to the business. In 1825, Eli Whitney Sr. died, leaving a large estate to his family but an even more munificent legacy to his country.

His life spanned a period that saw the people of the United States rise from discontented colonialists to armed revolutionists to a place secure among the nations of the world. In the political and military adventures of his lifetime, he played no direct part. But as a key factor in the development of *two* disruptive technologies, he figured largely in the economic transformation of this country from a colonial dependency, where handicraft turned out the few locally manufactured goods, to a rising industrial power, well on its way to manufacturing self-sufficiency, using a system that would become the most powerful on earth.

His career clearly revealed the impact of his society upon him. His ambition, his education, and the opportunities it provided him were as specifically American as the cotton gin itself. His life's work catalyzed cataclysmic results, including the Civil War, where the forces of southern plantation agriculture and northern industrialism, both of which he did so much to unleash, collided. But perhaps more important, his life revealed patterns of behavior characteristic of subsequent generations of American manufacturing entrepreneurs. Time has shown, of course, that although Americans may have embraced interchangeable parts and mass production earlier and more enthusiastically than most societies, the idea did not originate in the United States and nothing in the Americans' nature made them inherently more proficient in these techniques. A procession of Fords and Buicks descending the Yangtze River from the assembly lines of Chonqing, the loads of Dell Computers carried by the stream of Malaysian air freighters arriving at Dallas–Ft. Worth Airport, the Sony Play Stations from Japan, the flat-screen TVs from Korea, all these and more testify to global mastery of methods once thought peculiarly suited to America.

Guided by his ambition, seeing in it a polestar on which he could set the course of his life, Whitney perceived a market, assembled the assets necessary to meet it, and kept those assets employed by shifting into a new product when the old failed. Despite these manifold skills, Whitney's career demonstrated a truth known to every successful innovator and venture capitalist: building a better mousetrap doesn't bring the world to your door. In Whitney's case, the "better mousetrap," the cotton gin, brought him fame, but not fortune. Success, when it came, depended as much on the Yale "Old Blue" network and a federal government that tolerated cost overruns and decades of delay. Bolstered by the patient support of his fellow alumni and his national government, Whitney, striving for mechanization and standardization, blazed a trail that became a path and ultimately an expressway to prosperity traveled by generations of American manufacturers who followed him both in life and in the pages of this book, and by nimble businesses elsewhere, whose products we see more and more in America and around the world.

Chapter 3

The Grim Reaper

CYRUS HALL MCCORMICK

Cyrus Hall McCormick: the Grim Reaper as millionaire

Most of the important things I've learned (such as "problems rarely get solved; they mostly become obsolete") I first heard from someone I disagreed with at the time. Despite this, I'm inclined to find people who agree with me pretty smart. For example, I decided that the late British polymath—novelist, poet, composer—Anthony Burgess qualified when I read in a *New York Times* article two statements I absolutely endorsed: that he found Los Caracoles restaurant in Barcelona a diner's delight and that he preferred trains to planes. Like Burgess, I suspect every time I board a plane that I won't survive, and that I have worsened the odds by flying so often. I know that mathematically this makes no sense: each trip opens a new lottery in which the odds of drawing one of Eli Whitney's dreaded "blanks" run the same every time, regardless of past experience, just as the odds of tossing heads or tails are always 50-50, even if heads has come up a hundred times in a row.

I find trains a more civilized way to travel for many reasons, not least of which the fact that one meets interesting people and talks to them in a civilized way across a dining-car tablecloth, rather than the elbows-in, half-shouted, side-of-the-mouth manner necessitated by airplanes. Among interesting denizens of the dining car, I have found many Europeans, who ride trains here because they learned to savor the excellence of rail travel at home and because they come to America to see it, not to fly over it.

On one trip from Seattle to Chicago, I enjoyed the company of two elderly German couples who practiced their tourists' English on me while I inflicted my pidgin German on them. As the train ambled across North Dakota, our seats in the dome car gave us a close-up view of one of North America's most intriguing annual spectacles, the wheat harvest on the Great Plains. As we watched, the giant combines moved in echelon, like scarlet locusts cutting a half-mile swath through wheat fields that stretched in every direction as far as the eye could see. The combines' reels, rising above the waves of grain, and then plunging forward and down to stroke the stalks into the cutting knives, looked for all the world like paddle-wheels on the Ohio River towboats that I had watched as a boy. In the towns, the lines of trucks and strings of railroad cars at the grain elevators formed another link in the mechanized conveyer that moved the crop from field to market without the touch of a human hand.

The next day, as the train rolled through Milwaukee, one of my companions said to me, "And now the cities and factories begin, yes?"

"Yes," I replied, "I'm afraid so."

"That is not so much to see," he said. "In Germany you can see that also. In Essen, in Mannheim, in Frankfurt, you can see all the factories you want. But three thousand kilometers of forests and wheat fields, that you cannot see. I think you Americans have not as much to fear as you think you have."

That truth, of course, we often forget. Any people that can feed itself has less to fear than one that cannot. In New Zealand, where farming and fishing supply the lifeblood of the economy, agricultural news dominates the print and electronic media. Newspapers blast headlines such as "Dairying income tipped to leap," "Prospects for farming good despite continuing volatility," "Silver Fern Farms plans new cuts [of meat] for China's plates," and a story about "China's newfound taste for lamb." Advertisements for sheep inoculations and varmint poisons appear regularly on prime-time television, and appeals for a national charity feature a cow dancing to Ravel's

"Bolero." Cheap sea and air freight rates eradicated much of New Zealand's modest manufacturing sector (including Ford's rudimentary assembly plant); most of what remains involves processing wool, "sheep meat," beef, and dairy products. Every New Zealander acknowledges the centrality of agriculture to the country's quality of life, and many of them speak with a greater awareness of the United States as an agricultural powerhouse than do most Americans.

In the fields and towns of the Great Plains, my German train companions and I had witnessed the confluence of industrial technology, fertile land, and a benevolent climate into the river of agricultural productivity that makes many Americans well fed, even fat, in a lean and hungry world. However valuable crude oil may seem (its price has increased sixfold since the first edition of this book), no one can eat it, nor, once harvested, replant it. This harsh reality, which eludes so many Americans, has haunted the potentates of the petroleum-producing states. As a guarantee of survival for oneself and one's posterity, a wheat field in North Dakota makes a better bet than an oil well in the Persian Gulf or the Gulf of Mexico.

As we have seen in the case of Eli Whitney's cotton gin, the potential agricultural productivity of the American expanses presented manufacturers with a great opportunity. The generation of innovators that followed Whitney busied itself seizing the market for labor-saving machines inherent in a land so vast and a people so few. Dozens, then hundreds, of mechanics rushed to patent devices designed to perform the tasks traditionally handled by peasant hands in Europe. The northern states, which would not countenance slavery, suffered perpetually from a shortage of farm labor. Few people would work another person's land when they could farm their own, and those who would demanded high wages. Farmers themselves, and the editors of newspapers and magazines directed to the farm audience, recognized the necessity for mechanization, a need that intensified as settlement moved westward, creating larger farms that specialized in grain as a market crop.

In 1823, Jonathan Roberts, president of the Pennsylvania Agricultural Society, wrote in the *American Farmer* magazine:

> In practical husbandry, the expense of labor is a cardinal consideration. Since the year 1818, farmers have . . . felt that labor has been much dearer than produce. . . . A mitigation of this effect may be sought . . . by improved implements. . . . Nothing is more wanted than the application of animal labor [to machines] in the cutting of grain. It is the business on the farm which requires the most [speed], and it is always the most expensive labor. Such an invention can be no easy task, or the ingenuity of our fellow citizens would, ere this, have effected it.

In England, as the whirling machinery of Lancashire cotton mills sucked workers from the countryside, as emigration to the United States further depleted their numbers, and as political agitation fractured the tractability of those workers who remained on the land, the English press took up the cry. In 1834, the *Farmer's Magazine* of London wrote, "It is certainly a remarkable circumstance in the history of mechanical science in this country, that the art of cutting down the cultivated crops should be so inadequately supplied with instruments."

In fact, farmers of the 1830s still assaulted their foremost problem, harvesting the ripe grain, with weapons thousands of years old, the sickle and the scythe. From the Book of Ruth through American primitive painters, observers romanticized the harvest in story, song, and picture. But a brief sojourn in a wheat field on an August afternoon, laying about with a scythe, resulted in a demythologizing experience. Certainly neither farmers nor their laborers had any illusions about the brutal nature of the work. Furthermore, it had to go quickly, for about 10 days after ripening, the husks opened, the grains of wheat fell to the ground, and the crop was lost.

In such circumstances, workers could demand high wages and an expensive fringe benefit in the form of a wagon laden with refreshment to slake their thirsts. The hands preferred Monongahela whiskey, but the cost and the temperance scruples of many farmer-employers often dictated a substitute. The *Southern Planter* advised its readers, "The next best thing to the 'ra-al Monongaly' to string up the nerves of those who wield the scythe, is a drink composed of five gallons of iced water well mixed with half a gallon of molasses, one quart of vinegar, and two ounces of ginger." The *American Farmer* declared a recipe of five gallons of water, one-half gallon of molasses, and one-quarter pound of ginger, mixed and served hourly, "invigorating, refreshing, and safe, no matter how cold the water may be. The cooler the water, the more grateful will it be to the palate,—the more refreshing to the system, the surer of giving tone and strength to the harvester."

Even when toned, strengthened, and well strung up in the nerves, the scythe men and their helpers who bound and stacked the cut grain cost the farmer a lot of money. In 1830, it required six laborers to harvest two acres of wheat a day. Any machine that reduced this cost would find a ready market among farmers with large acreage, provided it sold at a reasonable price.

In the open spaces of the American Midwest, old Northwest, and Great Plains lay a potential wealth equal to that of the cotton fields in the South. It took three keys to unlock this bonanza: people, transportation, and machines. Immigration supplied the first, railroads and canals the second, and American manufacturing the last. The mechanical harvester, the machine that most facilitated the transformation of these open spaces into a cornucopia, emerged from a farm workshop in the Shenandoah Valley, the "Valley of Virginia," as folks styled it in the nineteenth century. Cyrus Hall McCormick, the harvester's inventor, contributed the first of a series of technological innovations culminating in the combine that mechanized the entire harvesting process, and his skill in manufacturing and marketing carried his firm to the top of the farm machinery industry and kept it there. In addition, McCormick's distribution methods were emulated by all successful competitors and subsequently adapted to other products, most particularly the automobile. The methods by which modern automobile firms manufacture and sell their product, itself the apotheosis of urban, industrialized societies everywhere, thus trace their pedigrees directly back to Eli Whitney and Cyrus McCormick, farm boys who sought their fortunes in serving an agricultural, rural economy.

Like Abraham Lincoln, Cyrus McCormick was born in 1809, the year that Eli Whitney finally completed his first musket contract for the U.S. government and Abel Stowel produced the first screw-cutting machine in America. McCormick's immediate ancestors followed a typical pattern of American immigration, migration, and settlement. His great-grandfather, a Scotch-Irishman, immigrated in 1734, and eventually settled in Cumberland County, Pennsylvania, on the west bank of the Susquehanna River near Harrisburg. Cyrus's grandfather, Robert McCormick, settled first in Juniata County, Pennsylvania, on the Juniata River, a Susquehanna tributary. In 1779, he removed himself and his family to Rockbridge County, Virginia, in the Shenandoah Valley, midway between Lexington and Staunton, where Cyrus's father, Robert, lived his entire life.

The McCormicks illustrated how topography determined patterns of settlement before the advent of railroads and automobiles. The East Coast of the United States benefited from a wealth of river systems that penetrated the coastal plain into the foothills of the mountains. Settlers clung to these waterways, floating their goods upstream until they reached open land. Whenever they could, they set up their farms along a stream because only by water could they profitably send produce any distance to market. Carting crops to town over primitive roads inflicted a bone-and-wagon-shattering ordeal, and worse yet, a prohibitively expensive one. The cost of hauling grain to market often exceeded its selling price. The same transportation requirements dictated the location of factories. A Senate report in 1816 declared, "A coal mine may exist in the United States not more than ten miles from valuable ores of iron and other materials, and both of them be useless unless a canal is established between them, as the price of land carriage is too great to be borne by either."

In addition to water routes, the location of the mountains shaped the direction of migration. In Juniata County, the first Robert McCormick had gone about as far west as a man could go without encountering the parallel spines of the Alleghenies, which run from southwest to northeast across the state. Transmontane migration with heavily laden wagons involved ticklish haulage, not so much because of the difficulty of dragging loaded wagons up the mountain (a slow but sure process), but rather because of their nightmarish tendency to hurtle downhill on the far side. The steep ridges of central Pennsylvania formed a teamster's horror in the days of wagons, and even now truckers dread them more in the winter than they do the gentle escarpments of the Rockies. When Robert McCormick decided he needed and could afford more space, he took the path of least resistance, moving southwestward across the Potomac River at Harper's Ferry, and then up its tributary, the Shenandoah, into the broad valley that bears its name. As the Pennsylvania mountains deflected the stream of migrants into the Valley of Virginia, the northern half of the valley filled with German and Scotch-Irish settlers.

A tough bunch, these Scotch-Irishmen who, like the Cromwellites a century before, marched with the Bible in one hand and a musket in the other, ready to smite their enemies with either weapon. Hating the British, and ever fearful lest some American version of British privileged oligarchy establish itself in this land, they rallied to the colonial banner in the Revolution and to the standard of Jeffersonian democracy afterward. Cyrus's grandfather fought with the colonial forces at Yorktown. Cyrus himself remained a staunch Democrat all his life, in marked contrast to most of his fellow industrialists, who hewed to the Whig, and then the Republican, line.

Deeply Calvinistic, these Scotch-Irish farmers saw in themselves the personification of Thomas Jefferson's declaration that "Those who labor in the earth are the chosen people of God, if ever He had a chosen people, whose breasts He has made His peculiar deposit for substantial and genuine virtue." Glorying in their religious faith, their political creed, and their virtuous occupation, the McCormicks and their neighbors went about their business "in an armor of militant self-righteousness." They also exhibited a talent for selectivity, fastening upon those texts that justified their behavior and ignoring others less convenient. For example, as farmers, the McCormicks could rejoice in Jefferson's celebration of them as a chosen people; as slaveholders, they ignored his warning that slavery made him "tremble for [his] country when [he] reflect[ed] that God is just." Robert McCormick could refuse, on religious grounds, to supply his harvest hands with their cherished alcoholic refreshment; the same scruples did not prevent him from converting his surplus corn to whiskey and selling it for 25 cents a gallon in distant bastions of Virginian sin such as Lynchburg and Richmond. Cyrus McCormick once gave $10,000 to found a Presbyterian church in Chicago; in the same year, he collected $110 rent from two aged slaves he still owned in Virginia.

Throughout his life, Cyrus expected the Lord to bless his endeavors and thought his faith vindicated when he thrived in the ferocious American marketplace. Crushing competitors, harassing railroads for rebates, besieging potential customers with advertising, he did battle confident of the continued assistance of his mighty ally. "Business is not inconsistent with Christianity," he said in 1845, as he set out to carry his reaper into markets beyond his native state. In meeting past obstacles, he reflected, "Providence . . . seemed to assist me in our business." In avoiding future pitfalls, "I believe the Lord will help us out." And so it came to pass, or seemed to anyway. In 1857, a millionaire and the dominant figure in the American farm machinery industry, McCormick rejoiced, "Providence is with us and will defend us as heretofore."

Before industrialization, generations of successful businessmen and farmers like Cyrus McCormick's ancestors had sought and found religious justification for private property; for borrowing and lending money at interest; for buying and selling labor and commodities at prices set by the market; for slavery; for saving, investing, and speculating; for the whole panoply of activities that built the mercantile, agricultural economy of preindustrial America. Most prosperous men found sanction, not stricture, in religion; some, like Eli Whitney, discarded formal religion altogether. Not surprisingly, the generations that presided over industrialization followed a similar course, sometimes adapting, with the help of cooperative clerics, the old creeds to the new needs; sometimes, as we shall see with Andrew Carnegie, finding an adequate faith in the new process itself.

Whatever absolute rules the Protestant deity might enforce at the heavenly bar, his earthly adherents propounded a pliable secular code, readily shaped to cover capitalism in its industrial as well as in its agricultural permutations. In religion, then, as in politics, Americans defended specific changes as the logical outgrowth of the impact of absolute values on a progressively evolving society. Cyrus McCormick, whose lifetime spanned the American age of industrialization, personified the extension of militant Protestant values from farm to shop, factory, and global business enterprise. Sallying forth to do savage battle with his competitors, confident that "Providence . . . will defend us," McCormick proclaimed "the feeling that should be cherished [is] unconditional submission and resignation to the will and hand of Providence . . . rejoicing that unworthy as we are, the law has been satisfied, and we may be saved by *faith.*"

By 1830, when Cyrus McCormick turned 21, his father had expanded the original 400 acres bought by Cyrus's grandfather in 1779 to a 1,200-acre estate. Called "Walnut Grove," it produced grain, fruit, timber, and limestone and had gristmills, a distillery, a sawmill, and limekilns to process its products. These installations furnished the farm with much of its needs. The elder Robert McCormick's move to Rockbridge County had carried him beyond the navigable headwaters of the Shenandoah, so transportation costs gave the McCormicks an incentive to process raw materials into more valuable and compact commodities before shipping. The same incentive induced Gustavus Swift in the late nineteenth century to ship dressed beef to the East Coast, leaving hooves, hides, and horns in Chicago, and it now makes oil refineries a tempting investment for petroleum-producing countries.

To help him work his extensive holdings, the younger Robert McCormick had acquired, by 1830, five children, nine slaves, and 18 horses. These assets made him a prominent man, influential in his community and his church, with extensive credit available when he needed it. And sometimes he did need it, for like most successful farmers past and present, he was land rich but cash poor. The McCormick farm, like the Whitney farm, had a workshop, including a blacksmith's forge. As he grew old and prosperous, the second Robert McCormick spent more and more of his time there, indulging a penchant for invention, particularly inventions that might lessen farm labor.

Like many another farm tinkerer in England and America, Cyrus McCormick's father invented a reaper, a horse-drawn device to cut the wheat in the fields. No grain farmer needed agricultural journalists to tell him what a boon such a machine would deliver. Unfortunately, it proved devilishly difficult to make one that worked. A number of variables needed accommodating: for example, a machine that cut wondrously in a flat field of dry wheat often bogged down in rough ground or in heavy, wet, or tangled wheat. The machines also tended to shatter their cutting teeth on the rocks that in the Shenandoah Valley often seemed to sprout as thickly as the wheat itself. In addition, if the cutting action had power enough to sever a swath of tough wheat stalks, it often proved so violent that it shook the kernels out of the husks, whereupon they fell uselessly to the ground.

Cyrus, who often helped his father in the shop and early demonstrated an inventive knack of his own, took up the task. He fashioned a reaper that operated successfully on a neighboring farm during the harvest of 1831. Later, Cyrus claimed to have realized at once that the machine could bring him a million dollars. If so, he had a more sanguine imagination than Eli Whitney, who had dreamed in terms of thousands, or perhaps he simply reflected the increased scale on which Americans could dream after the 40 years of expansion that took place between Whitney's invention and McCormick's. More likely, he simply indulged in the omniscience of hindsight, since he set aside the new gadget for several years while he pursued other and, as it turned out, worthless schemes to make his fortune. First he crossed the mountains into Kentucky, where he passed a fruitless year trying to sell a hemp-breaking machine that his father had invented. These days, hemp cultivation, banished from the United States on the grounds that it might somehow turn America into a nation of marijuana users, takes place largely in remote areas of the world like Bangladesh, but in the early nineteenth century many Kentuckians, including their most distinguished statesman, Henry Clay, thought hemp might do for Kentucky what cotton had done for states farther south, and the McCormicks perhaps envisioned themselves as the Whitneys of hemp.

After this venture failed, Cyrus McCormick returned to the workshop to improve his reaper. In 1834, satisfied that he had perfected it to a point of marketability, he received a patent for his machine. With patent in hand, and standing on the very threshold of success, McCormick once again detoured. Manifesting a weakness that reappeared throughout his life, he went haring off in pursuit of quick riches in a nearby iron mine and furnace. McCormick knew nothing about the iron business but plunged in with his energies and his resources, piling up lots of debt but little iron. In 1840, McCormick abandoned this boondoggle and returned to work on the reaper, but he never lost his penchant for get-rich-quick schemes.

Fighting his way to the top of the farm machinery business, McCormick displayed a knowledge of manufacturing, a subtle understanding of the market for his products, and a farsighted perception of the shape and direction of American agricultural development. These instincts, however, often deserted him when he confronted an opportunity to speculate. The glittering prospect of wealth lurking in the earth particularly addled him. Even late in life, when his business had made him a wealthy man, he poured $200,000 into a hole in the ground, investing in a gold mine that he never saw, complaining afterward of "the most *outrageous swindle* that could be perpetrated." Like many another entrepreneur, McCormick demonstrated that beyond the qualities that made him wealthy and successful, his personality included a large dose of childlike naïveté, which money and power only magnified.

In contrast with his leap into the iron business, McCormick crept forward cautiously with his reaper. In December 1839, he advertised in the *Richmond Enquirer,* declaring the reaper ready for general sale, and promising to fill any orders in time for the next harvest. Certainly he had incentives to get going. The machine worked, at least sometimes, and when it did, it halved the labor cost of harvesting. Many farmers had already seen it in action, and their testimonials, together with a number of articles in the press, aroused significant interest. In addition, a competitor, the first of many that McCormick faced in his career, had entered the field in 1833, six years earlier. This worthy, sporting the picturesque name Obed Hussey, had invaded McCormick's territory with a reaper of his own invention. Goaded to action, McCormick sold two machines in 1840, but his claims of perfection proved premature when both failed. Consequently, he withdrew from the market in 1841 to spend a year in the Walnut Grove workshop, getting the bugs out of the mechanism. In 1842, he reentered the market and sold six, in 1843, 29.

By 1844, McCormick believed that at last he had a machine good enough to capture a large share of the market. The market itself, however, had gotten on the move. The national government, through the process established by the Northwest Ordinance of 1787 and subsequent acts, together with its survey of the land, had converted the lands of former European North American empires first into territories and then into states. The process had transformed unorganized space into "property" that individuals could own and exploit. The Erie and other canals, the Great Lakes, and the rivers of the Midwest had opened the grain markets of the East Coast and Europe to western farmers. Furthermore, the railroad, as everyone knew, would soon open up those areas not reached by waterways. By 1840, a single county in western New York grew more wheat than all the New England states, and two New York counties outstripped Virginia and Maryland combined. The future lay even farther westward, in the great flat open spaces that stretched to the Rockies. In 1845, when New York led the United States by producing 16 million bushels of wheat, Ohio ran a close second with 13 million bushels. A steady stream of settlers, including immigrants from Europe and native New Englanders, poured west. "I sing New England," lyricized William Ellery Channing, "as she lights her fires in every Prairie's midst." In New England itself, some fires went out. In the 1880s, English poet Matthew Arnold saw long-derelict farms in the Connecticut River valley, depopulated in favor of the broad prairie expanses where "hundreds, nay thousands, of acres . . . enclosed by one fence [form] a campania of waving grain the like of which one may search the rest of the world in vain to find."

As the settlers spread west, they pushed the frontier of commercial agriculture ahead of them. Between 1840 and 1850, the population of Ohio expanded from 1.5 million to 2 million, of Indiana from 700,000 to 1 million, of Illinois from 500,000 to 900,000. During the same period, wheat production rose from 84 million to 100 million bushels. Because of a fortunate combination of factors, the demand for wheat expanded as rapidly as production. Population increase in the United States and in Europe, together with bad European harvests and a reduction of import duties on American grain, created a market that absorbed all the wheat American farmers could grow and then some.

"Western Farmer!" exhorted one American observer from his post overseas,

> what are you going to do for the Old World next year? Are you going to feed them, or let them die of hunger? If you cannot . . . grow *one thousand millions* of bushels . . . for them the coming season, and send it over . . . they will come after it themselves, and your prairies will swarm with them, as with an ocean of bull frogs. So be up now and at it. There will be no potatoes raised [in Great Britain] this season, and you must plant . . . for half the world.

Planting, however, didn't block the way to feeding "half the world"; harvesting did. With so much land available for settlement, farm labor grew scarcer despite immigration. One western New York farmer commented in 1845, "Many a farmer with an excited woebegone face have I seen this season, riding about in search of [workers] . . . but experienced [men] were few indeed." Not only the shortage of labor but also the large acreage of western farms made them ideal for mechanization. Westerners needed machinery and urged their eastern brethren to supply it. In 1842, the *Union Agriculturalist and Western Prairie Farmer* of Chicago wrote, "Inventors— here is a field for you to operate in; anything that you wish to have introduced into extensive use, which you know to be really valuable, you can bring here with a good prospect of success. Bring along your machines."

In June 1844, as the annexation of Texas, with its thousands of acres of cotton lands, failed its first test in Congress, Cyrus McCormick went west to the wheat fields and took along his machine. Jolting and swaying in crowded stagecoaches, wading through spittle and tobacco juice on the decks of canal boats, surviving the rancid food of travelers' hostelries, McCormick journeyed to western New York, Ohio, Michigan, Indiana, Illinois, Wisconsin, Missouri, and Kentucky, demonstrating the reaper as he went. In the Ohio valley, McCormick saw, as Whitney had seen in Georgia 40 years before, crops rotting in the fields for want of a machine to process them.

McCormick returned home and announced triumphantly that his machines had performed "without a failure and with the most perfect success." The western agricultural press echoed his enthusiasm. The Chicago *Daily Journal* declared the reapers

> just the thing for our prairies, where more grain is sown than can possibly be gathered in the ordinary way, and their comparative cheapness puts them within reach of every tiller of the soil. So indispensable will be their use that hereafter the sickle [and] the scythe . . . may as well hang themselves "upon the willow."

The Chicago *Daily Democrat* reported

> the . . . universal opinion of the farmers of the prairies [is] that the quantity of wheat grown [will be] greatly increased by the facilities for harvesting afforded by the Reaper . . . and if they can get enough of McCormick's Reapers, they can beat the world . . . growing wheat.

McCormick himself, as well as his machine, came in for lavish praise, a delicacy for which he developed an insatiable appetite. Even in the 1840s, he seemed destined for a place in the pantheon of greats, which the pragmatic Americans reserved not for thinkers who idled away their hours pondering recondite abstractions, but for those who could bring dreams into practical realization. The same American attitudes that had anointed an inventor as "The Artist of His Country," echoed 40 years later in an Iowan who lauded McCormick as one of the men bringing America into "the *'golden age'* of agriculture," as significant to mankind as the golden philosophical ages of yore. "The introduction of machinery for harvesting forms a new era in farming on the prairies," he declared, "and had the inventor chanced to live in old Greece or Rome they would have held a high place in mythology. . . . One such practical man as McCormick does more for his kind than a thousand theorizers on Guano [bird dung]." William H. Seward, one of McCormick's patent attorneys (and later Abraham Lincoln's secretary of state), also invoked the classical comparisons favored by educated Americans: "No General or Consul drawn in a chariot through the streets of Rome by order of the Senate ever conferred upon mankind benefits so great as he."

As a woeful procession of innovators has learned, it is one thing to have one's invention and one's talents applauded, but quite another to embody these in a successful business organization. Between the reaper and its market lay the welter of obstacles in manufacturing, transportation, and sales that had vanquished Eli Whitney in the 1790s. Moreover, by the time McCormick returned to Virginia in the fall of 1844, confident of a western market, his original patent had only four years left to run, with renewal uncertain. Farmers' hostility to monopoly in the form of patents had abated not a whit since Whitney's day. Their sentiments found powerful expression in

Congress, as did the opposition of competitors such as Hussey, each of whom had his champion in the nation's capital.

McCormick needed to produce a lot of machines in a hurry, and his small workshop at Walnut Grove, poorly located to supply the western markets, could not in any case turn out more than 40 or 50 a year. To get his demonstration machines to the western states in 1844, McCormick had had to cart them up the valley to Scottsville, Virginia, ship them by canal boat to Richmond, by freighter to New Orleans, and then by steamboat up the Mississippi. The expense of this circuitous route, added to the costs of manufacture and an allowance for profit, would price the machines beyond the reach of most prospective customers and presented a golden opportunity to western rivals, of which a dozen had appeared in Illinois alone by 1847.

To step up production swiftly in locations central to western markets, McCormick took a step that Whitney and Miller had considered and rejected: he temporarily licensed manufacturers in other cities to produce his machine. Such arrangements between patentees and manufacturers had become common by the 1840s. The manufacturer paid a stipulated fee for each machine produced (if the inventor had his way) or sold (if the manufacturer had his). McCormick made such arrangements in Brockport, New York; Cincinnati; Chicago; St. Louis; and elsewhere. At the same time, he enlisted his brothers William and Leander to push the Walnut Grove shop to its utmost. Together, these installations produced and sold some 1,200 machines between 1844 and 1848, when McCormick closed the Walnut Grove shop and opened a factory in Chicago.

Sub-manufacturing, however, worked poorly; the licensees proved slow in production and sloppy in workmanship. The nature of harvesting, seasonal work with a brief window of opportunity, meant that 10 days' tardiness in delivery amounted to a year's delay and the loss of a year's income; moreover, delivering a poorly made machine that broke down at the crucial moment or damaged the crop generated almost as much customer fury as delivering no machine at all. Consequently, when sub-manufacturing agreements expired, McCormick did not renew them. After 1851, his entire output came from his own factory.

Manufacturing involved only the application of known methods to achieve mass production. By the time McCormick moved to Chicago in 1848, manufacturers understood and had access to Whitney's legacy of machine-made interchangeable parts. McCormick could bring the required tools and a steam engine to drive them, hire experts to install and run them, and mass produce from the outset.

But selling the harvester presented unprecedented problems. Rarely had American business had to sell complex machines to nonexpert buyers. In the East, the better railroads relied more and more on designated purchasing officers who kept up with the increasingly complex railroad equipment. As time passed, the railroads' agents dealt directly with manufacturers, eliminating the commission merchants who had served as middlemen in the railroads' early years. But these transactions took place in a market populated by a relatively small number of expert buyers and sellers.

McCormick faced a market made up of thousands of independent farmers. Tough customers in every sense of the term, they refused to buy reapers the way McCormick bought gold mines, sight unseen. They demanded demonstrations, especially ones in which manufacturers pitted their products against one another. Success at such competitions demanded the presence of an expert at the reap-off to adjust the machines to local conditions and to make running repairs. In the early days, McCormick himself attended many exhibitions. As the search for markets and sub-manufacturers took up more of his time, he dragooned his brothers into service. Relying on family members or on old, trusted acquaintances had sufficed in preindustrial America, as it had for centuries in Europe. But mass markets made such nepotistic methods obsolete. No one had a family that large. For manufacturers who, like McCormick, produced volume goods for diffuse markets, mass distribution presented greater problems than mass production and forced the manufacturers to create organizations to handle sales as well as manufacturing.

Marketing the reaper involved more than competitions and displays at county fairs. After the move to Chicago in 1848, McCormick participated in fewer such events because of the often uncertain outcome. Sometimes his machine lost; sometimes biased local judges favored a competitor's product. The McCormick reaper did win its share of medals, prizes, and certificates of merit, which the company proudly displayed. But competitors did the same, and farmers, facing conflicting claims, often believed none. In addition, farmers found that results of hard daily usage fell suspiciously short of those in staged competitions. The result, as the editor of the *Farmers' Register* observed, was

> grave injury inflicted on deserving inventors themselves, as well as on the public by the *puffing system.* Every new invention . . . whatever may be its . . . merit or demerit, is ushered forth with puffs upon puffs. Dupes are made, and knaves who puff, and sell, profit at the expense of the fools who believe and buy. . . . The more discreet . . . who know the working of the puffing system, stand aloof, and trust [neither] true statements [nor] false.

Since reaper marketing demanded extensive personal contact, McCormick gradually came to rely more on a far-flung network of salesmen, on his company's reputation, and on his factory's ability to out-produce any competitor's, than on showboating before increasingly skeptical audiences at bucolic gatherings.

The reaper was, for its time, a delicate and complicated machine. In fact, nothing so complex had ever been widely marketed before. Few customers, moreover, could claim much mechanical expertise; unlike the manufacturers of railway equipment, McCormick sold to a nonexpert clientele. From the outset, McCormick salesmen had to instruct farmers in the use and care of the machine. Even the mules and horses that pulled it required breaking to the task; otherwise, they had a tendency to bolt across the fields, trying to escape the rattling contraption pursuing them.

In the 1840s, when sales numbered in the dozens, McCormick often urged his brothers to handle deliveries personally: "William or Leander could attend to . . . putting together, explaining, and having printed directions [for the machine]." Later, printed instructions accompanied every machine, explaining its operation, adjustment, the need for lubrication, the best technique for sharpening the cutting knives, and the replacement of broken parts.

Printed instructions or not, the machines often broke down, requiring repairs or adjustments that the farmers would not or could not perform. The early reapers acquired a reputation for fragility that constituted one of the major sales obstacles to be overcome. This reputation survived long after the reaper passed from the experimental stage. In the 1850s, for example, one farm journalist dismissed all reapers, even McCormick's, as of little value unless the farmer had "a Blacksmith shop at each corner of the field."

Breakdowns often resulted from farmers' attitude toward maintenance, an attitude similar to one once encountered by an automobile service manager friend of mine. A furious customer confronted him with a car that rattled, shook, and belched smoke. A quick check showed that the car had 64,000 miles on the odometer and no oil in the crankcase. "Did you ever change the oil?" my friend asked. "Change the oil! Why the hell should I change the oil?" the customer demanded heatedly. "I paid $8,000 dollars for this car. What the hell was wrong with the oil they put in it? I'll never buy this make again." Like this frustrated motorist, many farmers felt that a machine that cost so much should run by itself and forever. One bedeviled reaper repairman commented, "I am sorry I enlisted [for this job] . . . the Machiens are in the worst plight imaginable. I have found them outdoors and frozen down Just where they used them last." But even the most bullheaded characters needed coddling, as McCormick knew, lest they become enemies. In the early years, the factory supplied the farmers with the name of a nearby mechanic, along with the printed instructions. "I think it would be well to refer persons in the vicinity of Richmond to Mr. Parker for repairs," one of McCormick's agents wrote in 1845. "It is desirable to give satisfaction to all if possible, for now in the infancy of the reaper's existence a few dissatisfied persons might do you serious injury." But such casual arrangements with people who owed no particular allegiance to the company proved as unsatisfactory as agreements with sub-manufacturers. The need to provide reliable service over a widespread area contributed to the development of a network of company agents.

The company also had to supply spare parts. After the first few years, the parts were interchangeable, but the reaper's frequent redesign meant that parts for one year's model often would not fit another's. The company tried to meet this difficulty by furnishing a set of spares with each machine. When this proved unsatisfactory, it set up a parts department at the Chicago factory. Farmers could send a defective part to the plant, where shop men matched it against a collection of all the machines the company had ever built. Using drawings pulled from the files, the company shop then duplicated the part. This method proved slow, expensive, and unsatisfactory. The machines broke down during the harvest, precisely when most needed, just when few farmers could wait for the factory to duplicate and return the defective component. The company had to establish stockpiles of parts quickly available when needed.

Finally, the reaper cost a lot of money—an average of $130 before the Civil War. Few farmers had that kind of cash, and banks, which had no interest in consumer finance, would rarely lend it to them. The company, therefore, had to interpose itself as a credit intermediary, selling machines on the installment plan and using its own superior credit to borrow operating funds until farmers paid up. Obviously, the company couldn't restrict credit sales to members of the McCormick family, its friends, and its acquaintances; in effect, McCormick had to pawn his firm's resources and lend the proceeds to thousands of strangers scattered across the prairie outback. No small sum sufficed: by 1858, farmers owed McCormick half a million dollars; two years later this had grown to a million dollars.

To survive in this kind of risky business, the firm needed reliable credit information before the sale and aggressive debt collection after it. In the East, formal credit rating services, the forerunners of Dun & Bradstreet, appeared in the 1840s and 1850s, but these agencies supplied no information on the probity of midwestern farmers.

McCormick thus had to devise some structure to demonstrate the machines, sell and repair them, supply spare parts, evaluate credit, and make collections. During the Virginia years, McCormick had relied on a motley troop consisting of himself, other family members, newspaper editors (thought useful because of their potential value as publicists), and blacksmiths. These catch-as-catch-can arrangements worked badly enough in Virginia but broke down entirely after the company moved to Chicago and began mass production. Searching for a solution to this combination of marketing problems, McCormick found himself in unexplored territory, for no manufacturer had yet encountered similar vexations. McCormick had to have a widespread network of dependable agents, loyal to the Chicago factory and its products but familiar with local business conditions, farming practices, and, above all, the credit worthiness of prospective customers. No prototype of such a network existed; however, distribution of general merchandise, much of it sold on credit, had long since evolved in small-town and rural America, the province of merchants and storekeepers in the towns and peddlers in the countryside.

On this existing foundation, McCormick found he could build. Successful merchants, though he could know but few of them personally, at least belonged to a trustworthy category and had long experience with credit sales. Beginning with an adaptation of the merchant-peddler system of the 1850s, the company developed a sales and service system that evolved from a loose-knit assortment of agents and subagents (whose functions corresponded roughly to those of merchants and peddlers respectively) into a highly structured, closely regulated network of franchised dealerships. These marketing problems, ultimately encountered by all mass producers of goods with similar inherent problems of sales, service, and finance, thus contributed to the shift from personalized to bureaucratic business methods that invariably accompanied industrialization.

McCormick's new sales methods aroused the ire of his farmer customers, who regarded dealers as unwelcome intruders who disrupted the farmers' direct relationship with the company and had the gall to charge for the depersonalization. Responding to these attacks, denying that its agents acted as "parasitic middlemen," the firm used examples it thought its rustic critics could comprehend. His agents, McCormick argued, were as necessary to him "as clerks were to the owner of a store." After all, the company asked, "Would you, a farmer, sell a horse on credit to the first stranger who came along?" In the 1870s and 1880s, this plan translated into a network of franchised dealerships. Copied and expanded to a national scale by wagon and carriage manufacturers, it became the prototype for modern dealerships that sell automobiles and other consumer durables requiring demonstrations, service, parts, and financing.

The success of this system of sales and service, the first of its kind, and not simply the productivity of his factory, carried McCormick to the top of the farm machinery industry and kept him there despite fierce competition and the expiration of his patents.

In the beginning, the company's agents and subagents restricted themselves largely to sales and credit functions, leaving mechanical problems to the factory's parts and repairs departments, or to company mechanics sent out from Chicago after the season's production ended. As the years passed, the agents assumed these responsibilities as well. The company expected its agents to provide showrooms, to display the machines, to "travel thoroughly . . . through the wheat growing portions" of a specific district, to sell to "responsible and trustworthy farmers only," to hire "efficient assistant agents," to deliver machines, to "devote themselves actively to putting up, starting and setting to work the . . . reapers," and to make collections, as well as to stock spare parts and make repairs. Eventually the company got out of the repair business altogether, telling its agents that the factory "should not be made a graveyard for broken-down or imperfect machines. . . . Our rule . . . is that every general shall take care of his own wounded and bury his own dead." This directive meant that dealers also had to repair and resell trade-ins, although in practice they limited overhauls to whatever a paintbrush could accomplish. Dealers also had to perform auxiliary services, such as stocking twine for the binders (machines that tied the wheat in bundles as it was cut) that came on the market after the Civil War, and negotiating with railroads for rebates on shipments to their territories.

Originally, the company made year-to-year arrangements with their representatives. Soon, however, the principal agents became permanent company employees, working on a salary rather than a commission basis, restricted to the sale of McCormick products, and held responsible for hiring and supervising subagents. The agent's lot was not always a happy one. When the factory overproduced, he came under great pressure to push the machines into the market. This often led to sales to farmers who could ill afford further debts, through a process a Detroit car dealer once described to me as " taking bad paper to move old iron." McCormick thus engaged in a forerunner of the modern technique of restoring the market's vital signs by injections of consumer-credit adrenalin, a method that reflected traditional American confidence in the better days to come. In boom times, when factory output fell short of demand, angry customers swarmed the agent like hornets. Most burdensome of all, the company hounded its dealers to collect from the farmers, many of whom could not pay, and some of whom felt that old man McCormick with all his money could, like the dentist, wait.

Obviously, success as an agent demanded an aggressive character. The company exhorted its representatives to have "spunk," "grit," and "sand," to "spit on your fists," "make it hot for them," and "to keep on top of the heap." When the competition got hot, the company apparently required something more. One home office representative, commenting on the failure of a Minnesota agent, wrote,

> Edgar [has] trouble all over his dist[rict]. . . . The only reason I can assign is that he has too many *churchmen* for [sub-]agts. I believe in religion & temperance but it ain't worth a "cuss" to run the Reaper trade on in Minnesota: it requires cheek & muscle and I am sorry to say some "evasions" from the truth to successfully sell McCormick harvesters with the opposition we have. . . . You have got to fight the Devil with fire and it is no use trying to fool him on sweetened water.

As the field organizations expanded, the company offices in Chicago underwent an evolution of their own. A subdivision of labor soon separated the manufacturing function from the others. By 1859, the company's office had specialists who dealt exclusively with one aspect of business outside the factory, including agent supervision, collections, purchasing, shipping, repairs and spare parts, and accounting. In time, each of these individuals metamorphosed into a department with an office and field staff, thus nudging the company down the road from family to bureaucratic management. A printing department published a company newspaper called *The Farmers' Advance* that reached a circulation of 350,000 in the early 1880s. The company also published 800,000 thirty-page pamphlets annually, printed in five or six different languages, some 8,000 colored show cards, and repair catalogues listing spare parts and their prices.

From his first days in business, McCormick had pioneered in widespread advertising. As sales expanded, the policy continued with unabated vigor and soon boasted a specialized staff of its own. "Trying to do business without advertising," the company declared in *The Farmers' Advance,* "is like winking at a pretty girl through a pair of green goggles. You may know what you are doing, but no one else does." Advertising not only reached the market, but, as the company found, expanded it as well, persuading many a farmer to buy machines he neither needed nor could afford.

By fair means or foul, the whirlwind activities of the sales staff created a forced draft that kept the factory boilers at full steam. Production rose from 1,500 in 1849 to 4,500 in 1858 to 8,000 in 1868. In 1871, the original factory burned in the great Chicago fire. A new and larger one arose and then expanded as production rose to 10, 12, and 15,000 machines per year. All this made Cyrus McCormick a rich man. In 1849, profits totaled $65,000; in 1856, $300,000; in 1878, $600,000; in 1880, $1,200,000. Floods, droughts, Hessian flies, weevils, armyworms, wheat blight, chinch bugs, and grasshoppers beset the farmers, but the McCormick machine churned on.

By 1858, Cyrus McCormick had become a millionaire; when he died in 1882, a millionaire 10 times over. After 1858, McCormick devoted increasingly less time to the immediate supervision of his business. In fact, from 1858 until 1871, when he returned to supervise the rebuilding after the Chicago fire, McCormick spent little time in Chicago. Most of the day-to-day responsibility fell to his brothers: William ran the office, Leander the factory. Crying family unity, Cyrus had induced his brothers to come to Chicago in 1840, though both they and their wives lamented leaving the soil of Virginia. Like an Oriental satrap, McCormick arrayed his family about him, harrying his sisters and brothers-in-law to join the clan in Chicago as well.

But McCormick's zest for family unity stopped at the factory gate. During their first 10 years in Chicago, his brothers received only a salary, while Cyrus grew wealthy on the profits. Eventually they protested big brother's meanness. William demanded "something considerable more than a salary out of the business." Leander added, "I have done *not a little* for the machine and I am resolved not to be satisfied without a pretty strong interest if I remain in the business." These demands first came in 1857, but the brothers did not become partners until 1859, when they threatened to quit. By that time, they had become nearly indispensable to Cyrus McCormick, particularly since he had in mind spending less, not more, time on the reaper business.

Partnership, however, did little to heal the wounds of long exploitation. The brothers increasingly resented doing the lion's share of the work while Cyrus indulged his hobbies and perambulated the world collecting trophies and applause. "C.[yrus] H. is the picture of health," complained William's wife; "he takes it easy and thinks . . . he does the hardest of work." Exhausted by his responsibilities, William collapsed and died in 1865. Leander toiled on, but grew more embittered, particularly when Cyrus dragged his feet about admitting Leander's son to partnership.

In 1858, Cyrus McCormick married Nancy Fowler, a Presbyterian choir-singer 25 years his junior. The union further divided the brothers when Cyrus's wife proved a tough-minded woman with a strong business sense. She became his most, and often his only, trusted business confidant, to the anger and frustration of his brothers. McCormick legend has it that she, not they, persuaded him to rebuild after the Chicago fire of 1871. Unquestionably, her social pretensions and religious fervor encouraged him in the activities that diverted his attention from the business after their marriage. Leaving his brothers to "fight the Devil with fire" and supply the necessary "cheek," "muscle," and "evasions," McCormick reveled in the company of "churchmen" and lapped at the "sweetened water" of health spas. He developed a taste for musical soirees and enjoyed hobnobbing with moguls such as August Belmont and Cyrus Field, as well as playing power broker with political luminaries such as Samuel J. Tilden. In Chicago and New York, where he bought houses after his marriage, he dabbled in politics. In 1860, he maneuvered to get the Democratic nomination for mayor of Chicago, but failed. He served as chairman of the county central committee of the Democratic Party in Chicago. In 1864, he ran for Congress as a Democratic peace candidate and got trounced three to one. For years, he lusted for a role as political kingmaker, but the party bosses took his money, drank his wine, shook his hand, and ignored him.

He fared better in the religious world. Always a conservative, he financed churches and a seminary staffed by divines who shared, or at least professed to share, his negative views on abolition of slavery and revision of church dogma. In these matters, he showed plenty of cheek and muscle of his own. On one occasion, he cut off the salary, credit, and coal supply of a minister who transgressed the doctrine according to McCormick.

Urged on by his brother William, he invested in real estate, becoming the largest landlord in Chicago. To his gold-mining speculations, he added a series of ventures in railroads. For a man with such rigid criteria in selecting worshippers, McCormick joined some tacky predators on the hunt for the railroad dollar. In association with the gentlemen of the Crédit Mobilier, who plundered the stockholders of the Union Pacific Railroad, McCormick profited nicely; however, he himself got fleeced by the Southern Railway Association. In the Southern Association, McCormick, a diehard southern sympathizer and postwar contributor to southern causes, allied himself with Henry S. McComb, a rogue and a carpetbagger, though, like McCormick, a loudly proclaimed Christian.

The Civil War further separated McCormick from his business. A Virginian, a slaveholder, and an outspoken supporter of the southern cause, McCormick opposed, avowedly on constitutional grounds, forceful preservation of the union. But his legalese did little to deter the wrath of the public, or of the Chicago *Tribune,* which denounced him as a "rebel" and a "slave-driver." As a man with a lot of property that patriotic mobs might torch, McCormick issued a public statement in April 1861, declaring that his "utmost efforts were directed toward the maintenance of peace, believing . . . that the best interests of the country would be thereby promoted." Now that the war had come, however, he proclaimed his allegiance:

> Though a native of the south, I am a citizen of Illinois and of the United States, and as such shall bear true allegiance to the Government. That allegiance I shall never violate.

So much for his public position. Private behavior suggested quite a different point of view. Early in 1862, he sailed to Europe, ostensibly on business, but with the ulterior motive of soliciting intervention on behalf of the Confederacy.

His company meanwhile trimmed its sails to the winds of war and steered a prosperous tack. In the months before fighting broke out, the company reminded its southern agents to emphasize McCormick's southern birth, and the southern heritage of the reaper itself. Copies of Chicago newspaper articles denouncing McCormick went south to show that his position was "right" on slavery. While reminding Virginia agents that "our heart still yields allegiance to the 'Old Dominion,'" the company simultaneously told its northern representatives that it opposed secession and would rally to the "Stars and Stripes first, last, and always."

Like many northern manufacturers, the McCormicks had a relatively small southern market, but one that they hesitated to abandon. Weeks after Fort Sumter, the company stood willing to sell machines in the South, provided customers would pay cash. The McCormicks shared this attitude with other manufacturers on both sides of the Mason–Dixon Line. For example, as hostilities approached, Samuel Colt, an arms manufacturer born and raised in New England, offered to build gun factories for southern states and rushed his agents south to take orders. "Make hay while the sun shines," Colt urged his factory superintendents, ordering a step up in production. Weeks after Fort Sumter had fallen, Joseph Anderson, proprietor of the Tredegar Iron Works in Richmond, Virginia, submitted a bid for an artillery ammunition contract being let by the federal government. His company had had such contracts in the past, Anderson argued, had always filled them on time, and would do so now regardless of "politics." Thus, the McCormicks, like other manufacturers, subjugated patriotism to business until the troops drew impassable lines. Luckily for those on the north side of the lines, patriotism (or protestations of it) proved compatible with profits.

After a brief downturn in 1861 and 1862, the war proved a bonanza for the McCormick firm. Farm labor marched off to war; crop failures in Europe produced a soaring export market; government spending flooded the land with greenbacks. Finding themselves with a booming market, a greater shortage of hands than ever, and cash a-plenty, farmers rushed to buy machinery. Many paid cash for the first time in their lives, and they also paid long-overdue notes with inflated wartime currency. For years, the McCormicks, like other businessmen, had badgered their creditors for payment. Now the tables turned, bringing a situation where, as William McCormick wrote his brother, "creditors were running away from debtors who pursued them in triumph and paid them without mercy. . . . I . . . told you long ago," he added, that [the law that made greenbacks] legal tender would in the end be a good bankrupt law. "Money" *may* be brought by the bushel to pay . . . us. This legal tender law is . . . a great *leveler.* It will enable the creditor to pay his honest debts with scraps of paper.

Cyrus McCormick played no more role as "a great leveler" than the greenback dollar, despite his lifelong adherence to the people's party of Jefferson and Jackson. His career put a great distance between him and hoi polloi, and he liked it that way. Suspicious of all reform movements, he had no sympathy for the Granger organizations through which grain-belt farmers voiced their protests in the 1870s and 1880s. As a politician and a farm machinery manufacturer, McCormick tempered his public criticisms of the Grangers, who were, after all, potential voters and customers. On issues he thought irrelevant to his own self-interest, such as opposition to monopoly, McCormick publicly expressed sympathy with the Grangers' aims. Privately, he instructed the company's staff to stand fast against any demands that affected the McCormick Harvester Company directly. Rubbing elbows in Grange halls full of sweaty farmers had no charms for Cyrus. His wealth had opened the doors of society's inner sanctums, and he much preferred hobnobbing with the elite at watering holes like the Manhattan Club and Saratoga Springs.

Like many another citizen of the republic, McCormick relished the approval of the Europeans, the more aristocratic the better. In 1851, he exhibited the reaper at the Crystal Palace exhibition in London, winning a Grand Council Medal. In 1855, the French International Exposition awarded him the Grand Medal of Honor. Delighting in these baubles and others collected from lesser European states, he decided in 1866 that selection for the French Legion of Honor would make a crowning touch to his achievements, so he campaigned for the award. "I might," he wrote to a friend in France, "get the 'Cross of Honor' for the Invention & improvement of the Reaping Machine." His friend declared the award attainable "with proper management." McCormick's influential friends in France lobbied hard on his behalf, and on January 5, 1868, the Emperor Napoleon III made McCormick a Chevalier of the Legion of Honor. Thereafter, McCormick proudly wore the Legion's red rosette in his lapel. (What McCormick's fiercely independent Scotch-Irish forebears would have thought of his preening before a petty, third-rate French dictator one can only imagine, but it probably would have paled compared to their reaction when he tried to have his daughter presented to Victoria, queen of hated England.)

The citation that accompanied the award of the Legion of Honor acclaimed McCormick as the "inventor of the reaper." When he received it, he had invented nothing significant for 20 years. The original Virginia Reaper underwent more or less continual improvement and finally gave way in 1870 to a lighter, more efficient model called "the Advance." But these changes merely refined the original design. Over the years, the company expanded its line by adding a mower, a combination reaper-mower, a harvester that not only cut grain but also raked it automatically into piles, and finally a binder that cut the grain and bound it into bundles ready for threshing. All these machines incorporated new and patented ideas, none of them Cyrus McCormick's. When he sought to renew his original patent in 1848, his application failed for lack of novelty. In 1855, he sued a major competitor for infringement of his own patents, but lost.

These setbacks, however, made little difference. As his brother William remarked, "I have often said your money has been made *not* out of your patents but by making and selling the machines." As the most powerful competitor in the field, McCormick could simply buy whatever patents he needed to keep pace with competition. His factory and sales force did the rest. As he himself remarked on the subject of twine binders,

> The self binding part of these machines [was] invented by others, while they have been brought to the present state of practical utility, economy & adaptation to public wants in my works & by their operation in the field by men engaged with me in my business.

With such a powerful rival already in the field, few inventors could find the capital to commence manufacture on their own. It made more sense to license an established firm to use their patent in return for a royalty on each machine built. McCormick's opponents, not without some reason, denounced him as a "monied monopolist" who siphoned cash from the farmers' pockets into his own, and denounced his patent suits as attempts to "protect [himself] from the improvements of anybody else and so to stop the whole inventive genius of the country." The presence of wealthy potential licensees like McCormick, however, may have encouraged inventors rather than discouraged them and thus accelerated rather than retarded the diffusion of technology. If so, then in some ways big business preserved individual initiative on the one hand even while destroying competition on the other. In any case, McCormick's patent buying typified a pattern that appeared with increasing frequency thereafter.

Born at a time when farmers harvested their grain crops as they had since time immemorial, Cyrus McCormick died in 1882, having lived to see the mechanical reaper prove its worth in France's breadbasket, the "*Pays de Grande Culture*," the expanses of Australia, and elsewhere around the world. As with the British Empire, the sun never set on the McCormick reaper. He and his competitors had converted the American prairies from open space to the granary that fed the United States and sometimes much of Europe. In some ways his firm, which did so much to modernize the American agricultural economy, remained an anachronism at his death, stranded halfway between traditional family management and modern bureaucratic control. McCormick would neither relinquish control of his business nor exercise it consistently after 1858. Together with his brothers' disaffection, this led to diminishing efficiency and loss of direction.

By the time McCormick died, his firm had become something of a rudderless ship, its lack of direction masked by the fact that American farmers had entered a period of unparalleled prosperity that kept demand for farm machinery high. When McCormick's son prepared to enter the business in 1879, W. J. Hanna, who had succeeded William McCormick as head of the company's office, wrote that the firm

> practically has no head—every man in the office seems to do what is right in his own eyes—makes his own hours, and goes home when he pleases without leave. . . . A general laxity prevails, and that laxity extends to the

agents likewise. They are allowed far too much freedom, and feel quite independent of the *apparent* government of the office.

A similar laxity prevailed in the factory itself, as evidenced by the fact that despite significant increases in annual production, the cost of constructing each machine remained constant.

Despite these failings, McCormick, in reaching the diffuse market for farm equipment and expanding it through advertising and credit, had created a system of sales and service that became one component of the modern industrial firm in the United States and beyond. A complex man, McCormick shrewdly foresaw Chicago's future role as the hub of American agricultural commerce, but naïvely fell prey to swindles by gold mine and railroad promoters. Sometimes generous and forgiving, he contributed hundreds of thousands of dollars to his church and to Washington and Lee University; he became friends with generals Grant, Sherman, and Sheridan, who had scourged his beloved South during the war. But he turned mean and petty as well, particularly to his inferiors: he upbraided subordinates for wasting the company's money on unnecessary postage stamps or superfluous words in telegrams. Secretaries and servants never lasted long. When offended, he became a venomous, indefatigable enemy. A millionaire, he once declined to pay the Pennsylvania Railroad an excess baggage charge of $8.70 that he considered unjust, although his obstinacy meant that his wife and two small children had to cancel their trip. When the railroad subsequently lost the baggage, he instituted a suit for damages and pursued it for 18 years.

His character thus exhibited paradoxes common among his countrymen. Generous and stingy, ambitious and lazy, clever and naïve, energetic and narrow-minded, unscrupulous and self-righteous, he pursued self-aggrandizement, flattening obstacles human and otherwise that stood in his way. In the process, he multiplied humankind's ability to feed itself and made an enduring contribution to the American business system. Ultimately, his name disappeared into the corporate anonymity of International Harvester (formed in 1902), but his work lives on. The giant combines that move through wheat fields all over the world trace their ancestry to the clumsy little reaper born in the Shenandoah Valley of Virginia.

Chapter 4

The Star-Spangled Scotchman

ANDREW CARNEGIE

Andrew Carnegie: the Steel King as philanthropist

W e go back a long way, Andy and I. Even before I could read, I heard the story of this Scottish immigrant boy whose rise to wealth and power became part of the American "rags to riches" legend. When I went to school, the teacher directed me to the nearby Carnegie Library, where I discovered Zane Grey and Richard Halliburton, who convinced me that I might someday play shortstop in the major leagues or swim in the Panama Canal. (I'm batting 50 percent so far.)

In my salad days as an academic, Carnegie's life provided the material for one book, and one of his foundations supported the research for another, as a result of which I've appeared on television—the History Channel and PBS in the United States and the BBC in Scotland. Someday I expect I'll retire (though why any academic would retire I haven't discovered yet) on a pension fund for which Carnegie furnished the seed money. In the hiatus between the railroad and college, however, I had already discovered another aspect of Carnegie's handiwork, the steel industry.

Somebody told me you could find gold in that thar steel; you just needed to buy a truck and go haul it. Like Cyrus McCormick, I should have known better, but my mother never heard the country song telling mommas how to raise their babies:

Don't let 'em pick guitars and drive them ol' trucks;
Let 'em be doctors and lawyers and such.

It took a while to learn that pricey lesson on my own. A friend once asked my partner, "Is there any money in the trucking business?" "Damn right," he replied, "there's several thousand dollars of my money in it somewhere."

Although at the time I couldn't see the benefits that lay obscured in a stack of unpaid fuel bills, I realize now that I got a bargain. As an "independent owner-operator," I joined a fraternity for which the traditional equation of movement with individual liberty survives as a living creed. Though much truckers' conversation tends to be, as one cynic remarked, "lies about them waitresses and how fast them trucks will go," I nevertheless learned a good bit about independence, self-reliance, and the pros and cons of Brother James Hoffa, then president of the Teamsters Union. I also encountered the sometimes diabolical nature of government interference with individual initiative and cunning ways to avoid it. I learned how to fake the Interstate Commerce Commission logbook so as to drive as many hours a day as I could stay awake, regardless of what the law mandated; I mastered the art of running the rig's outside wheels over the curb instead of over the scales at a turnpike tollbooth, thereby holding down the weight and the toll; I memorized the locations of treacherous downhill grades, as well as the names of small towns where cops carrying flashlights and wearing white socks lurked to trap the unwary, conveying them first to the scales and then to all-night justices of the peace; I ate lots of bad food and saw lots of beautiful country; I explored mills (most of them now long gone) where steel poured out in a continuous ribbon at 30 miles an hour, and factories that made bathtubs and fence posts on assembly lines.

During long layovers between loads, spent in dozens of cinder-block modern motels, the desk clerks, chambermaids, and waitresses told me their life stories. Around the pools and bars of these hostelries, the natives—airline crews and working girls—regaled me with stories of trips around the world, while we all waited for our next haul. In fact, for a business that attracted the independent-minded who craved freedom of movement, trucking turned out to involve a lot of truckling: to the tyranny of the telephone; the vanity of the commission agent who arranged loads; and the cupidity of loading crews, whom I often had to bribe lest death take care of me before they did.

Steel hauling particularly involved protracted waits, both inside the mill and out. Twelve-hour delays happened too routinely to merit comment, 24 hours often, 48 hours on occasion. Some notorious mills starred in truckers' folklore; drivers widely circulated the tale of one wretch who had frozen to death in his truck while waiting to load at a legendarily lethargic plant. Drivers especially dreaded assignments to United States Steel (the direct descendant of Carnegie Steel), where confusion and indifference dominated everything. After lying beached for 24 hours, along with a school of other trucks, at Carnegie's original mill in Pittsburgh, I met a colleague who had become a history buff in his plentiful spare time. "I've been reading about old Carnegie," he said, "and if Andy could see this, he'd clean house in a hurry."

In fact "old Carnegie" would have found plenty to rile him, for by the 1960s, the American steel industry, insulated for decades by tariff barriers, war, depression, and lack of capacity among overseas producers, had grown bloated, arrogant, and inefficient. Burdened with obsolete methods and inefficient production, a slipshod mess worsened by management stupidity and perpetuated by lack of research, firms had tacit agreements that set prices and ignored costs, other than to pass them on to customers. This decay more or less characterized other mature American industries such as automobiles and shipbuilding. All of them lay virtually defenseless against any vigorous competitor that could enter the market, as time and Toyota, among others, soon showed.

Confusion and idleness, however, only hinted at the tentacular inefficiencies choking Carnegie's once-streamlined industry. Plying the turnpikes of Ohio, Pennsylvania, and New Jersey, endless lines of trucks shuttled back and forth, carrying steel from the mills of the Delaware Valley to the factories of Ohio, and from the steel mills of Ohio to the factories of the Delaware Valley. Many of the loads at opposite ends differed only in slight variations in weight. With steel products and their prices standardized, and since the manufacturers absorbed the shipping charges, then standardized by law, price competition played little part in the selling and shipping of steel. Assuming a dependable delivery schedule, a manufacturer in Philadelphia didn't care whether he bought his steel from a mill nearby or from one in Cleveland. Once sold, it made no financial difference to buyer or seller which trucking company hauled the steel. Competing for sales and loads, salesmen therefore showered purchasing agents and shipping clerks with emoluments such as Playboy calendars, dinners, and baseball tickets (Cleveland-based salesmen had a handicap: they couldn't give Indians' tickets away in those days).

The resulting inefficiency kept a lot of truckers busy burning a lot of fuel, but it also created a market opportunity perceived by one of my more acute brethren. Under his auspices, drivers gathered nightly at a truck stop outside Philadelphia, made a list of their loads and destinations, and then telephoned a similar group in Ohio. When a driver could match his load to a similar one on the other end of the line, he saved himself a long trip. Representatives from each end met at Somerset, Pennsylvania, midway on the Pennsylvania Turnpike, exchanged paperwork for the matching loads, and returned home. Next morning, each lucky driver delivered the wrong load, but the right paperwork. The system worked because all the steel looked alike and because the trucks got weighed on dispatch, but not on delivery. Eventually, of course, logorrhea overthrew discretion; the story got out, and established inefficiency deposed extemporaneous efficiency. Years later, after I had rummaged through Carnegie's life, I concluded that if Andy had been around, he would first have laughed, then fired the head of shipping and replaced him with the truck driver who found a better way.

Andy wanted things moving around his place, so he promoted hustlers and fired slackers. Sluggishness wasted time as well as money, and time was money, that he knew. Waste offended both his Scottish fetish for thrift and his American fascination with efficiency. These and other personal qualities he translated into management methods that created America's first manufacturing "Big Business," carried him from poor Scottish immigrant boy to richest man in the world, and made him a hero to his countrymen. Like Cyrus McCormick's, his firm's identity eventually disappeared into the anonymity of a corporate merger, but Carnegie himself left an indelible mark on American business and society. His career became a legend, inspiring to some, infamous to others. His wealth became a legacy to the people of both his native and adopted homelands. His system became, like Whitney's theory of production and McCormick's distribution methods, a component of the modern American industrial machine and a key to global competitiveness for any firm entering the arena.

Carnegie was born in November 1835, in Dunfermline, County Fife, Scotland. Andrew Jackson was president of the United States, which comprised 24 states and some 15 million people, 90 percent of them rural residents. The American economy remained overwhelmingly one of farming and trading, though industrialization had gotten underway and household manufacturing had begun its decline. Aside from the New England textile mills and a handful of other exceptions, however, manufacturing remained the province of small shops. Only the first thousand miles of what grew to be a railroad network of a quarter of a million miles existed. Cyrus McCormick had embarked on his ill-fated excursion into the iron business. Karl Marx was a 17-year-old middle-class student in Germany.

In Britain, the Industrial Revolution, powered by steam, swept across the land, eliminating the remaining pockets of traditional handicraft production. Dunfermline, a town of handloom weavers, lay squarely in its path. Its wake churned up the Chartist ferment, demanding political reform and legislative protection against rampaging capitalists. During Carnegie's boyhood, both the Industrial Revolution and the Chartist agitation engulfed Dunfermline. Industrialization succeeded, inflicting dislocation on the Carnegies and thousands of other Scottish families. Chartism failed.

In the bleak decade that became known as "the hungry forties," a quarter of a million British citizens gave up the unequal struggle against the machine and sailed to America. In 1848, the year that Karl Marx published the *Communist Manifesto,* calling on the "workers of the world [to] unite," the Carnegies joined the diaspora.

In the 13 years between Andy's birth in Scotland and his family's departure for America, Scotland had made a vivid impression on him, inculcating attitudes that affected his behavior the rest of his life. Measuring American realities against Scottish ideals, he found scope and outlet for his driving ambitions and developed a paradoxical character that reflected the contrasting worlds of his boyhood in preindustrial Scotland and his manhood in the mechanized United States. Carnegie, whose work made Pittsburgh the nineteenth-century American industrial city par excellence, replete with bleak factories, grimy air, and an unskilled labor force regulated by factory discipline and wages, grew up in a town as unlike Pittsburgh as any imaginable.

Dunfermline's prosperity and stability rested upon an ancient and honorable craft, the handloom weaving of linen. More than half the town's 11,000 inhabitants practiced this craft, handed down from father to son essentially unchanged for centuries. Self-employed, working hours of their own choosing in their own home workshops, earning good wages, the weavers saw themselves as men of substance and self-respect, indebted to no one and subject to no man's beck and call. As one of Dunfermline's more skillful practitioners, Andrew's father, Will Carnegie, enjoyed the respect of his fellow townsmen and the security of a home and family. In 1836, he had such a prosperous year that he moved his family to a larger house, bought three additional looms, and took on apprentices to work them.

But the very factors that made linen weaving such a special art—the large amount of skilled labor and time required to produce each piece—rendered the trade particularly susceptible to mechanization. By 1838, steam mills elsewhere produced goods in such volume that Dunfermline's handloom weavers found prices and demand sinking. This decline, discounted at first as one of the temporary slumps that occurred from time to time, soon proved an irreversible trend. In 1843, the decline became an avalanche when a steam mill opened in Dunfermline. The mill's whistle, sounding the beginning and end of the working day, screeched the death knell for Will Carnegie and his fellow artisans. Since he could no longer work for himself and would not work for others, Will Carnegie's world collapsed around him.

For young Andy, Dunfermline had seemed a magical place, filled with the romance of Scotland's past and the ferment of its present. Although the largest town in County Fife and the center of handicraft production, Dunfermline had a rural setting among hills and glens, overlooking the Firth of Forth. Relics and ruins of Scottish history dotted the landscape, as they still do. As a boy, Andy explored Dunfermline Abbey, Malcolm's Tower, monuments to Mary Queen of Scots, and the palace and tomb of King Robert the Bruce.

Carnegie's uncle George Lauder cast a troubadour's spell over the boy, peopling the ruins with the paladins of Scotland's past—William Wallace, Robert the Bruce, and Shakespearean heroes. To this heady brew the uncle added liberal doses of Scottish ballads and, above all, the poetry of Robert Burns. A self-respecting people must stay free, Andy learned, but real peace could come only through peaceful means. The Scots had shown themselves valiant warriors for centuries, the uncle argued, but heroic tales amounted to a poor return on all the valor and bloodshed. The United Kingdom had swallowed up Scotland's cherished independence; Scottish boys whose grandfathers had marched proudly under the cross of St. Andrew now tramped under the English flag along the highways and byways of the British Empire. Democracy, not war, could fashion the key with which a people could unlock the greatness that lay within them. The United States, Uncle Lauder told Andy, showed what a free people could do. Under his uncle's tutelage, Andy added Benjamin Franklin, George Washington, and Thomas Jefferson to his stock of heroes.

To the enchantments found in days wandering sun-dappled glens and among rain-streaked monuments, young Carnegie added the nocturnal excitements of Dunfermline's political agitation. Dunfermline enjoyed its renown "as perhaps the most radical town in the kingdom," according to Carnegie. Convinced that the People's Charter, with its provision for universal manhood suffrage, could bring to Scotland what the Constitution had provided the people of the United States, Carnegie's father and uncles joined the Chartist movement. In torchlit squares and lamplit parlors, Andy absorbed the guiding principle of the radical reformers: "Political equality, that is all we ask, and then everything else will follow: the prosperous yeoman, the respected artisan, the happy child. Give us the Charter and we can take care of ourselves." By 1847, when Will Carnegie told his son, "Andra, I can get nae mair work," Carnegie's boyhood had instilled attitudes that endured throughout his life: a reverence for the heroic figure, a faith in nationalism, and a belief in political equality as a remedy for mankind's woes. This mental equipment, fashioned in old, decaying Scotland, proved ideally suited to the challenge of young, booming America.

By 1848, the Carnegie family had fallen on desperate times. The father, recognizing that he would never practice his craft again, had sold his idle looms. The responsibility for the family's support had passed to the mother, who squeezed a meager living out of cobbling and storekeeping. Although Samuel Johnson once remarked that "the noblest prospect which a Scotchman e'er perceives is the high-road that leads him to England," the Carnegies looked not toward England, whence came Scotland's misery, but toward the United States, where many a Scot had already found hope. Margaret Carnegie, Andy's mother, had two sisters who had emigrated to the United States in 1840. The sisters had written home often, the tone of their letters reflecting the fluctuating economic climate of their new home:

> I wish I had . . . not come to America this soon—the banking system has made sad havoc . . . business is at a stand. . . . I would not advise any person to come who can get livelihood at home, as trade is very dull here, indeed many who are both willing & able to work find it impossible to find employment. [1842]

Later, the outlook brightened and America proved "far better for the working man. . . . You seem to breathe a freer atmosphere here." In the face of such conflicting advice, the Carnegies clung to their home as long as they could. Only when Dunfermline seemed to offer no hope for the future did the family abandon it. The mother borrowed the passage money, and on May 17, 1848, the Carnegies left Dunfermline on the trek:

> *To the west, to the west, to the land of the free*
> *Where mighty Missouri rolls down to the sea;*
> *Where a man is a man if he's willing to toil,*
> *And the humblest may gather the fruits of the soil. . . .*
> *Where the young may exult and the aged may rest,*
> *Away far away, to the land of the west.*

Many millions before the Carnegies had followed this siren song, and many millions more followed after. For some, the new land delivered all the song promised and more. For others, the "new world" proved not a fertile field, but a graveyard of their hopes.

Emigration traumatized all but the very young. In some individuals, the decision to emigrate signaled not a courageous determination to carry on, but rather the ultimate admission of defeat, the inability to cope with circumstances that some— those who stayed behind—found ways to surmount. Like Joseph Conrad's Lord Jim, or Herman Wouk's Tom Kiefer, who abandoned ships they thought sinking, only to find later that sturdier souls had remained aboard and kept the vessel afloat, some immigrants blighted the rest of their lives with the self-damnation of shame. To this category belonged Will Carnegie, age 43 at the time of sailing: reduced from proud, self-employed craftsman, patriarch, and prominent figure in his ancestral home to penniless nonentity, dependent upon his wife's labor and courage to keep the family together. Emasculated by his shattering experience in Scotland, Will Carnegie did not find manhood, exultation, or rest in "the land of the west." America needed handloom weavers even less than Scotland did; politics offered no foothold, for the Americans already had the Charter; religion provided no solace, for Will had long ago repudiated the Calvinist faith of his ancestors. In the last seven years of his life, as his will to live dwindled, Will became a vagabond peddler. He died a beaten man.

Many immigrants, however, responded energetically to their new surroundings. Like oysters converting the irritation of a grain of sand into the beauty of a pearl, they vindicated their flight in letters home that bristled with pride in the virtues of their new homeland and their own achievements there. Andrew Carnegie and his mother belonged to this group. Margaret, age 33, burned with shame at her husband's failure and despair; at leaving poor and defeated; and at having to beg, borrow, and sell out to get the passage money. Margaret determined that her sons would succeed where her husband had failed, and that she herself would someday return to Dunfermline in triumph. Andrew, age 13, aware of his father's failure and his mother's contempt for it, looked to the future for redemption of the past. Only the younger son, Tom, age 5, boarded the ship unburdened with the baggage of failure.

For the Carnegies, as for millions of other immigrant families, the presence in America of relatives, friends, and fellow countryfolk cushioned the shock of landing in their new home. A strong sense of community pervaded the Scots in America, regardless of their position in the old country. From the day of their arrival, the Carnegie family benefited from the aid of an informal Scottish community. Time and again throughout Andy's career, some Scot appeared at a crucial moment to lend a hand, just as the Yale "old-boy network" had so often rescued Whitney.

In New York, the Carnegies were met by the James Sloane family: Sloane himself a former Dunfermline weaver, Mrs. Sloane a girlhood friend of Margaret Carnegie. In Pittsburgh, Margaret's sisters welcomed them, and other Scots provided employment. Henry Phipps gave Margaret a job cobbling; Andy found work in the textile mill of a Mr. Blackstock, who gave preferential treatment to his fellow Scots. The job paid $1.20 a week. "I have made millions since," Andy later remarked, "but none of these gave me so much happiness as my first week's earnings. I was now a helper of the family, a breadwinner." He soon found a better job in the bobbin factory of John Jay, another Dunfermline expatriate.

At the bobbin factory, young Carnegie demonstrated many of the qualities that would carry him to the top: reliability, a willingness to work hard, an ability to perceive opportunities and to make the most of them. He attacked his pedestrian duties—dipping bobbins into oil and firing the factory boiler—energetically, although the oil smell nauseated him and the boiler frightened him (ironic reactions in a lad who later became an oil speculator and a railroad superintendent). Andy's employer rewarded his ardor with occasional stints in the office. There Carnegie learned the rudiments of accounting, acquiring the first in a set of management tools he assembled while still a young man. He polished this skill by enrolling in a night-school course in double-entry bookkeeping, trudging back and forth through snow to class at the end of 14-hour days at the bobbin factory.

Young Andy thus showed that he had plenty of pluck, but as all dutiful readers of Horatio Alger learned, pluck alone will not suffice; you need a little luck as well. Sure enough, luck ("Fortunatus," as Carnegie called it) arrived, and after only a year of waiting. "My Good Fairy found me in a cellar," Andy rejoiced. Naturally, the good fairy was a Scot, David Brooks, manager of O'Reilly's Telegraph office in Pittsburgh and a crony of Carnegie's Uncle Hogan. Brooks needed a messenger boy for the telegraph office, and whenever possible he hired Scottish immigrant boys. Uncle Hogan nominated Andy, who rushed home for parental consent. Margaret, who thought Andy's subterranean chores at the oil vat and coal bin beneath her son, rejoiced at the new opportunity. She and Andy quickly quashed Will's objections, and Andy presented himself at the telegraph office the next day. A momentous step, the new job not only let Andy escape to "paradise . . . heaven, as it seemed to me, with newspapers, pens, pencils, and sunshine," but more important, as he later recalled, "I felt that my foot was on the ladder and that I was bound to climb."

Opportunity had knocked and Andy, as he so often did, recognized the chance and flung open the door. In leaving the bobbin factory for the telegraph office, however, Carnegie did much more than exchange a tedious job for a more pleasant one; he moved from a business backwater to a mainstream, one then revolutionizing American commerce and industry. The railroad and telegraph together brought the first significant increase in the speed of commerce and communication in centuries. Passengers and goods, hitherto restricted by the snail's pace of wagons, coaches, canal boats, and steamboats, now rushed through weather and across mountains that often brought more primitive methods to a standstill. Communications, agonizingly slow and frustratingly uncertain in the past, now sped virtually instantaneously via the dots and dashes of Morse code. The rails and the wires battered down ancient barriers of space and time, opening land for settlement and markets for exploitation, an impact analogous to and multiplied today's permeating Internet, which in effect has put a telegraph key in the hands of anyone with access to a computer and requires no code beyond literacy.

Thanks to its ideal location, Pittsburgh thrived on America's economy of agriculture and industry. Transportation routes radiated from Pittsburgh like the spokes of a wheel. The Ohio River, together with the Pennsylvania and Ohio canal systems, tied the city to the emerging granary of the Ohio Valley and Great Lakes region and to the established cotton economy of the Mississippi Valley. The Conemaugh River reached eastward to the iron mines and furnaces on the slopes of the Alleghenies; the

Monongahela and Youghiogheny Rivers penetrated the coal deposits of Connellsville, Pennsylvania, and West Virginia; the Allegheny and Clarion Rivers flowed from the iron and oil fields to the north. As enterprisers discovered and developed these natural resources, the rivers funneled them to Pittsburgh, making the city an industrial center just as it had become a commercial center earlier. By 1849, when Carnegie moved to the telegraph office, the city's iron smelters and mills clouded its sky with smoke and fouled its rivers with slime.

From the clicking keys at the telegraph company, Carnegie learned firsthand of the rise and fall of agricultural markets, as well as the negotiations through which merchants and manufacturers joined hands to finance industrial enterprises. He got to know many of the city's prime movers personally by delivering messages to them. The telegraph office thus served as an informal but effective school of commerce and business methods. Bright and eager, Andy soon knew as much about Pittsburgh's business as anyone in town. He knew who sold what to whom, at what price, and on what terms. He learned who succeeded and who failed, as the credit standing of individuals and firms passed through his hands every day.

Distinguishing himself by coming early, staying late, and sweeping out the office when he had no messages to deliver, Andy soon garnered the rewards of virtue. His salary rose from $2.50 to $3.00 a week. The company promoted him, first to part-time telegrapher, then, in 1851, to full-time telegraph operator. (The superintendent who approved his promotion was James D. Reid, born in Dunfermline.)

As a qualified telegraph operator at age 16, Carnegie had achieved a position in the world that might have satisfied a lesser striver for life. He had a job that rewarded responsibility with respect, a salary large enough to support a family, and a prospect of future promotion. But for Carnegie, as for many another ambitious American—Thomas Edison among them—the telegraph office served as a stepping-stone to better things. It did, however, justify writing home to Scotland to boast of his success and the virtues of his new country. "I am past delivering messages now," he wrote to his cousin "Dod" Lauder in Scotland, "and have got to operating. I am to have $4 a week and a good prospect of getting more." In Scotland, he added, "I would have been a poor weaver all my days, but here, I can surely do something better . . . if I don't it will be my own fault, for anyone can get along in this country."

His success, he declared in an argument he would advance throughout his life, reflected the merits of the American political system:

> We now possess what the working classes of Your Country look forward to as constituting their political millennium. We have the charter [for] which you have been fighting for years as the panacea for all Britain's woes, the bulwark of the liberties of the people. . . . The best proof of the superiority of our system is . . . the general prosperity.

Under this benevolent government that existed by consent of the governed, the national treasury held a surplus; the public debt got paid as it matured; the western lands opened to the plow; 13,000 miles of railroad and 21,000 miles of telegraph existed, with thousands more on the way; pauperism rarely occurred. Only political equality, Carnegie thought, explained the contrast between the United States and the Canadas. They were settled by the same people at the same time under the same government—and look at the difference! Where are her Railroads, Telegraphs and Canals? her commercial marine and her unrivaled steamships? her fast clippers or her potent Press? We have given to the world a Washington, a Franklin, a Fulton, a Morse—what has Canada ever produced?

Carnegie's belief that the American environment made all the difference squared with his experience as an immigrant who got ahead, an experience common among many of his associates who fared far better in their new country than in the one left behind. This reality applied not only to his youth, but to the rest of his life as well. Many of his partners and managers at Carnegie Steel came from abroad and flourished in America, vanquishing many an old Yankee iron firm in the process.

While still a young man, then, Carnegie articulated the principle of interdependence between political equality and economic superiority that most of his fellow Americans, rich and poor alike, embraced. This equation served Carnegie as a two-edged sword: with one side he attacked other countries' systems as inferior; with the other he defended American institutions against criticism. The United States did most things right; the few lingering failings would improve or disappear because the system, by its very nature, corrected itself. That being the case, Americans could look forward to a brighter future for their children, and, as often as not, for themselves.

The credo not only excused economic abuses but also justified opposition to economic reforms, either by government intervention or by labor agitation. Should reformist intervention eventually become necessary, then, Carnegie argued, the political system would make it easy. Such a view most nineteenth-century Americans shared with Carnegie. Even in the twentieth century, when reform often seemed blocked or perilously delayed on every hand, Americans overwhelmingly preferred working through the existing political system to overthrowing capitalism in favor of some alternative economic arrangement.

In America—in its prosperity, democracy, opportunities, heroic figures, rich men humble enough to treat kindly the poor telegraph boy who conveyed their messages—Carnegie perceived Scottish radicalism incarnate, and it seemed good. Soon it got better.

In 1852, another good fairy appeared in the personage of Tom Scott, superintendent of the western division of the Pennsylvania Railroad. The Pennsylvania, whose tracks had replaced a cumbersome system of canals and inclined plane railroads across the Alleghenies, linked Pittsburgh, with its transportation network west and south, to the markets of the eastern seaboard. Scott needed a personal telegrapher and secretary; he hired Carnegie, the office hotshot, at a salary of $35 a month. The opportunity, more than the salary, lured Carnegie away from the telegraph company. "In my old berth," he wrote to his cousin in Scotland, "I must always have been an employee. The highest station I could attain was Manager of an office." Even before Scott showed up, he had resolved to accept any offer "which would be better for the future," even if it paid less than telegraphy.

Carnegie spent 12 years on the Pennsylvania Railroad, resigning as superintendent of the Pittsburgh division in 1865. His railroad service shaped the rest of his business life: on the railroad he assimilated the managerial skills; grasped the economic principles; and cemented the personal relationships that enabled him to become successively manager, capitalist, and entrepreneur. If he had exercised a conscious choice of training grounds in up-to-date managerial methods, Carnegie could have chosen no better than the Pennsylvania Railroad, which he had joined by chance. In America, the railroads pioneered sophisticated management structures, and the Pennsylvania, "The Standard Railroad of the World," led the way. Charles Francis Adams, a ferocious critic of railroads in general, called the Pennsylvania "that superb organization, every detail of whose wonderful system is a fit subject for study to all interested in the operation of railroads." And in fact, other American railroads and many abroad copied its methods and organization.

Carnegie, joining the Pennsylvania during its formative years, absorbed the methods that carried it to excellence. Necessity drove railroads like the Pennsylvania to innovate in management techniques. In size of physical plant, in cost of construction, in complexity of technology and operation, in number of employees, in revenues, and in expenses, they quickly dwarfed even the New England textile mills, the largest previous business enterprises. The railroads' voracious appetite for capital led to modern investment banking and the stock exchange. Their equipment needs created a market that called forth a whole industry to supply rails, locomotives, and cars. The railroads had to develop systematic methods to run trains without running them into one another, to hire and fire workers, to perform necessary maintenance, and to keep track of thousands of shipments and millions of dollars (much of it literally in nickels and dimes) that passed through the hands of hundreds of employees. All this Carnegie saw and learned. But above all, he absorbed the railroad's dual obsession as to costs: knowing them and reducing them.

Circumstances forced the railroads, more than any other business before them, to apply cost accounting to management. The railroads were built with other people's money; whether the year ended in a profit or a loss, investors had a right to know how much money came in and where it went. The Pennsylvania did this so effectively that a stockholders' committee reported that "a charge or entry of a day's labor, of the purchase of a keg of nails, or the largest order goes through such a system of checks and audits as to make fraud almost an impossibility."

Detailed cost accounting also greatly aided management decision making. In an operation as complex as the Pennsylvania Railroad's, even knowing which services made money and which did not constituted an analytical nightmare. Cost accounting pinpointed the sources of profit and loss. It also helped measure employee performance. In addition, it permitted cost-based pricing, enabling the railroads to assess charges that assured a profit. And a profit they had to earn, to avoid bankruptcy by meeting interest charges and paying dividends high enough to attract further investment. Costs also determined investment decisions. New equipment that could pay for itself by reducing cost or attracting business merited buying, regardless of price; otherwise, it wasted money no matter how little it might cost.

Scott, with Carnegie at his elbow, set about making the Pennsylvania a paying proposition by getting volume up and holding costs down. The structure that Scott developed to effect this policy involved a labyrinthine, departmentalized bureaucracy, a stream of paperwork inundating its desks. That maze, which Carnegie memorized, we need not wander into here. It suffices to know that from Scott, Carnegie learned the simple underlying principles, which he later applied to the steel business: install whatever arrangements necessary to know all costs all the time; to customers who can opt for a competitor's services, keep the price barely above cost and rely on volume to make a profit; with shippers lacking access to other railroads' services, charge the limit; promote cost-conscious subordinates and fire the others; if business volume strains capacity, drive your workers and equipment as hard as you can before hiring or buying more; buy anything that pays for itself and nothing that doesn't. The last two guidelines Carnegie fastened upon in particular, loading cars to capacity, marshaling them into the heaviest trains that locomotives could haul, and then running them as fast as conditions would permit (or faster, when a Casey Jones had the throttle). An adequate return on capital depended on the fact that it cost little more and paid a lot more to run big trains fast than to run small trains slowly. This fact dictated concentrating investment in more durable rails, more powerful locomotives, and cars with greater capacity, all contributing to reduce the cost of hauling each ton of freight, each sack of mail, each passenger.

When the Pennsylvania promoted Scott to vice president in 1859, he named Carnegie his successor as superintendent. This taxing position demanded 24-hour-a-day attention. As Carnegie described it:

> The superintendent of a division in those days was expected to run trains by telegraph at night, to go and remove all wrecks, and indeed to do everything. At one time for eight days I was constantly upon the line, day and night at one obstruction or the other.

Carnegie gloried in it.

When Scott offered the appointment, Carnegie said, "I was only 24 years old, but my model then was Lord John Russell of whom it was said he would take command of the Channel fleet" on a moment's notice. As superintendent, he demonstrated his expertise with Scott's cost-volume-velocity doctrines, the complex statistical analyses that had produced them, and the operating strategies that put them into practice. He burned wrecked cars to clear the line or laid new tracks around a wreck. He originated night train dispatchers to expedite 24-hour service and kept all telegraph stations open around the clock. When he forwarded to headquarters proposals for improved service at lower costs, he supported them with statistical analyses. He advocated double-tracking the entire main line between Altoona and Pittsburgh to reduce train delays and urged that train crews' shifts be lengthened from 10 to 13 hours to eliminate a change between the two cities. He kept trains full by cutting Pittsburgh commuter fares to meet competition, and by holding back the company's own coal and lumber shipments until traffic was light.

In 1865, Scott, following his own maxim of promoting cost-cutters, offered to make Carnegie general superintendent. Carnegie declined because he had bigger ideas; he had learned the lessons of crucial years. By 1865, when Carnegie left, the Pennsylvania Railroad had become the largest business firm in the world in revenues, employees, and value of physical assets. Carnegie had shown his mastery of the Pennsylvania's complex system by superintending the division most important in terms of revenues generated, and its most demanding in terms of operations. Carnegie came to the Pennsylvania a callow telegrapher; he left it a mature, polished manager trained to run a big business by the biggest business of them all. He came there a poor boy and left a rich man. This rise, too, he owed to Tom Scott, who liked to let "my boy Andy" in on things, and to his own genius at making the most of his chances. Carnegie justified Scott's faith, while validating Samuel Johnson's observation that "much can be made of a Scot, if you catch him young enough."

Tom Scott introduced Carnegie to the magic of capital investment, and Carnegie proved as apt a pupil in this art as he had in management. Scott showed Carnegie a trick better than the making of bricks without straw; he showed how a shrewd capitalist could make a lot of money without having any. Starting in 1856, literally without a nickel to spare, Carnegie built a fortune. By 1863, his investments provided him with an income of $45,000; to a friend who asked how he fared, Carnegie replied, "I'm rich; I'm rich." By 1868, even richer, he owned securities and partnership shares worth $400,000 that paid him $56,000 a year. Thus by age 28, Carnegie had followed two paths in the world of business, paths that had done much more than make him rich. By mastering the new art of large-scale management and by fathoming the mysteries of capitalism, Carnegie had prepared himself uniquely to benefit from the combination of big industry and big finance that drove America's economy to world prominence after the Civil War.

Ultimately, Carnegie demonstrated his skills by vanquishing or stalemating a formidable array of business rivals, including the entire American iron and steel industry, Cornelius Vanderbilt, John Murray Forbes, Jay Gould, John D. Rockefeller, and J. P. Morgan. His career as capitalist and speculator, however, began modestly. In 1856, Tom Scott persuaded Carnegie to buy 10 shares of Adams Express Company stock for $600, lending him the money. Carnegie, broke, a tyro at investment, shared his mother's Scottish distaste for debt. He took the plunge, nevertheless, because his hero told him to: "I had not $50 saved for investment, but I was not going to miss the chance of becoming financially connected with my leader and great man." His devotion paid Carnegie quick dividends in the form of a $10 check from Adams Express.

"I shall remember that check . . . as long as I live," Carnegie later recalled, "it gave me the first penny of revenue from capital—something that I had not worked for with the sweat of my brow. 'Eureka,' I cried, 'Here's the goose that lays the golden eggs.'" Here shone a new world indeed, the world of the capitalist, where one could make money without toiling for it. With Scott's guidance, Carnegie acquired a whole new perspective on money, scrapping the consumer's mentality in favor of the investor's. He learned to see money as a commodity, untrammeled by emotions; as something to use to make more money, not as something to spend; as something whose value depended on what it could earn, not on what it could buy.

Once gripped by the investor's mentality, no one can loll about like Silas Marner, basking in the glow from a pile of cash. Money idle, not invested for income and gain, becomes money wasted. Carnegie's Adams Express stock venture taught him an important corollary: it made no difference whose money he invested. If expected dividends exceeded the interest rate on a loan, it made good sense to invest borrowed money, and better sense yet if the value of the shares rose. The Adams Express investment paid dividends 10 times the interest on the loan during the first year that Carnegie held it. Money from credit thus served investors as readily as cash from savings, but, in both cases, only when one's estimate of the future proved sound. Englishmen had invested in colonial America not out of some Rousseau-like admiration for the beauty of wilderness, but out of the expectation that the wilderness could yield cash. The original optimism took root and flourished, becoming an inherent characteristic of American society. With its vast lands, enormous resources, and a people bent on proving themselves by making good, the United States augured well as an investment, first in agriculture and then in manufacturing. The country's rapid growth, furthermore, served to keep American capital at home while attracting massive sums from abroad.

The prospect of income, Carnegie learned, kept capital coming. Investors didn't want their principal back, for that only required finding another place to put the money. Indeed, shrewd capitalists lavished loans on reliable borrowers, rather than demanding payment. In the long run, of course, as the "derivative" and "sub-prime mortgage" driven depression of the first decade of the twenty-first century showed, a valid relationship must exist between the quantity of capital invested and the productivity of the assets—land, plant, equipment, patents—that it bought.

Scott's financial wizardry may have fascinated Carnegie, but it never mesmerized him. Moreover, he mastered the art of minimizing risks. Investors, like insurance actuaries, know that some of their clients will die on their hands. Some depend on spreading individual risks in such a way that in the aggregate, risk plays no part. Carnegie had an even better method, which he himself described: "I am sure," Carnegie said, "that any competent judge would be surprised how little I ever risked. . . . When I did big things some large corporation was behind me and was the responsible party." Most often, the "corporation" behind him was in fact the Pennsylvania Railroad. The Pennsylvania bought a lot of goods and services. Carnegie, in association with Scott and J. Edgar Thomson, the Pennsylvania's president, invested in firms that supplied them. This mixture, perfectly legal then though now outlawed by "conflict of interest" and "inside information" statutes, fireproofed the investors against risk. Carnegie's encyclopedic knowledge of the strong and the weak in the Pittsburgh business community proved almost as useful; the former telegrapher kept his data bank current as a railroad official. Carnegie rarely ventured beyond the financial magnetic field generated by the Pennsylvania dynamo; when he did, he carefully allied himself with a local businessman or financier of amply demonstrated shrewdness.

In 1858, Carnegie joined Thomson and Scott in financing the T. T. Woodruff Sleeping Car Company. The partners arranged to pay for their shares in installments, a common practice in nineteenth-century finance. Investors committed themselves to pay a specific amount of capital in a fixed number of payments over a specified period—sometimes at designated intervals, sometimes on call. During the War of 1812, Francis Cabot Lowell had induced skeptical Boston merchants to invest in the first integrated textile mill by offering just such a deal.

Advantages accrued to all involved. If the stockholders' list contained the names of the prominent and well-to-do, the firm got credit and customers more easily. (In England, businesses customarily trotted out an aristocrat or two.) Meanwhile, the firm in effect had the leverage of its total capital, but paid dividends on only a part. Another common arrangement, the right to apply all dividends to unpaid stock subscriptions, allowed managers to retain company earnings for business use, and when dividends paid remaining installments, shrewd investors acquired a large interest in many firms while putting up little actual money. Indeed, if bold enough, or well-informed insiders, they didn't need money of their own. Carnegie grasped precisely such an opportunity with the T. T. Woodruff Co. Without cash, he subscribed for a one-eighth share, "trusting," as he said, "to be able to make payments somehow or other." In truth, he had little need for "trusting." Carnegie knew that Thomson and Scott would see to it that Woodruff cars went on Pennsylvania trains. Carnegie got a bank loan to meet the first installment of $217.50, but he never made another payment. In the first year, dividends paid off the entire share balance; from the second year on, he received $5,000 or more annually until he sold out in the early 1870s.

Under a similar arrangement, Carnegie joined William Coleman, a wealthy ironmaster and elder statesman among Pittsburgh businessmen, to form the Columbia Oil Company in 1861. The Columbia Company sailed briskly into the booming flood of the oil that had recently gushed on the banks of Pennsylvania's Oil Creek. Carnegie subscribed for $110,000 worth of stock with $11,000 in cash, drawn from his Woodruff dividends. The $11,000 investment returned him $17,800 the first year and eventually brought more than a million dollars altogether.

Carnegie also became a partner in the Keystone Bridge Company, which opened for business in 1862. Keystone Bridge manufactured and erected iron railway bridges of a type patented by John Piper, supervisor of bridge construction for the Pennsylvania Railroad. The cost-conscious Pennsylvania seemed certain to replace its frail and flammable wooden bridges with iron because the trend toward heavier locomotives and trains, for which the Pennsylvania set the industry pace, demanded spans of ever-greater capacity. That the Pennsylvania would buy its bridges from Keystone Bridge seemed even more certain, since Keystone's partners included, in addition to Piper himself, the following Pennsylvania Railroad officers: J. Edgar Thomson, president; Thomas A. Scott, vice president; W. H. Wilson, chief engineer; Enoch Lewis, superintendent of transportation; Aaron Shiffler, bridge supervisor; J. H. Linville, bridge engineer; and Carnegie, superintendent of the western division.

Not surprisingly, the firm prospered immediately. Carnegie held a one-fifth share; the first and only assessment of $1,250 he borrowed from a bank. In 1863, Keystone paid him $7,500 in dividends, and it continued to do well throughout the Civil War. After the war, it did even better, expanding its operations from coast to coast, including construction of the Eads Bridge over the Mississippi at St. Louis, a nineteenth-century marvel still in daily use.

In the seven years that followed Carnegie's decision to leave the railroad for a full-time career as investor, he ascended into the stratosphere of high finance, winging it with the highest flyers in Europe and the United States. He sold $30 million worth of bridge and railroad bonds, some of them good, some of them not so good, some of them worthless; but all of them paid him a commission. He borrowed cheap and lent dear; he manipulated stock prices up and down, buying and selling to take advantage of the fluctuations; he took part in clandestine stock deals in the Union Pacific Railroad, Western Union, and the Pullman Company. He became the confidant of the Morgans and other moguls of finance; he became a wealthy man. Then, in 1872, he abruptly changed course, abandoning his career as a financier and speculator, liquidating his assets, and pouring the proceeds into a new steel mill.

Carnegie's decision to abandon finance for manufacturing had many roots, some in practical calculations, and some in conscience. Greed played a part, but a minor one. By 1872, he had assembled more than enough wealth to last him a lifetime; moreover, although the following year brought a panic that bankrupted many, Carnegie, like the Morgans, survived easily and moved on to greater riches.

By 1872, however, Carnegie had perceived a distinction between investment and speculation, and he developed a distaste for the latter. Investment, to Carnegie and others of a similar conservative bent, meant providing the capital necessary for a firm to produce tangible goods or real services—wheat, steel, railroad transportation. Carefully managed, such firms could be expected to generate a profit sufficient to pay a satisfactory return on the original investment. Of course, the point at which investment ended and speculation began posed a question on which men with conscience could differ, and which those without could ignore.

In the late 1860s and 1870s, with the Civil War over and the threat of sectional division apparently put to rest once and for all, a fresh burst of optimism swept through much of America. Limitless expansion became the order of the day: immigration, the Pacific Railroad Act, the Homestead Act, all pointed to swift settlement of the land between the Missouri and the Pacific. The business world took on a carnival atmosphere, as barkers of every stripe and hue, crying the boundless promise of the future, lured suckers into the capitalist big top. Promising to expand existing businesses or to create new ones, promoters hawked stocks, bonds, and partnership shares in massive quantities. In this era, only the jungle law "let the buyer beware" governed the investment marketplace. Would-be investors had nothing but their own wits to protect them against the most extravagant claims. Rosy forecasts of future profits frequently bore only a vague relationship, if any, to a firm's current or prospective earning power. As to the days ahead, even the most conservative forecasts depended upon variables so numerous and so imponderable that they had no more claim to validity than the predictions of astrologers and fortune-tellers, as many businessmen realized. The normally hardheaded railroad baron Commodore Vanderbilt, for instance, consulted a Staten Island mystic and invoked the ghost of dear departed swindler Jim Fisk for guidance in the stock market.

Many of the stockjobbers who swarmed into the capital markets on both sides of the Atlantic had at least a twinge of virtue. Many of these worthies trusted that the heat from the expanding national market would dry up virtually any quantity of stock, no matter how wet (overpriced) when issued. Sometimes they had it right. The Union Pacific Railroad, built at great cost across empty spaces in anticipation of massive but unpredictable freight and passenger traffic, eventually paid dividends and remains one of the country's healthiest railroads. But many other ventures, particularly when they involved borrowed money that required fixed interest payments, failed as overcapitalization proved itself a virulent complication of the speculative fever. Firms large and small foundered trying to keep their heads above their own water. Besides falling prey to well-intentioned but ill-advised promoters, investors also ran afoul of charlatans and mountebanks. Jay Gould and his brethren created stock purely for the purpose of selling it, neither knowing nor caring whether dividends would ever follow. Under their tender ministrations, once-healthy firms such as the Erie Railroad became bloated carcasses that not even the buoyant American economy could keep afloat. All these scenarios Carnegie saw played out in multiple variations. In a few cases, he served, wittingly or unwittingly, as a contributor. Although he liked to describe himself as a "first-class, steady-going securities man," he often dealt in paper of dubious value and knew it. He foisted bonds of the Davenport and St. Paul, the Missouri, Iowa, and Nebraska Railroads, and the Keokuk Bridge on European investors; all went bankrupt. Other ventures staggered along on the verge of collapse.

Later in life, Carnegie claimed that "I have never bought or sold a share of stock speculatively in my life," but he had, and often. At one time or another, he lied, concealing information and misrepresenting the facts, all in pursuit of speculative manipulation. In the end, however, the game palled. Speculative fever continued to sweep the country, but in Carnegie something—his radical past, memories of the abuses of Scottish landlords, thoughts of his father, perhaps—caused him to withdraw. When his mentor, Thomas Scott, plunged into the Texas and Pacific Railroad, the venture that ultimately led to his downfall, Carnegie refused to follow his "leader and great man" into the depths. When Jay Gould offered to buy the Pennsylvania Railroad and install him as president, Carnegie declined. Whether cured by shrewdness or conscience, Carnegie survived the speculative fever with an immunization that lasted him a lifetime.

His changing view of wealth also drove Carnegie out of finance and into manufacturing. In his early years, Carnegie pursued money as an antidote to poverty and the cold, hunger, and shabbiness that went with it. In 1863, he had rejoiced, "I'm rich; I'm rich." But by 1868, he no longer saw money as a guarantee of a rewarding life and feared, in fact, that continued pursuit of it might be his undoing:

> Man must have an idol—The amassing of wealth is one of the worst species of idolatry. No idol more debasing than the worship of money. Whatever I engage in I must push inordinately, therefore should I be careful to choose that life which will be the most elevating in its character. To continue much longer overwhelmed by business cares and with most of my thoughts wholly upon the way to make more money in the shortest time, must degrade me beyond hope of permanent recovery.

This memorandum, which Carnegie wrote for himself, not for public consumption, contained a program for self-improvement. He planned to arrange all his

> business as to make no effort to increase fortune, but spend the surplus each year for benevolent purposes. . . . Settle in Oxford & get a thorough education making the acquaintance of literary men. . . . Settle then in London & purchase a controlling interest in some newspaper or live review . . . taking a part in public matters especially those connected with education & improvement of the poorer classes.

These sentiments marked a transition in Carnegie's motivation. Once the personification of David Hume's maxim that avarice spurred industry, Carnegie now evinced more complex sentiments, similar to those expressed by John Ruskin in 1870: "Life without industry is guilt; [but] Industry without art is brutality." Other successful American businessmen testified to a similar change in motivation, one that reflected the shifting perspective of American society as a whole. James E. Caldwell, a utilities magnate, said, "As a younger man, I was urged on by the necessity for food and raiment." Later, he found commerce "a fascinating game," and creating a telephone system "highly entertained" him. Joseph E. Sheffield, a New England railroad builder and founder of the Sheffield Scientific School at Yale, related that originally "'getting gain' was a leading purpose" as well as a desire to *stand well* with my fellows and people." When he entered business, he hoped "to make money. But I distinctly recollect that my *pride of opinion* and great desire to be found *correct* in my *estimates* and *statistics* was paramount to all other considerations." As a wealthy man, "*unselfish* public spirited enterprise [became] far more intense than any hope of making money."

Most of Carnegie's plan for self-improvement he postponed; some of it never came to pass. He did, however, read extensively, attend plays and concerts, master the grammar of the English language, cultivate friendships with English literati such as Matthew Arnold and John Morley, and undertake a program of philanthropy.

Entering the steel business in 1872, Carnegie showed that business still fascinated him, but he had had enough of paper and speculation. "I wish to make something tangible," he said. He "had lived long enough in Pittsburgh to acquire the manufacturing, as distinguished from the speculative, spirit." Opening his own steel mill not only gave him the chance to make something tangible, but also to become his own boss, something he had wanted for many years. Leaving the railroad in 1865, he had commented, "A man must necessarily occupy a narrow field who is at the beck and call of others." He had set out "determined to make a fortune," and he had certainly made one, but he found that it had not freed him from "the beck and call of others." As a stock-and-bond salesman, he had still been a minion—a wealthy minion, surely, but nevertheless an altar boy to their sacerdotal majesties, the Barings, the Morgans, and others.

Starting his own business would make him his own master, and he meant to keep it that way. He sold no stock in Carnegie Steel, ever. To raise the initial capital he did take in partners, but he himself always retained the majority interest. In addition, he forced his partners to sign the "Iron-Clad Agreement," which enabled Carnegie to expel anyone he didn't like, but no combination of the other partners could force him out. In addition, the "Iron-Clad" prevented any partner from willing or selling his interest to anyone outside the company. By retaining absolute control, Carnegie kept a free hand to adopt any strategies he pleased, whether his partners approved or not. One of his policies in particular—using the firm's profits to finance expansion rather than pay dividends—drove many partners to distraction, but Carnegie stuck to it because it kept him and his firm clear of the stock market and its pitfalls.

Carnegie, like so many of his contemporaries, saw his business as an extension of himself, its reputation and his own inextricably intertwined. This fact fueled his obsession with controlling his own affairs. He determined to let none of his associates besmirch his own reputation by engaging in shady business dealings. It sometimes happened in spite of him: his first superintendent, W. P. Shinn, speculated in the pig iron market; his general manager, Henry Clay Frick, tried to trick him into selling his business to three notorious speculators, the Moore brothers ("those Chicago adventurers," Carnegie called them) and John W. ("Bet a Million") Gates, a hustler known to have wagered a thousand dollars on which raindrop would run down a Pullman car window first. Shinn, Frick, and other transgressors found themselves punished by expulsion.

Steel itself, as a tangible, solid product, the very foundation of progress, the web that bound the nation's vast expanse together in a commercial, political, and social entity, had an intrinsic appeal to Carnegie's newly realized sense of virtue. Steel also offered Carnegie a unique opportunity to utilize his manifold talents and connections. Always in touch with developments in the industry, Carnegie knew that railroads would soon replace iron rails with steel. In this development, as in so many others, the Pennsylvania Railroad would lead the way, for its president, J. Edgar Thomson, believed in "steel for everything." A huge market loomed—the Pennsylvania alone could keep several large mills going—and Carnegie not unreasonably expected to get his share of it. Metallurgy and machine technology had advanced to the point that mass production of durable steel rails seemed feasible.

Carnegie knew nothing of metallurgy and little about machinery, but he had learned on the railroad that he could hire any expertise he lacked. He did know something about the iron business from his experiences with Keystone Bridge and Union Mills, a firm he had purchased to supply Keystone's materials. Much of what he found out about the iron business and the traditional way it operated, however, he didn't like.

Developing Keystone and Union, Carnegie had found the iron industry organized much the same as the British textile industry. Each stage of manufacture from raw material to finished product took place in a separate independent production unit, often a small proprietorship or partnership. Iron furnaces smelted the ore into pig iron; forges and rolling mills converted the iron into bars and slabs; other mills then rolled plates, rails, and sheets, and cut nails. Separate factories fabricated tools, hardware, pots, and pans; foundries made stoves.

Specialized merchants who controlled this messy flow of materials from one manufacturing stage to another and then into the market dominated the industry. This dispersion of control added lavish expense for two reasons. First, every stage in the process added to the cost; second, the movement of material proceeded slowly through many hands and over a wide geographic area. The large quantity of material in the pipeline at any time kept a good deal of money–invariably borrowed money—tied up in inventory. The resulting finance charges boosted the cost of the final product. Such cost skyrocketed if the complicated supply train coupled to the kind of high-volume manufacturing plant Carnegie had in mind. In building his new steel mill, Carnegie planned to eliminate the cost and undependability of the traditional, dispersed operations by following the example of Francis Cabot Lowell, who had put all stages of textile manufacture under a single roof. In striving to reduce inventory costs, Carnegie embraced a strategy that has invariably characterized efficient industrial management in the United States and its overseas competitors. (The now-global effort to master the "just-in-time" system thus has an American ancestry stretching back deep into the nineteenth century.)

Carnegie also discovered to his dismay that most iron masters used bookkeeping systems unchanged since the Renaissance:

> I was greatly surprised to find that the cost of each of the various processes was unknown. . . . It was a lump business, and until stock was taken and the books balanced at the end of the year, the manufacturers were in total ignorance of the results. I heard of men who thought their business at the end of the year would show a loss and had found a profit, and *vice versa.*

Such primitive cost accounting consisted merely in dividing the year's expenses by the year's total output.

Obviously none of this would do; Carnegie wanted to build the largest steel business in the world, in the face of formidable competition from established mills at home and abroad. Such a business couldn't run like a corner grocery. "I felt as if we were moles, burrowing in the dark," Carnegie remarked, "and this to me was intolerable." He resolved to rectify and modernize these slipshod methods. To take the first step of learning all costs at all times, as at Keystone Bridge and Union Mills, he "insisted upon such a system of weighing and accounting being introduced throughout our works as would enable us to know what our cost was for each process."

Once he knew the costs, Carnegie set about mercilessly beating them down while driving production up. He pursued this campaign on many fronts. To reduce production costs in his planned steel works, he hired Alexander Holley, the world's foremost expert on Bessemer steel production, to design and build the most modern plant money could buy. When new technology appeared, Carnegie scrapped his existing equipment, striving always for machinery that could handle bigger batches and handle them faster, regardless of initial cost. Carnegie once ordered Charles Schwab, his first lieutenant, to tear out a three-month-old rolling mill when Schwab said he had found a design that would do the job more cheaply.

Carnegie's willingness to spend lavish sums of money on new equipment astounded his competitors. They didn't understand the principle of economies of scale. On one occasion, Carnegie recalled,

> the older heads among the Pittsburgh manufacturers [criticized my] extravagant expenditures . . . on . . . new-fangled furnaces. But in the heating of great masses of materials, almost half the waste could sometimes be saved. . . . The expenditure would have been justified even if it had been doubled. . . . In some years the margin of profit was so small that the most of it was . . . from savings . . . from the improved furnaces.

Another way to reduce the cost of each ton of steel manufactured involved accelerating the production process by the old Pennsylvania Railroad practice of "hard-driving," by getting the maximum output of steel in the shortest possible time, regardless of wear and tear on men and machinery. Cost accounting showed this method cheaper per ton than the British practice of coddling the equipment. The money generated by faster production more than paid for a new furnace.

Watching the hard-driving techniques that raised production at one Carnegie blast furnace from 13,000 tons to more than 100,000 tons a year, Sir James Kitson, president of the British Iron and Steel Institute, predicted that "it won't last. . . . The continual work at high pressure does not pay in the end." Kitson's mistake reflected tradition. British Industrial Commissions in the 1850s had noted this difference in attitudes toward labor and machinery between the United States and Great Britain. Cost accounting had few adherents in nineteenth-century British industry (and few enough in the twentieth century); manufacturers planned largely by instinct and custom. Carnegie planned on the basis of evidence. The British guesswork method usually kept costs high; Carnegie's produced rational policies that drove costs down. An exchange between English industrialist Sir Lowthian Bell and one of Carnegie's furnace superintendents highlighted the conflict. Bell condemned the "reckless rapid rate" of hard-driving "the furnaces so that the interior of each furnace was wrecked and had to be replaced every three years." The superintendent replied, "What do we care about the lining? We think a lining is good for so much iron and the sooner it makes it the better."

Another English visitor once told Carnegie, "We have equipment we have been using for twenty years and it is still serviceable." "And that," Andy replied, "is what is the matter with the British steel trade. Most British equipment is still in use twenty years after it should have been scrapped. It is because you keep this used-up machinery that the United States is making you a back number." This theme Carnegie repeated often, usually also tying America's commitment to industrial progress to the free climate created by its democratic political system. It formed the leitmotif in much of his writing, particularly *Triumphant Democracy,* published in 1886. The book began, "The old nations of the world creep on at a snail's pace; the Republic thunders past with the rush of an express."

Certainly things moved quickly in Carnegie's mills, where further savings accrued from rushing materials from one operation to another, for example, speeding the movement of steel ingots from blast furnace to rolling mill by pouring the steel into molds on moving flatcars. Sidney Gilchrist-Thomas, a British metallurgist, fascinated by such velocity and volume, remarked to Alexander Holley, "I would like to sit on an ingot for a week and watch that mill operate." Replied Holley, "If you want an ingot cool enough to sit on, you'll have to send to England for it."

Carnegie drove his men as hard as he drove his machinery. From the beginning, he employed supervisors who understood railroad accounting methods, or who could learn them quickly. An authority on railroad costs himself, Holley knew just what Carnegie wanted in the way of scales and checkpoints to keep track of production. As the plant's first superintendent, Carnegie appointed W. P. Shinn, former superintendent of the Allegheny Valley Railroad. Carnegie demanded that he receive weekly cost sheets no matter where he roamed, at home or abroad. By comparing this week's performance with last week's, or one man's with another's, he kept track of who produced quickly and cheaply and who did not. As one manager remembered, "You [were] expected always to get it ten cents cheaper the next year or the next month."

The system allowed Carnegie to control his firm's complex operations. He could make intelligent decisions about hirings, firings, and promotions even though he had "no shadow of claim to rank as inventor, chemist, investigator, or mechanician," and he did it while spending much of his time away from the mill. Carnegie had little scientific understanding of the new techniques, but he knew when one month's costs turned out lower than another's. He did not need to judge the scientific merits of technical excuses made by managers; he could compare a man's performance with that of others in the same position. He then demanded explanations in plain English.

Successful subordinates could expect quick promotion. "He may be just the man we need," Carnegie said of one suggested change. "If he can win the race, he is our race-horse. If not, he goes to the cart." Racehorses, if they ran long and fast enough, might ultimately join the firm's partnership. By the 1890s, even one-sixth of 1 percent of Carnegie Steel meant hundreds of thousands of dollars to the chosen. "Mr. Morgan buys his partners," Carnegie boasted, "I raise my own." Through this arrangement of multiple partnerships (a common form of business structure in Scotland, but unusual in the United States, where few partnerships had more than two or three members), Carnegie expected to generate loyalty and results. The system also sometimes fostered jealousy, treachery, bitterness, and despair, but some 40 employees rose through the ranks to partnership, including at least one immigrant who spoke no English when first employed, and one who, like Carnegie, began his career as a telegrapher.

Choosing subordinates increasingly bedeviled American entrepreneurs in the nineteenth century. Finding competent lieutenants often proved vital to success. When Eli Whitney tried to run his arms business unaided, he nearly destroyed himself and his firm. Cyrus McCormick needed help from the beginning. Carnegie, who had learned on the railroad what round-the-clock operations meant, knew that he had to delegate authority (and create departments and ranks that went with them) to achieve cost-based management in his steel business. He nevertheless kept the ultimate authority in his own hands. Manufacturers, then, did not leap from old-style family management to a full-fledged modern bureaucratic arrangement; rather, they yielded grudgingly to necessity. A gradual evolution resulted. Outside of the railroads, the predominant structure remained a hybrid, a mixture of family ownership and operation with the slow passing of some responsibilities to salaried managers.

Desperate for help, but reluctant to surrender control, businessmen usually exhausted their family's resources before involving outsiders. In 1818, Eli Whitney, with no heir yet born, wrote his nephew, begging for help in "getting on with my affairs which have been so numerous, embarrassing, and oppressive that I am almost driven to delirium. I find that it is absolutely impossible for me to accomplish . . . the most pressing necessit[ies]."

Cyrus McCormick, as we have seen, pressed his brothers into service. Carnegie did likewise, dragging his brother Tom into his business, first as a partner, ultimately as general manager. An old axiom says the best horses get ridden hardest; in business, this often meant that the most trusted became the most abused. Andrew Carnegie, like McCormick, spent much of his time away from the mill—in the early years, on business, later in global gallivanting and hobnobbing with the gentlefolk. In their absence, these potentates expected their siblings to keep the home fires burning, profitably. "We must work like sailors," Andy exhorted from his European spa, writing to Tom, holding the fort in Pittsburgh. "I'm sure you have had a trying time of it," Andy added, "and often you must have felt disposed to throw up the game [but] the more I find myself drinking in enjoyment, the deeper is my appreciation of your devoted self-denial. . . . It is a heavy load for a youngster to carry," but after all, Tom should realize, "if you succeed, it will be a lasting benefit to you."

Cyrus McCormick, idling away the Civil War in an English haven, accused his brothers, running the firm in Chicago, of "cruel treatment" when production fell below the absent magnate's expectations. He demanded that Leander not neglect the factory while building a new home. Such strains often broke family ties or broke down family members, as William McCormick's breakdown, Leander's hatred for Cyrus, and Tom Carnegie's early, bibulous death all demonstrated. Business quarrels shattered many an American family into feuding factions, often hastening the decline of family management.

When relatives proved inadequate in number, talent, or disposition, businessmen usually turned next to friends. Some of Carnegie's enduring partners in the steel business he had known since childhood. If forced to turn to strangers, an entrepreneur naturally sought, above all, to find people he could trust, which most often meant people like himself. What Tom Scott saw in Carnegie—a reflection of himself when young, poor, bright, and ambitious—Carnegie saw in Charley Schwab. As the scale of business enterprises ballooned, such mentor–protégé relationships proliferated between men of common background and outlook. Ironically, one of them, the alliance between Pierre du Pont and Alfred Sloan, produced the ultimate substitute for family control—the vast, shareholding, depersonalized bureaucracy of General Motors.

As the succeeding chapters document, sooner or later every growing firm founded by an individual, a family, or a partnership confronts a similar dilemma: how to manage a company grown too large for an informal organization to control effectively. Survival then depends upon the success or failure of the strategy chosen. Invariably, whatever role the founders' descendants play, size leads to bureaucracy, or to failure, and sometimes to both. In the end, bureaucracies emerged as a dominant fact of American business life, but paradoxically they often resulted, in part, from entrepreneurs' struggles to perpetuate family ownership and management in an economy that made such traditional methods increasingly inapt. Carnegie Steel, while typifying such transitional organizations, functioned better than most. Its blend of traditional ownership and modern, cost-based management gave Carnegie the best of both worlds.

From the 1870s through the 1890s, Carnegie, costs always in mind, drove his firm relentlessly. He hired a chemist to determine which ores to feed to which furnaces; he built open-hearth furnaces; he bought mines and quarries and coke smelters to supply raw material, and railroads to haul them to his mills; he refused to fix prices, meanwhile undercutting his competitors, and buying many of them. When the railroad market softened, he shifted some of his capacity to the rolling of structural beams and angles such as those used in the Brooklyn Bridge; in America's first skyscraper, the Home Insurance building in Chicago; and in Chicago and New York's elevated railroads.

Through booms and recessions, Carnegie Steel rolled on. By 1900, it alone produced more than the entire British steel industry. As volume rose, costs fell and profits soared. The first ton of Carnegie steel cost $56 to produce; by 1900, the cost fell to $11.50. In 1888, the firm made $2 million; in 1894, $4 million; in 1900, $40 million. A contemporary observer declared, "Such a magnificent aggregation of industrial power has never before been under the domination of a single man." Carnegie himself cried, "Where is there such a business!"

Carnegie savored his triumph all the more because he achieved it despite the frenzied efforts of promoters and financiers to defeat him. By the 1890s, the capacity of the American steel industry exceeded the market. In other industries confronting this situation, financiers such as J. P. Morgan tried to stabilize prices by controlling production. They set up holding companies that ended competition by merging the capital and control of the most powerful competitors. The trust (as holding companies were popularly called) traded its certificates for the stock of members; its total capitalization usually depended much less on the aggregate earning power of its constituent parts than on the total sum necessary to induce all the proprietors to sell.

One by one, manufacturing trusts lumbered into the field in the late 1890s. Several made overtures to Carnegie's firm. When some of Carnegie's partners, weary of the struggle, wanted to sell out, Carnegie would have none of it. In 1897, Illinois Steel, a Morgan creation, suggested a pool to divide the business in heavy steel. "Our policy in my opinion," Carnegie wrote his partners,

> is to stand by ourselves alone. . . . Take orders East and West. . . . As for Illinois Steel: if you do arrange with them you are simply bolstering a concern and enabling it to strike you in the near future. . . . We have made the fight, the enemy is at our mercy, now do not let us be foolish enough to throw away the fruits of victory.

Another behemoth, Federal Steel, lurched from the Morgan workshop in 1898. Carnegie spurred his partners on to battle:

> Surely my views about going into the trust are well known. . . . The Carnegie Steel Company should never in my opinion enter any Trust. It will do better tending to its own business in its own way. . . . We hope our competitors will combine, for an independent concern always has the "Trust" at its mercy.

In 1899, yet another trust, American Tinplate Company, threatened to stop buying Carnegie's steel unless he agreed not to sell to other tinplate manufacturers. Carnegie refused: "In these days of Trusts and other swindles I do not favor the contract. . . . I do not believe it is legal; I do not believe it is right. I think the Carnegie Company should keep a pure record. . . . I believe that independent concerns will soon beat the trust." When American Tinplate and other trusts began to cancel orders for Carnegie's steel in 1899, he wired his partners, "Crisis has arrived, only one policy open: start at once hoop, rod, wire, nail mills. . . . Have no fear as to result, victory is certain."

Carnegie's confidence had a solid foundation. He knew that none of these "paper concerns" could survive in competition with his efficient, streamlined establishment. It amounted to, as a congressional committee later described it, "a contest between fabricators of steel and fabricators of securities; between makers of billets and makers of bonds." Carnegie himself described Federal Steel as "the greatest concern the world ever saw for manufacturing stock certificates. . . . But they will fail sadly in steel." Such a trust, in fact, could survive only in the absence of efficient competition. Many of Federal's companies had only a creaky collection of obsolete machinery (some of it dating back to the Civil War), scattered randomly around the country and vastly overcapitalized. National Tube, for example, had a capital stock of $80 million on which to try to pay dividends. Julian Kennedy, Morgan's expert on steel works (and a Carnegie-trained man), told Morgan that National Tube's 19 plants had a real market value of only $19 million.

In 1900, Carnegie prepared to annihilate this upstart. Carnegie's firm owned a patent for manufacturing seamless tubes. The firm designed a tube plant that would employ the closest thing to continuous flow manufacturing yet achieved in the steel industry, showing how far the industry had advanced from the scattered units and lump businesses Carnegie had found decades before. "How much cheaper, Charley, can you make the tubes than the National Company?" Carnegie asked Schwab, who answered, "At least 10 dollars per ton." "Well," said Andy, "go and build the plant then."

When Carnegie announced his plans to build a tube plant, "he became an incorporated threat and menace to the steel trade of the United States," according to one of Morgan's partners. Morgan, capitulating, asked Carnegie to name his price. Carnegie, satisfied with his victory, anxious to undertake his long-delayed plans for philanthropy and self-improvement, and having no son to whom he could pass on the business, was finally ready to retire. When he sold out, he apparently had little faith in the future of the newly formed United States Steel Corporation, for he insisted on his payment in gold bonds, thus acquiring a mortgage that insured his right to reclaim his property should the trust fail. He had beaten the trust once and could do it again if needed. "I believe you would have captured the steel trade of the world if you had stayed in business," a congressman remarked to him later. "I am as certain of it as I can be certain of anything," Carnegie replied. Elbert Gary, who became chairman of United States Steel, observed, "If the management that was in force at the time had continued, the Carnegie company [might] have driven entirely out of business every steel company in the United States." Time bore out the wisdom of his caution. In U.S. Steel, as Carnegie had perhaps anticipated, competition gave way to collusion and complacency, and the enterprise as a whole, far from rising to the efficiency of its Carnegie Steel component, sank toward the level of its least efficient unit.

Carnegie retired to a life of philanthropy and promotion of peace. Looking back on his career, he could savor many triumphs: his rise to wealth through hard work and shrewd investment; his triumphant return to Dunfermline in 1881, when he and his mother had ridden atop a palatial coach and four in triumph through the town they had once fled in poverty, passing under banners reading "Welcome Carnegie, generous son"; his friendships with luminaries such as Herbert Spencer, Matthew Arnold, William Gladstone, and Woodrow Wilson; his successful marriage and the daughter it produced; and, last but not least, a bulging file of letters that he labeled "Gratitude and Sweet Words." He had also known his share of disappointment and tragedy: the failure of his father; the alcoholic death of his brother; and, above all, the catastrophe of the Homestead strike, which his callousness had precipitated. But he had fashioned a philosophy that gave him peace. Years before, he had read Herbert Spencer and found an explanation of the fundamental life process that made sense to him in light of his own career:

> Light came in as a flood and all was clear. Not only had I got rid of the theology and the supernatural, but I had found the truth of evolution. "All is well since all grows better" became my motto, my true source of comfort. Man was not created with an instinct for his own degradation, but from the lower he had risen to the higher forms. Nor is there any conceivable end to his march to perfection. His face is turned to the light, he stands in the sun and looks upward.

Buttressed by Spencer's philosophy, Carnegie could endure his mistakes and rejoice in his successes, secure in the belief that by following his own star, he helped move society as a whole toward its bright destiny. Finally, he justified his fortune by giving it away. He saw himself as the trustee of wealth, not its owner. "The man who dies rich, dies disgraced," he wrote in 1889. After retiring, he lived up to his own creed.

If Andy could see what's left of United States Steel today, he probably would think things had gone to hell since he left the business. But if he looked elsewhere in the American economy, he'd probably feel better, for wherever efficient manufacturing goes on in the United States, the Carnegie heritage survives. In the rest of the world, the passage of time has shown the utility, indeed the necessity of cost-based management in any truly competitive arena. When changes in political economy (as in China after Mao), or expansion of productive capacity (Japan since the 1950s), or mastery of technological sophistication (South Korea in the 1990s) meet market opportunity, such as the opening of American markets since the 1950s and 1960s, dynamic competition ensues. When it does, the principles and practices that propelled Carnegie to success necessarily soon follow. In his time, Carnegie saw much of the world and remarked upon its peculiarities. If he could see it now, he'd see convergence in industrial practices far and wide, a vivid legacy of his life's work.

Chapter 5

The Most Useful American

Thomas A. Edison

Edison at age 40 with an early phonograph. Both had a long run ahead

Despite my preference for trains, I fly a lot. On planes I meet lots of college parents and spend considerable time arguing that when the fate of the universe passes into the hands of their children, things will improve, not collapse. I have admired my students for 40 years; I think they comprise the most decent generation of people this country has yet produced. I don't fret that they watch bad TV; their grandparents spent their childhoods reading comic books and wasted many a Saturday afternoon gazing rapturously at movie screens filled with puerile nonsense; their parents read many a trashy book and watched many a television program that make today's shows look like Royal Shakespeare Company festivals.

Some detractors find it stylish to predict dire consequences looming from young people's supposed inability to read, write, or conjure with numbers. The Cassandras usually document their gloom with statistics of scores on standardized tests that supposedly measure a student's aptitude for college, graduate school, medical school, law school, business school, and I know not what all else. Neither this apparatus nor its results impress me, although I personally have benefited enormously by playing the system. The testing industry makes lots of money, and employs an army of test writers, scorers, and assorted others in a Princeton headquarters more elegant than the Taj Mahal. The tests themselves prove little except how well a student takes tests, and no one has the vaguest idea what any of it means in any other context, despite elaborate pretensions to the contrary. One potent precedent for my skepticism: Thomas Edison thought such tests absurd and mockingly devised one of his own entitled the "ignoramometer."

Today's college students can read. Students in fourth-rate colleges now read more than students in citadels of intellectuality did a generation ago, and although the worst of them can't write any better than the worst of them ever could, the best of them write so well that I'm repeatedly dazzled by their skills. In reality, students today read and write all the time, thanks to blogs, text messaging, twittering, and social networking sites such as Facebook—not Shakespeare or Milton perhaps, but every authority on teaching reading that I've encountered says, "Let them read anything they'll read." So, not to worry.

Much student conversation takes place in code, such as TTYL, LOL, and OMG (the latter two added to the Oxford English Dictionary in 2011!), but all language is a code to which each generation adds and subtracts, as witness business people using "this point in time" instead of "now," changing "impact" from a noun to a verb, and bloviating in such jargon as "askings," "learnings," and "mandatories." Each generation thus creates its own literacy, a blend of past and present. In the twenty-first century, computer literacy has joined the traditional repertoire required of functional citizens. Nearly all students arrive at college already equipped with it; their elders struggle—often in vain—to retrofit it. As for mathematics, if, in fact, most students know none, that results from rational calculation, not lack of intelligence; calculators cost less than corn flakes.

Today's college students simply come prepared in a different way from the generations that preceded them. Not worse, different. Calling them uneducated smacks of an ignorance of the ways the world has changed. As I told one of my sneering colleagues, we may feel smug about the elegance of our intellectual preparation, but polylingual poet Samuel Taylor Coleridge would have dismissed us as barbarians.

My students have provided me with a lot of rewarding surprises, not least of which is discovering that many of them truly love history for its own sake and enjoy researching the past. Although Larry Page and Sergey Brin, Google's founders, haven't yet achieved their goal of making all the world's knowledge instantly available, they've gotten far enough that gifted undergraduates produce in a few days research that would have taken my generation of graduate students weeks (if not months) to assemble. Having grown up imbibing the logic of computers, the younger generations often produce better search results than their more timid elders.

The more passionate history students I have known included one who worked as a guide at the Greenfield Village and Henry Ford Museum in Dearborn, Michigan. Among other relics of the American past, Henry Ford had Thomas Edison's Menlo Park laboratory brought intact to Greenfield Village. And I do mean intact: every plank, every nail, every bottle, every machine, indeed the very earth on which it sat Ford ordered exhumed, and the whole collection brought to Michigan. When Ford triumphantly presented his handiwork to Edison, the inventor, who had not seen the laboratory in 40 years, said, "You got it 99 percent perfect." "What's wrong with it?" asked the crestfallen Ford. "We never kept the floor this clean," replied Edison.

My student, whose sense of the drama of the past together with her considerable thespian abilities made her a favorite with the visiting throngs, particularly liked to show people through Edison's laboratory. Steering her charges through the labyrinth of mysterious apparatus, shelved chemicals, and the workbenches and tables on which Edison had often napped, she would sometimes abandon the prepared script, carefully researched by the museum's staff, in favor of an extemporaneous discourse, authored, or so she claimed, by Edison himself. The living Edison, blunt, cranky, and deaf, had relied heavily on shouts and obscenities when communicating to his subordinates; however, his pneuma displayed both a gentler temperament and subtler methods, inspiring his cicerone by spiriting his thoughts into her mind. Fascinated visitors often asked their guide what use Edison had made of this or that mysterious apparatus, now squatting obscurely in some dusty nook or cranny. Invariably, she rendered an explanation, often in elaborate detail, only afterward realizing that she had never noticed the relic before and had no personal knowledge of it whatever.

So where did she get her information? "From Edison," she told me. "I'm just his amanuensis." Well, who can say otherwise? In 1920, Edison, then in his seventies, explored the possibility of communication between the quick and the dead. The subject generated widespread interest in the era following a war that had killed millions. Edison, having tried nearly everything else (and perhaps thinking that he himself would need celestial contact in the near future), began searching for an appropriate technology. "I don't claim," Edison told a reporter from *Scientific American,* that

> Our personalities pass on to another existence or sphere. . . . I [think] it is possible to construct an apparatus . . . so delicate that if . . . personalities in another existence or sphere . . . wish to get in touch with us . . . this apparatus will . . . give them a better opportunity to express themselves than . . . tilting tables and raps and Ouija boards.

One of his assistants, Edison observed, had died while working on the apparatus, and "he ought to be the first man to use it if he is able to do so."

If Edison ever received news from the other world, he kept it to himself. He may have trumped up the whole business, for his character included a wide streak of whimsy and perversity. Genuinely iconoclastic in scientific matters, Edison enjoyed spreading consternation in other areas as well. The fundamentalist clergy and their fervent followers formed a particularly attractive target, since Edison, like many another inventor before and after him, had often stirred the wrath of the faithful by carrying worldly business into the precincts of the Heavenly City. Samuel Morse's telegraph, for instance, had provoked many a sermon and letter to Congress on the lines of "If God had intended words to be sent over wire, He would have . . . " This opposition Morse tried to negate through his choice of "What hath God wrought?" as the first official message.

In 1910, when asked what a personal God meant to him, Edison replied, "Nothing," a statement he repeated at suitable intervals. What he really believed no one can know, but he unquestionably enjoyed spreading distress among archenemies of the inventive mind. Suggesting the possibility of an apparatus delicate enough to communicate with the departed may have served as just another excursion into provocative posturing. But maybe not. He didn't get the job done in his lifetime, but Edison the ghost may have finished what Edison the man began. If so, it wouldn't be the only time that Edison succeeded where others failed, and not the only revolution Edison ever facilitated.

Americans have evinced an ambivalent view toward things revolutionary. In the political sphere, we have embraced the notion that our first revolution did the job so well that neither justification nor excuse has arisen for one since; consequently, we haven't wanted, needed, or had any more ourselves and often opposed them among folks elsewhere. Even when steadfastly resisting political overturn in either thought or deed, however, Americans have celebrated the interrelated revolutions in transportation, communication, and energy that remade their society. As technological advancements broke the shackles that had limited transportation and communication to the pace of wind and water and accelerated them to the speed of sound and light, most Americans rejoiced and called it progress. Fundamental to this change and to the expansion of manufacturing capacity, a two-stage revolution reshaped the ways humans converted potential energy to power. In the first stage, steam supplanted human and animal muscle, wind, and water as the source of power to drive tools and machines; in the second, electricity and the internal combustion engine took over.

American industry thus developed in three distinct periods, demarked by the prevalent energy source of the time. Eli Whitney belonged to the first era. The first cotton gin, a machine "which required the labor of one man to turn it" could also "be turned by water or with a horse." On the other hand, manufacturing cotton gins, muskets, or anything else in volume required "machinery moved by water," and this imperative dictated the location of manufacturing sites at a place with "a good fall of Water in the Vicinity." Above all, in the early days, the most useful of these waterfalls lay in close proximity to where the stream became navigable to the sea, for only water made transportation of heavy materials economically feasible. It also greatly facilitated matters if these riparian resources adjoined settled areas with labor and markets available.

In Whitney's day, this happy combination occurred most often on rivers from the Potomac northward. There the mountains lay close to the sea and ribbed the land between with rocky ridges that eroded into a staircase of waterfalls ideal for powering machinery. Many rivers compressed a great vertical fall into a short lateral distance. In 20 miles of Pennsylvania and Delaware countryside, for example, the Brandywine River drops farther than Niagara Falls. In some cases—the Brandywine at Wilmington, Delaware, the Passaic at Paterson, New Jersey—the last fall drops into tidewater. South of the Potomac, the fall line lies far from the coast in a region that remained, in Whitney's time, largely a wilderness. From there to the ocean, the rivers flow lazily through soft southern soil and limestone.

American manufacturing, born in this era of waterpower, began life in the valleys of the Brandywine, Connecticut, Merrimack, and other rivers of the north, not the James, Cape Fear, Savannah, or Chattahoochee. Southern cotton became cloth at mills in Lowell, Waltham, and Chicopee, Massachusetts, far removed from the raw material source. Whitney, retreating from Georgia to a suitable locale familiar to him, manufactured cotton gins and muskets in New Haven, Connecticut, for markets that lay far away.

In the second period, steam power liberated Cyrus McCormick and Andrew Carnegie from some of these locational restrictions. Although both men situated their works on navigable waterways and used them to transport raw materials and finished products, the railroads played a crucial role in their firms' massive expansion. Railroads created much of McCormick's market, carrying settlers to the land and their produce away from it, while enabling McCormick to distribute his machines in the huge landlocked regions of the wheat belt. Carnegie Steel used railroads so extensively to bring raw materials in and carry finished products away that it became the largest single railroad customer in the world.

In deciding where to build his plant, neither McCormick nor Carnegie had to consider access to waterpower. Steam engines worked anywhere you could get fuel to them, and Chicagoans rightly regarded McCormick's steam-powered plant as a symbol of the new industrial age. A visit to McCormick's factory in 1851 moved a local newsman to a rhetorical rhapsody:

> An angry whir, a dronish hum, a prolonged whistle, a shrilled buzz, and a panting breath—such is the music of the place. You enter—little wheels of steel attached to horizontal, upright, and oblique shafts, are on every hand. . . . Rude pieces of wood without form or comeliness . . . upon little railways, as if drawn thither by some mysterious attraction. [The wheels] touched them, and *presto,* grooved, scalloped, rounded, on they go . . . transferred to another railway, then down comes a guillotine-like contrivance—they are sawn, bored, and whirled away, where the tireless planes without hands, like a boatswain, whistle the rough plank into polish . . . smooth shaped and fitted for its place in the Reaper or the Harvester. The saw and the cylinder are the genii of the establishment. They work its wonders, and accomplish its drudgery. . . . Below, glistening like a knight in armor, the engine of forty-horse power worked . . . silently . . . but shafts plunge, cylinders revolve, bellows heave, iron is

twisted into screws like wax, and sawed-off at the rate of forty rounds a second, at one movement of [the engine's] mighty muscles.

Cyrus McCormick's 1851 factory, with its power tools turning out interchangeable parts and its "little railways" moving components from one operation to another, fulfilled the system of manufacturing that Eli Whitney had envisioned. Driven by its power plant that could function almost anywhere, McCormick's establishment served as a rudimentary but unmistakable prototype of the modern factory that lay at the heart of American industrial productivity. Carnegie's Edgar Thomson steel works, which opened a quarter of a century later, carried the evolution one step further. Steam-powered machinery made it possible to expand volume and speed up production so much that by the end of the nineteenth century, Carnegie's mill produced as much in one day as an 1850 Pittsburgh establishment could produce in a year. Steam drove the fans that put the blast in the hard-driven furnaces; steam-powered rollers shaped the rails and beams; steam cranes and locomotives shunted the material from one operation to another and from the plant to its customers.

Outside the factory, however, the world progressed more slowly. For all of the impact on American business, steam engines hardly touched on life in the American home, whether city or farm. There, human muscle and horseflesh, as always, supplied the power that got the chores done. Before electricity, most urban Americans lived dark, smelly, tattletale gray, washed-by-hand lives in homes and streets lit by guttering wicks and flickering gas lamps, reeking of coal, human excretion, and horse manure. Farm families, enduring numbing toil and embittering isolation, struggled with an existence far removed from the romantic Jeffersonian myth of the happy yeoman. Many rural families lived lives far more evocative of seventeenth-century English philosopher Thomas Hobbes's phrase "poor, solitary, nasty, brutish and short," lives starkly chronicled in the novels of Willa Cather and Ole Rölvaag and graphically depicted in *Wisconsin Death Trip*.

How profoundly Edison's work transformed these daily American lives is suggested by a partial list of the projects in which he engaged as inventor, manufacturer, perfector, or promoter. These included the electric light and all the associated apparatus needed to generate and distribute electricity, first for lighting and then for the whole paraphernalia of electrical appliances; the phonograph; motion pictures; electric traction motors and storage batteries that powered streetcars and delivery wagons and got horses and their droppings off the streets; and the "Edison effect," the phenomenon that led to the vacuum tube, the keystone of wireless telegraphy, radio broadcasting, and television. Small wonder that the public acclaimed Edison as the "most useful American."

Edison also contributed directly and significantly to America's industrial development by perfecting a system to send multiple telegraph messages in both directions over the same telegraph wire, by lighting up factories as well as homes, by devising new methods to manufacture and pour cement, by developing the prototype of the modern industrial research laboratory, by inventing the mimeograph machine, and by innumerable other contributions to technology. On average, Edison produced a patentable device every two weeks of his adult life. Together, he his colleagues, his rivals, and his imitators literally and figuratively electrified America by devising a power source driven by falling water, steam, or the internal combustion engine to generate a cheap, flexible energy, as well as the equipment to step voltage up to drive the heaviest industrial machinery, or down for use in every household.

Edison, along with those who perfected the internal combustion engine, thus presided over the last energy revolution we have so far had, although he suspected that others lay ahead. Today, groping for new sources of energy, we travel paths that Edison surveyed speculatively long ago. In 1922, he noted in his diary the possibility of atomic energy: "It may come someday. As a matter of fact, I am already experimenting along the lines of gathering information at my laboratory here. . . . So far as atomic energy is concerned there is nothing in sight just now. Although tomorrow some discovery might be made." On this subject, as on many others, Edison displayed his uncommon faculty ("a pipeline to God," some called it) for sensing that a thing might work without at the moment seeing how. Some of his visions—helicopters and hovercraft, for example—remained just that, visions, in his lifetime. But many became realities that changed American life; indeed, few men could claim to have witnessed so much change or to have contributed so much to the process.

When Thomas Edison was born in 1847, James K. Polk was president; 29 states contained 21 million people (85 percent of them living in rural areas), served by 5,000 miles of railroad. When he died in 1931, Herbert Hoover was president; 48 states had a total population of 124 million (56 percent of it urban), and 430,000 miles of track. Industries unheard of at Edison's birth had reshaped American lives by the time of his death. In 1931, 26 million motor vehicles traveled 216 billion miles over 830,000 miles of paved highway; scheduled airlines flew 43 million revenue miles; Americans had 20 million telephones and made 83 million calls a day on them; 17 million families had radios, served by 612 broadcasting stations; 68 percent of American households had electricity and had purchased more than $300 million worth of electrical appliances and radios every year since 1925; altogether, Americans consumed 110 billion kilowatt hours of electricity, almost half of it in factories, where electric motors furnished more than half the total horsepower used.

Almost at its beginning, the tempest of change stirred by the introduction of steam power buffeted Edison's life. His birthplace, Milan, Ohio, owed its prosperity to a canal that carried Ohio farmers' produce to Lake Erie and thence to eastern markets. In 1854, the Lake Shore Railroad, building west, bypassed Milan. The canal dried up and the town with it; Edison's father's timber business, collapsed. Samuel Edison removed his family to Port Huron, Michigan, set up a new business, and sent his son off to school. The local schoolmaster (no Eli Whitney he) pronounced young Thomas "addled," enraging Edison's mother, who declared the teacher a fool and carried the boy home, determined to teach him herself. This exercise of parental discretion rescued Edison from a style of learning he found "repulsive."

Under his mother's supervision, Edison escaped from the rote learning of the schoolhouse to an early exposure to classics such as Edward Gibbon and William Shakespeare. He read Thomas Paine and experienced an epiphany similar to Carnegie's encounter with Spencer:

> It was a revelation to me to read [Paine's] views on political and theological subjects. Paine educated me then about many matters of which I had never

before thought. I remember very vividly the flash of enlightenment that shone from Paine's writings. . . . I went back to them time and time again, just as I have done since my boyhood days.

Newton's *Principia,* however, proved heavier going; young Edison soon found himself lost in "the wilderness of mathematics," developing "a distaste . . . from which I never recovered." In fact, mathematics roused his perversity throughout his life and he continued to dismiss it as merely a necessary adjunct to his trade. "I look upon figures as mathematical tools," he declared, "which are employed to carve out the logical results of reasoning, but I do not consider them necessary to assist one to an intelligent understanding of the result." Later he added, "I am not a mathematician, but I can get within ten percent in the higher reaches of the art." Besides, he concluded with savage satisfaction and a wisdom conventional among successful entrepreneurs, "I can always hire mathematicians, but they can't hire me." (Stung by the truthful arrogance of these and other sallies, his critics coined the pejorative term "Edisonian" to denote the trial-and-error methods forced on Edison and others by their lack of theoretical background.)

The books that most fired young Edison's imagination, however, Richard Parker's *Natural and Experimental Philosophy* and the *Dictionary of Science,* launched him on the road to invention. Spending all his pocket money on chemicals, bottles, and other apparatus, Edison fled below stairs to carry out the experiments described in these magical books. According to his father, Edison "never knew a real boyhood like other boys" because "he spent the greater part of his time in the cellar." Like most sorcerers' apprentices, Tom produced some jarring results, leading his father to predict, "He will blow us all up!" Edison's mother, like Carnegie's, stood behind him. "Let him be," she urged; "[he] knows what he's about." "My mother was the making of me," Edison later recalled. "She understood me; she let me follow my bent."

In 1859, fate in the form of the railroad boom once again took a hand in young Edison's life. It found him, like Carnegie, toiling away in his cellar. The Grand Trunk Railroad, building a line from Portland, Maine, through Canada and across Michigan to Chicago, reached Sarnia, Ontario, across the St. Clair River from Edison's hometown, Port Huron. The railroad established a car ferry to shuttle its trains across the river and built a branch line from Port Huron to Detroit. Finding himself this time squarely in the path of railroad-borne progress, young Edison leapt aboard.

Declaring himself grown and independent at age 12, Edison became a "train butcher," selling candy, fruit, and vegetables on the morning trip from Port Huron to hustling Detroit and the evening Detroit newspapers on the return journey. No commuter hustling train, between stops to get workers to and from suburbs and city, this "rattler" belonged to a now-extinct species known as the "way passenger train." It left Port Huron at 7 a.m. and took 4 hours to cover the 63 miles to Detroit; in the evening, it left Detroit at 5:30 p.m. and arrived back at Port Huron at 9:30. The train paused at each station, loading and unloading passengers, baggage, and express parcels before sauntering down the line.

Thus at an age when, nowadays, we think children capable of little more independent action than flicking on a television set (or perhaps hacking into the Pentagon's computers), Edison developed the pattern, continued throughout his life, of working 16-hour days and making the most of them. He set up a garden in Port

Huron and hired boys to tend it to supply him with produce to sell on the train. He used the six-hour layover to peruse the scientific volumes in the Detroit library. In the train baggage car he set up a printing press and published a sheet called the *Grand Trunk Herald,* containing local news and gossip, which he peddled to the passengers. In 1862, he found a way to enlist the telegraph as an aid to his entrepreneurial energies. Hearing of a bloody battle fought at Shiloh, Edison persuaded the editor of the Detroit *Free Press* to supply him with 1,500 newspapers on credit. He then cajoled the railroad's Detroit telegraph operator into sending the headlines to all the stations down the road, where the stationmasters chalked the bulletins up on the train board. As the evening train worked its way north, at each station Edison found a mob so eager to buy his newspapers that he raised the price from five cents to a quarter and sold out his entire stock. "You can understand," he recalled, "why it struck me then that the telegraph must be about the best thing going, for it was the telegraphic notices on the bulletin boards which had done the trick. I determined at once to become a telegraph operator."

The chance came through an incident worthy of Horatio Alger's imagination. Standing on the platform at Mt. Clements, Michigan, Edison saw the station telegrapher's son about to be run over by a passing freight train. Edison, the boy's father remembered, threw

> his papers . . . upon the platform, together with his . . . cap, and plunged to
> the rescue, risking his own life to save his little friend, and throwing the
> child and himself out of the way.

Unlike Horatio Alger's characters, the grateful father had neither fortune nor daughter to bestow upon his benefactor, but he gave what he had, teaching Edison the telegrapher's art.

Soon mastering the rudiments of the craft, Edison easily secured a regular job because operators left the railroads and telegraph companies in droves for the higher pay and greater excitement of the Military Telegraph Corps. In 1863, he began an eight-year career as a "boomer," an itinerant telegrapher who, like similar-minded brethren among railroad brakemen and locomotive firemen, worked for a while at one place and then restlessly moved on to another, motivated by an independent spirit that Jimmy Rodgers, Leadbelly, and others wove into American folklore:

> *I went down to the depot and I looked up on the board;*
> *It said, "There's good times here, but there's better down the road."*

Joining this mobile brotherhood (also, like the passenger train, now largely extinct), Edison traveled far and wide, working in Louisville, Nashville, Memphis, New Orleans, Fort Wayne, Indianapolis, Cincinnati, Detroit, and a dozen other, smaller towns in the United States and Canada. Serving a variety of railroads and telegraph companies, Edison became a first-class operator and developed a style of his own. One of his colleagues later recalled that

> a memorable experience of this episode [of my life] was to listen to what
> might be called the autograph of a certain operator . . . at Indianapolis

named Edison. The telegraphic style of the [future] great inventor . . . was unique [in] its lightning-like rapidity. . . . [E]ven . . . expert telegraphers . . . often had to . . . ask him to repeat.

Like most boomers, Edison had idiosyncrasies that made him something less than an ideal employee and often got him fired. For some, the weakness lay in drink, for others, a tendency to leave the apparatus unattended while they pursued gambling or more pernicious pitfalls of the flesh. For Edison, his scientific curiosity ensnared him; it often led him to conduct experiments on the telegraphic apparatus itself, or to lose himself in his bottles and chemicals when trains needed dispatching or telegrams awaited forwarding.

Finally, in 1868, Edison wandered to Boston, where he took a job with the Western Union Telegraph Company. Now 21 and wise in the ways of the road (though woefully naïve about cities and the business carried on in them), Edison manifested personal traits that never subsequently changed: slovenly dress, a tireless indifference to night and day that made his work habits the despair of those who tried to keep up with him, a gaudy vocabulary (as essential as good eyesight to survival around a railroad, as Carnegie also had learned), and a national reputation for his skill matched only by his cockiness. Ace telegraphers, like gunfighters, confronted challenges at every turn, but Edison, who could send faster than anyone else could transcribe and transcribed faster than anyone else could send, proved hard to shoot down.

On his first night in Boston, his fellow operators manipulated their assignments so that Edison had to take a message from "the fastest man in New York." The New Yorker began slowly, but "soon," Edison said,

increased his speed, to which I easily adapted my pace. This put my rival on his mettle, and he put on his best powers. . . . At this point I happened to look up, and saw the operators all looking over my shoulders, with their faces shining with fun and excitement.

After some minutes of this, Edison "thought the fun had gone far enough . . . [so I] opened the key and remarked: 'Say, young man, change off, and send with your other foot.'"

Working at night, studying in the daytime, Edison delved into Michael Faraday's *Experimental Researches in Electricity.* Bristling with confidence, armed with a thorough knowledge of the practical and theoretical aspects of telegraphy, Edison decided to become an inventor. Displaying the hallmark of the practical technologist, he looked for some situation in which the application of telegraph technology might improve the status quo. In the factory of Charles Williams, who later made Alexander Graham Bell's first telephone, Edison devised an apparatus to record votes instantaneously in legislative assemblies. To his amazement, he soon discovered that his potential customers, both in the Massachusetts legislature and the federal Congress, reacted with horror to this device that threatened to accelerate the traditional, glacial pace of their proceedings. "Young man," they told him in Washington, "if there is any invention on earth that we don't want down here, it is this." With his feathers thus singed, Edison determined to waste no further time inventing things that, however useful, did not have an immediate commercial application. With this determination, he set himself apart from the legions of inventors who pursue gadgetry for its own sake, sure that technical elegance will lead to fame and fortune, but destined to learn that capitalism provides "no philanthropic asylum for indigent inventors," and that solutions looking for problems find only blind alleys.

The incident of the automatic vote recorder taught Edison a lesson often disregarded by otherwise prescient individuals before and since: those who deal in ideas ahead of their time doom themselves to oblivion, not success. Success most often goes to those who perfect innovations long overdue, often a "sustaining technology" that better serves a market that already exists. Thus, after his first failure, Edison concentrated his efforts on developing equipment to improve telegraphic services where they had already proved useful and profitable. In January 1869, he placed a notice in *The Telegrapher* announcing that "T. A. Edison has resigned his situation in the Western Union office, Boston, and will devote his time to bringing out inventions." The first of these, an improved stock ticker, supplied current market quotations to brokerage houses. This device found a ready market and made Edison some money, which, establishing another lifelong pattern, he immediately plowed back into other experiments. When these new enterprises failed, Edison decided to emulate the American capital market and migrated from Boston to New York, arriving, penniless, in May 1869.

In New York, Edison for a time fell upon lean days, existing largely on a diet of apple dumplings until fate once again rescued him. Poor but not unknown in his own field, Edison found a friend in Franklin L. Pope, chief engineer of the Laws Gold Reporting Company, one of two firms that had a stranglehold on the lucrative service of furnishing gold and stock market quotations to brokers in New York. Pope let Edison sleep on a cot in the company's battery room. Edison thus chanced to be on hand one day when the central transmitting machine broke down. Pandemonium at once ensued as runners from dozens of brokerage houses rushed into the office demanding instant information. Both Pope and Dr. S. S. Laws, the firm's proprietor, succumbed to the hysteria of the moment. Edison, keeping his head, located the trouble and soon repaired it. Impressed and relieved, Laws hired Edison at a salary of $300 a month, two and a half times his wage as a first-class telegraph operator. But Edison, who had no more mind than Carnegie to restrict himself to the "narrow field" delineated by "the beck and call of others," soon resigned and set up a partnership with Pope. Pope, Edison & Company advertised its services as electrical engineers, specializing in "the application of electricity to the Arts and Sciences." Edison offered to design instruments "to order for special telegraphic services," and to perfect "the application of Electricity and Magnetism for Fire-Alarms, Thermo-Alarms, Burglar-Alarms, etc."

Despite this grandiose advance billing, Edison in fact continued to concentrate on a narrow range of telegraphic instruments. By this time, the principle had become well established that capitalists saw patents as things to buy or evade as circumstances dictated. As a man whose fertile mind spun off a series of practical improvements for an industry embroiled in cutthroat competition, Edison soon found himself courted by the emerging titans of telegraphy, particularly the moguls at Western Union, who wanted nothing less than a monopoly of the industry in the United States.

It proved easier to plan such a monopoly than to accomplish it, even for Western Union, masterminded by Ezra Cornell and Amos J. Kendall, and backed by the vast financial resources of a Vanderbilt-Morgan syndicate. Competitors flocked to an industry that offered glittering prospects for profits, a national market of continental dimensions, plentiful supplies of capital, and new technology that improved almost daily. They appeared from far and wide to challenge Western Union's hegemony. Western Union mounted a two-handed counterattack, gathering in existing rivals with one hand while reaching out with the other to snap up new inventions before they could help the competition. Thus, when Edison designed an improved stock printer and organized a service to rent it to subscribers, Western Union bought him out for $5,000. The company then proceeded to add Edison to its stable of inventors, which included among others Elisha Gray (who subsequently created a working telephone simultaneously with Alexander Graham Bell).

Edison did not become a formal employee of Western Union, but General Marshall Lefferts, one of Western Union's executives, gave him a series of practical problems to tackle and supplied the money to finance his research. With the money from the sale of his stock ticker supplemented by Western Union's subsidy, Edison could afford to become a freelance inventor, a scientific soldier of fortune free to pursue any problem that intrigued him, as well as to accept specific assignments from Lefferts. Although Edison operated under an informal understanding that Western Union would have first refusal on any patents he might obtain, he could in fact double-cross his patron by selling his inventions to anyone he chose.

Some months and several inventions later, Lefferts called him in and offered him $40,000 for the work done so far. Edison accepted and, knowing nothing of banks (or so his version of the story goes), sat up all night in his Jersey City boardinghouse, fearful that some footpad might relieve him of his newfound wealth. The next day, with a friend's help, Edison penetrated the mysteries of banking sufficiently to open a deposit account, but to his dying day he retained the deep-seated suspicion of bankers and banking (not unjustified by dismal historical experience in every century of America's existence) that characterized many Americans (Henry Ford a spectacular example) of rural midwestern origins.

Now possessed of more wealth than he had ever dreamed possible, Edison moved across the river to Newark, New Jersey, and opened a factory to manufacture the new stock tickers for Western Union. Earlier, when he had received the $5,000, Edison had written home to his irascible father, "Don't do any hard work and get mother anything she desires. You can draw on me for money. Write me . . . how much money you will need . . . and I will send the amount on the first of [the] month." Old Sam's astonishment at finding his vagabond son rich enough to pension off his parents increased when Thomas, now ensconced in his Newark factory, wrote, "I have one shop which employs 18 men and am fitting up another which will employ over 150 men. I am now what you Democrats call a 'Bloated Eastern Manufacturer.'"

Between 1869 and 1875, the inventor-cum-bloated-manufacturer continued to improve the telegraph. Financed by Western Union and by the Mephistopheles of late nineteenth-century American finance, Jay Gould, Edison churned out improvements, patented them, and then set up factories to produce the equipment. Inevitably, he became embroiled in the suits and countersuits with which the corporate rivals battered one another. He had to endure character assaults in and out of the witness box, hearing himself branded as a man who had "basely betrayed" his Western Union patrons, as a "rogue inventor," a "professor of duplicity and quadruplicity," and as a "young man [with] a vacuum where his conscience ought to be."

Since Edison sometimes accepted support from several companies simultaneously to work on the same problem and then sold the results to the highest bidder, some of these accusations bore an element of truth. Since he considered himself more swindled than swindling, Edison's conscience emerged relatively unscathed. "Everybody steals in commerce and industry," he reflected. "I've stolen a lot myself. But I knew *how* to steal. They don't know *how* to steal—that's all that's the matter with them." His excursions into the freebooting world of high finance, which included a fleecing at the hands of Gould and a particularly ferocious courtroom denunciation by a master of legalistic histrionics, Roscoe Conkling, did, however, persuade him that the denizens of Wall Street made up an even more rascally lot than small-town bankers, another view later vehemently espoused by his disciple, Henry Ford.

However reprehensible these characters, Edison had to deal with them, for in the late nineteenth century, technology became so complex and so expensive that no inventor could hope to progress far without access to capital markets and the men who manipulated them. The day when an Eli Whitney could create a revolutionary machine using hand tools to shape bits of wood and wire, and could then test his creation by turning a crank, had not entirely passed, as Edison later proved with the phonograph. But most electrical apparatus required months of experimentation to perfect, expensive precision equipment, a well-financed factory to manufacture, and elaborate facilities to test (to try a system of long-distance transmission that required a far-flung network on which to transmit). Consequently, Edison and other inventors found themselves clutching at financiers, however distasteful the embrace.

Many brilliant inventors had a business sense that would have embarrassed children. Edison, who started shrewdly enough in his days as a railroad vendor, apparently lost his somewhere along the way. For years, he admitted, he kept nothing but payroll accounts. "I kept no books," he said. Sometimes he simply handed clerks fistfuls of cash with which to pay bills, but usually he settled his debts with personal notes. When the notes came due, he "had to hustle around and raise the money." This chaotic system avoided "the humbuggery of bookkeeping, which," he said, "I never understood." Later, when his empire grew so large that some form of financial organization became unavoidable, he put his affairs in the hands of Samuel Insull, a bounder with ideas so original that in later life his handiwork helped precipitate the Great Crash of 1929 and inspired a whole new category of preventive legislation.

In the wide-open booming economy of the late nineteenth century, alliances of capitalists and technicians could often make fortunes. The alluring prospects brought forth an endless stream of innovations across the whole spectrum of business activity, described by *Scientific American* as "a gigantic tidal wave of human ingenuity." Not surprisingly, the inventors often came out on the short end; promoters Ezra Cornell, Theodore Vail, and J. P. Morgan made fortunes out of the telegraph, the telephone, and the electric light that dwarfed the returns to Samuel F. B. Morse, Alexander Graham Bell, and Thomas Edison, who invented them. As the golden stream flowed by, Edison did, however, manage to siphon off enough to finance projects that filled even his monumental working hours. On an upper floor of his Newark factory, Edison established a laboratory, filled it with apparatus, and staffed it with technicians. Their enthusiasm for the work, or for Edison himself (some of his most talented associates migrated to Newark specifically to associate themselves with the great man), sustained them so that they thrived on working conditions that Edison summarized by saying, "We don't pay anything and we work all the time."

Work all the time they did, as Edison, driven by inspiration or financial necessity, turned his team onto one project after another. Some of these quests he originated, including one that produced the first mimeograph machine. (These personal projects gave him special satisfaction. After completing one of them, he noted it in his journal as "invented by & for myself and not for any small-brained capitalist.") Some involved improving upon the work of other inventors, such as the automatic telegraph, invented by George D. Little and brought to Edison by Edward H. Johnson, an entrepreneur who had bought Little's patent. Other projects, including the telephone, came at the behest of corporate sponsors like Western Union. Whatever the inspiration, he followed the same method. Rounding up everything known on the subject, Edison listed all the alternatives that he and his staff could conjure up; then he set his team to work creating the apparatus necessary to test them all. Edison proved a driving master of the hunt. Once, when confronted with a breakdown in a new model stock ticker, Edison summoned his staff: "Now, you fellows," he told them, "I've locked the door, and you'll have to stay here until this job is completed." It took 60 hours, an extreme case, but Edison commonly expected his men to toil until they could work no more, then nap on a workbench, the floor, or in some out-of-the-way corner until they could rouse themselves enough to work again.

The employees tolerated this regimen because the boss worked as hard or harder. In addition, his charismatic, mercurial character generated excitement and kept the staff entertained. "Mr. Edison had his desk in one corner," one of his workers said, "and after completing an invention he would jump up and do a kind of Zulu war dance. . . . He would swear something awful. We would crowd round him and he would show us the new invention and explain it to the pattern maker and tell us what to do about it." Once, returning from a day spent in negotiations with New York lawyers and capitalists, who used a language Edison described as "as obscure as Choctaw," he rushed into "the workshop with a whoop, fired his silk hat into an oil pan, and was preparing to send his fine coat after it, when someone laughingly pinned him down." Edison then gladly resumed his normal persona, "as dirty as any of the other workmen, and not much better dressed than a tramp."

By 1876, America's centennial year, Edison's combined labors as inventor and manufacturer had brought him solvency, even modest wealth. The hard-won principles of modern manufacturing—repetitious reproduction of undifferentiated components, constantly monitored by cost-control accounting—always bored Edison. Nevertheless, he understood them and applied them to his own enterprises, despite his public pronouncements on the boredom of bookkeeping. Even the magic of economies of scale, which Andrew Carnegie, across the mountains in Pittsburgh, would soon teach the iron trade of the world, held no mystery for Edison. When he first began to manufacture light bulbs, for example, they cost $1.40 each to produce, but Edison priced them at 40¢, knowing that volume production would soon bring costs down.

But manufacturing, which demanded constant attention to a single project, could not long absorb a man with Edison's cast of mind: "I never think about a thing any longer than I want to," he said. "If I lose my interest in it, I turn to something else. I always keep six or eight things going at once, and turn from one to the other as I feel like it." In 1876, therefore, Edison abandoned his manufacturing ventures and moved his equipment and his staff to the hamlet of Menlo Park, New Jersey, then a remote spot 25 miles south of Newark. At the Menlo Park laboratory, Edison institutionalized his role as creative inventor, establishing what amounted to an invention factory, where he planned to produce technology to order while simultaneously pursuing his own interests.

At Menlo Park, Edison continued to restrict his organization to projects that promised to make money and make it quickly. One commentator called Edison "the first great scientific inventor who clearly conceived of inventions as subordinate to commerce." By adhering to this maxim, Edison became, as German economist Werner Sombart observed, "the outstanding example of a man who made a business of invention itself." As such, he contributed to the dynamic blend of technology and capital that drove American manufacturing to world prominence in the late nineteenth century.

Edison himself made no bones about his role:

> I do not regard myself as a pure scientist, as so many persons have insisted that I am. I do not search for the laws of nature, and have made no great discoveries of such laws. I do not study science as Newton and Faraday and Henry studied it, simply for the purpose of learning truth. I am only a professional inventor. My studies and experiments have been conducted entirely with the object of inventing that which will have commercial utility.

He insisted upon a similar focus among the members of his staff. Criticizing one of his subordinates, Edison said:

> I set him at work developing details of a plan. But when he [notes] some phenomenon new to him, though easily seen to be of no importance in this apparatus, he gets sidetracked. . . . *We can't be spending time that way!* You have got to keep working up things of commercial value—that is what this laboratory is for. We can't be like the old German professor who as long as he can get his black bread and beer is content to spend his whole life studying the fuzz on a bee!

At Menlo Park, this pragmatic formula brought dynamic results and considerable income, which Edison, as always, reinvested in new apparatus and further research. He continued to enjoy corporate patronage. Western Union, for example, in 1876 belatedly perceived the telephone as not just a gadget but also a dangerously competitive form of communication. It once again engaged Edison, this time to create a system that evaded the patents held by Alexander Graham Bell and his

Edison at his laboratory:old; rich; and feisty

backers. Edison soon produced one that, after the inevitable, protracted legal wran-
gles, brought him $300,000. It also required a second trip to England (he had gone
once before in an unsuccessful attempt to sell his telegraphic apparatus to the
British post office), where he supervised its installation and testing. Unlike so
many of his countrymen—McCormick, Carnegie, T. S. Eliot, Henry James, to
name a few—who found European society sophisticated and invigorating, Edison
thought the English slow and unimaginative. "The English," he said, "are not an inventive people." This shortcoming he explained by one of the crackpot formulas
that so endeared him to the American press and public: "They don't eat enough pie.

To invent, your system must be all out of order, and there is nothing that will do that like good old-fashioned American pie."

The phonograph, which Edison and his helpers constructed late in 1877, exemplified Edison's dedication to the profit motive. The talking machine excited the public imagination, bringing newspaper reporters, scientists, and other interested parties on pilgrimages to the wilds of New Jersey. Edison enjoyed showing visitors around and performing parlor tricks to convince the many skeptics that his apparatus did not depend on some chicanery such as ventriloquism, but actually reproduced the human voice. Arthur Clarke, coauthor of *2001: A Space Odyssey,* a man who predicted communications satellites 20 years ahead of time, claimed that "any sufficiently advanced technology is indistinguishable from magic." The public reaction to the phonograph certainly mirrored such a viewpoint. Edison, dubbed "the Wizard of Menlo Park," reaffirmed that title in the public imagination by subsequent sorceries, particularly the electric light.

Edison basked in the publicity generated by the phonograph but didn't let it blind him to the needs of his purse. He set the phonograph aside for some years in favor of the telephone and the electric light, which offered superior commercial possibilities. The invention of the incandescent electric light, which brought Edison enduring, worldwide fame, resulted from his belief that he could harness electricity to tasks other than communication. Steam engines could generate plenty of power, but no easy means existed to transmit it beyond the confines of a factory. In addition, the country contained many remote areas where a shortage of fuel or a small market made steam power uneconomical. Edison thought that electricity, which flowed through wires like water through pipes, generated at a central location and then sent through transmission lines, could power branch-line railroads or do the heavy work at isolated mines and quarries. Edison turned his attention to the potential of electric lighting during a visit to the workshop of William Wallace, a dynamo manufacturer in Ansonia, Connecticut. After watching Wallace's experiments with arc lights, Edison left Wallace with this parting shot: "I believe I can beat you making electric lights. I don't think you are working in the right direction."

Edison's boast flowed from one of his intuitive perceptions. Since the 1850s, the arc light had illuminated streets and lighthouse beacons but had inherent disadvantages— glare, obnoxious fumes, and the need for frequent adjustment—that made it impractical for use indoors. Sensing a market as vast as that for cotton, inventors on both sides of the Atlantic struggled to eliminate these quirks, but Edison's nimble mind leapt to another track altogether. He would make light not through an electrical arc—passing a current across a gap from one conductor to another—but by incandescence—that is, passing a current through a continuous conductor of sufficient resistance to glow. Other men had tried this idea before, but none so far had succeeded in overcoming the practical problems involved. Edison returned to Menlo Park and set to work at once to exploit this vast and waiting market.

When Edison started his search, indoor lighting depended on the burning of candles, coal gas, or kerosene, only the latter two economical on a large scale. Both had objectionable features: they shed a feeble light, stank, and often started fires. The business of distributing gas, furthermore, had often fallen to monopolies of local companies. This aroused the traditional venomous American response to such situations and opened a lucrative market for kerosene that John D. Rockefeller sought in the interests of his own growing monopoly. Kerosene refiners, moreover, had access to a large market where no competition existed, for kerosene lanterns served the darkened dwellings of rural America, where half the population still lived and where no gas company, not even a monopoly, could operate profitably. Nowadays, our reflexive association of petroleum with the automobile obscures the fact that Rockefeller built his empire and his fortune on kerosene, not gasoline; that the United States was the Saudi Arabia of the nineteenth century; and that Rockefeller's machinations excited hostile suspicions around the world ("that greedy little prune-faced peasant," one Frenchman called him) as great as the trepidations with which we now await the latest bulletin from the Organization of Petroleum Exporting Countries, the next *Exxon Valdez* shipwreck, or the next offshore drilling debacle.

So the market existed already, and Edison went after it. Difficulties he found in plenty: determining the right-shaped bulb, perfecting a filament that would glow without breaking, developing pumps to create a near-perfect vacuum in each bulb. Once successful, laboratory methods had to "scale up" into mass production. A system to supply electricity Edison had to develop from scratch: not a single generating station existed; not a foot of wire was yet strung.

Edison confidently predicted that he would succeed "in six weeks." But the weeks became months, and as time and equipment ate up money, Edison had to seek outside help. In the fall of 1878, he founded the Edison Electric Light Company to finance research, take out patents, and license their use. The new firm's backers included Western Union and, almost inevitably, a Morgan partner. With adequate financial backing, and with the marathon labors of his laboratory team guided by the calculations of a theoretical mathematician, Francis R. Upton, whom Edison had grudgingly hired, the Wizard ultimately fulfilled his own prophecy. In the last week of 1879, Edison put on a spectacular display of incandescence at Menlo Park, lighting the grounds and the laboratory with long strings of bulbs. Special Pennsylvania Railroad trains brought newspaper reporters and throngs of pilgrims to witness the miracle.

Electricity went on to light much of the world, but after that triumphant week in December 1879, Edison's own role in it declined. The tremendous amount of capital required to manufacture equipment and generate and distribute electricity forced Edison to yield more and more control of his electrical company to financiers such as Morgan. In addition, his initial demonstration of electricity's potential sparked a swiftly ramifying technology so complex that Edison could not keep up with it. Hundreds of other experimenters flocked to the field, one of whom, George Westinghouse, developed a system of alternating current that supplanted Edison's direct-current method. Within a few years, Edison's technical skills no longer had relevance to the booming American electrical industry.

J. P. Morgan soon combined the bulk of American electrical manufacturing firms (most of which bore Edison's name in some combination) into one of his pet behemoths. He called his new creation "General Electric," thus erasing even the inventor's name from the masthead. A few weeks later, Edison exposed his bitterness when his secretary, Alfred Tate, asked him a question about electricity: "Tate," Edison replied, if you want to know anything about electricity, go out to the galvanometer room and ask [Arthur] Kennelly. He knows far more about it than I do. In fact, I've come to the conclusion that I never did know anything about it. I'm going to do something now so different and so much bigger than anything I've ever done before, people will forget that my name ever was connected with anything electrical.

People of course did not forget, nor did Edison do anything much bigger than he'd done before, but he kept trying. The fortune he made in electricity disappeared into a fruitless attempt to separate low-grade iron ore by magnetism. When the money ran out, he said, "Well, it's all gone, but we had a hell of a good time spending it." Undiscouraged, he returned to the phonograph, perfected it, made another fortune, and yet another in motion pictures. He devised a practical electrical storage battery, which he manufactured profitably.

Although he continued his driving pace at work, he found more time for his personal life. His first marriage, in 1871 to Mary Stilwell, a worker in his Newark factory, suffered from his neglect; it produced three children, two of whom came to unhappy ends. In 1884, Mary died of typhoid fever. Two years later, he remarried. His new bride, Mina, though only 19 (Edison, like Whitney, McCormick, and Carnegie, apparently preferred young women), showed sterner stuff. She forced Edison's life into a semblance of order, demanded companionship, and insisted that he fulfill his family responsibilities, a regimen that he increasingly enjoyed as the years passed. In these more normal family circumstances, the children of the second marriage thrived. (One of them, to Edison's wry amusement, became a theoretical physicist.)

As the first quarter of the twentieth century passed, Edison found himself revered as an American folk hero, a role he relished. Newspaper reporters, as always, found him excellent copy, like Carnegie almost always good for some iconoclastic statement. When a clergyman asked him if he should install lightning rods on his church spire, Edison answered, "By all means, as Providence is apt to be absent-minded." Edison also supplied reporters with quotable aphorisms: "Genius is one percent inspiration and ninety-nine percent perspiration."

In his declining years, Edison found an increasing fascination in nature's miraculous powers. He gloried in the perfection of an oak leaf and enjoyed showing a burned thumb that had healed perfectly, observing that "the life entities rebuilt that thumb with consummate care." He enjoyed camping trips with Henry Ford, Harvey Firestone, naturalist John Burroughs, and the entourage of reporters that accompanied their caravan. Tutored by Burroughs and encouraged by Ford and Firestone, Edison developed a strain of giant goldenrod, searching for a source of raw rubber that would thrive in the United States. As he grew older, the driving force of creativity wound down into more relaxed forms of puttering and rumination. Often asked when he planned to retire, he usually responded, "When the doctor brings in the oxygen tank." After the World War I, however, he retired in fact, if not in name.

When he died in 1931, the world mourned the passing of an original mind and Americans the loss of their "most useful citizen." During his lifetime, theoretical scientists had deprecated the contributions of men like Edison and Alexander Graham Bell, the latter caustically described by theoretical physicist James Clerk Maxwell as an elocutionist who "to gain his private ends [became] an electrician." Professor Emory A. Rowland of Johns Hopkins University said that "he who makes two blades of grass grow where one grew before" might do humankind some good, but "he who labors in obscurity to find the laws of such growth is the intellectual superior as well as the greater benefactor of the two." Perhaps, but in Edison's lifetime and to a large extent through the force of his own efforts, practical science became inextricably enmeshed with American industry, nourishing its growth by the constant infusion of updated technology.

Edison's example persuaded progressive corporate managers that their firms must have "invention factories" of their own. From General Electric, the Bell System, and Du Pont, the idea of integrated research facilities spread across the spectrum of American industry and ultimately into the government. With its complex of individual, corporate, and government-sponsored facilities, the American economy channeled a higher percentage of its income into research and development than did any other in the world. Science tied to industry facilitated prodigious (if often wasteful) growth, created terrifying weaponry, and gave humankind a powerful ally in its eternal combat with darkness, isolation, and hunger.

Today, we ponder these awesome consequences with mixed emotions, but our predecessors welcomed the convergence of science and industry, seeing it as evidence of America's superior contribution to the elevation of humankind. Scientific change meant human progress, and practical scientists were American heroes. Americans needed no Kants or Spinozas to transcribe the music of the spheres, but practical men who could

> *Bring the balloon of the mind*
> *That bellies and drags in the wind*
> *Into its narrow shed*

where it could do some useful work.

In the tradition of earlier Americans who had dubbed a mechanic "the artist of his country" and a reaper manufacturer a "hero in the classical mold," one of Edison's contemporaries celebrated a society in which "the chemist, the mineralogist, the botanist, and the mathematician are fellow laborers with the practical farmer and the manufacturer," and "vain and unprofitable theories no longer engrossed the attention of men of science." Other peoples might view "an active and feverish imagination . . . as [a] distinguishing mark of [the] philosopher," but not hardheaded Americans. For them, "philosophers are businessmen," and Edison, who made invention a business, was repeatedly named "America's most useful citizen" by his fellow compatriots.

Of course, the direct and indirect impacts of Edison's inventions made themselves felt far beyond the United States. Electricity went on to light and power much of the world. The phonograph and motion pictures, paradigmatic "disruptive technologies," revolutionized the music and popular theater industries at home and abroad. Meanwhile, Americans' pride in their scientific creativity and the technologies it spawned paradoxically nurtured the seeds of foreign competition. By focusing on "things of commercial value," capitalist innovators defined "technology" as something for which a market exists and thus, by definition, something for sale. This process has served to decouple science from technology, at least in national terms. American science and technology have emerged in products developed in Japan (VCRs), Korea ("mpeg" digital video format), China (Tibet railway), and elsewhere, as knowledge proliferates and diffuses in globalizing markets.

Many said when Edison died, and have often said since, that the world would never see his like again. In a world run by huge bureaucracies and staffed by scientists trained for years in arcane disciplines, so these lamentations go, such individualists have no place, and useful scientific perceptions lie beyond the reach of minds not formally trained. I think such obituaries for individualism premature. On April 17, 1978, *Newsweek* magazine carried a story about an obscure inventor named Stanford Ovshinsky. In 1968, Ovshinsky had predicted that solar energy would eventually become feasible through the development of cheap, electronic switches that would convert the sun's heat into electrical current. "Electronics experts," *Newsweek* reported,

> were highly skeptical on two counts, and theorists could not imagine how the amorphous semiconductors could possibly work. And they and others regarded Ovshinsky as a scientific outsider. He had no college degree, let alone one in physics; his only apparent talent seemed the ability to publicize [himself]. Ten years later, Professor David Adler of the Massachusetts Institute of Technology admitted, "Almost every statement Ovshinsky made in 1968 has now turned out to be true."

In late 2006, *The Economist* selected Ovshinsky for one of its annual "Innovation Awards," citing his invention of the nickel-metal-hydride battery, as well as his work on solar panels and hydrogen-powered cars. (Fast company, given that other winners included Sergey Brin; Larry Page; Herbert Boyer, co-founder of Genentech; and the iPod team at Apple.)

Thus, the role of individuals in the making of history, even scientific history, has surely survived Thomas Edison, even though big business bureaucratized systematic industrial research by creating research and development departments and sequestering them in places like the Bell System Laboratories and the Du Pont Experimental Station. But, as we shall see in the case of Edwin Land, here and there Tom Edison's notion of an "invention factory" survived and flourished.

Chapter 6

The Insolent Charioteer

HENRY FORD

The tinkerer turned debonair: Henry Ford at the tiller of his first automobile.

M y paternal grandfather looked just like Henry Ford, a fitting likeness, because he saw Ford as one of his folk heroes. Sometimes after Sunday dinner, he would take me by the hand and together we'd sit in the willow-tree swing to "watch the Fords go by." Just as Carnegie's ancestor regaled him with the wondrous deeds of Scotland's champions, so mine filled me with the marvels of Henry Ford and the cars he built.

They had a lot in common, these two septuagenarians, enough so that my grandfather could identify with his hero, finding in both their lives much of the right and good in America. Both had hated the farm with its confinement and drudgery; both had gone to the city and made good, though my grandfather's post on the L & N Railroad surely represented a more modest order of success. To Grandfather, Ford remained a simple man, an honest man, his virtues manifest in the products he made: plain, cheap, durable, and simple enough for anyone with a basic set of tools and an ample supply of elbow grease to fix. Wealth, moreover, hadn't changed Henry at all. In his Dearborn mansion, he still square-danced with his wife; he sponsored the "Ford Hour" on the radio, which played only "good music, not trash."

Above all, Ford bristled with that cherished (though more imagined than real) American trait, individualism, which caused him to despise all the right things. Ford hated bureaucrats and statistics and had personally led a raiding party, armed with crowbars, that had routed the statisticians and smashed the machines in a bureau someone had created behind his back. He hated interference in his affairs. When his stockholders meddled, he bought them out. When Franklin Roosevelt and the NRA tried to tell him what he could make and how he must sell it, he told them to go to hell and made it stick. When labor unions tried to organize his plant, he turned guards and dogs and fire hoses on them to beat them and drive them off, not because he hated workers (after all, hadn't he paid them $5 a day when the going rate was $2?), but because he wouldn't let outside agitators tamper with his freedom or his workers. "What can a union give them," he asked, "that they don't already have?" Unions and union leaders, Ford declared, perpetrated a hoax on the workers in order to levy a tax, in the form of dues, on their hard-earned wages. The dues then financed the leadership's "union salaries[,] liberating them from the necessity of work so that they can devote their energies to subversive activities."

Best of all, in my grandfather's eyes, Ford detested bankers and Wall Street. He, like his hero Edison, never trusted them, dealt with them only out of necessity and with great reluctance, and rejoiced at the day that his wealth put him beyond their reach forever. For Ford and my grandfather (who kept his money hidden in jars in the cellar), Andrew Jackson and all his legatees in the populist American tradition had it right. Bankers *did* conspire to defraud and mystify honest, toiling Americans out of the fruits of their labor. Bankers made nothing, grew nothing, and waxed fat swindling those who did. Edison and Ford had given us electric lights and cars that ran; bankers, as any intelligent person knew, had given us the Great Depression, then more than a decade old. Too bad more of the scoundrels hadn't jumped off bridges; maybe we'd have recovered sooner. (Had he lived into the twenty-first century, Ford would have seen history repeat itself.)

In the virtuous American tradition, Ford opposed monopoly and by single-handedly defying an early patent cartel had protected America's most important industry from its clutches. A gentle man, once he'd used the back door of his mansion for weeks rather than disturb a nest of robins that had taken up residence in front. A kind fellow, he'd built Henry Ford Hospital for the people and spent thousands on special medical care for the daughter of one of his supervisors. A generous citizen, he'd personally kept the city of Inkster, Michigan (and who knew how many others) afloat through the Depression by contributing millions of dollars of his own money to the city's coffers.

Of course the great Henry Ford had a side I didn't hear about in those Sunday afternoon sermons. Besides bankers, he had other hatreds, less appetizing, though no less in the American tradition, including a loathing for Jews, whom he saw as the mainspring of the international bankers' conspiracy. A core of meanness, savagery, and cruelty counterbalanced, perhaps overbalanced, his gentle traits. He belittled, humiliated, and destroyed his only son and heir, Edsel. He hired a thug, Harry Bennett, as a bodyguard for his grandchildren, admired Bennett's ruthlessness, made him the second most powerful man in the company, and sanctioned his creation of a private Ford Gestapo to bludgeon maverick workers into line or off the property. He ordered old, trusted associates (some with 40 years' service) fired for quixotic reasons and hid from them afterward.

He lived, in fact, a life of paradoxes, as I learned in schools far removed from my grandfather's front-yard swing. A pacifist who, like Carnegie, genuinely despised war and spent freely to oppose it, Ford nevertheless accepted the Grand Cross of the Supreme Order of the German Eagle from Adolf Hitler. The presentation came on Ford's 75th birthday, July 30, 1938, by which time the Nazi dictator clearly presented the most ominous threat to the peace Ford cherished. Himself a recluse who resented intrusions on his privacy, Ford authorized the creation of a "Sociological Department" to Americanize his foreign workers and teach all of them habits of thrift, as well as to educate their families in proper marketing, hygiene, and housekeeping. Run by a tame clergyman, Dean Samuel Marquis, the Ford Sociological Department extended its franchise, as bureaucratic agencies will, dictating the workers' private behavior in molds that Ford himself endorsed—temperance, abstinence from tobacco, fidelity for the married, and celibacy for the single—and maintaining a Big Brotherish vigilance to ferret out transgressors.

None of this intruded on my childhood delight in such a fabulous character. A more balanced view came years later; meanwhile, other influences intensified the Ford spell. My grandfather's loyalty to Ford automobiles (unbroken, after a brief, youthful flirtation with Willys) passed to my father (who never owned anything else) and then (with an occasional, unrewarding apostasy) to me. Where I grew up, and in the southern expanse beyond, Ford meant *the* car: tough, full of character, and above all fast; nothing could keep up with a Ford V-8. Moonshiners, bank robbers, and honest folk all sang a popular hillbilly anthem:

> *We're Ford men and we all know*
> *Ford's a good car and really will go.*

My first car, a 1935 Ford with a rumble seat, I bought for $50, and I've owned a lot of others since. Older, wiser, and in some ways sadder, I have a more balanced view of Messrs. Ford and their cars, but old loyalties die hard. I wouldn't buy a foreign car or a Chevrolet under any conceivable circumstances; when Ford gas tanks exploded or Ford transmissions slipped from park to reverse, I had the urge to confront the Ford in charge as a disillusioned young fan once confronted his hero, Shoeless Joe Jackson of the Chicago Black Sox, and demand, "Say it ain't so." In 2009, when Ford alone among American automakers avoided bankruptcy and a federal government bailout, I felt a sense of satisfaction, reinforced in 2010 when Ford topped the quality rankings for volume producers. As a car owner, I guess I'm nothing but a mannish-boy.

As a historian, however, I have surely changed my view of the car's progenitor: I find the person less admirable, but his achievements more remarkable. Henry Ford numbers among the few who historians can say personally changed the face of America. His career had an impact so gigantic and so paradoxical as to defy comprehension or description. (On the desk where I write sit three yard-high stacks of books, each of which has tried to measure some dimension of Ford and his work; virtually all claim partial success at best. And this represents only part of the Fordiana in print; Ford must rank with Washington, Lincoln, and Franklin Roosevelt as one of the most written-about Americans in history.)

Henry Ford, the person most responsible for twentieth-century America, was a child of the nineteenth century, with nineteenth-century ideas that held him in thrall throughout his life. Indeed, one might argue that Ford pushed those ideas to the maximum industrial capacity they could achieve. Like Frankenstein starting with good intentions, however, he created with his skill and ideas a monster that his talents could not control, with consequences that he could not foresee but came to fear. With the right talent and ideas for his time, Ford became the first (though not the last) billionaire on the strength of a company that he solely owned and controlled. As his fortune and fame grew, his countrymen, charmed like my grandfather by his simple and quintessentially American virtues, conceded to him a reputation for profundity he rarely merited outside the workshop.

In Ford, whose intelligence did not expand with his fortune, the foibles of the ordinary nineteenth-century rural American—bigotry, ignorance, mulishness—became dogma, then mania as senility set in. Enamored of his role as homespun sage and proud of his crank notions, he broadcast his quirks to the world through the newspapers and radio stations of his empire, and in three books that expanded his philosophy of production into a blueprint for society that rivaled *Brave New World* in its sterility. Together with the decline of his company from the mid-1920s on, Ford's views—ignorant, absurd, despicable—reduced him, in the eyes of many, from Edison's rival as "Most Useful American" to an object of ridicule, distaste, or loathing. "Ford has to his debit," wrote one critic, "more erratic interviews on public questions, more dubious quotations, more blandly boasted ignorance of American history and American experience, more political nonsense, more dangerous propaganda, than any other dependable citizen we have ever known."

Harsh words, but some of them true enough. Ford once admitted under oath that he couldn't identify Benedict Arnold, couldn't explain the Revolution of 1776 or the basic principles of the American government, and dismissed these questions as trivial because he found all history "more or less bunk." Later, proclaiming himself as "very much interested in the future, not only of my own country, but of the whole world," and as having "definite ideas and ideals that I believe are for the practical good of all," he bought the Dearborn *Independent* so that he could give his views "to the public without having them garbled, distorted, or misrepresented." Under Ford's aegis, the *Independent* then launched an anti-Semitic campaign that, among other niceties, denounced investment banker and presidential advisor Bernard Baruch as the "pro-consul of Judah in America," a "Jew of Super-Power," and the head of an international Jewish conspiracy. Seeking an even broader platform for his wisdom, Ford ran for the Senate in 1918, but lost. (The prospect of Senator Ford tickled his friend Edison no end. Ford, Edison opined, would provide the first silent senator in American history: "He won't say a damned word," Edison laughed.) Undaunted by defeat in his campaign for the Senate, Ford then pondered a run for the presidency in 1924 until cooler counsel prevailed.

The list of Ford's personal follies could be (and has been) extended to fill a book, but these tales—comical, unpleasant, or wicked—largely stemmed from the latter stages of his life, long after he had secured his place in industrial history. (When the Dearborn *Independent* launched its anti-Semitic campaign in 1920, Ford, age 57, had already built 6 million vehicles.) His views, moreover, on society, history, race, politics, and religion had a tiny impact on America compared to the consequences of his major creations: the cheap car "for the great multitude" and the system of production that made it possible.

By succeeding in his declared goal of making

> a motor car for the great multitude . . . large enough for the family but small enough for the individual to run and care for . . . constructed of the best materials, by the best men to be hired, after the simplest designs modern engineering can devise . . . so [cheap] that [any man] making a good salary will be [able] to own one

Ford catalyzed the automotive revolution in American life. But that revolution had consequences far beyond any that Ford envisioned or intended. By creating a machine that made it possible for every man to "enjoy with his family the blessings of hours of pleasure in God's great open spaces," Ford enabled his fellow Americans to break away from cities and rail lines. But legions of them moved into suburbs that devoured many of "God's great open spaces," carpeting them with settlements whose inhabitants suffered, alone in their cars, the curse of hours of commuting on crowded, narrow highways. In addition, by freeing rural Americans from the drudgery and isolation of country life, Ford galvanized an urban economy that caused many a farmer to abandon the land altogether.

Hating management bureaucracies, banks, stockholders, and Wall Street, Ford assembled a business so formidable that his rivals at General Motors had to compete by cementing together thousands of stockholders, millions of Wall Street dollars, and an impersonalized, efficient organization into the world's most powerful corporation.

Wedded to the traditional concept of family ownership, Ford so fanatically pursued personal control that he nearly destroyed both his company and his family's chance to hold onto it. Embracing, indeed personifying, the American creed of individualism, Ford created a system of mass production that stripped his workers of all vestiges of individuality and reduced them to robot machine tenders. Sentimental to the point of bathos about the charm and simplicity of an earlier America replete with small farmers, simple machines, and tiny shops, Ford shaped an economic society that threatened to obliterate these artifacts of its past. Aghast at the outcome of his own efforts and fearful that these cherished symbols might vanish, he spent millions on a museum designed to preserve them for posterity—the Henry Ford Museum and Greenfield Village, where my student heard Edison's messages from the beyond.

Symbolically, he built his museum, as he had built his industrial goliath the River Rouge plant, in Dearborn, Michigan, near the spot where he was born on July 30, 1863. Ford's father, a farmer like Eli Whitney's, made a decent but not sumptuous living. By the time Henry was 13, his mother and three siblings had died, leaving his father a widower with five surviving children. Like Whitney, Henry detested farm life and often shirked his chores in favor of tinkering. "Chicken is for hawks," young Henry said, "Milk is a mess." His father, like Edison's, feared that Henry had "wheels in his head." "John and William [the other two Ford sons] are all right," he told a neighbor, "but Henry worries me. He doesn't seem to settle down and I don't know what will become of him."

An increasing obsession with things mechanical "became of him." From fixing farm tools, Henry moved on to water wheels, turbines, and watches. At 16, he fled the farm for Detroit, where he got two jobs: an apprenticeship in a shop that repaired steam engines and part-time work fixing clocks and watches. He soon moved on to apprenticeships at the Flower Brothers machine shop and at the Detroit Drydock Company where, at age 17, he qualified as a journeyman machinist. Up to that point, his life had followed a course common to many American boys of his time. Approaching manhood, he had acquired a smattering of the three Rs and mastery of a craft that would furnish a decent living.

Henry Ford, however, had an uncommon gift—he understood the logic of machines. He could look at one, see its purpose, understand its workings, and imagine ways to improve it. Unlike Edison, who had the same acute mechanical instincts, Ford's mind rarely lent itself to original creation; he mastered the art of adapting and improving the ideas of others, becoming an innovator, not an inventor, "a natural-born mechanic," as Edison described him. Given a task to perform, a problem to solve, Ford himself might not originate a solution, but he knew an answer when he saw one, even if he saw it in a piece of scrap lying in the sand. Once, while searching for ways to build lighter cars, Ford went to an automobile race at Palm Beach: "There was a big smashup and a French car was wrecked. . . . After the wreck I picked up a little valve strip stem. It was very light and very strong. I asked what it was. Nobody knew." It was vanadium steel, as Ford made it his business to learn, an alloy that gave three times the strength per weight of ordinary steel. Applied to the Model T, "vanadium steel disposed of much of the weight" and furnished the last of the "requisites for the universal car."

These instincts and a burning ambition to succeed made Ford a man apart. Moving from job to job brought Ford an ever-expanding knowledge of the machines of American industry, including steam and internal combustion engines. He worked for Westinghouse, repairing steam traction engines that powered threshers and sawmills. In 1885, Henry repaired an internal combustion engine at the Eagle Iron works in Detroit. Then, or soon thereafter, he decided that by applying such an engine to a self-propelled vehicle he could fulfill a long-held ambition, "to make something in quantity." While still a boy, he had considered making watches: "I thought I could build a serviceable watch for around thirty cents and nearly started in the business. But I did not because I figured out that watches were not universal necessities, and therefore people generally would not buy them." This observation marks a difference between late-nineteenth-century American society and the early twenty-first, when most Americans, conditioned by decades of industrial time discipline, feel it necessary to know the time all the time. It also marked the young Henry Ford as already a market-oriented entrepreneur.

Just how Ford foresaw automobiles' future as "universal necessities" that "people generally" would buy, Ford himself may not have known for sure. It seems to have derived from his understanding of innate American restlessness (which he himself shared). As Ford said, "Everybody wants to be someplace he ain't. As soon as he gets there he wants to go right back," or as Bill Knudsen, one of Ford's production men, observed, "Everybody wants to go from A to B sitting down." In addition, Ford, who had no formal training in economics and laughed at those who did, perceived something that had eluded most of the erudite brethren of the dismal science: the American public had enormous potential buying power that would increase as industrialization expanded.

Whatever the source of his insight, it differentiated Ford from all but a handful of the dozens of mechanics experimenting with motor cars on both sides of the Atlantic, most of whom saw self-propelled vehicles as a luxury to build and price for the rich. Even in the United States, with its traditional notions of equality, only Ford, Louis Chevrolet, Ransom Olds (Oldsmobile) (all three mechanics with grease under their fingernails) and Billy Durant (Buick, Chevrolet, General Motors) saw the car's potential as a mass consumer product and found ways to make it a reality. Companies owned by members of Detroit's pre-automotive elite often restricted their firms to the luxury market (i.e., people like themselves). Producers such as Lozier Motor Company (which boasted it made "Quality Cars for Quality People" and that "PRICE has always been the LAST CONSIDERATION") failed repeatedly.

In 1889, Ford married Clara Bryant, a "neighbor girl," and acquired a source of strength and support in a marriage that endured, as all marriages were supposed to, through sickness and health, wealth and poverty. Fifty years and a billion dollars later, the New York *Herald-Tribune* reported the following:

> Clara never dyed her hair purple or had her face lifted or won the prize at the Beaux Arts Ball. Henry . . . had had his share of odd notions [but] never bet twenty grand on a dice game, never had to be psychoanalyzed . . . and has never been reported by the gossip writers as carrying the torch for either a countess or a showgirl. More, they still dance with each other. It may be that, in more manners than one, they are the richest people in the world.

In 1891, Henry took his bride to Detroit, where he got a job with the Detroit Edison Company, rising eventually to chief engineer. In 1896, he met Edison himself, told the great inventor of his tinkering with a "gas-buggy," and received what Ford later called decisive encouragement: "There is a big future for any light-weight engine that can develop a high horsepower and is self-contained. . . . Keep on with your engine. If you can get what you are after, I can see a great future."

He already had some of what he hankered after: two months before, in the wee hours of June 4, he had finished his first gas-buggy. Finding it too big for the woodshed door, he broke down a wall and pushed the car into the rainy street. With Clara holding an umbrella to shield him from the rain and a friend bicycling ahead to warn off nocturnal horseback riders, Ford started the engine and took his first test drive. The Ford car had taken to the road.

The Ford Motor Company, however, took longer to get rolling; it got under way in 1903, after several false starts. In 1899, Ford left Detroit Edison. Financed by local capitalists, including the mayor of Detroit, Ford established the Detroit Automobile Company. In keeping with an American practice that dated back to the 1790s Rhode Island textile partnership between the merchant capitalist Moses Brown and the mechanic Samuel Slater, Ford paid no cash for his shares but contributed his designs and expertise. The company built 25 cars and then failed. A new effort, the Henry Ford Motor Company, appeared in 1901. Ford owned a one-sixth interest in the company, but he soon found himself at loggerheads with his backers. Ford claimed they wanted to build expensive cars while he remained adamantly committed to a cheap one. The financiers, protesting that Ford wasted his time and the company's money building racing cars instead of production models, brought in master machinist Henry Leland to get things moving.

Racing then, as now, furnished a powerful vehicle for an automobile manufacturer to publicize his creations. Ford, who always had an eye for publicity, especially free publicity, certainly craved fast cars, and knew how to build them. In October 1901, Ford challenged Alexander Winton, whose car held the American speed record, to a match race and beat him. In 1902, Ford's famous 999, Barney Oldfield at the wheel ("Who does he think he is, Barney Oldfield?" my grandfather used to snarl when someone passed him), set a new American speed record, made Ford a local hero to Detroiters, and marked him as a comer in the industry.

Whatever the source of friction between Ford and his backers, Leland's presence no doubt intensified it. Ford may well have had a vision of the kind of automobiles he wanted to build and doubtless wanted to build them in quantity, but he didn't yet know how to go about it. The idea of interchangeable parts had not yet penetrated the automobile industry; like everyone else's, Ford's early cars were custom-made, one at a time, like firearms before Whitney. Leland, a master machinist trained in the post-Whitney firearms industry, had embraced interchangeability, knew how to achieve it, and instructed the industry's pioneers (including Alfred P. Sloan of General Motors, as we shall see) in the art. In 1908, Leland dazzled the British Automobile Club (and much of the rest of the automotive world as well) with an updated version of Whitney's interchangeability demonstration. After disassembling three Cadillacs, Leland mixed the parts, reassembled the cars, and drove them 500 miles without a breakdown. That same year, Henry Ford demonstrated how thoroughly he had absorbed Leland's doctrine by mass-producing the Model T, but in 1902, the two geniuses clashed. Leland, one former employee observed, "figured he could tell Ford what to do, but Mr. Ford wasn't the type to take it."

As his backers discovered, Ford didn't accept tutelage gracefully, particularly along the lines of what he could and couldn't, should or shouldn't, do. He never became such a man, either. Charles Sorenson, whose 40 years of service gave him the all-time longevity record among Ford's lieutenants, recalled that "Mr. Ford never caught me saying an idea he had couldn't be done. If I had the least idea that it couldn't be done, I wouldn't announce myself on it to him. . . . I always felt the thing would prove itself."

Ford's fixation with cut-and-try methods (a trait that, like anti-Semitism and an obsession with applied technology, solidified his friendship with Edison), bolstered by a wide streak of perversity, never faltered. The very fact that some "expert" (defined by Ford as "a man who knows all the reasons why a thing can't be done") told him he couldn't do something often goaded him to prove the contrary. Together these qualities served him well in the pioneering days when success meant doing all sorts of things that no one had done before, but they proved a great liability in later years when he refused to emulate the methods by which his competitors overtook and surpassed him. (Ford's perversity took bizarre forms on occasion. He nearly destroyed his English subsidiary by refusing permission to make the Model T with a right side steering wheel to accommodate the English practice of driving on the left-hand side of the road. No need to change, Ford said. The English would come to their senses eventually, and then Ford would have a head start.)

Frustrated in his purposes, Ford quit. (Leland stayed to build the Cadillac Motor Car Company, which he sold to General Motors, and then Lincoln, which, ironically enough, he eventually sold to Ford.) With the automobile craze underway and the country prospering, Ford soon found new capital for the Ford Motor Company, formed in 1903. A. Y. Malcomson, a coal dealer, and Ford each had 25.5 percent of the stock, with the balance divided among 10 others. These included the Dodge brothers, whose machine shop supplied most of the parts; C. H. Bennett, who had made his money with the Daisy air rifle; and Albert Strelow, who refurbished his Mack Avenue woodworking shop to provide the company with a factory building. Altogether the firm had $28,000 cash to begin with and never raised another penny by selling stock until after Henry Ford died.

The original list of shareowners soon dwindled. Malcomson sold his 255 shares to Ford and another backer for $175,000; Strelow, in what must rank as one of history's great miscalculations, sold his 50 shares for $25,000 which he lost, McCormick-like, in a phantom gold mine. The magnitude of Strelow's mistake showed in 1920 when Ford bought out his remaining stockholders. Rosetta Couzens, who owned one share that had cost her $100 in 1903, got $262,000 for it. By 1906, Ford owned 58.5 percent of the stock and controlled the company. He could now do as he pleased, and did. He got the company off to a blazing start by taking one of his cars out on a measured mile of cinders laid on the frozen surface of Lake St. Clair and driving it at just under a hundred miles an hour, surely a hair-raising ride for someone now 40 years old. Capitalizing on this feat, Ford's office manager advertised, "Don't experiment—Buy a Ford." Sure enough, plenty of people did just that.

From 1904 through 1908, Ford produced this model and that, striving for popular acceptance through reliability and low price. In the years 1904 and 1905, Ford sold 1,745 cars. In 1905, the company paid $288,000 in dividends on the $28,000 cash investment made just two years earlier. In 1906, Ford, now in control, concentrated on the Model N, a $600 car, overriding the opposition of the minority shareholders. In the years 1906 and 1907, the company sold a record 9,000 cars and took in $5.8 million. That same winter, in a locked room at the back of the plant, work began on the Model T, the "universal car," for which Ford felt certain a huge market existed, greater than anything that anyone (with the possible exception of General Motors' promoter Billy Durant) had ever dreamed.

Ford's conception of the mass consumer market, the hallmark of twentieth-century industrial maturity, bespoke his nineteenth-century experiences. A utilitarian man, raised in the cash-poor austerity of rural America, Ford thought consumer demand represented primarily the human drive for necessities. The rich could afford whatever they wanted, but ordinary people saved their money to buy what they had to have. In a country such as the United States, with its vast distances and large rural population (more than half of all Americans still lived in the country when the Model T first appeared), the need for simple, dependable transportation seemed obvious to Ford. Given the chance to buy an automobile that met these specifications at a price they could afford, people would seize it. And they'd continue to seize it, for luxury tastes and luxury incomes might come and go, but the common people and their needs went on forever.

In order to make the cars cheap enough, Ford knew he'd have to make a lot of them. That he thought he could do this resulted not only from his growing knowledge of cheap methods of production, but also from a conception of market dynamics he shared with Carnegie and a few other nineteenth-century proponents of efficient mass production. Unlike many of his contemporaries, driven by fluctuating demand that alternately taxed capacity or idled facilities into combinations that tried to allocate markets and control production, Carnegie thought the market infinitely elastic; he thought that at some price you could continue to sell everything you could produce. "Take orders at any price that keeps the mills running full," Carnegie exhorted his subordinates. If "demand [falls] short of the capacity to produce [and] a struggle . . . ensue[s] among producers for orders," cut the price: "The sooner you scoop the market the better." During recessions, the same policy must prevail—undercut the market: "When you want to capture a falling stone," Carnegie declared, "it won't do to follow it. You must cut under it, and so it is with a falling market." For such a strategy to succeed, a firm had to reduce costs along with prices, but that, Carnegie thought (and with reason), he could manage. His policy kept Carnegie Steel profitable through the depressions of 1873 and 1893, the worst the country experienced before his retirement.

Ford, like Carnegie, thought that a low enough price would find a market large enough to absorb all his output. Henry, however, had no intention of waiting for a falling market to force prices down. The market lay out there, waiting, and he meant to go get it by cutting prices as fast as reduced costs would allow. (Sometimes even faster. On occasion, he cut the price below cost and told his subordinates to "find a profit" on the shop floor unless they wanted bankruptcy and unemployment. He himself couldn't have cared less; he and Clara had all the money they needed and then some.)

The Model T and a primitive assembly line at Highland Park, about 1914.

Ford also perceived, sooner and more clearly than most, that industrialization not only reaches customers, but also creates them. The mill hands who rolled Carnegie's rails didn't buy them, but automobile workers bought automobiles, as did their barbers, grocers, and garbage men. Some fraction of the wages Ford paid eventually returned as profits, a fact that permitted, even dictated, a policy of high wages, as he explained to those who predicted bankruptcy when he raised thousands of his workers to $5 a day in 1914. For a man with little formal education and none whatever in economics, Ford responded with a sophisticated summary of effective demand and the relationship between productivity and income:

> I have learned through the years a good deal about wages. I believe . . . our own sales depend . . . upon the wages we pay. If we can deliver high wages, then that money [will] make storekeepers and distributors and manufacturers and workers in other lines more prosperous and their prosperity will be reflected in our sales. Country-wide high wages spell country-wide prosperity, provided, however, the higher wages are paid for in higher production.

The ways in which Ford got his higher production stamped a grim image on the other side of the bright five-dollar coin. The five-dollar day brought a mob of workers to the

Ford gates (in the dead of a Detroit winter, as it happened; when the thousands of disappointed applicants threatened to riot, Ford guards turned fire hoses on them). Ford could pick and choose among prospective employees and tyrannize his current workers into faster production with the threat of firing. His analysis of the source of effective demand, however, anticipated economist John Maynard Keynes by two decades—not a bad effort for someone whose monetary and banking theories mingled superstition, paranoia, and populist humbug.

Once he had designed his utilitarian, universal car, Ford "froze" the model to avoid the expenses of retooling and set out to reduce costs by increasing manufacturing efficiency. This resulted, of course, in the automobile assembly line, first developed by Ford and his aides, Sorenson, Knudsen, Pete Martin, and others, who came to the plant on Sunday so as not to interrupt current production. By trial and error, they developed the system of dragging the chassis across the floor to stations where parts, brought by pulley, conveyor, or inclined plane, got bolted on. Ford's detractors called the assembly line the brainchild of his assistants, but Sorenson, who participated, said that although individual contributions came from others, Ford "sponsored" the general idea and approved the specific combination of operations. (He got the idea, so one legend has it, while watching the disassembly of hog carcasses as they rolled down a packing-plant trolley.)

Unlike the Model T itself, the assembly line evolved slowly, through improvements introduced throughout the car's 18-year production run. Ford applied four basic principles to increase efficiency: the work must be brought to the worker; the work should be done waist high so as to eliminate lifting; waste motion, human or mechanical, must be minimized; and each task must be reduced to the utmost simplicity. The combination resulted in a prodigy of production and cost efficiency and obliterated skill and the worker satisfaction that went with it:

> As to machinists [said one analysis of Ford methods], old-time, all-round men [in other words, men like Ford himself], perish the thought! The Ford Company . . . prefers machine-tool operators who . . . will simply do as they are told to do, over and over again, from bell-time to bell-time.

The Ford system, *Fordismus,* as the admiring Germans called it, thus updated the revolution in production methods begun by Eli Whitney. The skill of shaping wood and metal, once an art as individualized as the fingers that practiced it, was drawn from artisans' hands and lodged in machine tools, leaving the workers with tasks as repetitious and uninspiring as a metronome's.

The system also produced cars (15 million of them by 1927), sales volume ($7 billion), and profits (in 24 years, the company's net worth rose from the original $28,000 to $715 million, including a cash surplus of $600 million). The company outgrew one plant after another, moving from Mack Avenue to Piquette Avenue (1904) to Highland Park (1910) to, finally, River Rouge (1919). With each move, Ford expanded his capacity to manufacture his own parts, cutting out dependency on outside suppliers. This process culminated in the fully integrated behemoth at River

Rouge, supplied by an empire that included ore lands, coal mines, 700,000 acres of timberland, sawmills, blast furnaces, a glass works, ore and coal boats, and a railroad. The Rouge poured out parts that supplied its own assembly plants, as well as a network of others scattered around the United States.

The Rouge concept appealed to Ford's individualism by making him nearly self-sufficient; moreover, the power and symmetry of it all excited him. The plan also had a hard, underlying economic purpose. Inventory costs had always bedeviled manufacturers; as production capacities increased, inventory costs kept pace until huge amounts of capital sat in materials awaiting processing or assembly. Ford intended to reduce this burden to a minimum by projecting the precision timing of the assembly line itself back into the operations that supplied it. If, for example, he could mine and ship each day the iron ore required for one day's car production, he need have none stored anywhere. By organizing all his supply lines the same way, Ford created a system of moving inventory that, when it worked, eliminated the need for warehouses, storage facilities, and stockpiles.

Even with a final product as simple, unchanging, and undifferentiated as the Model T, the arrangement demanded a marvel of scheduling and performance. It produced such savings, however, that his competitors at General Motors adopted it, ramifying it to accommodate the geometric complexities introduced by annual model changes and proliferating options. They also improved it by forcing suppliers, at their own risks, to conform to production schedules, thus avoiding the fixed costs and diverse management problems of an enterprise integrated all the way back to the raw materials—all this before computers existed. Ford's successors at his own company have since developed the "moving inventory" into a computerized, global art, scheduling, for example, the arrival of parts from 14 countries around the world to match production schedules in Thailand.

In Ford's own time, *Fordismus* achieved marvels of cost reduction and production. The price fell steadily from the original $850, finally reaching a low of $263 in 1927. Through 1926, Ford sold half the new cars made in the United States, while producing one every 45 seconds for years and years. And what a car! With its high clearance and planetary transmission, the Tin Lizzie went anywhere, through mud and snow, on roads or off them. Drummers hauled their wares in it; farmers plowed with it or jacked up one wheel and used it to drive threshing machines. It inspired poems:

> *Yes, Tin, Tin, Tin,*
> *You exasperating puzzle, Hunka Tin,*
> *I've abused you and I've flayed you,*
> *But by Henry Ford who made you,*
> *You are better than a Packard, Hunka Tin*

jokes:

> *"Why is Henry Ford a better evangelist than Billy Sunday?"*
> *"Because he's shaken hell out of more people than Billy ever did"*

"Lizzie Labels" that festooned the car with:

> *"Barnum was right"*
> *"You may pass me, big boy, but I'm paid for"*
> *"Follow us, farmer, for haywire"*
> *"Girls, watch your step ins"*

and great tales of running repairs made with chewing gum, bobby pins, and baling wire.

Owners could, in fact, disassemble the car with the toolkit of pliers, screwdriver, and adjustable wrench that accompanied it from the factory. Having located the defective parts, the owner could take them, like parts from McCormick's machines, to the dealer and exchange them for new ones. The Model T thus not only established the peculiar American tradition of the automobile as personal billboard (only in America are bumper stickers a commonplace), but also made a rudimentary knowledge of automobile mechanics part of the socialization process once undergone by virtually every American male. (A former World War II German *Landser* once told me of his amazement at learning, when taken prisoner by the American army, that nearly every G.I. knew enough to keep jeeps and trucks moving. In his unit, broken-down vehicles had sat for days waiting for the mechanic to arrive.)

On a weightier plane, the Model T called whole industries into being to build highways, vulcanize tires, and refine gasoline. Auto workers' wages, as Ford predicted, nourished service businesses and helped create a market for other mass-produced consumer goods—washing machines, refrigerators, electric irons, indoor plumbing, sewing machines. No wonder that Edison, asked by the New York *World* to comment on the $5 a day, replied, "Let the public throw bouquets to the inventors and in time we will all be happy." The automobile also brought local, state, and federal governments into new arenas where they have remained and expanded ever since: building, maintaining, and marking highways; testing and licensing drivers and vehicles; and enacting and enforcing safety and performance standards for cars and trucks.

Ford himself, of course, grew wondrously rich and persuaded of his wisdom in all things. The best thing about his system, he frequently boasted, was that making money inevitably resulted as a by-product of the company's main purpose, "to do good." "Your controlling feature," a reporter once observed, "since you have all the money you want, is to employ a great army of men at high wages, to reduce the selling price of your car so that a lot of people can buy it at a cheap price, and give everybody a car that wants one?" "If you can do all that," Ford declared, "the money will fall into your hands; you can't get out of it."

It could not, of course, go on forever. By 1927, the Model T had saturated the market for utility cars at any price. The very prosperity that Ford had done so much to generate had created a new kind of market that he didn't understand, a market made up of people who could afford to buy cars with features they wanted, whether they needed them or not. More and more people demanded warm, closed cars, with self-starters and soft seats, in a variety of colors. Those who would settle for less had an enormous supply of used Model Ts to draw on. General Motors, guided by Alfred Sloan's clear perception of this new demand, supplied it and stimulated it, presenting Ford with a challenge to which he could not, or would not, muster an adequate response.

The Henry Ford of 1927 had not the energy of the 1903 model. Now 64 years old, wealthy beyond impoverishment, and rigidly set in his ways, he professed not to know what Chevrolet did. "What's more, I don't care," he added. In 1927, he shut down River Rouge for a year while he designed a new car, the Model A, and retooled his plants to produce it. The shutdown presented his competitors with the entire automobile market, including the lowest-priced segment, which Sloan had hitherto conceded to Ford for years to come, if not for perpetuity.

The Model A regained some of the lost ground, but its fixed design soon fell back in the market under the onslaught of the annual model changes adopted by General Motors and Chrysler. In 1932, Ford brought out the V-8, his last significant innovation. By that time, his company had fallen to third place, and the country had descended to the depths of the Depression. Sales, which had reached 1.7 million Model Ts in 1923 and 1.4 million Model As in 1929, fell to 325,000 V-8s in 1933. At this sales level, the massive, vertically integrated structure, efficient only when car production ran full blast, became an albatross of costs that obliterated profits. Between 1927 and 1933, Ford lost almost $85 million.

The Depression bewildered Ford. The time-honored strategy of combating falling demand by cutting prices had always worked during previous slumps, including one in the years 1920 and 1921 that nearly bankrupted General Motors. Now it brought only more losses. Nothing in Ford's experience had prepared him for such a market, and he could think of no way to deal with it (he had, of course, plenty of company in his perplexity). Flailing about, he blamed the hard times on bankers' conspiracies and the laziness of the unemployed; then, aping Hoover's Secretary of the Treasury Andrew Mellon, he praised the Depression as "a wholesome thing," which he hoped would last a long time, "otherwise the people wouldn't profit by the illness." "If we could only realize it," he pontificated, "these are the best times we ever had."

The firm staggered on through the Depression, continuing to lose money, but held together by its $600 million bank account, the loyalty of die-hard customers, and the quality of the V-8 engine, much beloved by bank robbers such as Clyde Barrow for its speed. Remaining old-timers like Martin and Sorenson kept the line running; Harry Bennett and the Depression kept the workers running on the line. Above the shop floor, the company became an increasingly obsolete shambles. Ford had no cost accounting system worthy of the name, no market research other than dealer comments, and no system of product development to meet the fierce competition mounted by its cross-town rival, General Motors.

Henry Ford presided over the chaos with an iron and capricious hand, his mind lapsing more frequently into the twilight of senility. Even in his lucid moments, he devoted much of his energy to projects irrelevant to the fundamental weaknesses that sapped his company's strength. He lavished attention on his collections of Americana at the Greenfield Village and Henry Ford Museum; he built airplanes and dabbled in dirigibles; he set up small, water-powered shops at outlying villages in Michigan, where farmers could work in the off season making Ford parts.

When the war came, Sorenson turned the Ford system to the building of bombers and built thousands of them. The war exacted a heavy toll from the company's dwindling managerial resources. Pete Martin died, followed in 1943 by Edsel, the son Henry had given a million dollars in gold as a 21st birthday present, but could never quite bring himself to entrust with the company. In 1944, Ford fired Sorenson, the last of the original pioneers.

Peace found the Ford Motor Company in desperate straits, its plants and products obsolete, its labor force ferociously antagonistic, its management in the hands of a senile octogenarian and the vicious corporal of a goon-squad guard. It also had, as time showed, more assets than met the eye: enormous cash resources; a postwar market willing and eager to buy any car available after a four-year interruption; and, above all, the founder's grandson, Henry Ford II, who saw the company as his legacy and vowed not merely to save it, but to return it to its former glory.

Eventually this combination wrought a resurrection by subjecting the Ford production methods to the organizational disciplines perfected by its rivals. The founder did not live to see the good days return to the Rouge; he died in his Dearborn mansion, Fair Lane, on April 7, 1947. The eulogies that followed dwelt on Ford's epitomization of American qualities. Despite his dismissal of history as "bunk," Ford had indeed shown a sense of America's past. A hostile attorney, bent on embarrassing him, had once asked Ford, "What was the United States originally?" Ford, pausing to unlimber a jackknife and commence sharpening it on his leather shoe sole, replied, "Land, I reckon." Whatever the country was before his time (and who could improve on his answer?), many observers then and since have argued that, for better or worse, he changed the country as much as anyone ever has.

"Abraham Lincoln and Ford," read one eulogy, "mean America throughout the world—log cabin to White House—machine shop to industrial empire." "Only in America," declared another, "could he have built an empire of such vast extent. . . . Mr. Ford's eighty-three years give us a vivid, bright example of the opportunity in his lifetime. . . . In [this] one man, with his foibles as [with] his wisdom, is summed up the opportunity and the spirit of America."

Perhaps, but in fact Ford's career coincided with that of automotive pioneers elsewhere, all of them focused on an idea whose time had clearly come: applying the internal combustion engine to create a self-propelled vehicle to run on highways, not railroads. Among others, Karl Benz in Germany, Herbert Austin in England, Louis Renault in France, and Giovanni Agnelli in Italy succeeded in building companies that survive in the twenty-first century. All of them adopted *Fordismus* to some degree, but Ford himself drew on ideas from abroad, for example, vanadium steel from France and the internal combustion engine from Germany.

The automobile may have seemed to Ford uniquely suited to the vast American spaces, but from the outset, he saw it as a product for the world and today his company has plants on every continent. As Ford predicted, the motor vehicle has shown mass appeal to any society that can afford it, as witness the successive "automotive revolutions" in Japan, Korea, and China since the 1950s, and soon to come in India, with all that that implies.

Chapter 7

The Patriarchal Pioneer

PIERRE S. DU PONT

The Patriarchal Powdermaker: Pierre du Pont in 1915.

One day in 1940, my father came home and triumphantly announced that he had gotten a job at Du Pont. Thus ended many years of unemployment, underemployment, and misemployment, a soul-lacerating experience for a man (and millions like him) whose self-respect required the opportunity to support his family by practicing his trade of sheet-metal work, a skill in which he took great pride. Quite a job he'd found: Du Pont, accepting his credentials as a master craftsman, started him at the top rate for mechanics, more than doubling what he'd earned on his previous job. Better yet, he announced, "Du Pont never lays anybody off. It's a lifetime job." And so it proved; he never lost a day until he retired 30 years later. In the interim, he repaid the company's fidelity by going to work through fair weather and foul, in sickness and in health.

Giddy with new-found prosperity, the Livesay family put on a microeconomic demonstration of the power of employment to stimulate business, by building a house, buying a car (a Ford, of course), journeying to the supermarket every Saturday night for the week's groceries (meat! butter! ice cream!), then riding around like rich folks, listening to Mark Warno and "Your Lucky Strike Hit Parade." My father, who always had a nice sense of the ludicrous, particularly enjoyed hearing the Metropolitan Opera's Lawrence Tibbett sing "Don't Fence Me In." Although I only dimly sensed the implications of the Great Depression, I certainly knew when it ended—my father became a lot more fun to live with.

I didn't know it at the time, but we owed our salvation, ironically enough, to Adolf Hitler, whose blitzkrieg had sent the British and French scurrying for massive supplies of gunpowder. Du Pont, as it had 25 years before, responded quickly to the call of crowns and pounds and guineas. It threw together a cannon-powder plant in New Albany, Indiana, across the river from our Louisville home. It made for a hell of a way to end the Depression and a brutal validation of John Maynard Keynes's theories of government deficit spending to counter recessions, but the Livesays, like millions of their fellow citizens, had no mind to quibble over what then seemed distant abstractions. We kept busy enjoying the upsurge in our fortunes.

The Du Pont presence in my life took a quantum jump after the Second World War. Following his discharge from the U.S. Navy, my father reported back to the company. The demand for gunpowder having dried up and the Indiana plant with it, the company assigned him to its Chambers Works plant at Deepwater, New Jersey. There I found that Du Pont, which hitherto I had simply thought of as the place my father worked, now permeated my entire environment, for the company dominated Deepwater and the neighboring communities as totally as, albeit more benevolently than, any cotton mill ever dominated a southern hamlet or New England town.

Everyone worked for Du Pont, or for businesses that depended on people who did. Social structures and residential patterns reflected one's position with the company. Adults played at the Du Pont Country Club, children at the Du Pont YMCA. Much of the population lived in company-owned houses. Some boys came to high school wearing street-style safety shoes bought for them by their fathers at the plant store, a humiliation almost too great to endure.

The company pervaded not only the community's social and economic atmosphere, but also the very air it breathed. Most of the time the area for miles around the Chambers Works reeked with a stench so monumental that it often made it difficult to eat. Complaints—to parents or to local authorities, no one complained to the company— usually met a retort on the order of, "You're eatin', ain't ya?"

I soon found that the company also defined the aspirations of most of the boys in high school. (I can't remember that anyone worried about the girls' futures.) All but a handful of the boys expected to go "into the service" or "to the plant," and the company duly absorbed most of each year's graduating class. Most locals thought Du Pont a benevolent employer, providing lifetime security and total care, but without demanding too much in return. The reputation apparently approximated reality; when, on a whim, I went to my 25th high school class reunion and asked my classmates what they were doing, most of them replied, "Still messin' around down the plant." They knew they needn't elaborate.

Most high school discussions about career plans revolved not around whether one would work for the company, but how to avoid certain legendarily unpleasant operations within the plant. These included some dye manufacturing operations wherein, rumor had it, one's skin gradually turned the color of the product; the tetraethyl lead area, where people sometimes went mad and vanished to God-knew-where; and, above all, those operations (no one ever seemed to know for sure just which ones) where workers had to submit to semiannual cystoscopic examinations, rumored to inflict excruciating pain and sometimes to cause impotence. (Later years have validated some of those fears: secret World War II work on uranium had left unsuspected and dangerous levels of radiation; some commonly used chemicals such as benzidine have been identified as carcinogens, prompting a program of bladder cancer testing for Chambers Works employees; scorecard.com in 2002 ranked Chambers Works among the top 10 percent of the "Dirtiest/Worst Facilities in US.")

I escaped this lugubrious lottery by crossing the river into Delaware and going to work for the railroad. My father had passed down his lifelong love for trains, unrequited because of the Depression, making me susceptible to the same whistles that had lured Carnegie and Edison. Moving from New Jersey to Delaware resembled moving from one of the Duke of Northumberland's coal mines to his hometown, for I found myself surrounded by manifestations of the ducal Du Pont presence. By automobile, you could leave Wilmington in three directions, two of them on highways built by du Ponts. My paycheck said Pennsylvania Railroad, but I deposited it at a Du Pont bank. I read Du Pont newspapers. I saw plays at a Du Pont–sponsored theatre, listened to the carillon bells on Alfred I. du Pont's estate, and strolled among orchids and watched dancing water fountains at Pierre du Pont's botanical garden. The Du Pont Building topped the Wilmington skyline; the best hotel was the Du Pont Hotel. When I went to college, I went to the University of Delaware, itself a recipient of massive Du Pont largesse. Moving on to graduate school, I learned my trade under the masterly and beneficent guiding hand of Alfred D. (for du Pont) Chandler Jr., whose lifework included systematic analysis of the corporate structures that his family built, structures that had great impact on the broad, sweeping development of American industry and played no lesser role in my own life.

While still in Delaware, I myself joined the company for a time, working at night as a laboratory technician at the Du Pont Experimental Station while going to school in the daytime. Edison, although he might have found things too tidy for his taste, would have felt right at home at the Experimental Station, an establishment dedicated to Edison's kind of science—practical, profitable science. However, the Edison method of having the same team carry a project through from the first glimmering of an idea to the final glow of practical realization had long since given way to a subdivision of effort based on type of product and stage of development. Experimental scientists translated ideas into small-scale laboratory processes. If the product looked as though it might have a profitable future, it passed from the creator's hands to a team of engineers and technicians, who tried to duplicate laboratory results in factory conditions. If they succeeded, the company acquired the data necessary to make cost projections and to secure patents. With this system, Du Pont developed nylon, Orlon, Dacron, Teflon, and a host of other products that kept it in the forefront of the world's chemical manufacturers.

The company's products intrigued me less than its personnel policies and the people who carried them out. Du Pont labored continuously to persuade its workers that their fortunes meshed with the company's, and that the company, however big, cared about each of its workers individually and personally. Frontline supervisors carried this policy to the shop floor in two forms: group pep rallies, and conversations with individual workers that invariably began with the boss putting his hand on your shoulder and asking solicitous questions about your personal affairs.

All these theatrics fooled nobody as to their underlying purpose: the company wanted to keep production up and unions out. The workers, nevertheless, tolerated it all with more or less good grace. After all, the company did pay well, never laid anyone off, and fired people so rarely that nobody I worked with could remember when it had happened last. That all this benevolence depended on the company's continuing to make a healthy profit the workers understood so clearly that its ceaseless inculcation insulted the meanest intelligence.

In accepting the proposition that they and their employer had similar self-interests, my coworkers at Du Pont displayed an attitude characteristic of most American labor throughout the country's history and fundamental to the shape and success of the American business system. Du Pont capitalized upon this attitude, encouraging it with management practices that made their plants more congenial and financially rewarding places to work than the sirocco of a Carnegie Steel mill or the treadmill of a Ford assembly line. Whatever its faults, my colleagues felt, as my father had 30 years before, that in Du Pont they worked for a company apart, one of the best among American industrial employers. (They also felt their children should become lawyers, or doctors, anything but factory workers; they also insisted on doing my share of the work while I studied for exams, and told me when I left for graduate school, "You got out, so don't ever come back. Your old man sold his life to The Company; don't you sell them another one." Good advice, as it turned out; lifetime employment has gone the way of the 5¢ ice cream cone, and the Chambers Works, where 8,000 people once worked, employed 800 in 2010.)

Certainly the policy of encouraging positive views among its workers characterized other companies as well, General Electric for example. But in most giant American firms, where separation of ownership from management meant that the stockholder-owners numbered in the distant thousands and the managers worked for the company like everybody else, such paternalism resulted either from forceful action by labor unions or from employers' learning that enlightened self-interest dictated peaceful labor relations (and kept unions out). At Du Pont, in contrast, these policies began with the business itself, for they reflected the views of the original founder, Éleuthère Irénée du Pont de Nemours, who established the company in 1802 as a small powder mill in Delaware. The modern company as I encountered it—huge, diversified—superficially bore little resemblance to the firm in its infancy. But in fact, the history of the Du Pont Company involved many continuities besides its personnel policies, the survival of family control foremost among them.

The architect of the modern firm, Pierre S. du Pont, great-grandson of the founder, grew up steeped in family tradition. While transforming the family firm from a powder manufacturer to a diversified international chemical producer, Pierre du Pont created management structures and techniques that set the paradigms of corporate modernity then, and in some senses still do, but his desire to preserve the good things from the company's past guided him as much as his determination to secure its future. Admired, emulated, and studied by practitioners and analysts of the American business system, Pierre's firm long remained synonymous with progressive methods in research, development, production, and management. The company's management itself, at least at the higher levels, retained an awareness of its links to the past. And rightly so, for few firms illustrated more graphically the way in which tomorrow inevitably evolves from yesterday.

The history of the du Ponts in America began in 1799, when Pierre's great-great-grandfather and namesake, Pierre Samuel du Pont de Nemours, removed his family from the perils of Revolutionary France to the haven of post-Revolutionary America. Thus began a story that, like Whitney's impact on European cotton mills, McCormick's effect on cereal agriculture, Carnegie's use of Englishman Bessemer's smelting process, Edison's gift of light to a dark world, and Henry Ford's perception of the global automotive market, vividly illustrates the ongoing linkage of American business to the rest of the world.

For most fleeing aristocrats, emigration meant abandoning their property and the lifestyle to which it had accustomed them, but the du Ponts brought a portable asset that quickly restored their fortunes in the New World: they knew how to make better gun and blasting powder than anyone in the United States. Both products found a ready and continuing market in a country with a frontier to pacify and mountains to move. The Du Pont powder mill prospered almost from the first day that the original Pierre's son, Éleuthère, opened its doors.

By investing capital, hiring workers, and turning out a needed product, the du Ponts thus contributed to the growth of the American economy soon after they arrived. Theirs was not an isolated case; among the millions of immigrants, many arrived with talents they could put to work at once. The newcomers included skilled craftsmen and experienced farmers, as well as technical experts such as Samuel Slater and Paul Moody, who brought the secrets of mechanized textile production with them from the mills of old England to those of New England. The American economy benefited from the presence of these talented immigrants from its beginnings, and has ever since. By incorporating those who, like Slater and Moody, sought greater personal opportunity, and people like the du Ponts who fled political or religious persecution, the American business system acquired at little cost a capital asset of inestimable value.

This siphon, which later brought Enrico Fermi and Albert Einstein, among others, to America, continues to flow, as a stroll through the research laboratories of any major corporation or university will soon demonstrate. (At Du Pont, the supervisor of the project I worked on, an English-born, University of Manchester–trained chemical engineer, had left England convinced that the doors of British industry would remain forever closed to the likes of him, the son of a Liverpool bus mechanic.)

Éleuthère du Pont situated his powder mill on the swift-flowing Brandywine at Wilmington, damming the river's flow to supply power for the works. The Brandywine nurtured one of the centers of American manufacturing. There, in the eighteenth century, Oliver Evans built the first mechanized, automatic flour mill. Through the first half of the nineteenth century, as business boomed, other mills sprang up along the river's banks, grinding flour and gunpowder, rolling iron plates and paper. Blessed with such a prolific tumbling tributary, Wilmington's commerce swelled with firms that furnished shipping, insurance, and banking facilities to the manufacturers upstream; with factories that built mill machinery; and with shipyards that used the local supply of iron plates to such good advantage that the other Wilmington river, the Christiana, became known as "The American Clyde" (after the Scottish river where the British Empire's largest shipyard built majestic ocean liners, including the original Queen Mary and Queen Elizabeth.)

In the heart of this burgeoning valley, the du Ponts built an enclave of their own consisting of powder mills; homes for workers, and, on the high ground above the river, residences for family members. The powder mill community also contained a variety of stores; a doctor; and blacksmiths', coopers', and carpenters' shops that made it nearly self-sufficient. Company wagons, shuttling back and forth to Wilmington, provided the necessary connection to the world outside.

Within the company preserve, life developed cohesion and continuity as The Company served the family and vice versa. With the exception of a restless handful, male du Ponts stayed in the valley, knowing from childhood that when the time came, a place in the company's managerial ranks awaited them. The workers' community, too, developed considerable stability as a result of the company's policies. The du Ponts felt a seigneurial sense of responsibility for their dependents; moreover, powder making required skilled labor for dangerous work. The company had to behave as a benevolent employer to keep worker turnover low, thereby minimizing loss of life and production. *Noblesse oblige* thus combined with business pragmatism in a policy of furnishing workers with good housing and with stores and shops that charged reasonable prices, in addition to the Du Pont practice of paying good wages, providing pensions, and guaranteeing disability or survivors' benefits for the inevitable casualties.

Such self-sufficient communities that centered on a manufacturing establishment, a variation of the centuries-old manorial organization developed in European agriculture, characterized many American manufacturing industries in their formative years. Early entrepreneurs often had to enlist a labor force for their mills and then provide housing and services. The passage of time tended to disintegrate these communities as cities enveloped factories, and urban transportation enabled workers to move away from their work. In the nineteenth century, this process overtook the Du Pont community: the workers moved away from the Brandywine enclave. The family, however, remained—isolated, self-contained, relying on one another rather than on outsiders. Pierre du Pont recalled that his father, who was born in 1832 and died in 1885, never had a bank account in all the years he lived along the Brandywine.

Pierre himself entered into this tightly knit community in 1870. In the outside world, John D. Rockefeller set up Standard Oil, and the country struggled to recover from the ravages of the Civil War (from which Du Pont, as powder supplier to the Union, had prospered mightily). In the Du Pont enclave, however, little had changed in the 68 years since the company's founding. Family and firm had expanded, both spreading along the river's banks, but the growth of the Brandywine manufacturing region and the attendant doubling of Wilmington's population scarcely affected the du Ponts. Wilmingtonians regarded them as respectable, reclusive, wealthy, and prominent, but by no means the most wealthy or most prominent among Delaware's citizens. In fact, those circles of Wilmington society whose eminence and wealth dated back to colonial times regarded the du Ponts as *parvenus*. The larger community's opinion meant little to Pierre. Like most du Pont children before him, he remained within the confines of the family reservation, taught by governesses in his home, swimming in the Brandywine, finding his playmates among his cousins and the 10 younger brothers and sisters who arrived in rapid succession.

Although some of his uncles and cousins found a life circumscribed by the family circle confining and broke away, Pierre himself drew comfort and reassurance from the family's solidarity. Shy to a fault ("For fault it is," he himself admitted) as a boy, he remained so, reflecting later in life: "I myself have been aware of my shyness since earliest childhood." Although the twists and turns of his career took him far afield, he remained always a Brandywine du Pont, gravitating toward the reassurance of familiar surroundings; once returned there for good, he strove to perpetuate the environment that had nourished him in childhood. Even in matrimony he stayed within the familiar circle, marrying his first cousin Alice Belin in 1915.

As the son of Lammot du Pont, first lieutenant to General Henry du Pont, senior partner in the firm, the young Pierre had good reason to contemplate the future with equanimity, promising as it did to carry him along the well-worn path to the upper reaches of the company's hierarchy, if not to its very top. In 1880, however, Lammot du Pont burst free of the family cocoon. Convinced that the future lay in the manufacture of dynamite, not black powder, and frustrated in his attempts to convince General Henry to change the company's policy accordingly, Lammot decided to establish his own business, the Repauno Chemical Company, to manufacture the new explosive. By selling his interest in the family partnership, Lammot raised one-third of the capital; the other two-thirds came from the Du Pont Company itself, and from Laflin & Rand Powder Company, one of Du Pont's friendly competitors. The dynamite works required location in an unpopulated area. Lammot chose a site in the swamps of New Jersey directly across the Delaware River from Chester, Pennsylvania, midway between Wilmington and Philadelphia.

Having removed himself from the company's affairs, Lammot thought it symbolically important to remove his family as well. In the spring of 1881, Pierre's mother told him the family was moving to Philadelphia. The news, which meant that Pierre must soon confront an alien world, came as a shock. "No order of banishment could have been more sorrowfully received," he recalled.

In Philadelphia, Pierre attended Penn Charter School, where he established a record of inconspicuous excellence, earning the nickname "Graveyard" from his classmates. In the Quaker atmosphere that pervaded Penn Charter, Pierre absorbed a tolerance for divergent religious views, a respect for theology as an ethical system, but a profound and enduring skepticism toward all brands of religious mysticism.

In March 1884, the Repauno plant blew up, killing Pierre's father, leaving Pierre, at age 14, the male head of the family, a responsibility he accepted gravely and fulfilled for many years. His father's death also brought Pierre under the influence of the relative who became his guardian, Alfred Victor du Pont, a resident of Kentucky. Unlike the Brandywine du Ponts, most of whom considered an apprenticeship at the mill an appropriate and sufficient education for any powder man, Alfred Victor advocated a technical education. Back on the Brandywine, General Henry might rest content with methods that had sufficed for generations, but from his better vantage point, Pierre's guardian watched as the fusion of systematic science with manufacturing replaced the rough and ready methods of the past. Alfred Victor's own business interests, which included converting horse car lines to electricity and manufacturing steel rails for city railways, involved him in industries where science made swift inroads. What Carnegie's chemist Dr. Fricke and Edison's mathematician Francis Upton had done in steel and electricity, others must soon do across the whole spectrum of American industry, exemplifying Louis Pasteur's maxim that "science and the applications of science [are] bound together as the fruit of the tree that bears it."

Persuaded by his guardian's logic, Pierre followed three of his cousins to the Massachusetts Institute of Technology. Quiet and studious, his timidity with strangers eased by the presence of cousins and younger brothers at nearby colleges and prep schools, Pierre did well at MIT, graduating in 1890. Although he left college with some regret, Pierre rejoiced that his long exile had ended and he could now launch the only career he had ever seriously contemplated, a job with the family firm.

On September 1, 1890, Pierre went to work at the Upper Powder Yard on the Brandywine, a beginning he regarded as appropriate and auspicious: "This is where my father, grandfather and great-grandfather had entered the company's employ." His mother intensified the sense of homecoming. Delighted to rejoin her family and friends, she moved from Philadelphia, reestablishing the family seat on its original Delaware soil.

Though satisfied that the elements of his life had returned to their proper niches, his experiences at the mill soon raised doubts that swelled to disenchantment. Pierre's light and inconsequential official duties left him free to roam the works. Measuring the firm's equipment with his MIT-trained eye, he found it disconcertingly primitive:

> The laboratory, so-called, was in deplorable condition. . . . A common kitchen range and one small spirit lamp were the only means of heating for chemical work. No gas or electrical facilities [existed]. . . . Any unusual impurity [in] the distilled water . . . was accounted for by the words "She must have boiled over." The laboratory contained no chemical reagents for making ordinary tests.

Despite the deficiencies, everything at the Brandywine mills got "sufficiently well accomplished" to suit the old-line management, and it got done by equipment that everywhere duplicated the antiquity and obsolescence of the laboratory. Disquieting as Pierre found all these anachronisms, the head of the firm, Eugene du Pont, General Henry's successor, cherished them, as mountaineers did the old-time religion, as "good for our fathers and good enough for me." This complacency derived from the nature of the powder business, for here jousted no steel or railroad industry, no fiercely competitive Carnegie or Vanderbilt cutting prices to scoop the market. Instead, a cozy cartel, the Gunpowder Trade Association (one of the few that ever worked in the United States), tightly controlled the powder markets by setting prices and allocating production quotas. As one of the first in the field, and as one of the largest, Du Pont had always had a share big enough to assure prosperity for the firm and wealth for its owners. Du Pont, Laflin & Rand, and other major firms maintained order by buying one another's stock, thereby acquiring a voice in each other's management and access to their books, which made it impossible to violate price and market agreements on the sly.

With its market (which always included the U.S. government) assured through control and allocation, Du Pont felt little need of new products or better methods of production. The laboratory served as a place for testing, not research; cost accounting could remain perfunctory, since a cursory knowledge of costs sufficed. Pierre thus found the powder business, as Carnegie had found the iron business 40 years before, a "lump business, run the same way since time immemorial."

The older generation proved unreceptive to suggestions from Pierre and his contemporaries. His younger brother Belin, also an MIT graduate, wrote Pierre in disgust that "even if the [plant] should burn down, they would probably build it up just as it is now or if any changes were made I am sure I would not be consulted." Later, Belin added, "there will be only one way of your doing . . . well with [the company] and that is: eventually becoming the head of the business and changing their entire business methods, so that the business will have a chance of making money as it should."

Pierre's elders could not fathom the restlessness and impatience that afflicted his generation. Younger du Ponts should do as younger du Ponts had always done: bide their time and await their inevitable accession to power. In 1899, when he demanded a partnership and an executive position, Pierre reported that

> Cousin Eugene simply said that [someday] when things were organized there would be several good places to be filled and thought that I could fill any of them. No special place was mentioned and no salary offered or any mention of giving or selling me an interest in the company.

In the nine years that he had spent with the firm, Pierre had made no progress except insofar as his elders had moved inexorably that much closer to their demise. The fact that in the intervening years he had supplemented the skills learned at MIT by acquiring a fundamental understanding of the world of finance and cost-based management methods only intensified his frustrations. These added skills had resulted from his guardian's death in 1893, which made Pierre trustee of his younger brothers' and sisters' estates; a stockholder in Alfred Victor's enterprises; and an associate of his guardian's partners in the steel rail business, Tom Johnson and Arthur Moxham. Johnson tutored Pierre in the mysteries of investment, explaining different kinds of securities and the workings of the stock market, an education Pierre badly needed, for when he had become trustee of his siblings' estates, he recalled, he "hardly knew the difference between a ledger book and leger-de-main."

Arthur Moxham, president of the Johnson Company (the steel rail firm), introduced Pierre to the Carnegie method of management. Moxham, Pierre related, "was a master of cost sheets and orderly management. He visited his plant frequently and was interested in details but was always accompanied by the line man in charge through whom every question or recommendation passed. His cost sheets were fascinating." Part of the fascination stemmed from the fact that Moxham could easily disaggregate the company's gross revenues and expenses, showing what contribution each operation made to the overall result. Nothing like this had penetrated the musty accounting houses on the Brandywine, but Pierre "became hopeful that the business of [the] Du Pont Company could be presented in such clear manner."

Moxham's cost sheets "proved" that the Johnson Company should move from Johnstown, Pennsylvania, to Lorain, Ohio, buy a large tract of land, and erect a new mill. Johnson's choice of location showed the acuity of the firm's methods, for Carnegie and Schwab chose it seven years later as the site for a new pipe mill; however, Moxham's plans tripped over the economic stringencies of the Depression of 1893, which confounded normal American optimism by worsening as the years passed.

In January 1896, the Johnson Company teetered on the brink of bankruptcy, its ambitious plans stymied by the weakness that so often felled fledgling American business, a shortage of working capital. Potentially the firm embodied all the components necessary for long-run success: it had products—steel rails and electric traction motors—demanded by the booming street railway and interurban industry; it had a new mill and the patents, technical expertise, and management skills requisite to efficient production. These assets boded well for the future, but only if the company could survive the present by finding the cash necessary to pay current bills. Pierre's cousin, Coleman du Pont, superintendent of construction at Lorain, wrote him that the firm had to find $750,000 and find it in a hurry. Coleman asked Pierre to come up with $100,000 somehow.

With much of his own and his siblings' estates invested in Johnson Company securities, Pierre turned to willingly enough. He found the money at two local banks that did business with the Du Pont Company. For the next two years, the two cousins scrambled to keep the Johnson Company afloat, Pierre scurrying about renewing loans in Wilmington while Coleman tried to raise production and efficiency in Lorain, even bringing in the great guru of the efficiency cult, Frederick W. Taylor, in a vain attempt to wring profits out of minimal production.

Despite these energetic efforts, the future still remained problematical when, in 1898, salvation of a sort appeared in the form of J. P. Morgan's latest Frankenstein monster, Federal Steel. By gorging his creature on a large if indiscriminate diet of independent steel producers, Morgan hoped to force-feed Federal Steel into a giant big enough to challenge Carnegie. The Johnson chieftains unloaded their mill on this corporate glutton, retaining only their real estate and an electric railway.

In the transaction, Pierre sustained a financial loss, receiving only $28,000 for securities nominally worth $120,000. But he and Coleman had gained experience that subsequently more than compensated for their misfortune. Pierre had learned the virtues of cost accounting as a management tool and the perils of insufficient working capital; Coleman had run a large industrial enterprise and had learned Carnegie's gospel of efficiency engineering from one of its foremost apostles.

Four years later, the cousins got an unexpected opportunity to apply their hard-won knowledge to the Du Pont Company. In 1902, Du Pont found itself in a predicament that besets virtually every American family firm at one time or another: the senior partners had grown weary and anxious to retire, but either had no heirs, like Carnegie, or thought the younger generation ill suited or ill prepared to take over. One younger du Pont, Alfred I., another of Pierre's innumerable cousins, had acquired a seat on the board of directors and a partnership in the firm, but the senior members had "formed an exceedingly low estimate of Alfred['s] good judgment and business ability." Coleman had the necessary qualifications, but certain family rivalries precluded him.

At this critical juncture, family firms usually underwent a transformation: selling out to a competitor, as Eli Whitney's heirs sold to Winchester; diluting their ownership by selling large blocks of stock to the public, as Edison's sons did; or succumbing to the ardent wooing of trust builders like Morgan, as did Carnegie and the McCormicks. Whatever the course taken, family ownership invariably receded, and family management usually ended. (The problem of succession, of course, continues to confront all new firms when the founders die or retire, and the very life of the business depends on resolving it effectively. McDonald's and Walmart, for example, met the challenge brilliantly when Ray Kroc and Sam Walton left the scene; Wang Computer disappeared with the founder; and multitudes of Apple stockholders wonder who can possibly fill Steve Jobs's shoes when the time comes.)

The crisis of succession had come to different families at different times: to Carnegie's after one generation, to McCormick's and Edison's after two; Whitney's lasted three. At some point, however, the day inevitably arrived when even the most fecund industrial families could not perpetuate their dynasties. Through one of those fascinating interactions of events that historians love to examine but can rarely explain, an extraordinary number of American business families arrived at this critical turning point simultaneously at the turn of the century. This factor, among others, accounted for the disappearance of more than 2,600 individual firms between 1898 and 1902 and, together with a swelling concern for the consequence to individual Americans of the ending of the frontier and the abuses of big business, contributed to the *fin de siècle* mentality of despair, rooted in a sense of loss.

The Du Pont Company, which by 1902 could look back on a century of unbroken family domination, presented an unusual case of longevity, but it now seemed certain to join the anonymous multitudes. Despairing of an internal solution, the directors entertained a motion to sell to their largest competitor, Laflin & Rand. Alfred, whose alleged limitations blocked him from succession in his own right, managed to amend the motion so that it called for sale "to the highest bidder." He then announced to his startled colleagues that he himself would buy the business. One of his shocked elders told him that he simply could not have the company. "Why not?"

Alfred demanded. "I pointed out," Alfred said later, "the fact that the business was mine by all rights of heritage, that it was my birthright; I told him that I would pay as much as anybody else, and furthermore, I proposed to have it."

This appeal to family tradition rallied Colonel Henry du Pont to Alfred's support: "Gentlemen, I . . . understand Alfred's . . . desiring to purchase the business, and . . . it has my hearty approval, and I shall insist that he be given the first opportunity to acquire the property." Pulling Alfred aside, he said, "I assume of course, although you said nothing about it, that . . . Coleman and Pierre are, or will be, associated with you in the proposed purchase?" Told that they would, the Colonel added, "With the understanding that Coleman and Pierre are associated with you in the proposition I assent to it most cordially and will do everything in my power to bring it about."

Alfred, whose role in the company diminished almost from the moment the sale was consummated, had planned carefully, struck hard at the appropriate instant, and preserved the company as a family firm. When he had approached his two cousins about joining him in the purchase, Alfred had found enthusiastic allies, but allies whose awareness of his limitations as a businessman led them to set certain conditions. Coleman agreed to participate, but only if he got the largest block of stock, assumed the presidency, and could bring in Pierre as treasurer to manage the firm's financial affairs. Pierre, who had left his time-serving job with Du Pont in 1899 to preside over the liquidation of the Johnson Company's remaining assets, and then moved on to buy a street railway in Dallas, jumped at the chance to play a major role in the future of the company that he too considered his birthright. Telling his brothers the good news, Pierre wrote,

> The wheel of fortune has been revolving at pretty high speed on the Brandy Wine during the last week or two with the result that Coleman and Alfred and I have made E. I. du Pont & Co., an offer to buy out their property and I today received verbal acceptance of the Proposition. . . . I think there is to be some tall hustling to get everything reorganized. We have not the slightest idea of what we are buying, but in that we are probably not at a disadvantage as I think the old company has a very slim idea of the property they possess.

The older generation's pleasure at keeping the firm within the family and the younger generation's belief that the company had a profit potential far beyond anything achieved by its conservative management combined to facilitate the practical arrangements of the sale. Both parties agreed on a price of $12 million, paid by exchanging bonds for the outstanding stock held by family members. The three new owners then issued $20 million worth of stock and divided it among themselves. This arrangement promised the sellers a continued income at the established level (as investors they wanted assured income, not return of the principal) in the form of interest on the bonds, as well as protecting them, like Carnegie did, with a mortgage on the property in case the new arrangement went haywire. It also gave the buyers complete control of the company without their having to raise any cash. Whether the young cousins' stock would have any real value depended entirely on their abilities to squeeze increased income from the property. This they at once set out to do, first taking an inventory to find out just what they had actually bought. Alfred returned to his accustomed post supervising production at the powder mill. Coleman and Pierre surveyed the company's properties. These by then included additional mills in Iowa, Pennsylvania, Tennessee, and New Jersey, each operating more or less independently of the Delaware facility, with much duplication of effort.

The cousins soon decided to buy up their major competitors, beginning with Laflin & Rand. That erstwhile competitor labored in the midst of a succession crisis of its own. The terms of sale followed the pattern established by the original Du Pont transaction: a combination of bonds and stocks that gave the former owners income and the new owners control without any cash changing hands. Once the du Ponts had their largest competitor, the others tumbled like a row of dominoes. Certain opportunists, however, carpentered together new firms overnight, hoping for lucrative sales to the emerging powder trust. As one Du Pont executive wryly observed, the belief had become widespread that "there [was] no better investment than to 'sell to the Trust.'" The young du Ponts assiduously avoided such dubious bargains. Within two years, nevertheless, they had sufficient plants to supply 60 percent of the explosives market. The reason for the 60 percent limit (the same target set for U.S. Steel by its chairman, Judge Elbert Gary) went beyond mere avoidance of possible antitrust prosecution.

Arthur Moxham had, at Pierre's behest, brought his steel-industry expertise to the new powder company. His explanation of the 60 percent limit reveals the rich Carnegie heritage in American manufacturing philosophy: "If we could by any measure buy out all competition and have an absolute monopoly in the field, it would not pay us." Moxham knew that future demand for explosives might prove highly "variable." Ownership of all capacity would mean that "when slack came [Du Pont] would have to curtail product to the extent of diminished demands." Better, he continued, to "control only sixty% of it all and [make] that sixty% cheaper than the others." Then, when "slack times came we could still keep *our* capital employed to *the full.*" As Carnegie had once urged his subordinates to "cut the price, scoop the market, run full," now Moxham declared, "If you make cheaply . . . you [can] count upon always running full."

To tend to the next chore, guaranteeing efficient production, the cousins set about whipping their facilities, which ranged from the efficient to the ragtag and bobtail, into a profitable consolidation. They created a hierarchical, bureaucratic management structure and found people to staff it. Committees and departments specialized in particular functions such as finance, or particular products such as black powder, dynamite, or smokeless powder. An auditor recruited from the steel industry adapted its cost sheets and other accounting devices for use in the powder business. Once developed, such cost sheets exposed inefficient plants, soon closed, and inept employees, soon fired.

Howls of protest arose from individualists used to doing things their own way in an old-fashioned business. The cousins, confident of their course, steamrolled over all objections. Subordinates who tried to buck the company's new auditors got told to shape up or ship out. To keep in the forefront of technological developments, the company set up a permanent development department, soon subdivided into three divisions: Competitive Products, Raw Materials and, most important of all, Experimental. Within two years, then, the cousins had brought off a corporate revolution, one that uniquely combined traditional and modern aspects of American business. As in the past, traditional family ownership continued, but the three principal owners had become bureaucratic corporate managers.

Thus the accumulated wisdom and experience of America's industrial pioneers transfused new life into the old company on the Brandywine. With its streamlined organization, standardized, companywide procedures, and updated research and development departments, Du Pont achieved a modernity then matched only by firms in the electrical industry. Almost overnight, it had metamorphosed from an anachronism into a firm capable of pioneering on its own.

Alfred remained content to limit his horizons to black powder production. Coleman developed a tendency to divert his energies to politics and to outside investments, a proclivity that intensified as the years passed. Pierre thus came to serve as the chief architect of the company's continuing transformation. He found no contradiction in melding traditional ownership with modern management. Indeed, preserving family control remained his first priority. It dictated a policy of conservative financial management coupled with hard-nosed operating efficiency.

The demands of such efficiency soon carried Pierre beyond cost sheets and organization charts. He had to restructure the family's relationship to the firm, retaining the clan as the company's principal capital resource while discontinuing the long-standing practice of automatically promoting family members to management; nevertheless, not all the company's top jobs went to talented outsiders. Pierre fiercely believed that a du Pont should always head the Du Pont Company; moreover, no organization chart, not even Du Pont's, could wholly abolish nepotism. Pierre insisted, however, that a family member's performance on the job, not his family status, should determine his position. Thus, the Du Pont Company would not be headed by the best man around, but rather by the best of the du Ponts, who, given the family's size, should have abilities more than good enough.

By recruiting some family members, sidetracking others, and combing the ranks of the numerous du Pont in-laws, Pierre created a respectable talent pool. Maintaining the family's solidarity behind the firm while reshuffling its members' roles called for an evenhanded diplomacy for which Pierre's temperament singularly qualified him. It also demanded a stellar performance from the company itself, for nothing so maintained peace as a steady flow of dividends and bond interest. A high return on investment with minimal use of outside capital became the guiding principle to evaluate both current operations and future projects. Every project had to fortify the company's capital fund by providing high dividends, as well as substantial retained earnings. Expansion and modernization, as well as diversification into other products, all demanded by Pierre's aggressive subordinates, went forward only as the company and the family together could supply the necessary capital. Even expansion of output required careful planning because of its drain on working capital. Pierre's experience with the Johnson Company had shown him how such a drain could undermine even a solidly based firm. He preferred passing up tempting market opportunities to borrowing short-term capital at ruinous rates. "The impairment of working capital," he told his associates in 1904, "will be credit suicide and the shortest road to financial embarrassment."

Translating such conservative, family-oriented finance into company policy proved no easy task. Demands for capital strained the combined resources of the family and firm. Keeping costs down required not only modernization but also vertical integration to reduce the cost of raw materials by, say, buying nitrate mines and manufacturing acids. Confronted by these and a bewildering array of other demands for capital, Pierre followed a plan analogous to Carnegie's. He and the executive committee delegated the authority over daily operations to department managers and their subordinates, and then they relied on statistical controls to evaluate the results. The departments had wide and unfettered discretion to solve quotidian problems, including labor disputes, but anything that required a significant capital expenditure required executive committee approval. Such capital demands taken together always exceeded the company's resources, so the executive committee had to devise a consistent method to evaluate each request. For Pierre, return on investment always remained the overriding consideration. This meant that efficiency, not volume, must prevail. The company, Pierre thought, must give preference "to such improvements as will furnish cheaper raw material or cheaper production leaving as a second consideration the actual increase in the volume of business." He thus echoed Carnegie's maxim that if a firm watches its costs, "the profit will take care of itself" because reduced costs fall straight to the "bottom line," which, like Coyote of Navajo legend, is always waiting and always hungry.

By declaring that the company must invest its money where it would produce the greatest return whether or not more production resulted, Pierre du Pont had arrived at one of the fundamental rules for the survival of a business in a capitalist economy. In the economy as a whole, demands for capital almost always exceed the supply. Consequently, capital flows from areas of low return to more promising sectors. A firm must use its capital to finance efficiency while shutting down inefficient plants or else eventually go under, unless rescued by outside intervention. In the late twentieth and early twenty-first centuries, succor, in the form of the federal government, sometimes arrived to prevent bankruptcy in firms, such as Lockheed, Chrysler, Penn Central Railroad, Chrysler, General Motors, and AIG, whose collapse might have had unacceptable political, economic, or military consequences. In Pierre's time, however, no company enjoyed the immunity of the indispensable, nor did the federal government run a business rescue service.

On the contrary, Du Pont faced an indifferent, sometimes downright hostile, government. Du Pont had long furnished most of the powder bought for the U.S. armed forces. In 1906, however, it found itself in danger of losing the privileged position enjoyed by major arms contractors since Eli Whitney's time. Branded publicly as the "Powder Trust," it faced the same attacks that befell other corporations similarly defined, such as Rockefeller's Standard Oil. The next year, the government launched an antitrust suit that eventually forced Du Pont to divest itself of significant holdings, in the process creating two new competitors, the Atlas Powder Company and the Hercules Powder Company. In 1908, Congress compounded the threat by authorizing expansion of the government's own powder manufacturing capacity. The government's two-pronged assault against his company hardened Pierre's conviction that Du Pont must spend every dollar where it would do the most good.

The company's relatively small size invited ever-greater caution. Du Pont's domination of the explosives market made it a dangerous trust in the eyes of both the public and antitrust prosecutors, but in fact it was a relatively puny member of that despised category. Prior to 1915, Du Pont's capitalization never exceeded $63 million, minuscule compared to the billions of dollars tied up in U.S. Steel, Standard Oil, American Tobacco, and other giants targeted by trustbusters. As late as 1914, Du Pont's gross receipts totaled less than the *net profit* made by Carnegie Steel in 1900. A company Du Pont's size could not afford unproductive investments. Pierre's strict evaluation of capital expenditures in terms of probable return made good general business sense; it also reflected the realities of his company's situation.

Maintaining investment profitability meant predicting both future costs and prices. Du Pont's cost-accounting techniques and experience in the explosives business allowed the company to forecast manufacturing costs with tolerable accuracy. Forecasting prices, however, proved another matter altogether. It required predicting market behavior, an art that to most American businesses seemed as mystical as voodoo. Carnegie, with no stockholders to placate, could freely "take [the] orders East and West" that kept his mills "running full" until the market rebounded. Ford, confident that *Fordismus* would drive costs steadily down, pushed production while trusting efficiency to produce profits whatever the price. For Pierre du Pont, cautious by nature and especially about family financial resources, such nineteenth-century attitudes smacked of folly and courted suicide.

Past experience had shown American businessmen the difficulties of controlling the market; antitrust laws had made it an offense even to try. But what one could not control, Pierre thought, one might nevertheless predict. From the outset, Pierre himself prepared forecasts of the company's profits for the year ahead, translating these into estimates of the amount of money available for capital investment. He demanded forecasts of future capital requirements from his department heads, assuming that such estimates would rest on prognostications of future market behavior. Not surprisingly, the first efforts yielded primitive results. In 1906, for example, Hamilton Barksdale requested an appropriation to expand the company's dynamite capacity. Barksdale forecast the dynamite market by simply taking actual sales in 1905 and adding a 15 percent increase every year through 1909. Time and practice, however, upgraded market forecasting to a viable management tool, if not to an exact science. Data from actual sales tested the accuracy of past predictions, and future forecasts got revised accordingly. Pierre's insistence made market forecasting an integral tool of Du Pont's management strategy. After the fashion of other successful techniques, its use by other industries made it an important component of the American system of management. Pierre du Pont's obsession with maintaining his family's control had thus led directly to one of the last significant additions to modern American management methods.

Under such guidance, the Du Pont Company expanded from its modest beginnings in 1902 to become one of the world's 10 largest corporations for a time. It diversified from explosives to the manufacture of hundreds of other products; yet, as generations of managers passed through the company's offices, the carefully estimated rates of return on investment remained their guiding principle. Market forecasting and a management structure that combined centralized financial control with decentralized operations helped

Pierre du Pont run a big firm efficiently and profitably in a fluctuating, highly competitive market. Just how big and efficient these firms could become, a subsequent generation would demonstrate at Du Pont and General Motors. Market forecasting became a common management tool for determining investment strategies. It still plays a central role in the competition for capital among corporate divisions; moreover, it constitutes an essential component in the business plans required of entrepreneurs by venture capitalists.

Du Pont, however, under Pierre's restraining hand, grew slowly until the enormous profits of World War I provided an unexpected infusion of capital. From 1904 to 1912, the company's annual gross receipts rose from $26 million to $36 million. In 1913, after the court-ordered dissolution that created Hercules and Atlas, business fell to $27 million. In 1916, the European slaughter multiplied receipts twelvefold, to $319 million. Altogether, between 1914 and 1918, the company's sales totaled $1.1 billion: net profits, according to the company's figures, totaled $238 million. (In fact, they may have made more; the Nye Congressional Committee, which investigated the munitions industry, thought so. Pierre, testifying in 1934, laconically told the inquisitorial senators, "I am not trying to fight the figures, because no matter what the figures are, the profit was very large.") So large, in fact, that the company's earlier lean capital diet yielded to an investment banquet that vastly exceeded any conceivable needs of the explosives business. Soon Du Pont had a controlling interest in General Motors as well as its own full-scale diversification program.

Pierre met the wartime bonanza with customary wariness. Like most American businessmen, he first saw the war not a harbinger of prosperity but an unwelcome interruption to business stability. His view also reflected the company's past experience. Spain's sudden collapse during the Spanish-American War had stuck Du Pont with expanded facilities, warehouses full of unsold powder, and canceled contracts. The outbreak of World War I had at first brought a decline in business. The company sold less in 1914 than it had the year before. The du Ponts, along with much of the rest of the world, expected the fighting to end quickly. In August 1914, Pierre's brother wrote an executive of an English dynamite company, "I do hope this unfortunate war will soon be over and appreciate that it must be more of an inconvenience to you than to us." The same month, the company approved the expenditure of a paltry $16,000 to expand smokeless powder capacity, but not until "the receipt . . . of large additional orders for Smokeless Powder either from Foreign Governments or our own government."

Even when the war raged on and large orders materialized, Pierre held fiercely to his conservative approach. Sentiment remained secondary to profits; indeed, Pierre declared himself ready to sell to all comers who could meet the company's terms. In February 1915, he wrote Coleman that should the Germans come "forward with orders in quantity similar to the orders of the Allied Nations [Du Pont] would be willing to sell." With the Allies, Pierre drove hard bargains to assure a copious return on wartime investment. A French contract for 8 million pounds of cannon powder brought one dollar a pound, twice the price charged the U.S. government. Furthermore, Pierre demanded 50 percent in advance, 30 percent when the powder went to the drying house, and the final 20 percent before shipment. Such terms forced the French to supply all capital necessary for expansion while guaranteeing that the company would get paid for all finished orders even if the war ended unexpectedly. Throughout four years of war, though the price declined, the terms remained essentially the same.

Just as European capital had financed much of America's nineteenth-century industrialization, especially railroad construction, the World War I Allies financed a massive expansion, not only of Du Pont's facilities, but also of its labor force, particularly the engineers who designed and built the new plants. Pierre also initiated an aggressive program to ensure that peace would not idle the expanded capacity. In September 1915, Du Pont bought the celluloid-manufacturing Arlington Company to provide a postwar outlet for some of the company's expanded output of solvents and nitrated cotton. As the cash poured in, the company accelerated its diversification, sometimes by buying going concerns, sometimes by acquiring patents for processes its munitions plants could readily adapt. Wartime profits laid a sound foundation for postwar development. When peace came, Du Pont had extended its range of products to include celluloid, artificial leather, dyes, paints, and varnish, and it owned huge, debt-free plants for their manufacture, a transformation largely funded by the taxpayers of Britain, France, and the United States, with enough left over to buy a controlling share of General Motors. Thus doth government and business wax mighty together.

America's entry into the war did nothing to soften Pierre's policies or his demands. He thought it only reasonable that Du Pont should have protection against risk whenever it made a large investment, and he saw no reason to make an exception for the U.S. government. He demanded contracts that would provide all the capital necessary to build new plants, a suitable profit both on construction and subsequent manufacturing, and enough extra money to pay bonuses to key supervisors. Years before, Andrew Carnegie's success in binding the loyalty of key personnel by rewarding them with shares in the business had impressed Coleman du Pont. Pierre, who had adopted the plan enthusiastically, thought its fine peacetime results made it all the more appropriate in wartime. That the French and the English had caved in to this demand, Pierre thought, had facilitated the company's prodigies of production and manufacture: "I do not think [it] could have been done without the stimulus of our bonus plan." The U.S. government must do the same, Pierre said, "not only because we would be unwilling to undertake the work [otherwise] . . . but [also] because we could not hold the men in our service unless such outlay be made." (Perhaps the English and French should have paid such bonuses to the Tommies and *poilus* in the trenches.)

Pierre's demands outraged the public and some government officials, particularly Secretary of War Newton D. Baker, who declared at one point, "We have made up our minds . . . to win this war without Du Pont." One proposed contract led Baker to declare that "his mind could not conceive of the services of anyone being worth such a price." Startled by such hostility, Pierre insisted that his company wanted only "reasonable compensation for [its] services." He planned to argue the company's case in *Outlook* magazine, naïvely assuming that the "facts" would lead the people to rally to the company's support.

Luckily, *Outlook*'s editor gave Pierre's preliminary draft to Elihu Root, formerly a secretary of war under McKinley and Theodore Roosevelt. Root gently instructed Pierre in the facts of life: "The attitude of a very large element of our people is still such toward the great corporations that there is some possibility of stirring up a feeling that the War Department was championing the cause of the plain people as against 'Big Business.' " Ultimately, cool heads prevailed on both sides. The War Department realized that it needed Du Pont powder; Pierre accepted the fact that he must join in a great patriotic crusade. The company responded with its practiced celerity, throwing up plants, churning out powder, gathering profits less than those on Allied contracts, but plenty large enough to add significantly to Du Pont's swelling surplus.

On May 1, 1919, shortly after the war's end, Pierre du Pont retired from the presidency of the company, satisfied that he had fulfilled the goals set when he and his cousins had taken control. "I am firmly of the opinion," he told the board of directors, "that we have now reached another turning point . . . ; therefore it would seem wise to place responsibility for future development and management of the business on the next line of men." To his intense gratification, "the next line of men" included his younger brothers: Irénée, who succeeded to the presidency, and Lammot, who became first vice president and chairman of the executive committee. Without children of his own, Pierre had assumed paternal responsibility for his brothers and sisters since their father's death. All of them had called him "Dad" since childhood, so his younger brothers served as surrogates for the sons he never had. With control of the company passed on, and with family ownership still firm, Pierre retired satisfied with a trust fulfilled, a legacy enriched, a heritage preserved. The great wealth that he himself had accumulated always remained secondary to these benisons.

Rich, efficient, run by a modern organization that had proved its mettle in wartime, the Du Pont Company remained solidly du Pont. Pierre, his family obligations more than met, looked forward to retirement into the quiet, private life he preferred. A botanical garden at his estate and philanthropies for his beloved Delaware had already begun to absorb his attention.

As it turned out, Pierre's retirement plans had to wait. Suddenly, in 1920, General Motors teetered on the brink of bankruptcy. With both his family's and his firm's investments at stake, Pierre reluctantly engrossed himself in the auto company's affairs. He maneuvered a complete reorganization, assumed the presidency, and promoted the rise to power of Alfred P. Sloan. His collaboration with Sloan on the reorganization helped make General Motors the paragon of American corporate efficiency for much of the twentieth century. Not until 1928 could Pierre du Pont retire to his flowers and his charities. He died 26 years later, in 1954, survived by his company and the far-flung du Pont family, both of which he had guarded so well.

Chapter 8

The Organization Man

ALFRED P. SLOAN

Alfred P. Sloan Jr.

A s a third-generation Ford man, I grew up with an intense, innate distaste for General Motors (GM) and all its products, especially Chevrolets. My father argued the case for Ford superiority with references to arcane technical deficiencies hidden in the Chevrolet innards. But of such things as vacuum-assisted gearshifts I knew nothing and didn't need to learn. Chevrolets were no good because they weren't Fords, and that was reason enough. It baffled me that my maternal grandfather, who otherwise seemed perfect, preferred the hated rival and always had one sitting, to my embarrassment, in his driveway.

Such childhood prejudices die hard. Political scientists tell us that people tend to vote the way their parents did, and I suspect the same sort of loyalty to one corporation or another affects buying patterns as well. Certainly they did in my case. When I grew old enough to become a consumer, I assiduously avoided GM products. No Frigidaire appliances for me, despite the fact that in the part of the country where I grew up, folks used Frigidaire as the generic name for all refrigerators. As for cars, the idea of buying one from GM never occurred to me.

My first intimate acquaintance with General Motors' products, therefore, came through occupational necessity, not consumer choice. In the 1950s, the Pennsylvania Railroad dieselized, to the distress of an army of steam-locomotive sentimentalists for whom the Pennsylvania's classic engines had held a cherished place, but to the intense relief of operating railroaders like me, who had an all-too-painful acquaintance with the cantankerous inefficiencies of steam. In the freight yards where I worked, the Pennsylvania installed diesels from three manufacturers: Baldwin, Alco, and General Motors. Each brand had its own peculiarities. The Baldwins, everybody's favorite, had "a lot of heart." They combined quick acceleration, good braking, and a lot of pulling power. The Alcos, powerful but slow, would "pull the world if you could couple one up to it." The GM locomotives seemed to me just like Chevrolets. They did everything acceptably, but unspectacularly. They started slowly, stopped grudgingly, and were notoriously "slippery" on wet rails. Watching one of them spinning its wheels one rainy day, I called the engineer on the radio and asked him if the engine had run out of sand. "I don't need sand," he answered, "I need a Baldwin. *This* bastard would slip if the *rails* were made out of sand."

I discovered, however, that my negative view of GM's locomotives wasn't shared by the men who maintained them. Engine-house foremen told me sulfurously that the railroad should junk everything else and buy all General Motors products. "They're easy to work on," one foreman told me, "the parts are always in stock, and if you have a problem, GM will send a man out from LaGrange [Illinois, then headquarters of GM's locomotive division] right away. Those people are organized." Indeed they were—so organized that they eventually drove competitors clear out of the locomotive business and, but for the later entry of General Electric, would have monopolized the field.

GM's financial resources alone sufficed to make it a formidable competitor in any field it cared to enter. Long the largest corporation in the world (and, despite recent difficulties, still #15 in 2009, with gross revenues of $105 billion), its annual income exceeded that of many countries. With its vast assets, it could buy whatever technology it needed to enter any promising market, and often did. GM got into the appliance business by buying the Guardian Refrigerator Company in 1918, into aircraft engines by acquiring the Allison Engineering Company in 1929, and into diesel locomotive manufacturing by absorbing Winton Engine and Electro-Motive Engineering in 1930. In each case, General Motors acquired patents and expertise that brought it into a young industry at the forefront of existing technology.

Technology alone, however, doesn't guarantee success. Indeed, as Alfred P. Sloan, principal designer of General Motors' modern organization, observed, "American industry has always drawn from a common pool of technology." As Whitney and McCormick, Edison, and Ford after him learned, no American manufacturer can expect to enjoy more than a brief technological advantage over his competitors. Carnegie showed that industrial supremacy depends upon coupling technology to systematic organization. Pierre du Pont improved the mix, and Alfred Sloan brought the union to its most fertile consummation at General Motors.

Behind my engine-house foreman's observation of General Motors' superiority lay the ability of the GM organization to translate technological development into a full-blown industry. A Dayton engineer named Alfred Mellowes created the original Guardian refrigerator by harnessing the heat-absorbing properties of vaporizing gas. This principle had intrigued inventors before Mellowes, but none had succeeded in turning it into a marketable product. Mellowes himself hadn't mounted much of a threat to the iceman when Billy Durant, then GM president, visited the shoestring Guardian operation in 1919. "This man's got an idea," observed Durant, after threading his way through the clutter; "the rest is a lot of junk. . . . I'll tell you what I'll do. I'll organize a company with one hundred thousand dollars new capital and give you people a quarter interest." Two years later, Guardian, renamed Frigidaire, had run up losses of $2.5 million. Sloan turned the operation over to GM's Delco-Light Division. Delco-Light "had a fine sales force spread over large areas of the country, and some unused manufacturing capacity," as well as access to GM's research staff and capital. Four years later, Frigidaire had more than half the booming American mechanical refrigerator market. GM's capital, research facilities, manufacturing know-how, market research, and sales techniques had turned Mellowes's rudimentary idea into a household necessity.

When GM bought Winton Engine, the diesel locomotive hadn't yet become practical. The necessary research and testing, which Winton's limited budget had held to a snail's pace, rushed ahead, financed by GM's petty cash and driven forward by Charlie Kettering, the doyen of GM experimenters. For Kettering, one of his colleagues observed, the diesel challenge "was just like the sound of a bell to a fire horse." For GM, the diesel locomotive, once perfected, opened a new market to exploitation by the company's manufacturing and sales techniques.

Realizing that diesel locomotives had more in common with automobiles than with steam engines (a fact that eluded some manufacturers to their dying day), GM discarded the traditional industry practice of building locomotives to custom specifications. It designed a standard model to mass-produce at low cost, built several demonstrators for railroads to try, and, taking a leaf from Henry Ford's book, told prospective customers, "You can have any model you want as long as it's this one." To the diesel's efficiency, GM added the whole panoply of customer enticements developed in the mass production and marketing of harvesters and automobiles: long-term financing, speedy delivery, interchangeable parts, and factory-trained maintenance men.

As time passed, GM offered more models but kept them simple and cheap by building them from standard components. As locomotives aged, GM offered to take old models in trade or to rebuild them, even to rebuild competitors' products with genuine GM parts. Trade-ins, of course, they refurbished and resold.

Within 20 years, these methods had revolutionized the locomotive industry and, to a degree, the railroad business as well. The once-crude Winton Diesel had grown into a profitable General Motors division. For GM, this growth didn't count as a revolutionary development, but as a matter of routine. In fact, Alfred Sloan found his greatest pride in having created an organization that could attack such challenges systematically. Sloan, he and others thought, exemplified the "Organization Man" *par excellence*, a fully evolved specimen of the modern executive for whom the organization, not the product, provided the indispensable ingredient of success. (Sloan wasn't the first manufacturer to recognize the necessity for organization, of course. Whitney's failure to profit from the cotton gin resulted largely from a failure of organization; his subsequent success derived from his systematic conception of production [as well as patient government support.]) Each of the actors I have introduced after Whitney made lasting contributions to the organization of some aspect of American industry: McCormick to sales and distribution, Carnegie to cost analysis, Edison to applied science, Henry Ford to mass production, Pierre du Pont to market forecasting and diversification, and all of them to inventory control. Before Carnegie, however, organization came second, as merely the means to cherished ends—making some particular product and maintaining family control.

In Carnegie, a transition of emphasis from product to organization appeared. Unlike his predecessors, Carnegie, no mechanic and no expert on his firm's product, knew how to get steel made, not how to make it. "My preference was always for manufacturing," he said, but his strength lay in his organization. "Take away everything else," he declared, "but leave me my organization and in ten years I'll be back on top."

Pierre du Pont's career plots the shift clearly, for he discovered that the organization he designed to perpetuate his firm's dominance of a single product could adapt to control a diversified operation. For the shy, retiring Pierre, the boardroom and the executive office formed more natural habitats than laboratories or factories. In his hands, organization charts, more comfortable to manipulate than tools or people, became the blueprints for survival in the complex world of twentieth-century American industry. Although certainly neither inhumane nor insensitive, Pierre's decision to exclude inept family members and admit outsiders to Du Pont management reflected his view that no one person mattered more than the organization, whereas the organization as a whole had capacities greater than the sum of its individual human parts. At Du Pont, top-level management subordinated the imperatives of research, manufacturing, and selling to the guiding principle of return on investment, lessons forgotten by businesses only at their peril, sometimes their mortal peril.

Viewed narrowly, Pierre's handiwork can seem the logical outgrowth of manufacturers' endless struggle to match production to shifting, uncontrollable market demands in a way that kept their assets profitably busy. Whitney solved the problem by relying on the government as a customer, a solution not available to people such as McCormick, who found himself perpetually bedeviled by having made too many machines or too few. Carnegie and Ford relied on efficiency, believing they could always drive prices down to the point at which demand revived. For them, as for many other American manufacturers, the assumption that the American economy would forever expand seemed validated by experience. It took a long time for most to realize that excess capacity had supplied one of the driving forces behind the trust movement that ultimately absorbed Carnegie's and McCormick's firms, and hundreds of others. Pierre du Pont's vision, informed by his experience at the Johnson Company, was clearer: firms had to calculate markets, not assume them; the business had to shape strategies based on statistical realities, not romantic obsessions.

The ascendancy of corporate organization men fitted into the larger historical patterns of the time. American business, like American society, had become infinitely larger and more complex than in Whitney's day. As the variety of products proliferated, the trickle of innovation became a flood, and every aspect of mass production manufacturing became subdivided and specialized. Business had to develop more complex organizations to function at all, let alone at a profit.

At the same time, for government, developments in the economy presented challenges never contemplated by the Founding Fathers. Beginning with the Depression of 1873, increasing numbers of Americans across the entire social spectrum developed doubts about the effects of unregulated business. In the last quarter of the nineteenth century, supposedly "beneficial" competition seemed paradoxically to have brought not "the best of all possible worlds," but instead monopolies and combinations designed by J. P. Morgan and others to eliminate altogether what they denounced as "ruinous" competition. In reaction, farmers formed alliances such as the Patrons of Husbandry (the "Grange"), workers joined unions such as the Knights of Labor, and the Populist Party emerged to demand government intervention in the economy. Even some despairing railroad executives joined the cry for regulation of shipping rates. The response, in the form of the Interstate Commerce Act of 1887 and the Sherman Antitrust Act (1890), brought the federal government into the economy in then-unprecedented ways and ushered in a string of regulatory acts that have continued ever since.

These developments in business and government formed part of a larger pattern in the late nineteenth century, when a quest, sometimes even a mania, for order pervaded America, infecting some business owners as well as political reformers, doctors, engineers, and farmers. Although the prospect of achieving stability through combination fascinated financiers such as Morgan, the sheer (if often delusional) tidiness of trusts often led to merger for merger's sake, even in industries where combination made no sense. For every International Harvester that threshed its way to success, a U.S. Cotton Duck waddled into failure. In other cases, the merger process created "paper concerns," as Carnegie derided them, saddled with massive quantities of bonds and stocks on which no management could hope to pay interest and dividends. Nor were such mistakes limited to amateurs or small fry. Morgan himself, for example, put together U.S. Shipbuilding, which sank upon launching.

Management, sometimes in consultation with Frederick Taylor and others of the new breed of efficiency gurus, tried to raise productivity through organizational tinkering, with mixed results. The symmetry of organization and flow charts, so easily redrawn, often seemed to convert hope to reality in the office, while mutiny and confusion reigned on the shop floor. Henry Ford, driven by a different mania, created yet another sort of industrial order. Fired by the excitement of turning his company into one vast conveyor belt carrying raw materials from his mines to his plants in his ships and his railroad cars, Ford pushed through the complete vertical integration that worked well enough while prosperity prevailed, but became an expensive albatross on his neck when sales declined in a gutted market. Ford's plan, like many others that proved wanting in hard times, typified the traditional optimistic attitude of American businessmen, an attitude nurtured in the expansive climate of the nineteenth century. A Carnegie, an Edison, a Ford found it hard to imagine that much could go wrong for long, and impossible to plan on such a pessimistic basis.

For Alfred Sloan, however, as for Pierre du Pont, the true test of an organization lay in its ability to prosper during slack times. They regarded recessions as inevitable, however bright the long-term outlook. The Depression of 1893 affected them both deeply: du Pont because of the Johnson Company's vicissitudes, Sloan because he encountered a dismal job market when he left MIT in 1895. He spent his first working years with the Hyatt Roller Bearing Company as it skated along on the brink of bankruptcy. Even when prosperity returned and the automotive industry galvanized the economy, Sloan, supplying bearings to myriad automobile manufacturers, saw how failure relentlessly stalked the weak and poorly organized. In the free-for-all early automotive market, Hyatt's customers and competitors went under frequently, their weaknesses exposed by a decline in the market or exploited by a better-organized rival.

In a series of transactions between 1916 and 1918, GM absorbed Hyatt; Sloan became a vice president and a major shareholder in GM, making his wealth a hostage to the company's fortunes. "I found myself," he recalled, "with rather little cash and a devil of a lot of stock." He also found himself in the midst of corporate chaos slackly tolerated by Billy Durant, the GM founder and chairman, another old-style optimist who planned only for success. Alarmed, Sloan pressed Durant for systems, order, and organization, preferably along lines laid out by Sloan himself. Durant responded with smiles, encouragement, and inaction.

Then the automotive market collapse of 1920 swept through the ramshackle GM structure. In its wake came Pierre du Pont and a Du Pont–trained salvage crew, determined to pick up the pieces, reorganize, and preserve the stockholders' investment. The arrival of the Delaware cavalry and its calm, high-collared, pince-nez–wearing leader pleased no one more than Sloan. Seeing General Motors as a potential customer for vast quantities of Du Pont products, the du Ponts had put $67 million into GM stock—a princely sum, to be sure, but the money had come from surplus war profits that the du Ponts could find no better place to invest. They could have lost it all without damaging much but their pride. Sloan, on the other hand, had a measure of desperation in his organizing zeal. "Everything I had in the world," he later recalled, "was in General Motors."

In Pierre du Pont, Sloan saw a savior. Pierre knew nothing about making automobiles, but he brought an unmatched reputation for business probity, massive financial clout to tide the company over its immediate crisis, and a determination to reorganize for stability and security. If anyone could bring system to the GM muddle, Sloan thought du Pont could. The two were kindred spirits, similar in temperament, both MIT trained; and both believed in basing decisions on facts, not brainstorms.

Sloan had long found Durant a trial to work with. He described Durant as a "genius," no complimentary term in Sloan's lexicon, for it denoted men who gloried in the "kind of thinking" that relied on "hunches." Sloan himself "much preferred the slow process of getting all the available facts, analyzing them as completely as . . . possible, and then deciding our course." He worked most comfortably with men who, when "confronted by a problem . . . tackled it as [he] did [his] own, with engineering care to get the facts." Durant, on the other hand, said Sloan, "would proceed on a course of action guided solely, as far as I could tell, by some intuitive flash of brilliance. He never felt obliged to make an engineering hunt for facts." Durant, moreover, "could create but he could not administer," and his breezy, backslapping manner and boundless optimism grated. Sloan by nature had a quiet, retiring, cautious character; his coterie often called him "Silent Sloan."

Admittedly not "a Durant man," Sloan did not think Durant the man for GM. The company "had become too big for a one-man show. It was . . . far too complicated. The future required more than an individual's genius." To realize "the potential industrial force under the General Motors emblem" required not "boldness and daring," but "the most competent executive group that could be brought together." Such a group meant first of all "a new president to take the place of Mr. Durant." Sloan knew just the man he wanted: "[Pierre S. du Pont] was the one individual . . . who had the prestige and respect that could give confidence to the organization, to the public, and to the banks, and whose presence could arrest the [growing] demoralization." Sloan, of course, also knew of the "capability for business leadership [Pierre] had shown . . . in the Du Pont Company." Sloan also found Pierre personally compatible; indeed, his description of du Pont would have served for himself: "tall, well built, and reticent," a man "who would not put himself forward."

Pierre, as we know, was reluctant to take over. He soon found in Sloan, however, an alter ego who had the knowledge of the automobile industry that he himself lacked. Sloan, moreover, was a man with a plan, the same plan of reorganization that Durant had dismissed. Couched in the organizational language that Pierre used like a mother tongue, Sloan's blueprint became the basis for GM's reconstruction; Sloan himself became Pierre's right-hand man, the operational head of the company, with the title of vice president of operations. Together, in 1921, these two spare, taciturn MIT graduates set about the business of reshaping a helter-skelter collection into a smoothly functioning organization, tuned for systematic growth in a fluctuating marketplace. For Pierre du Pont, the GM challenge capped an already masterful career; for Alfred Sloan, it represented the opportunity he had worked for since boyhood.

Alfred P. Sloan was born in 1875, five years after Pierre du Pont. The son of a coffee and tea importer, Sloan grew up in comfortable, but not opulent, surroundings. A studious boy with a bent for mathematics and science, young Alfred became something of a child prodigy, finishing high school at the Brooklyn Polytechnic Institute a year ahead of his class. He passed the entrance examinations for MIT, but the school delayed his admission for a year because of his youth. Once admitted, he got himself back on schedule, becoming a "grind" who "worked every possible minute" and graduated in three years.

Even for a student as promising as Sloan, the Depression in 1895 made it a grim time to look for a job. But through his father's friendship with John E. Searles, kingpin of the American Sugar Refining Company, Sloan found work as a draftsman at the Hyatt Roller Bearing Company in Newark, New Jersey. In John Wesley Hyatt, his nominal superior, Sloan met an old-style, self-trained, lone-wolf inventor, a man Sloan described as "scientifically illiterate." Hyatt had not done badly for an illiterate. He had invented celluloid, the first practical plastic, hoping to make his fortune by substituting celluloid for ivory in billiard balls. A later invention, the roller bearing, had more potential for real money. Wherever metal turns upon metal, some sort of antifriction bearing is required. In industrial America, a land of turning shafts carrying increasingly heavier loads, the market potential for a device such as the Hyatt roller bearing seemed unlimited.

Yet Hyatt encountered real problems in bringing the roller bearing to a marketable stage. These problems illustrate the increasing complexity and interlocking of scientific disciplines that beset late-nineteenth-century manufacturers. Roller bearings depended on metallurgy to make a metal hard enough to bear loads without wearing, on petroleum chemistry to develop lubricants that would not break down or catch fire when subjected to the bearings' heat, and on mechanical engineering to develop machines that would turn the bearings to precision tolerance in large volume and at low cost.

The real power at Hyatt, as at so many fledgling American manufacturing firms, lay not with the inventor, but with the man who put up the money, John Searles. Searles eventually wearied of the unending drain on his finances and withdrew his support. Sloan's father came to the rescue, put up $5,000 to keep the business alive, installed his son as president, and gave him six months to show a profit. Sloan cut costs and raised production by installing systematic controls and procedures at the Hyatt plant, relocated between a junkyard and a city dump in Harrison, New Jersey. With the aid of a hustling sales manager who had mastered the drummer's ancient arts of wining, dining, and bedazzling the customers, Hyatt cleared $12,000 at the end of the first six months and went on to bigger and better things.

As the turn of the century approached, Sloan realized that the fledgling automobile industry could become his most important customer. He had a product that every automobile manufacturer could use, because every car rolled and every engine turned on some kind of bearing. Early automobile producers spent much of their time scrambling around looking for people to manufacture necessary components. A company such as Hyatt, already turning out a needed product, came as a godsend. Sloan and his sales manager followed developments in the automobile industry closely. Any new manufacturer they aggressively solicited for his business. Sloan, for example, first wrote Henry Ford in 1899, nine years before the first Model T.

Among a hurly-burly of such fledgling component suppliers, Sloan's firm rose steadily to the top. Hyatt offered carmakers an invaluable service, for Sloan's development organization could design bearings tailored to fit specific needs. In addition, Sloan's manufacturing organization established a reputation for punctual delivery of orders, vital for an industry in which assembly waits until all the parts arrive. Sloan kept up with rising demand by driving the workforce hard, concentrating on efficiency, and plowing profits back into expanding capacity.

Business often took Sloan to Detroit, where he met most of the automobile industry pioneers, including Henry Ford, the Dodge brothers, Ransom E. Olds, the Fisher brothers, Charles Nash, and others. This rough-and-ready crew consisted largely of "shirt-sleeve mechanics" turned manufacturers. They gathered daily at the Hotel Ponchartrain bar, the automobile industry's watering hole, to exchange shoptalk and rumors. Sloan never felt comfortable in such an environment ("A couple of cocktails [were] just about my limit"), but he endured it for the sake of personal contacts and keeping abreast of industry news. If you waited at the Ponchartrain bar, Detroiters said, anybody you wanted to see in the automobile industry would turn up within two days.

Sloan admired these pioneers but felt at ease with few of them. His contempt for the "scientifically illiterate," a rare disease in those days, tinged his outlook and caused him to rank his peers according to the degree of science with which they approached their work. He respected Henry Leland because "quality was Leland's god" and because the old man, micrometer in hand, taught professional engineer Sloan the real meaning of precision by rejecting an order of Hyatt bearings. "Mr. Sloan," Leland told him, "Cadillacs are made to run, not just to sell." Thanks to Leland, who insisted, "You must grind your bearings. Even though you make thousands, the first and the last should be precisely alike," Sloan acquired a "genuine conception of what mass production should really mean" even before Henry Ford made it the hallmark of the industry. When manufacturers began demanding parts machined to interchangeable precision, Hyatt, unlike many competitors, had his firm ready and prospered accordingly.

Sloan found another kindred spirit in Charles Stewart Mott, a mechanical engineer trained at the Stevens Institute of Technology. Mott manufactured axles, and as a Leland disciple learned to make them fully interchangeable. Naturally enough, Mott turned to another precision manufacturer for the necessary bearings. Soon, Sloan said, "Mott and Hyatt were interdependent to an extraordinary degree." This relationship required close cooperation between the two firms' chiefs, who established an easy rapport. "I liked to work with Mott," Sloan said. "His training had made him methodical" and endowed him with that quality Sloan cherished above all others, "engineering care [for] the facts."

Between 1905 and 1915, as automobile sales soared from a handful to more than 800,000 units, Sloan and Mott prospered, their firms following parallel and often convergent courses as volume suppliers of precision parts. Gradually, the industry took a new shape. As dozens of manufacturers expired, the survivors concentrated in and around Detroit. Major car manufacturers began to draw their suppliers into closer corporate and geographic relationships. In 1913, Mott moved most of his production facilities from Utica, New York, to a new plant in Flint, Michigan, at the behest of his largest customer, Billy Durant. Mott financed the move by selling a share of his business to GM.

Sloan watched in alarm as Durant wove Mott's firm into his corporate web. The emerging configuration of the industry seemed to menace his life's work, his father's fortune, and his own. "I had put my whole life's energy into Hyatt," he recalled; "everything I had earned was there in bricks, machinery, and materials." By driving profits back into expansion, Sloan had, by 1916, transformed the shabby Harrison building into a 750,000-square-foot plant, turning out 40,000 bearings a day. The "works were highly organized . . . as nearly scientific in . . . operations as a business could be." "An effective cost system" monitored efficiency; chemists and metallurgists kept the company abreast of scientific developments; "every step in the [manufacture] of raw material into antifriction bearings was checked by scientific methods." To serve the customers, Hyatt had "three sales divisions, each with its own engineering and sales staff." The Newark office "promoted the use of our bearings . . . in all classes of machinery." A Chicago outlet handled the tractor industry, and one in Detroit dealt with the company's mainstay, the automobile industry.

Despite all this efficiency, capacity, and diversity, Sloan feared for his firm's health. He lay vulnerable to the expansion strategies of the two automobile giants, Ford and GM, which together supplied the bulk of Hyatt's business. Either or both might decide to dispense with Hyatt's services anytime, in which case, Sloan said, "our company would be in a desperate situation," stuck with excess capacity, an idle plant, and horror of horrors to a dedicated capitalist, unproductive capital.

The Ford Motor Company grew entirely through internal expansion, using its profits to establish its own parts-manufacturing plants. Henry Ford had the capital by 1916 to do anything he pleased, including going into the bearing business overnight on a scale that would not only supply his own needs, but also make him a devastating competitor for the remaining market. Ford showed no signs of such a move, but, given his vast resources and mercurial temperament, his past behavior offered no reassurance for Sloan's future. One thing Sloan knew for certain: Ford wouldn't buy Hyatt Roller Bearing. When Henry did something, he did it from scratch his own way. Looking for future security, Sloan had to look elsewhere.

GM, following a course diametrically opposed to Ford's, bought up existing producers through exchanges of stock. Thus Durant, an even more unpredictable character than Ford, might deal Hyatt a crippling blow by absorbing and building up a competitor. In 1916 as before, plenty of people, including bearing manufacturers, stood ready to clean up by "selling to the trust." When Durant invited him to lunch and offered to buy him out, Sloan found himself one of them. After some negotiation, they settled on a price of $13.5 million.

In his two autobiographical volumes, Sloan retrospectively explained his decision with ineffable logic as a Hobson's choice, providing an emblematic illustration of the changing climate of American enterprise in the early twentieth century. In the prime of life, rich, successful, and controlling owner of his company, Sloan headed no gimcrack operation, thrown together in hopes of a quick sale to the trust, but rather a prosperous, efficient enterprise with an enviable record for quality and dependability.

It speaks to the times that Sloan lacked the fierce pride of ownership that characterized so many of his predecessors. They had seen their firms as an extension of themselves. Had Sloan had a son to carry on, he might have acted differently, as Carnegie might have in 1900. Andy, however, would never have accepted a subordinate's role in United States Steel. Sloan, on the other hand, craved wealth and power and saw a chance to multiply both by joining a vastly larger organization. Identity and independence as a manufacturer seemed to him a small forfeit for such an opportunity. Many of Sloan's contemporaries faced the same choice: Charles Mott, the Fisher brothers, and Charles Kettering (inventor of the self-starter) chose to join GM. Henry Ford (who turned down an $8 million offer from Durant in 1908), Charles Nash, Walter Chrysler, and the Dodge brothers opted for independence and went their own ways, some to glory, some to oblivion.

Since Sloan's day, many a successful entrepreneur has made the same choice he did, becoming part of a process that the economist Joseph Schumpeter saw as the harbinger of capitalism's doom. According to Schumpeter, and other mavens who followed him, capitalism depends on individual initiative, which when successful builds firms that only a bureaucracy can manage; but bureaucracy inexorably stifles individual initiative, ending in a fatal hardening of the corporate arteries—a classic dialectic at work. Throughout his years at GM, Sloan defended a contrary view, arguing that even the biggest corporate structure could encourage, not extinguish, individual effort. "General Motors," he declared, "was built on initiative." The corporation's resources, first of all, multiplied the possibility of individual satisfaction through achievement. "After all," Sloan said, "what any one individual can accomplish is not great, but through the power of organization the effect of a few may be multiplied almost indefinitely." As supporting evidence, Sloan cited the career of Charles Kettering. Working at first alone in a barn, Kettering invented the self-starter. Later, backed by GM's resources and aided by technical staffs at Du Pont and Standard Oil, Kettering developed quick-drying paints that enabled the company to offer cars in a variety of colors; perfected tetraethyl lead for gasoline that permitted high-compression engines; synthesized Freon, the first practical refrigerant for home use; and perfected the diesel engine.

According to Sloan, GM also preserved individual incentive through promotion and stock bonuses to reward individual contributions to the firm's success. Pierre du Pont had brought the bonus plan to GM; Sloan became an avid booster and expanded the plan over the years. Bonuses not only made company men of individuals "by encouraging executives to relate their own individual efforts to the welfare of the whole corporation," but also insured them against financial loss as a result of trading independence for corporate loyalty. "By placing its executives in the same relative position . . . that they would occupy if they were conducting . . . their own . . . business," intoned Sloan, "[the company] provides opportunity for accomplishment through the exercise of individual initiative and opportunity for economic progress commensurate with performance."

That the GM method worked Sloan thought irrefutable. In business, success furnishes the ultimate proof, and Sloan endorsed the views of Walter S. Carpenter Jr. of Du Pont, who observed in the early 1960s that "the Du Pont Company and General Motors . . . the most prominent exponents of the bonus plan have been extraordinarily successful." They had excelled in the "assembling and retention of an organization of outstanding men."

There, in Carpenter's last statement, lurks evidence of a fundamental shift in American outlook, a shift symbolized by Sloan's career. It suggests how a nation that had long prided itself as a place where "everyman" could act as "his own boss" could embrace a system where virtually everyone worked for someone else. It shows how a country of "independent yeomen, shopkeepers, and mechanics" could transform itself into a society of interdependent employees, bureaucrats, and corporation men, yet persuade itself that the new arrangements preserved, or even—to men like Sloan—strengthened the cherished American tradition of individualism.

Sloan believed that high salaries, bonuses, and the chance to multiply one's own efforts through the corporation's financial and mechanical leverage preserved individualism for executives. In the case of the workers, steady wages and increased leisure time more than compensated for the loss of independence and artisanal pride. For a time he seemed right. On such meat some Caesars fed and waxed mighty, though others gorged, coarsened, staggered, and ofttimes died of bloat. In any case, society today more closely reflects Sloan's bureaucratized perception than those of Jefferson, Ralph Waldo Emerson, Ayn Rand, and other apostles of self-reliance.

All this lay far in the future when Sloan agreed to sell to Durant; he somehow concluded then that the massive GM organization offered a more satisfying channel for his ambitions than did the continuation of his own business. Durant, no fool, sensed Sloan's drive for power. He sweetened his proposition by offering Sloan the presidency of United Motors, a GM parts-manufacturing subsidiary, thus giving him the chance to run four companies instead of one.

So the year 1916 began Alfred Sloan's tempestuous four-year association with William Crapo Durant, a fabulous character in American business history. Unfortunately for Durant, historians of business organization largely portray him as the bungler who made the mess that Sloan and Pierre du Pont had to clean up. But Durant deserves more than parody. A man of extraordinary vision, like Henry Ford, he foresaw the automobile as a necessity for the masses at a time when other manufacturers considered it a rich man's plaything. Early in the game, Durant told his peers, "Gentlemen, you don't realize the purchasing power of the American people. I look forward to the time when we'll make and sell one million cars a year."

Durant, in fact, had a more sophisticated presentiment of the American car market than Ford, who refused to the bitter end to abandon his conception of the automobile as a simple utility vehicle. Americans, Durant believed, would buy all sorts of cars, from the spartan to the sumptuous, as their incomes permitted and their pretensions dictated. Anticipating the day when the automobile would sell as a status symbol as well as for its utility, Durant tried to build a manufacturing empire to supply every buyer's craving.

In his early years, Durant followed an orthodox, relatively conservative path of development. He had already accumulated money and skill in becoming the country's largest carriage manufacturer, complete with specialized parts plants and a nationwide distribution network. In 1904, he bought the small, bankrupt Buick Motor Company in his hometown of Flint, Michigan and soon turned it into the country's largest car producer. Durant redesigned the car, built new assembly plants, attracted parts suppliers including sparkplug maker Albert Champion to Flint, and outsold Ford 9,000 cars to 6,000 in 1908.

In 1908, when the Model T took to the road, Ford rattled off to a seemingly insurmountable lead. Durant, boiling with frustration and impatience at seeing his competitor steal a march, threw caution aside. For Durant, the Ford method of growth seemed much too slow. He couldn't, or rather wouldn't, wait for retained earnings to finance new plants. Instead, he decided to buy existing facilities. In 1908, he formed GM, combining Buick, Cadillac, and Oldsmobile. Ford's success had brought a bullish atmosphere to the industry, but he hadn't the least notion of letting outsiders in on the best thing going by selling stock. In those circumstances, GM looked to frustrated investors like a heaven-sent opportunity. Durant had little trouble raising capital or finding sellers who would accept GM shares in payment. In its first two years, GM's profits rose from $29 million to $49 million.

Durant, confident that ever-expanding sales would always provide plenty of working capital, spent the money as fast as it came in. In 1910, however, he found himself caught short when the market paused. Undaunted, he secured $13 million from a syndicate of bankers. The rescuers exacted a stiff price—$15 million in notes, plus $6 million worth of the company's stock as a "bonus." In addition, they demanded that Durant turn over his voting rights to a voting trust (of bankers, needless to say) for five years and ousted him as president. Still unchastened, Durant joined Louis Chevrolet to form the Chevrolet Motor Car Company. Chevrolet, raised lean and efficient on a slim capital diet, produced a sporty car that sold well. On the strength of Chevrolet's performance, Durant found a new source of money in John J. Raskob, once Pierre du Pont's secretary, now risen to chairman of the Du Pont Company Finance Committee. Raskob, a poor boy made good, shared Durant's roseate view of the future of the American economy in general and of the automobile industry in particular. He invested in Chevrolet and persuaded Pierre to do the same.

With his pool of Chevrolet profits fortified by this freshet from the bountiful Du Pont fountains, Durant began quietly buying GM stock. His former banker friends unwittingly aided him by paying no dividends, although their efficient interim management generated substantial profits. Parsimony exacted its price; the stock fell from $100 a share to $24. Then the five-year voting trust expired. Durant showed up at the next meeting and soon proved, to the bankers' dismay, that he and his Chevrolet Motor Company owned a majority of GM's stock. In the reorganization of the company, Pierre du Pont became chairman of GM's board, but with his marriage and a flood of Allied powder orders on his mind, Pierre left control of operations to Durant, who immediately resumed expansion.

Between 1915 and 1920, GM grew by leaps and bounds, corralling car builders and a herd of parts manufacturers. Buick, Oldsmobile, and Cadillac were joined by a clutch of lesser firms such as Cartercar, Marquette, Ewing, Randolph, Welch, and Oakland, and other marques long since gone to their rewards. Sloan's United Motors Company, set up as a GM-controlled holding company to acquire parts manufacturers, bought out, in addition to Hyatt, New Departure (ball bearings), Remy Electric and Delco (lights, ignition parts), Harrison Radiator, Klaxon (horns), and others.

In a quandary, as we have seen, to find an outlet for their wartime surpluses, the du Ponts in 1918 shoveled in another $25 million to fuel expansion, acquiring now a quarter interest. Raskob persuaded Pierre that the price of the stock was cheap, dividends good and sure to improve, and, not least, that GM would buy all its paint, varnish, and artificial leather from Du Pont. Durant also agreed to turn GM's financial management over to a committee appointed by the du Ponts. Pierre chose Raskob as guardian of the Du Pont interest, which proved the equivalent of appointing a rat to guard the cheese. Raskob, for all Pierre's confidence in him, turned to putty in Durant's hands. Durant continued on his merry way, wheeling and dealing; Raskob followed along, paying the bills. Amid the exuberant and uncoordinated hully-gully, only a few division chiefs kept their heads. Sloan methodically brought order to United Motors while forwarding his constant suggestions for overall reorganization to Durant. Harry Bassett ran a tight ship at Buick. Like Sloan, he introduced systematic cost control in production and tried to establish a rational marketing scheme.

That chaos prevailed should not obscure the fact that Durant, too, had an overall plan, one so brilliant that it laid the foundation for the reorganized firm's subsequent rise to the top of the corporate heap. First, he assembled a full line of cars that catered to a variety of tastes and pocketbooks. Second, he diversified by manufacturing refrigerators, electrical generators, tractors, and trucks in addition to automobiles. Third, he integrated by absorbing parts manufacturers to supply the car-building plants. His successors validated all these policies by continuing them.

Durant failed because he didn't create a strong enough central organization to coordinate the properties once acquired, analyze their performance, and shape up the laggards. He let most of the acquisitions operate as independently after they joined GM as before. Consequently, Du Pont accountants discovered that only two of the automobile divisions (Buick and Oldsmobile) consistently made money, and, worse, most of them competed with one another. No market forecasting took place; therefore, no real production planning existed. Each plant simply built as many cars as it could, hoping to sell them all. Furthermore, GM had no purchasing policy or inventory control. Each division manager bought materials independently, sometimes from GM-owned parts makers, but often not.

When Sloan and du Pont took over, they found that the company's various divisions had inventories that totaled more than $200 million. This tied up an amount of working capital almost double the Du Pont Company's total assets and, needless to say, contributed massively to GM's perpetual cash shortage. Outside of Cadillac and Buick, the GM car divisions had paid little attention to quality control. Many of the company's products had acquired a shoddy reputation. GM could survive these weaknesses only as long as an expanding market or optimistic investors kept the cash coming. In 1920, both sources dried up and Durant fell.

Whether Durant, given enough time, would have turned from a strategy of mere combination to one of real consolidation one can only guess. His record at Buick and Chevrolet suggests that he knew how to run an efficient operation, and even Sloan admitted that Durant might have tightened up GM eventually. But sometime between 1904 and 1908, Durant seems to have undergone a fundamental change in outlook. Perhaps Ford's competition led him to abandon caution for haste and daring, reversing the progression toward conservatism that supposedly accompanies aging.

Psychologists have had a lot to say about the critical middle years in men's lives, and some have suggested that most creative men do their best work either early or late, but rarely throughout their lives. If successful manufacturers can be considered creative, and my sample of them representative, then such men present an exception. By and large, their original, successful work continued through their middle years. Indeed, their careers suggest that the ability and stamina required to mount a sustained effort of long days over many years often forms a component of entrepreneurial success.

On the other hand, Durant numbers among the many industrialists for whom the middle years brought a sharp change, manifested by some irrevocable choice, bold move, or galvanizing of effort. Whitney had turned 33 (middle-aged for his time) when he gave up on the cotton gin and contracted for the entirely new task of making thousands of muskets. McCormick transplanted himself and his factory to Chicago at 39. Carnegie gave up his career flogging securities and, as he said, "put all [his] eggs in one [steel] basket" at 38. Edison, passing 40, turned away from electricity, which had occupied him from boyhood, sold his General Electric stock, and concentrated on developing the phonograph, motion pictures, and his iron ore separation scheme. Henry Ford at 39 decided to break with his luxury-car-minded backers and form a new company to "build a car for the great multitude." Sloan sold Hyatt to GM at 41. As we shall see, Henry Ford II in his early 40s supplanted his hired managers and took charge of his company; Edwin Land introduced the Polaroid camera at 38.

So Durant's indefatigable daring and drive were not unique, but his policy of expanding first and organizing later undoubtedly led to his downfall. Sloan, with Pierre du Pont's solid backing, immediately set about reorganizing the company. Durant's tripartite plan—variety (several kinds of cars), diversification (into other products), and integration (to control sources of components)—remained company policy, but subordinated to a more fundamental principle: "The primary object of the corporation," said Sloan later, articulating a fundamental capitalist creed, "was to make money, not just . . . make motor cars." Furthermore, Sloan argued, just making a profit didn't justify continuation of any operation:

> The profit resulting from any business considered [alone] is no real measure of the merits of that particular business. An operation making $100,000 a year may be . . . very profitable [,] justifying expansion and . . . all the additional capital that it can profitably employ. On the other hand, a business making $10,000,000 a year may be . . . very unprofitable . . . not only not justifying further expansion but even justifying liquidation. . . . It is not, therefore, a matter of the amount of profit but of the relation of that profit to the . . . invested capital.

This positive declaration of the rate-of-return principle, a principle Durant had ignored, naturally struck a resonant chord in Pierre du Pont, for whom it had long been gospel. Their basic unity of thought cemented the working relationship between the two men. (Indeed, Sloan later declared that he and Pierre had disagreed only once on an issue relating to the company: John Raskob's acceptance in 1928 of the chairmanship of the Democratic National Committee, while still a GM officer.)

Sloan, as he expected, had a most useful partner in his rebuilding campaign. Du Pont cash and credit with the Morgan house furnished working capital to carry the company over the market crisis of 1920–21 and provided investment capital for expansion and modernization. A swarm of Du Pont accountants, led by Donaldson Brown, buzzed through the GM labyrinth, taking inventory, analyzing the profitability of current operations, and installing standardized accounting practices everywhere. Du Pont engineers surveyed the company's plants, did efficiency studies, drew plans for reconstructing old facilities and building new ones, and supervised the work.

With the capital situation under control and statistics flowing, economy measures began. Purchasing stopped until inventories ran down. Newly installed central controls prevented any recurrence of scarcity or glut. Chevrolet became a GM division, whereas unprofitable lines such as Scripps-Booth, Sheridan, and Oakland wafted off to automobile Valhalla. Remaining divisions got orders to buy parts from GM subsidiaries or explain why they didn't.

Donaldson Brown adapted a Du Pont concept, "standard volume," to the automobile industry. Standard volume supplied a hypothetical statistical yardstick that showed the detailed costs and profits that should result from normal levels of production. When compared to actual performance, this yardstick could tell who produced efficiently and who didn't. Personnel soon got shifted accordingly in a barrage of promotions, transfers, marching orders telling them what to do and how to do it, and walking papers telling them to get a job elsewhere. Many of Durant's cronies departed; fresh talent, including Ford protégés Norval Hawkins and William Knudsen, arrived.

Sloan wanted to preserve the good qualities of GM's tradition of divisional independence, even while holding all operations subject to policies established by central authority. He further split GM's multiple operations into divisions according to function—Chevrolet, Oldsmobile, research, parts, accessories, and so on. Each division operated semi-autonomously according to the instructions of the Executive Committee. That body labored continuously to "determine the functioning of the various divisions constituting the Corporation's activities, not only in relation to one another, but in relation to the central authority."

Striking the appropriate balance between centralization and decentralization involved a lot of trial and error. A constant reshuffling of organization charts ensued, based on statistical results, a process that goes on to this day, encouraged by the availability of computer software that makes redrawing organization charts easier than drawing with an "Etch-A-Sketch," and necessitated by the company's recent struggle to make vehicles people want to buy. Mercifully, we need not dissect Sloan's reorganization process here. After all, as Sloan himself said, "The language of organization has always suffered some want of words to express the true facts and circumstances of human interaction." Suffice it to say that Donaldson Brown's yardstick did indicate when and where the firm's units met rate-of-return goals and when they didn't. A little centralization here and a little decentralization there toned up the structure accordingly.

Once adequately equipped to judge results, Sloan went about improving them. He told Charlie Kettering's research team to improve the cars and ordered divisions to develop quality controls to make sure they stayed improved. He reorganized the product line so that each division produced for a particular price level without competing with the others. The bottom level he left, for the time being, to Ford, since Henry had such a hammerlock on it. As Sloan said, "No conceivable amount of capital short of the United States Treasury could have sustained the losses required to take [Ford's] volume away from him at his own game." (Ultimately, the availability of used cars, the Depression, rising consumer tastes for automotive luxury, and Ford's own obstinacy did the job for them, thus sparing GM the expense.)

With better quality in the works and product lines established, Sloan, borrowing another tool from the Du Pont kit, installed market forecasting. As the company learned to evaluate the four principal variables that affected demand—growth, seasonal variation, general business conditions, and competition—it translated market forecasting and predicted rates of return into prices, production, employment, inventory levels, and capital investment. Once institutionalized in statistical bureaus, market forecasting supplied the finishing touch to the GM organizational structure and philosophy. Completed in the late 1920s, the GM structure, Sloan later recorded, "remained essentially unchanged," and the policies it represented became "the general practice in American business."

This immensely powerful engine of production, however, did not suffice. Sloan coupled it to a refurbished dealer network and a panoply of techniques designed to stimulate sales. Annual model changes featuring this or that gimmick aimed, Sloan admitted, "to make you dissatisfied with your current car so you will buy a new one." Liberal trade-ins, GM-sponsored financing, advertising blitzes, searchlights, parades, banquets, balloons, indeed the whole carnival of the modern hard sell, combined to push GM's products into the market in ever-increasing numbers until 1929.

In 1922, Sloan's first full year in operational control, GM sold 457,000 cars and trucks and netted $61 million. In 1923, the figures rose to 800,000 vehicles and $80 million profit. In May of that year, Pierre du Pont declared that the corporation had achieved "stability," turned over the presidency to Sloan, and retired "to his enormous hothouses at Longwood Gardens, [to] pluck orchids and figs, to sit in the evening on his broad plaza and watch his $500,000 fountain swish and spurt in beams of many-colored lights," to listen to his $250,000 organ, and to pursue his philanthropic campaign to improve his native state.

As president of GM, Sloan more than fulfilled Pierre's expectations. Cars rolled out and money poured in. In 1929, GM sold 1.9 million cars and trucks, netting $248 million after taxes for a 16.5 percent return on assets. These results, however, came during the boom of the 1920s, the kind of climate in which even Durant had made money. The Depression provided the acid test for Sloan's methods. Not until 1939 did sales return to the 1929 level; in 1932, they fell to less than a third of the 1929 figures. GM nevertheless made a profit and paid a dividend every year because, as Sloan said, "We had learned to react quickly" to a changing market and adjust production, employment, and inventories immediately "through [our] system of financial and operating controls." Through depression and war, and on into an era of increased government presence in its affairs, Sloan's organization kept plowing ahead, "making money and not just making motor cars." After Sloan, the GM presidency passed to a series of men whose names few of the public ever knew and fewer still can remember. In this anonymity Sloan no doubt saw affirmation of his ideals, for he thought the organization more important than any one man. Reflecting on his life's work, he observed that "it is imperative for the health of the organization that it always tends to rise above subjectivity." He had perhaps earned the right to boast that the structure he had built "was designed to be an objective organization, [not] the type that gets lost in the subjectivity of personalities," though time has cast doubt on its wisdom.

To Sloan himself, perhaps the ultimate proof of his achievement lay in the fact that the organization continued to thrive for many years after he departed. To those who study American business, however, the ultimate validation of Sloan's principles, particularly those that apply to inventory control and focus on ROI, appears in their widespread application (even as GM itself has lost sight of them) by firms such as Dell that have grown into major competitors in the globalized economy of the twenty-first century.

Sloan thought himself a creative man, as many of his gray-flannel- and double-knit-leisure-suited successors in business bureaucracies have since thought themselves. Designing something as ephemeral as an organization or, worse yet, some minuscule part for an assembly-line-produced gewgaw may seem poor stuff in a creative tradition that included such handcrafted gems as the ax handle and the clipper ship. Sloan, however, faced a problem that to his mind taxed human creativity to the utmost: how to enlist for GM's benefit the same sustained, driving effort, rooted in self-interest and self-respect, that people gave their own businesses. That he succeeded in the face of the company's massive bureaucratic structure, diffuse absentee ownership, and minute sub-division of tasks, he regarded as a creative triumph: the organization chart as work of art. Whatever one thinks of the consequences, Sloan and others like him succeeded where Schumpeter thought they would fail.

Until the last third of the twentieth century, the most successful modern American corporations seemed to have bureaucratized the entrepreneurial function without destroying it. Time has recently shown, however, that although individual companies may devise strategies and structures that keep the Schumpeterian menace at bay, like rust it never sleeps. Bureaucratic arteriosclerosis lurks ready to beset the smug, the unwary, the lazy, the complacent, as the histories of firms such as Sears, IBM, Xerox, Chrysler, Kmart, and many others have shown. Time also showed that much of the vaunted American efficiency of Sloan's time rested on an absence of lean, mean competition that, when it arrived from Germany, Japan, and elsewhere, exposed even GM as tethered to the unwieldy accretions of its past. Bonuses once awarded for meritorious performance had become entitlements paid whether or not the company made a profit; successful, innovative executives who broke the mold of the GM stereo-type faced an uphill struggle and an uncertain future. For example, John Z. Delorean revived the Pontiac (from near oblivion to number three in the industry by 1964) and Chevrolet (first brand ever to sell 3 million vehicles in one year, 1972) Divisions in the 1960s and 1970s. However, as the GM Heritage Center biography puts it, "DeLorean refused to conform to the GM leadership idea of how a highly-paid executive should look and behave. . . . [H]e fancied himself part of the jet-set, hanging out with Hollywood celebrities." In 1973, he resigned in frustration.

Sloan died in 1966 and thus did not live to see the atrophy that hobbled his once supple organization, even as younger firms demonstrated the timeless vitality of his organizational principles. Sloan, it seems, tried to play his role so that when it ended and he slipped through the curtains, no one ever again would occupy center stage. Happily, he did not entirely succeed, as the society that produced such enterprising individualists as Carnegie and Ford continued to produce them, including some such as Kroc, Walton, and Dell who started from scratch, not in the ranks of anonymous bureaucracies. Even in those faceless structures, however, stars rise now and again to brighten the landscape. We need organizations that produce, and they doubtless require organization men to run them, but it would be a dull firmament that had no stars. Fortunately, novas still burst forth now and again, Henry Ford's grandson one of them.

Chapter 9

Avatar of the Worldwide Car

HENRY FORD II

The old order passes: Henry and Clara Ford with grandson Henry Ford II at Greenfield Village, 1946

Speaking of his generation, the generation that fought the Civil War, Justice Oliver Wendell Holmes remarked, "Through our great good fortune, in our youth, our hearts were touched with fire." In Holmes and many of his contemporaries, the flame of individualism, a legacy of generations of Americans before them, burned brightly; for them the vehicle of progress remained, as always, individuals.

A bold faith that, and, perhaps excepting a trust in some supreme, benevolent power, the most noble faith that humankind can embrace. It became a difficult creed to sustain in an era when proliferating bureaucracies subordinated personality to the collective needs of the nation-state and the giant corporation, engines that seemed to develop purposes and directions of their own. Individualism survived, nevertheless, as a legend protected by the hothouse climate of national power, magnified to near-omnipotence by the (real or imagined) American rescue of the Allied cause in World War I, and by the national prosperity that endured until 1929.

The hearts of my generation, in our youth, were touched with cold, the cold of fears that lapped over us in waves. First, the fear of want and hunger permeated the Great Depression, haunting not only those who had no work today, but also those whose jobs might vanish tomorrow. The anguish and despair with which our parents contemplated the possibility that the American system had broken down beyond repair communicated itself subtly to my generation, which knew nothing of the Depression's causes and all too much about its effects.

Then came the terror of Pearl Harbor and the months that followed. Looking back, it seems silly that we ever imagined that Japan and Germany, with most of the rest of the world arrayed against them, could possibly win the war. But I remember when we expected Japanese invaders on the Pacific Coast and when torpedoed oil tankers burned within sight of the Atlantic shore. I remember the anguish of the defeats at Bataan and Corregidor in the Philippines, and the exultation of the victories at Guadalcanal and El Alamein. For a time, at least, it seemed we might lose the fight, the men who went off to it (including my father, two uncles, several cousins—virtually every male member of my family between 18 and 45), and with them, our whole way of life.

Peace brought further traumas: the fear of lapsing back into the Depression; the emergence of the powerful, implacable, treacherous Soviet enemy; and the dread, literally, to end all dreads, the looming certainty of atomic holocaust. All in all, it didn't look too good for humankind. As for the individual's power to avert these cosmic disasters, why, it seemed to shrink with each tiding. Big Problems demanded Big Antidotes that only Big Government could supply: for depressions, the Full Employment Act of 1946; for the Russian bomb, bigger bombs and plenty of 'em; for segregationist Arkansas and its governor Orval Faubus, the 101st Airborne Division; for the Cold War, the Berlin Airlift, the Marshall Plan, "Containment," NATO, SEATO, "Brinksmanship." I had a firsthand experience with the last, a real taste of anomie incarnate. In 1958, my unit of the 82nd Airborne Division got briefed for an assault (ultimately aborted) on Lebanon, a place few of us had heard of and none of us cared about. "Any questions?" ended the battery commander, jabbing his swagger stick into the sand table. "Sir," asked one "crack trooper" (as *Time* invariably called us), "who the hell is the enemy?" "Never mind that," came the reply. "That's not your problem. We'll tell you who to kill." Ten years later, in college, it dawned on me that he didn't know the answer any more than we did.

For me, college darkened the whole prospect. Outside the ivied walls there came Cuba, and then Vietnam. Inside I met a Greek chorus of mandarins and savants who proclaimed (with footnotes) the inevitable rise of the impersonal mass in some form or other, and the ensuing decline of the individual, the certainty of whose downfall was exceeded only by his inherent bestiality. Catechized by *Canticle for Liebowitz;* plowed under on *Animal Farm;* enshrouded in *Darkness at Noon;* abused by *The Power Elite;* lost in *The Lonely Crowd;* blown away by those titanic trumpeters of Götterdämmerung—Hegel, Marx, Weber, and Schumpeter—I moved on to graduate school, where I pondered the "Invisible Hand" of Adam Smith and the *Visible Hand* of Al Chandler, both these hands indiscriminately turning Matthew Josephson's *Robber Barons* and Alan Nevins's "Industrial Statesmen" into grist for the mills that churned out William Whyte's *Organization Man* as River Rouge turned out Model Ts.

"Man," as Mick Jagger said, "what a mess. I was shattered." My grandmother's assurance that I and everyone else had come into the world trailing clouds of glory crumbled under the massed assault of gloom and doom. True, life went on, and true, for me it got better—fellowships, friends, and lovely Baltimore evenings at Memorial Stadium watching the Orioles play. The first years in graduate school seemed to me the best I had ever known, and the seedtime of friendships that would last (and have lasted) a lifetime. Listening to my colleagues discourse on the evils of the present system and the beauties of the socialist nirvana to come, and watching the unfolding Nixon obscenity, the spreading inferno in Vietnam, and the burning of Baltimore's inner city, leached away most of my optimism.

For a time I considered self-exile to England, where eccentricity, if not individualism still seemed cherished, or withdrawal into professorial sanctuary, where romanticizing the past could anesthetize the grim present. Poverty, however, precluded flight to England, and the vibrant presentism of the University of Michigan's undergraduates cut off retreat to the rear. Gradually, optimism returned, fed by calmer counsel, such as cartoonist Walt Kelly's Albert the Alligator, telling his swamp friends, "Man can't live his whole life worrying about ten seconds of boom and whango," and Pogo Possum, pulling up in flight from the cry, "Run for the hills; the dam is bust!" to ask, "Wait a minute; is the swamp even *got* a dam?" I also found comic relief in memories of unsophisticated but shrewd former colleagues, such as a picturesque railroad conductor named "Dirty Neck" Burke, who heard me fretting about the menace of the Congo with its feuding chieftains, Kasavubu and Lumumba. "I'll worry about them guys," observed Burke (who never read a pundit such as Walter Lippmann unless he appeared in *Racing Form*), "when I hear they can swim five thousand miles."

Life isn't that simple, of course, nor as simple as the "Domino Theory," "I have in my hand a list of Communists . . . ," "We gave China away," "Make the World Safe for Democracy," or "Bring 'Em On," catchy slogans used by rabble-rousers, paranoids, and bullies such as Senator Joe McCarthy to spread fear, like fungus, among us. But individuals and simple slogans, more than arcane theorizing, *have* galvanized mass movements. Consider, for instance, the historic impact of "Christ is risen!"; "There is but one God and his name is Allah!"; "Workers of the world, unite. You have nothing to lose but your chains!"; and in my own lifetime: "Ein Reich! Ein Volk! Ein

Fuehrer!"; "Never Again!"; "We shall overcome"; "Hell no, we won't go!"; "Four More Years!"; and "Iraq Has Weapons of Mass Destruction!" (Wait a minute, is the swamp even *got* a dam?)

I myself found more motivation in optimism than in paranoia. Studying history as an adult, I concluded that the epitaph for the individual bawled so widely in my formative years, had come prematurely. He, and now increasingly she, still lived, hopeful and influential. Even among giant corporations, those bastions of depersonalization whose bureaucratization of the entrepreneur's function Joseph Schumpeter diagnosed as capitalism's fatal disease, idiosyncrasy still raised its warty head now and then, and personality sometimes prevailed. Indeed, in the ability of the occasional strong character to convert bureaucracy to an instrument of his personal will, capitalism finds, for better or worse, a source of regeneration. Numerous examples come to mind, and some of them—Thomas Watson's IBM, Sol Linowitz's Xerox, Edwin Land's Polaroid, Michael Dell's Dell Computer, Ray Kroc's McDonald's, Sam Walton's Walmart, Steve Jobs's Apple—have had a dynamic impact on American society and its economy. Moreover, each of them grew and prospered in the face of preexisting, efficient, bureaucratized competitors.

The story of Henry Ford II's ability to reshape the Ford Motor Company to embody his own vision presents an outstanding such case in the history of American business. Not just large, Ford by any standards merits the term "enormous." Consistently one of the largest manufacturing firms in the world in the twentieth and twenty-first centuries, Ford in 1977 ranked third among U.S. industrial corporations in sales ($38 billion), fourth in assets ($19 billion) and net profits ($1.7 billion), eighth in 2005 with $172 billion in sales, and eighth again in 2009 with $118 billion (twice the sales of Microsoft and three times those of Apple). Ford operates a global manufacturing, assembly, and marketing empire that obviously could not function without a complex managerial bureaucracy to coordinate its intricate operations.

If ever a firm's structure presented an insuperable obstacle to individual domination, Ford would seem a prime candidate. In fact, the contrary situation has prevailed through most of the company's history. Despite the obviously necessary delegation of much authority to subordinates, through the 1960s and 1970s industry observers and company employees, from vice presidents in Dearborn to the plant manager in Upper Hutt, New Zealand, knew that Chairman Henry ran the company, just as they knew in 2005 that Bill Ford held the reins. Henry Ford II knew his own mind and power and never hesitated to interpose both, even against the advice of his managers, their staffs, and the sophisticated network of computers the company used constantly. He proved himself willing, more than once, to bring a Lincolnesque ending ("Seven ayes, one nay; the nay has it") to executive committee meetings by inquiring, "Whose name is on the building?"

For more than 30 years, Ford dominated the company's affairs, not only in broad policy making, but also at lower organizational levels, frequently intervening in personnel decisions down to the third level of management. The company's policy and products thus reflected Ford's personal view of business's social responsibilities to the community, his philosophy of international trade, and his opinion on the kinds of cars the public would buy. Ford served as the first chairman of the National Alliance of Businessmen, which tried to find industrial jobs for the hard-core unemployed, and he prodded his company to set an example in this area for all American industry. His cash, willpower, and persuasiveness powered the Detroit renewal effort. His company throve in the European market and probed for profitable openings in the underdeveloped world using structures and tactics developed from studies that he personally instigated and approved. No new model entered the Ford line without his personal imprimatur. He once gave direct orders to Ford Division General Manager Donald Frey to abandon plans for a seven-passenger limousine, bypassing the three officers between himself and Frey on the organization chart. As Arjay Miller, one of a legion of Ford Motor Company ex-presidents, once observed, "The first thing you have to understand about the company is that Henry Ford is the boss. . . . He was always the boss from the first day I came in [1946], and he always will be the boss until he decides to retire."

In addition to running his company, Ford lived a life of conspicuous celebrity. Opinionated, outspoken, leading a pyrotechnic personal life, he seldom stayed out of the news for long. He was the only American businessman of his time whose name recurred on "10 best-known American" lists and other such gauges of notoriety, and the only head of a *Fortune* "Top 500" firm that most Americans could identify. His friends included not only the moguls of the automotive world in the United States and abroad, but also race-car drivers, beautiful women, and a New York City police reporter. He had close ties with three of America's most prominent black leaders: Whitney Young of the Urban League, whose father got a $300-a-month job as an electrical engineer from the original Henry Ford at a time when few blacks could find such jobs anywhere; Carl Stokes, former mayor of Cleveland, ex-assembly line worker; and Coleman Young, mayor of Detroit, partner with Ford in the city's resurgence, and former organizer for the United Auto Workers during the union's most violent period of confrontation with Henry's grandfather and his "Enforcer," Harry Bennett.

Chairman Henry's achievements loom even larger in light of the circumstances in which his leadership of the company began. In the fall of 1945, when Henry II's mother and grandmother joined forces with him to persuade his legendary grandfather to turn over the reins, the Ford Motor Company was sliding rapidly down the razor blade of business life. It seemed only a matter of time—and not much time at that—until the Ford name joined the long list of family firms that passed from the American business scene as a result of a secession crisis. Bankruptcy or, more likely, sale to a competitor seemed inevitable.

Ford didn't suffer from an inability to make cars—enough old hands like Meade Bricker remained to keep the line going—or sell them—you could sell anything in the car-starved, cash-flush market of postwar America—but rather from not knowing what it cost to make them. In fact, no one at Ford knew what it cost to do anything, or even whether the company's massive wartime government contracts had yielded a profit or loss.

The company had no cost-accounting capability whatever. Three decades before, as Model T production rose and unit costs fell, Charlie Sorenson had shown Henry I his calculations that demonstrated economies of scale. "That's enough, Charlie," said Ford. "Don't show me any more figures; I've got the smell of the thing now." Thereafter, Ford concentrated on design and "running full" in the Carnegie manner. He despised accounting (a seedy offshoot of the banking conspiracy), wouldn't use accountants, and wouldn't let anyone else bring them in either. Once while Henry was out of town, his son Edsel authorized construction of a new office building with the fourth floor set aside for an accounting department. When Henry returned and heard the news, he left without comment but sent a nocturnal raiding party that cleared the floor of the offending desks, telephones, and office machinery. Next morning Ford told his son, "Edsel, if you really need more [office] room, you'll find plenty of it on the fourth floor." For the old man, dividing the number of cars produced into the year's total expenditures served as cost accounting enough; consequently, in 1945, the firm ran the same way as had the pre-Carnegie iron trade, as a "lump business."

For a long time, it didn't matter; as long as new plants and bank balances kept going up, income obviously exceeded expenses. Plenty of great fortunes had been made—by English textile manufacturers and by the early du Ponts, for example—in blissful ignorance of costs. Henry Ford's was not the first, though surely the greatest and probably the last. When the time arrived—during the declining market of 1920 and thereafter—when such information became important, the elder Ford simply didn't care. Like his friend Edison, money per se neither intrigued nor motivated him. In 1945, moreover, the Ford Motor Company, despite its size, remained a family-owned firm, with no debts to pay and no outside stockholders to hold management accountable. ("The good thing about going public," a Seattle entrepreneur once told me, "is that you get stockholders' money. The bad thing is you get stockholders.")

In 1945, Ford Motor Company also had not a whisper of market forecasting ability. Old Henry didn't believe much in statistics and scoffed outright at the notion that past data could indicate future truth: he thought the idea a hoax on the face of it. (It's tough for me, who listened to Robert McNamara's "body counts" and the projections he made from them during the Vietnam War, not to warm to the old codger on that one.) Besides, if someone had somehow divined accurate cost data and market predictions, the company couldn't have used them. Above the shop floor, the lines of authority disappeared into a tangle of untitled executives with no clear-cut responsibilities and with positions often obtained not by ability, but from personal relationships with Harry Bennett.

Ford's free-form arrangements worked fine in the halcyon days of the Model T, but they failed to withstand the competitive onslaught of GM, kept in constant fighting trim by Sloan's statistical guidelines. In Ford's increasing chaos of the 1930s and 1940s, only the company's enormous cash reserves, the residual goodwill of dealers, and the loyalty of die-hard customers (many of them attached to the V-8, which Chevrolet didn't offer until 1955) kept the firm afloat until young Henry arrived at the top. The steady decline of the company's bank balance and its fading third place in sales provided graphic evidence of past decay and grim omens for the future.

Confronting this mess, 28-year-old Henry Ford II had paper credentials that one could only charitably have called so much as modest. From a childhood spent playing with locomotives and automobiles on his grandfather's estate, he had gone on to an undistinguished academic career at private schools and at Yale. In college, he switched from engineering to sociology when the former proved "too tough," but he failed to graduate even from that curriculum because he got caught turning in a custom-written term paper. Back in Dearborn, he went to work for the company, learning the business as a "grease monkey in the experimental garage and a checker in the dynamometer room." In 1941, he entered the navy, where he filled inconsequential stateside posts.

When his father Edsel died in 1943, the navy released him to return to the company, where, like almost everyone else in the Ford executive ranks, he had no defined duties or authority. Between his return in 1943 and his assumption of the presidency in 1945, Ford later described himself as "green and searching for answers." He found some, mostly bad: the company had foundered, and Bennett would have to go before anyone could do much about it. He did, however, discover one person he could trust, John Bugas, a former FBI agent and Ford's head of government relations. Bugas helped him find a few more. But altogether they numbered too small a crew to try to overhaul such a leaking hulk.

Henry II did have certain other intangible assets, as he soon proved. He had his heritage in the automobile business; he had grown up in it and had never considered any other career. Detroit, where folks often call car building "a disease, not a profession," doesn't think any amount of technical skill or bureaucratic finesse will avail without a dose of gasoline in the blood, and this young Henry certainly had. He also had a goal—perhaps a vision would better describe it under the circumstances—of returning his company to its former preeminent position in the industry, while keeping it, like Du Pont, a family firm. He showed the ability to assess realistically his own capacities, which included a talent for assuming and exercising authority surprising in someone with no previous managerial experience except as undergraduate manager of the Yale crew. He also radiated a strong personal charisma that came in handy when recruiting a new team.

As soon as young Henry became president, he fired Harry Bennett and his cronies. To begin the salvage process, he rounded up what trustworthy old hands he could find at Ford. Then he recruited public relations specialist Earl Newsom and public opinion pollster Elmo Roper to begin repairing the company's image, tarnished by years of anti-Semitism and antiunion thuggery. But none of these could tackle the most pressing problem: installing a cost-accounting system, locating the hemorrhages, and applying tourniquets before the company bled to death. Something had to happen in a hurry, for the company lost $10 million a month through the first half of 1946. And always, across town, lurked the intimidating presence of GM—rich, efficient, powerful, capable of swallowing the market if Ford should falter.

In this menacing competitor, however, Ford found the instrument of his company's resurrection in the person of Ernest R. Breech, president of Bendix Aviation, a GM subsidiary. Bright, ambitious, thoroughly versed in the GM method, Breech had found himself shunted from the GM fast track onto the Bendix siding by, ironically enough, ex-Ford man William Knudsen, who (according to Sloan) thought Breech a "financial man," not a "car man." It took several visits and a liberal application of the Ford charm to lure Breech from his perch on a high branch of the GM corporate tree, but in the end, he succumbed. His task—restoring order and doing so profitably—required so thoroughgoing a reorganization as to nearly undo him, as Breech admitted to his biographer. Driving to work one morning in 1946, a month after he took the job, he felt suddenly struck by the magnitude of the shambles and pulled off the road to gather his wits: "For the first time in my life I was overwhelmed.

Not afraid, but very disturbed. Our problem seemed almost insuperable. Things were in a mess. It would take years to get them under control." More specifically, he diagnosed Ford's ills as "rundown plants, obsolete products, almost nonexistent financial control, an inadequate engineering staff, and just sufficient cash [flow] to meet daily [needs]." (He might have added to the list the worst labor relations in the industry and a poor public image.)

Breech's prescription approximated what one would have expected from a GM manager (and, not coincidentally, included a list of the contributions to American industry made by several of the principal characters in this book):

> What we [needed] was precisely what . . . any firm [needs] to be competitive . . . above all . . . competent management, flexible and big enough to respond swiftly to changing market conditions [Sloan, Pierre du-Pont]; research and engineering adequate to meet . . . modern product competition [Edison, Whitney]; plants and machinery efficient enough to compete with the best . . . [Henry Ford I, Carnegie]; and a financial control system which supplies some forecasting [Sloan], that keeps operations efficient, and is geared to produce peak profits [Du Pont].

Few Ford employees' experience had prepared them to administer (or swallow easily) this massive dose, so Breech raided the ranks of his former employer. GM, with as much depth at every position as the Michigan football team down the road in Ann Arbor, had talent to waste and wasted plenty of it. Dangling the prospect of meaningful responsibilities and swift promotion, Breech lured hundreds of supervisors from GM to Ford. Not all of them worked out, but many had the time of their lives. One of them subsequently observed that he "had more downright fun and progressed further in his first six months with Ford than he had in 16 years" with a GM division.

Ford himself contributed to the recruiting program, reversing a longstanding company policy of not recruiting college graduates (another of old Henry's fetishes translated into company policy). He also hired the so-called Whiz Kids, a group of 10 former air force statistical analysts who sold themselves as a package in the postwar job market. The Whiz Kids included Tex Thornton, who later put together the Litton Industries conglomerate; Arjay Miller (later dean of Stanford's business school); Robert McNamara (John Kennedy's secretary of defense), who rose to the presidency of Ford Motors; and J. Edward Lundy, who became a Ford executive vice president of finance.

The galaxy of new talent encountered reactions ranging from entrenched resistance to cooperative bewilderment at the new methods. When they asked the controller's office for financial projections for six months ahead, they might as well have asked for a projection of lunar eclipses. Willing but unable, the controller replied, as the Pentagon apparently replied to Secretary of Defense McNamara's demands for body count data 20 years later, "What do you want them to be?" Gradually, however, the new management turned the company around. Henry Ford II made peace with the labor unions; Newsom rebuilt the company's public image. Breech's system analyzed costs, and the company assaulted them by revamping and expanding its obsolete plant, spending money with a dedication Carnegie would have relished—$4 billion between 1945 and 1962 redesigning and reengineering the basic Ford, as well as adding new models to broaden the base of competition.

By the end of 1946, Ford had started making money and went on to make more, a total of $5.5 billion during Breech's tenure, which lasted until 1960. GM remained far ahead in total sales, but Ford regained second position and even managed to outsell Chevrolet once in a while. Mistakes happened along the way, some of them—such as the Edsel, which chewed up two or three hundred million dollars—humdingers. The GM decentralized, divisional structure proved inappropriate at Ford and subsequently got revamped into a functional arrangement—product development, manufacturing, and marketing. On the whole, however, Breech did everything asked of him. In the eyes of many, he literally saved the company. One observer declared:

> When the history of the Ford Motor Company is finally written, it should be noted in bold type that Ford was saved from imminent oblivion or at least a complete change of ownership by Mr. Ernest R. Breech. . . . In my opinion this rescue operation under forced draft while in competition with the most successful company in the world, ranks with Alfred Sloan's structuring [of] GM as the outstanding corporate achievement of the 20th century.

Earl Newsom put it more succinctly, "There would be no Ford Motor Company today if it hadn't been for Ernie Breech."

No one, of course, is indispensable, not even Breech. The second Henry nevertheless owed him a great deal, which he acknowledged in print, salary, stock options, and business deals that made Breech a millionaire many times over, and by naming a Ford ore ship after him. Breech left Ford in 1960 (of his own free will, he and Henry claimed; forced out, according to Detroit's underground telegraph) and went on to a successful career reorganizing TWA while grappling with Howard Hughes, a tycoon who made Henry Ford II look like St. Francis of Assisi.

In 1960, with his company prospering, solidly organized, and well stocked with executives capable of assuming control, Henry Ford II might well have retreated from the killing regimen demanded of active automobile executives. (Skeptics should spend a week in the Ford World Headquarters parking lot, logging people in and out. Don't forget to show up on Saturday and Sunday; the automobile industry pays its executives well, but from those to whom much is given, much is expected.) He could have turned to many other pursuits instead: avuncular board chairman, philanthropist, art collector, jet-set playboy, adviser to presidents, and sponsor of urban redevelopment, for all but the first of which he demonstrated a proclivity. In fact, he took the opposite course, reclaiming the reins from his hired help and taking firm hold of the company's operations.

Ford regarded the Breech years as more than a period of renaissance for his company; in effect, he himself accepted them as a period of apprenticeship in its management. By 1960, he had learned enough. "I've graduated, Ernie," he reportedly told Breech, who commented at the time, "Henry doesn't need me anymore." Ford, no ball of fire in college ("I was flunking engineering," he remembered, "and they said sociology was easy so I transferred, but I flunked that too"), became an apt pupil in Dearborn. "He listened," Breech said, "he took advice, and he learned. He may not have been a great student at Yale, but he certainly was a great student of how to become an executive and he became one."

After taking over, Ford ran the company with an eye-catching flamboyance, personally making decisions about products and people in a manner sometimes arbitrary, capricious, or even cruel, but with a haste that often left competitors in the dust. Ford made and unmade top executives with lightning speed. Some—Miller, McNamara—left with their shields; others—Jack Reith, Bunkie Knudsen, Lee Iacocca—departed upon them. Ford may have acted out of vanity: Knudsen and Iacocca projected strong images of their own, whereas J. Edward Lundy, who spoke with a powerful voice inside the organization but remained a nonentity to the public, survived more than 30 years. Or he may simply have protected the family position at the top while his son Edsel, born in 1949, learned the business. (His appointment in 1978 of his younger brother, William Clay Ford, as prince regent supported the family-continuity hypothesis.)

Whatever his reasons, Chairman Henry's personnel policies, although producing casualties and tension in the ranks, created enticing possibilities for advancement as well. Ford executives down the line often reflected the attitude of junior British navy officers in the days of sail, who used to drink to "long, bloody wars; oceans of gore; promotions galore." As one Ford aspirant told me:

> The exciting thing about this company is that if you come up with an idea, no matter how big, you know the money can be found, and you know who the man is that has to be convinced. In a situation like that you can dream any kind of dream. At GM, it's hopeless. Everything has to be passed up the line through a dozen committees, but the credit doesn't pass back down.

Mavericks did actually seem to survive more often at Ford than its competitors. GM produced few if any Iacoccas, brazenly hustling the boss with bright ideas such as the Mustang. Several emerged at Ford, including William Bourke, who vaulted from Ford Asia-Pacific to Ford of Europe to a Dearborn vice presidency in five years.

Ford's decisive vote on which cars to make could lead to mistakes, as the Edsel undeniably proved, but could also expedite a success such as the Mustang, which leapt from drawing board to showroom to an insurmountable sales lead before GM could get its committees together to mount a competitor. Henry claimed to have a feel for what the American public would buy (the ultimate attribute of a consummate "car man") and a string of winners—Falcon, Mustang, Maverick, Pinto, Cougar, Capri, Granada, Fiesta, Fairmont—suggests he often did. The company had particular success with cars and trucks that expressed individualistic flair, whereas the great mass market for conservative sedans remained Chevrolet's happiest hunting ground, perhaps because buyers gravitated to the company that reflected their own self-image. Perhaps the very quirks of Henry Ford II's personality, like those of his grandfather before him, by resonating with the traditional American admiration for stubborn independence, became salable commodities.

Certainly his penchant for speed and motor racing, another inherited trait and a widespread American enthusiasm, contributed to strategies that widened the market for Ford automobiles. The V-8 engine had long made Fords top dog in American stock car racing, a position usurped after the war by the Hudson Hornet and others. Ford didn't like losing, and he responded to Lee Iacocca's pitch that racing could sell cars. In the 1960s, Ford fielded factory teams in several racing categories, and in partnership with English engineer Keith Duckworth developed engines (including the Cosworth) that won at Indianapolis and on the European Grand Prix circuit.

An inveterate reader of racing magazines, Henry knew that the Daytona Five Hundred and the Twenty-Four Hours of Le Mans represented the top of the greasy pole in American stock car and European road racing respectively. He wanted to win both and told his engineers to design equipment that would. So they did that. In 1963, Fords took the first five places at Daytona. Le Mans came harder, but failures in 1964 and 1965 preceded four successive wins that gave the company enormous publicity and the boss the chance to hold court in the grand marshal's box, posing for pictures in a Ford jacket and holding the trophy aloft. Having won the big prizes, Ford withdrew to a lower profile, but Ford engines in Wolf-Fords, Coyote-Fords, Lotus-Fords, and other hybrids continued to win a lot of races around the world through technical collaboration between the company and racing-car designers.

The grandson with his own racing car: Henry Ford II squints into the Le Mans glare, June 1967

Less spectacular, but equally influential in the long run, Chairman Henry played a major role in revamping the company's overseas operations into their current multinational structure. Throughout the 1950s, and increasingly after 1960, the firm's international strategies reflected Henry's philosophy of global economics. Ford Motor Company had earned its first export dollar in 1903 and remained active outside the United States thereafter. The complex evolution of the company's overseas facilities continued throughout the twentieth century. By 1960, three companies, Ford of Canada (which owned subsidiaries in the British Commonwealth countries outside Great Britain itself), Ford of England, and Ford of Germany, existed as self-sufficient, essentially autonomous divisions, each producing its own line of cars, occasionally drawing on Dearborn for technological assistance, and submitting, sometimes reluctantly, to its coordination of export markets outside the three companies' defined domains. International sales had historically contributed an important share of the company's total business: 9 percent (by units sold), 1911–20; 12 percent, 1921–30; and 24 percent in each succeeding decade through 1960, as well as a significant share of its profits—20 percent in 1962, for example.

Despite this record, Ford judged his company's international structure inadequate for the future. It consisted, in his words, of "a collection of individual national organizations." Efficient enough for their own bailiwicks, such structures had horizons too limited to deal with "the day [not] far off when organizations even of the scope of North America and Europe will prove too limiting." Furthermore, the national companies' facilities, concentrated in the industrialized countries of the world, could not hope to penetrate the potential markets of the underdeveloped world, where the people, "deeply committed to fast industrialization," demanded local manufacture or assembly as a prerequisite for doing business. "Whether we like it or not," Ford declared in 1961, "Africa, Latin America, and Asia are going all-out into the industrial age." In these statements and others, Ford revealed himself as not a parochial American industrialist, but as an internationalist who saw the whole world as a potential market for Ford products. Widely traveled in the service of the company (he made trips to Europe in 1948 and 1952, and frequently thereafter traveled around the world to the company's facilities), he broadened his perspective as an alternate delegate to the United Nations in the early 1950s. Robert McNamara, speaking not only of his experiences with Ford at the company but also as head of the World Bank, declared, "There's no doubt that he's one of the best informed businessmen in the U.S. on the rest of the world."

Like his grandfather's, Ford's worldview envisioned a global market for Ford vehicles: not a market in which American manufacturers could plunder less fortunate peoples, but rather one in which American industry stood to benefit from worldwide industrial prosperity. In the 1920s, the elder Ford had said, "We ought to wish for every nation as large a degree of self-support as possible. Instead of wishing to keep them dependent upon us for what we manufacture, we should wish them to learn to manufacture themselves and build up a solidly founded civilization." Forty years later, his grandson declared, "If we want to share in those [emerging] markets, rich and vast as they will someday surely be . . . we [will] have to go in with our tools and know-how and help them get the things they want."

In a statement as rare among American industrialists of the time as his opposition to the Vietnam War, he had already publicly advocated free trade in an industrializing world:

> I believe this country should step forth boldly and lead the world toward freer trade. . . . We need competition the world over to keep us on our toes and sharpen our wits. [The truth of this statement Toyota, Volkswagen, and others soon drove home.] The keener the competition, the better it will be for us. . . . People cannot keep on buying from us unless we buy from them, and unless international trade can go on, our business will stagnate here at home. . . . Competition is the keen cutting edge of business, always shaving away at costs.

In the 1960s, Ford transformed the structure of his overseas affiliates according to his philosophy by creating local manufacturing facilities in many countries. In implementing these and other plans for global organizations, the company benefited from steps already taken by its chairman, who foresaw globalization before the term found common usage. In 1948, Ford II had instructed his overseas subsidiaries to sell worldwide in any market they could find. During the 1950s, he began buying up the affiliates' stock, much of which the company had sold to local investors during the 1920s. By 1962, the parent company owned 75 percent of Ford of Canada, 99 percent of Ford of Germany, and 100 percent of Ford of England. In 1961, dead end with secure control of the subsidiaries, he moved further toward an integrated international structure, stepping up overseas investment so that for the first time it exceeded domestic capital expenditure. He informed his subordinates that "[T]o further the growth of our world-wide operations, each purchasing activity of the company or an affiliated company should consider . . . sources . . . not only in its country but also . . . in other countries." To break down local resistance to the new policies, Ford dispatched American executives to key posts overseas. In 1962, for example, Americans headed 8 of the 12 European sales, assembly, and manufacturing companies. Service abroad soon became dead end at many companies, but a prerequisite to a Ford management career; by the 1980s, no one reached the Ford upper echelons without foreign experience. In the years since, many foreign nationals have reached the top executive ranks at Ford World Headquarters in Michigan, including two who rose to CEO.

In Europe, Ford of England and Ford of Germany made money and gave Ford Motor a foot in each of the European free-trade camps, the Common Market and the European Free Trade Association (EFTA). Even so, Ford found this arrangement wasteful and inadequate, because each subsidiary company produced a range of vehicles that not only duplicated and competed with one another, but also used no common parts. Chairman Henry ordered the creation of Ford of Europe to integrate the European companies into a single unit, producing a single line of cars assembled from common parts flowing from all over the region and, in time, from all over the world. "Implicit in this change," he said,

> was a growing recognition that the entire company needed to think more and more in world-wide terms and that the foreign subsidiaries no longer

could be thought of as a collection of individual national organizations. This applied particularly in Europe where eventual expansion of the Common Market seemed certain to require a strongly integrated approach.

In the years after 1967, Ford of Europe struggled toward the vexingly difficult goal of a product line built of internationally interchangeable parts. In doing so, it adhered to the original plan's assumptions that the European vehicle market would expand, the Common Market would survive and incorporate Britain and the rest of EFTA, and European consumers (and eventually consumers worldwide) would accept cars that had no local national identity. Manufacturing, at the same time, became more decentralized with the construction of single-product factories such as a transmission plant in Bordeaux, France, and an engine plant in Taubate, Brazil. The output of these works flowed to a network of assembly plants in Europe, Asia, Latin America, the United States, and elsewhere. By supplying major components for the entire product line, this system fulfilled Ford's contention that "the entire web of components and end products [will] become increasingly multi-national."

Of course, such a complex restructuring of going concerns met (and still meets) many obstacles, such as national pride, a dogged persistence of local consumer idiosyncrasies, the integration of metric and English systems of measurement, shortages of components, labor disputes, and product defects. The company persevered with its original plan, however, and for a time maintained its position, first achieved in 1965, of leading the world in sales by U.S. companies outside North America.

Ford's gamble on the Common Market's viability and Britain's entry into it paid big dividends. At a time when many American firms, frightened by the decaying British economy or the specter of its semi-socialist government, left the United Kingdom or curtailed operations there, Ford not only stayed, but poured in tens of millions of dollars in additional investment. The resulting capacity increased the company's ability to compete in the British market and provided a source for components priced in (then) cheap pounds, many of which went into cars sold for ever-dearer Deutschmarks, guilders, and other appreciating continental currencies until the Euro supplanted them.

In an equally bold move, Ford decided that Spanish political stability would survive its dictator Generalissimo Franco's death and invested billions of dollars there. The company in effect bet that Spain's relatively low labor costs, its undeveloped but potentially large domestic market, and its probable entry into the Common Market would recoup the investment. Ford gambled that thousands of Spaniards would abandon their "casual Mediterranean lifestyle" to toil on the assembly line and that Spanish entrepreneurs would set up supplier industries and dealerships. Spaniards repaid the company's investment with production and profits, and they feted Henry Ford II himself with a tumultuous, flower-strewn welcoming parade when he arrived in Valencia on a tour of inspection. Chairman Henry clearly belonged to that group of Americans cited by French journalist-politician Jean-Jacques Servan-Schreiber in 1968 as the only people who fully comprehended the potential of the Common Market from the beginning.

In the latter part of the twentieth century and into the twenty-first, of course, Ford Motor Company has, like other manufacturers, struggled to create and maintain a viable global structure in an industry where capacity often exceeds demand. That complex story we need not pursue here, and all the better because a detailed account of Ford's search for profit in Asia, a strategy that involves the purchase of Mazda and a joint venture in China, among other things, would fill a volume of its own. No matter the eventual outcome for the Ford Motor Company itself, time has already shown the accuracy of Henry Ford II's vision of the globalized automobile market. Transnational operations expand every year, often articulated by mergers and acquisitions such as Chrysler-Daimler-Benz, Renault-Nissan, and others; the search for a "worldwide car" continues (and sometimes seems on the brink of success, as when one sees the Ford Focus on the streets of Liege and London, Paris and Portland, Beijing and Bombay, Ulaan Bataar and Urumqi, Moscow and Milan, and when advertisements announce the American debut of the Fiesta, the closest an American car company has come to a "universal car" since the Model T). Ford's strategy of "cross-hauling" components from country to country and region to region, facilitated by computerized tracking of components and the intermodal container's reduction of shipping costs, has spread to other industries under the aegis of firms such as Dell and McDonald's.

Henry Ford II had such confidence in himself and his organization that he often said he could compete with the Japanese on our home ground or theirs, a prediction borne out by his successors in 2010 when Ford topped all volume manufacturers, foreign and domestic, in quality rankings. Other American producers must do the same, or foreign firms will someday constitute the bulk of the "American" automobile industry.

Surely Henry Ford II did remarkable things. His determination, and his ability to choose the right person at the right time, brought one of America's venerable manufacturing companies back from the brink of oblivion equipped with techniques of management, production, and sales refined by generations of manufacturers from Whitney to Sloan. By taking personal charge of his revivified firm and dominating its complex bureaucracy, Ford turned a giant corporation into an enormously potent instrument of his own will. By translating his philosophy of international business and economics into company policies, he made the Ford Motor Company a global empire and a genuinely multinational firm in which the Ford family, as he always intended, retained a controlling ownership. In 1980, he retired, turning the company over to his handpicked successors, Phil Caldwell and Don Peterson. Soon the company rode the breakthrough Taurus to unprecedented sales and profits. The year Henry Ford II died, 1987, the Ford Motor Company made more money than GM, a fitting memorial to his resurrection of a pioneer American industrial firm.

Whether the Ford empire will survive, and whether a Ford will head it, time will tell, but history has recently repeated itself. In 2001, William Clay ("Bill") Ford, Henry Ford II's nephew, became CEO. In 2006, a year in which the company lost $12.6 billion, Bill Ford, like his Uncle Henry 60 years before, found himself overmatched and brought in help from outside. Alan Mulally, then president of Boeing Commercial Airplanes, an engineer and a former Sloan Fellow at MIT's Sloan School of Management (a nice bit of historical symmetry, that), took over as CEO in straits as dire as those confronting Ernie Breech in 1946. Though a long hard road stretched ahead, by 2010 Mulally had brought Ford Motor back from the brink, had avoided the last-gasp bankruptcies and federal bailouts that kept Chrysler and GM alive, and had restored the company to modest profitability.

Henry Ford II's career showed that even in an age when business, government, and labor seemed to spawn ever-larger units and power ran to bureaucracies and committees, an individual could still have a crucial impact. Whether this constitutes the vaguely defined "individualism" that Americans nostalgically cherish as part of their heritage depends, I suppose, on one's outlook. Time has, however, already demonstrated his central contention that the automotive market would globalize, and that no company without a global strategy could hope to survive in it.

Certainly the late twentieth century boasted few Henry Ford IIs to serve as the caretakers of a national mythology, but the operative question may not be how many existed, but how many suffice to keep a legend, and the hope it expresses and sustains, alive. Statistically, few nineteenth-century Americans actually made the trek from rags to riches, but Carnegie's spectacular career demonstrated that some did. Millions of Americans, basking in the reflected glow of Andy's well-publicized triumphs, could see the modest improvements in their own lives and those of their children as part of the same glorious and in their minds uniquely American progress toward a brighter world. Learning English, finding a job, puzzling out the labyrinth of a strange city, bringing in the first crop on a homestead farm, buying a home, sending a child off to college—in retrospect these accomplishments may seem modest compared to the opulence squandered in Carnegie castles and Frick mansions. In hindsight, the meanness, squalor, and drudgery of everyday life in industrializing America may make it seem that most ordinary people lived on a dung heap from which a handful of plutocrats quarried diamonds. But for people of the time—most of them, at least—their small successes seemed interlinked with the greater ones, and millions of people who never heard of Herbert Spencer, let alone read him, could feel with Carnegie that all was well because all got better.

Henry Ford II's life told a different but equally compelling story of individual relevance in a bureaucratized world. His life validated for many the legend that a strong enough character could put a stamp on even a giant bureaucracy. Surrounded by flashy cars, escorting beautiful women, able and willing to tell anyone he pleased to go to hell, "the Deuce," as many of his workers called him, incarnated modern American machismo. This independence of spirit many of his workers admired. ("He's a mean son-of-a-bitch, but he's a man," they told me in several languages around the world).

For better or worse, then, Henry Ford II's image—in fairness to him neither entirely accurate nor wholly of his own making—fits the surviving, cherished tradition of personal independence. In that tradition, people keep trying to make it, and some of them, such as Edwin Land, Michael Dell, Ray Kroc, Sam Walton, Bill Gates, Steve Jobs, and others, make it really, really big.

The Philosopher Scientist Edwin Land, with Some Account of His *Doppelgänger*, Steve Jobs

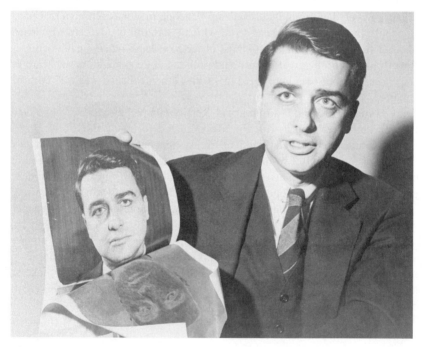

Edwin Land

L ike many an academic, I'm a frustrated novelist. I even wrote a novel once; the manuscript and a set of rejections squat on the shelf in front of me. My problem is plots. I have trouble concocting reasonable ones; mine wander from the pedestrian to the wildly improbable.

Here, for example, I offer one such excursion from the mundane to the implausible. I'll make the hero the son of a prosperous Jewish scrap dealer in Connecticut, thus subtly establishing a background blended of ethnicity, social mobility, and Yankee ingenuity. As a boy my hero, as boys so often do, will grow up in awe of his father. This makes for a banal plot situation, truly, but one that lets me establish motivation by saying that my hero, at an early age, decides to outstrip his father's achievements.

The father, in classic American style, wants to launch his son on a loftier trajectory than his own, so he sends the lad off to a fancy prep school, far removed from the family scrap yard. At prep school, the young fellow becomes something of a prodigy in science, but just to prove he's not one of those weird prodigies, I'll also make him an athlete. In fact, I'll make him a track man, which shows his competitive but nonviolent nature, and that he prefers individual achievement to submersion in team efforts.

After prep school comes college, and since I can send my hero anywhere I want, I'll send him to—O Bastion of Genius, O Citadel of Knowledge—where else?—Harvard.

Now for a twist in the plot. During a school vacation, the boy goes to New York. Wandering through Times Square, as all good tourists must, he finds himself blinded by the glaring lights of the Great White Way. Dazzled by the myriad bulbs flashing away on billboards and theater marquees, and fearful that in his blindness he may get run over by an automobile, our hero decides to find some way to cut down all that glare without diminishing the brilliance of the spectacle that radiated it. Instantly, he perceives his chance for fortune.

I once read in a "how to" book for writers that you may employ only one explanation by coincidence per story, so I guess I'll use mine here. The boy has grown up in a town with few scientific books, but fortuitously he did come into possession of one, R. W. Wood's *Physical Optics*. He has thus become fascinated with light and its behavior and can see the coruscating brilliance of Times Square as a problem in physics, not just a spectacular pain in the eye. Even as a coincidence this may seem a bit far-fetched, but I have, after all, the citable precedent of the boy Thomas Edison finding inspiration in the pages of Richard Parker's *Natural and Experimental Philosophy*.

Pursuing his vision, the lad drops out of Harvard and moves to New York, where, supported by indulgent parents, he conducts experiments in a makeshift laboratory set up in his Fifty-fifth Street room. When these jury-rigged facilities prove inadequate, he avails himself of a well-equipped laboratory at the Columbia University Physics Department, gaining unauthorized access by sneaking in through an unlocked window. On these nocturnal prowls, he enjoys the assistance of a young female companion, who, to add a dash of classic romance, subsequently becomes his partner in a marriage that endures a lifetime.

After three years of this, he returns to Harvard. At that august institution, the powers-that-be soon realize they have a genius on their hands and, although he is technically only a sophomore, turn over to him and his bride the laboratory and materials needed to carry on their work. Three additional years of labor at last bring results. One semester short of graduation, our hero leaves college forever, sets up his own business backed by family capital, and patents a process for reducing glare.

Soon giant corporations beat a path to his door: Kodak buys light filters for its cameras; American Optical signs him up to manufacture glare-free sunglasses. The barons of Wall Street, ever seeking profitable places to put idle capital, get wind of the young genius and his tiny company. They come, they see, they are conquered. They supply a million dollars in fresh capital; moreover, the young entrepreneur (now 28) so impresses these hard-bitten money moguls (let's call them Rockefeller, Kuhn-Loeb, Harriman, and Warburg, just to make them recognizable) that they give him the cash on terms that leave him in complete control of the company, free to do anything he wants so long as he remains in its service 10 years.

To make this part of the story even more incredible, I'll have it span the worst years of the Great Depression by having my hero go back to Harvard in 1929, drop out of school again and enter business in 1932, get his first big contracts in 1935, and conquer Wall Street in 1937.

Freshly funded, the company moves from its basement headquarters in Cambridge to a succession of larger factories and laboratories. During World War II, the firm prospers, devising this and that bit of optical equipment for the military. Near the end of the war, the hero has yet another vision, this one of a product that few people need but that almost everyone, as our genius foresees, will turn out to want. No one, including our hero, knows how to make this product, but he, like Edison before him, has a knack for knowing that a thing *can* be done. In due time, this vision becomes a reality. On the wings of it, and a succession of others that spring from his fecund mind, our protagonist rises from an obscure scientist to a figure of world prominence, gazetted with medals and honorary degrees at home and abroad, becoming in the process one of the half-dozen richest people in America. His company, an extension of his genius, follows an equally meteoric path, spreading around the world while its securities become a "glamour stock," one of the highest of the high fliers.

It makes a good story, but I have a feeling it wouldn't sell as fiction. In reality, of course, it's the story of Edwin Land, founder and presiding genius of the Polaroid Corporation, and, in the form of newspaper and magazine articles, not to mention the company's products, it has sold quite well indeed. As an "incarnation of the American dream" (as one of Land's biographers called it), it doesn't match Carnegie's story, for Land rose, as so many other successful entrepreneurs, not from rags, but from respectability to riches. It's a remarkable tale, nevertheless, not so much because of the man's flashes of brilliance, but rather because of his ability to translate his visions into industrial realities and sell them to his subordinates, his stockholders, and the buying public. In this and many other ways, as contemporaries often observed, Land's career much resembled Edison's.

To a degree remarkable in a corporate, bureaucratic age, Land dominated the Polaroid Corporation, making it embody his personal will. His dominance manifested itself in the titles—chairman (chief executive officer), president (chief operating officer), and director of research—that he held from the company's founding until 1975. He then relinquished the presidency, with its control of day-to-day affairs, to

William McCune, an old associate, but retained his other posts and did not finally retire until 1980. As the head of a firm doing a billion-dollar-a-year business, Land obviously had to rely on a staff of professional managers, and the day soon passed when he knew every employee personally; nevertheless, every product Polaroid made during his active career reflected a vision of its founder and research that he personally conducted or supervised.

Land makes a hard person to write about, an obsessive ferociously dedicated to his own privacy. He once declined to supply a *New York Times* reporter with the names of his married daughters, though they were obviously a matter of public record. Mark Olshaker, his first biographer, got no closer to an interview with Land than a few sessions with Polaroid's director of publicity. A second, Victor McElheny, vainly pursued a Land interview for 30 years. Although Land continuously made news after World War II, he remained notoriously unwilling to give press conferences, submitting only to one in 1947 and then one more 24 years later in 1971.

As a sop to the investment community, Land occasionally and grudgingly granted an audience to a reporter from the *New York Times, Forbes,* or *Fortune,* but the results scarcely justified the effort involved. Asked to elaborate on his methods, his point of view, or his processes, Land responded circuitously, in terms of individual eccentricity:

> I find it very important to work intensively for long hours when I am beginning to see solutions to a problem. At such times *atavistic competences* seem to come welling up. [italics added] [Perhaps as a result of eating pie, like Edison]

philosophical treacle:

> We are ultimately as concerned about the success or failure of the society as we are about the success of our own enterprise. Indeed, we are convinced that we [these are imperial "we's," no doubt] cannot succeed . . . unless our society is successful

or technical opacities:

> This departure from what we expect on the basis of colorimetry is not a small effect but is complete . . . the factors in color vision hitherto regarded as determinative are significant only in a certain special case. What . . . misled us . . . is the accidental universality of this special case.

Obscure stuff, all that, doubtless clear enough in Land's mind, but hardly a contribution to any layperson's guide to business success. Not that Land couldn't muster brevity, but his frequent one-liners didn't help much either. Asked once what problems he had encountered developing the SX-70 camera, Land answered, "There are no problems in science, only opportunities." Pressed by a *Fortune* reporter to explain Polaroid's success, described by the reporter as "one of the great miracles of business, fully documented and widely publicized, but still awesome to contemplate," Land replied winsomely, "Virtue and a good product are invincible!"

His stockholders fared little better at extracting information, despite the fact that at the annual shareholders' meeting (his only regular public appearance), they theoretically had a clear shot at him. Land dominated the meetings, tantalizing the faithful with vague but glowing allusions to miracles to come, occasionally bewitching them by delivering one such as the OneStep instant color camera or an instant home movie system. These unveilings combined many of the features of Sloan's new model introductions with all the subtleties of television late-show commercials; they featured fanfares, dancing girls, babies, dogs, and demonstrations by Land himself. The audience then divided into groups and trooped away to try their own luck with the new gadgetry. After blazing away at the babies, the dancers, the dogs, and each other (but not at Land; shooting him, even with his own cameras, was strongly discouraged), the multitude reassembled.

Thus softened up, the stockholders usually bore the balance of the meeting with becoming docility. The occasional obstreperous outburst got a cold reception from Land, who, though he called his stockholders his "partners," clearly thought they should remain of the silent variety. Pressed for specifics about future products, Land might retort that he had no obligation to give any and would hold that ground until loyal followers shouted the dissident down. At the 1977 meeting, after rhapsodizing about the fabulous achievement of the instant movie system (Polavision) with its "rather miraculous cassette," Land confronted one skeptic who wanted more than the song-and-dance act. The extravaganza aside, the "partner" declared, all that really counted was the new system's impact on "the bottom line" of the balance sheet. "The only thing that counts is the bottom line?" Land sneered. "What a presumptuous thing to say. The bottom line," he declared with finality, "is in heaven."

Given Polaroid's uneven dividend record and the stock's fluctuating market value ($24 to $60 per share in the first three months of 1979, for example), it may often have appeared to some Polaroid stockholders that they had more hope of a celestial than an earthly reward, despite their company's glamor status. For a stockholder to ask his firm's chief executive about the profit potential of some new product did not in itself herald a revolt. Stockholders exercise the prerogative routinely at annual corporate clambakes, though in fact they have little recourse regardless of the reply. But Land's brand of tartness *was* rare; stockholders expect, and usually get, some soothing, if uninformative, response. Land could rebuke such impertinence and get away with it; most of his "partners" saw his aloofness as part of his charisma, an aura powerful enough to cement stockholder loyalty against the mundane centrifugal forces of disappointing earnings.

Land could serve "pie in the sky, by and by" because his "partners" ate it up. "Polaroid and . . . Dr. Edwin Land [the title by virtue of his honorary degrees]," wrote a *New York Times* market analyst in 1973, "continue to dazzle Americans, who clearly regard him as a latter-day Henry Ford." Considering the "uneven . . . earnings over the years," the column went on, some stockholders obviously felt attracted because the "founder is an original," not "because of the results."

The Polaroid Corporation constituted, of course, much more than a carnival and its founder something more than a charismatic crank. From its million-dollar funding in 1937, the firm grew in 30 years to the 230th largest American industrial corporation (in terms of sales), and to an even better standing in assets (180th) and net income

(140th). To achieve such growth, Land needed qualities even of a visionary, snake-oil merchant and purveyor of sonorous platitudes. Even Land's instant perception of a technical solution (plastic or glass with a molecular structure that eliminates glare) to Times Square's incandescence, although extraordinary, certainly had precedents. In fact, the legal validity of an inventor's "visionary flash" dated back at least to George Westinghouse. Land united inventive genius and personal charisma with a hard-headed business sense that included a shrewd grasp of the market, a conservative approach to business finance, and an ability to select and inspire talented subordinates, a combination that distinguished him from all but a few scientists and inventors. From these qualities and his exercise of them emerged the fascinating interplay of Land's innate personality and many of the values and traditions of American society.

However much he came across as a philosophical cornball, Land, like Carnegie, Edison, Ford, and others before him, genuinely believed that his firm's success depended on and contributed to the success of his society. Nor did he see any contradiction between business and aesthetics. "I am first of all an artistic person," he said in 1975:

> I'm interested in love and affection and sharing and making beauty part of everyday life. . . . I'm lucky enough to . . . earn my living by contributing to a warmer and richer world. . . . And if I use all my scientific, professional abilities in doing that, I think that makes for a good life.

And not just a good life for him, but potentially for everyone, everywhere. Land, like most scientists and generations of Americans, scientific and otherwise, saw science as the key to unlock the chains of misery and ugliness. "It bothers us at Polaroid," he said in 1972, "to see a world that could be ever so much more tender and beautiful if the full potential of science were realized."

Like Henry Ford, who argued that if you "do good" in business, "the money will fall into your hands; you can't get out of it," Land defined profit as an inevitable result of good work, not the reason for it. "If anything characterized [Polaroid and drove] the analysts wild," he exulted, it was the fact that "we grow and grow and grow, not on the basis of bottom line but on the basis of faith that if you do your job well[,] the last thing you have to worry about is money, just as if you live right, you'll be happy." Land thus advocated the belief in the harmony and symbiosis among work, virtue, profit, beauty, technology, and progress that, if not unique to Americans, has characterized them to an extraordinary degree throughout their history and has so often served entrepreneurs as motive and justification.

Land saw utility and beauty as synonymous and often described such mundanities as cameras and film cassettes as "miraculous" and "beautifully self-contained." Moreover, they opened vistas of art and communication for mass enjoyment. As Ford could visualize the Model T, in all its utilitarian ugliness, as opening to "the great multitude . . . the blessing of hours of pleasure in God's great open spaces," so Land could see his cameras removing "all mechanical obstacles between . . . people . . . and the exercising of a new art" and opening "a domain . . . in which friends can share the deep satisfaction of creating together and in which strangers while photographing together can explore the pleasant periphery of friendship."

Beneath Land's idealism, however, there lurked a hard-won awareness that all these glorious benefits ultimately depended upon market acceptance, not technical excellence.

That acceptance, he learned, does not come automatically, however much potential beauty some gadget may have in the eye of its creator. Failure to understand that stark reality of capitalism bars the path to commercial success for many scientists and inventors. Among those who do realize it, as Land came to, the perception itself may become an insuperable obstacle. Many scientists, seeing their mission as exploring the frontiers of knowledge and sharing their discoveries with humankind through swift publication, sequester themselves in universities where publication also brings the peer recognition that defines scientific success.

Scientists seeking a market beyond academia, however, often find their ideals painfully contradicted by an axiom of capitalism: ideas have market value only if they become property, usually a patent, or better yet, a web of patents, and thus eligible for property's protections. Publication, by law, constitutes "disclosure," and disclosure precludes a patent. The scientist's inclination to share thus clashes with the capitalist's instinct to monopolize, sometimes with tragic results. Polymer chemist Wallace Carothers left the Harvard faculty for the Du Pont research labs in 1928. In 1931, his team invented neoprene, the first synthetic rubber; by 1936, the team had done much of the research that led to nylon; in 1937, despite having been the first industrial chemist elected to the National Academy of Science, Carothers committed suicide.

For many, perhaps most, inventors, realizing the omnipotence of the market does not lead to acceptance of it. Often this rejection results from learning that getting to market will require human and financial resources they don't have, that getting those resources will require surrendering ownership, and that loss of ownership will mean loss of control. Few inventors, moreover, have embraced the venture capitalists' and entrepreneurs' credo that control depends on performance, not ownership, that 10 percent of a success beats 100 percent of a failure, and so on and on.

Finally, even among scientists and inventors who understand market realities and accept them, that comprehension does not in itself confer the talents and resources needed to overcome the obstacles that stand between their creations and the market. That Land knew and accepted these actualities set him apart from most scientists and inventors. His ability to translate his mounting insights into a thriving business marked him as one of the few technically creative people who, like Whitney and Edison before him and Steve Jobs after, had the entrepreneurial skills to put inspiration on a commercial basis, to reap profits from brainstorms. The combination occurs rarely, but when it does, it often produces dramatic results, as Land's career demonstrated.

In the late 1930s, having mastered the art of manufacturing glare-reducing glass, Land stalked a quarry much bigger than the limited market presented by camera filters and sunglasses. The virtues of applying the Polaroid system to automobile headlights and windshields, thus reducing glare and the bloody crashes it produced, seemed so obvious to Land that he could not imagine the automobile industry declining to avail itself of such a boon. Decline it did, however, citing expense and complexity, a Detroit dirge that has became all too familiar over the years and has played a part in its decline.

With that chance gone a-glimmering, Land cast about for some other product with mass-market potential. He came up with the "Vectograph" system of motion pictures, the so-called 3-D movies, successfully demonstrated at the 1939 New York World's Fair. Although cardboard Polaroid glasses had less profit potential than automobile headlights, they nevertheless offered enough possibility to make visions of sugarplums dance in anyone's head. After an interruption for World War II, during which the firm battened on federal contracts for various light-filtering devices, Polaroid pressed on with the Vectograph, and for a time millions of Americans, little cardboard glasses perched on their noses, leaped and squirmed about in darkened movie houses, dodging spears and darts flung and spat at them by Hollywood aborigines. In the early 1950s, the fad died, of its own absurdity, trashy movies, and competition from that emerging giant, television. Polaroid, like the makers of hula hoops later, suddenly found itself stuck with warehouses full of the silly things. (Lately resurrected by a fresh onslaught of multidimensional cinematic mayhem and Super Bowl commercials.)

Twice, then, the firm had come to a dead end, both times by relying on another industry as the market for its products. Understanding the market implications of a product for which the customer (the automobile industry in this case) and the end user (the automobile owner) differ presents a challenge most businesses confront. Developing or failing to develop an appropriate strategy has often made the difference between success and failure. "We learned," one of Land's lieutenants later recalled, in a statement later echoed by Michael Dell, "that the best way [was] to sell as directly to the consumer as possible." More accurately, they had learned that in trying to sell components requiring further manufacture or assembly ("producers' goods"), they had shattered their tiny lance on the leviathan automobile industry's nearly impenetrable armor of resistance to ideas, even good ideas, from the outside (the NIH, or "Not Invented Here" syndrome). "Consumer goods," products that left the factory ready for the end users with no further processing required, seemed a better prospect. Fortunately, by the time the 3-D movie craze subsided, Land had begun producing by the million just such a product: the instant camera.

The instant camera had resulted from another of Land's flashes. On vacation with his wife and three-year-old daughter Jennifer, in New Mexico in 1943, Land took a picture of the little girl, who at once demanded to see the result. Times Square all over again: Why not a combination camera-developer that anyone could simply aim and shoot, which would then disgorge a fully developed color picture? Snapshots while you wait; who could resist such a marvel? Almost no one, Land thought, for his vision ignited a "fantasy" that the instant camera would "be as widely used as the telephone" and could "have the same impact as the telephone on the way people live." Here Land had the best kind of market perception: a better way to serve an existing demand. Americans took untold millions of pictures a year, enough to make Eastman Kodak an industrial giant and to support a panoply of ancillary retail services such as selling and developing film.

Almost at once, Land sensed he could make such a camera, though he knew it would take time: "By the time Jennifer and I returned from our walk," he said, "I had solved all the problems except for the ones it [took years] to solve. Within an hour," he added, "the camera, the film and the physical chemistry became so clear" that he could rush to a friend and describe in detail "a dry camera which would give a picture immediately after exposure." Such a creation required cramming the whole apparatus of darkrooms—tanks full of chemicals, rinsing baths, enlargers, and printers—into the innards of a small, inexpensive camera. Then came the challenge of flogging the product into a market dominated by Eastman Kodak, an old, established, technically proficient, productively efficient firm with resources that dwarfed pygmy Polaroid's.

None of these obstacles deflected Land. If he could imagine the camera, he could make it: "All that we at Polaroid had learned about . . . polarizers and plastics, and . . . viscous liquids, and . . . microscopic crystals . . . was preparation for [that] day when I suddenly knew how to make a one-step photographic process." And if he could make it, he could sell it. After all, "Virtue and a good product are invincible." What Kodak might or might not do didn't matter. Within six months, Land had worked out the essential technical details of the developing process and had begun to erect the battlement of patents necessary to defend his handiwork against marauding competitors. Land, like many an inventor predecessor, might have made his fortune by selling his patents, thus avoiding the vexations of manufacturing and distribution, but for him, making and selling the camera presented "opportunities" that Land himself could exploit, not "problems" to slough off to some more able firm.

When World War II ended, and with it most of the lucrative military contracts for filters and lenses that had assured the firm's prosperity, Land had rejected the precarious role of peacetime military contractor. Instead, he bet everything on the instant camera, gambling that he could win a race between product development and bankruptcy. It came down to the wire: by 1947, business had declined to less than a tenth of the wartime level, whereas research expenses had skyrocketed, producing three consecutive years of heavy losses. On February 21, 1947, however, Land dazzled the Optical Society of America by demonstrating his instant camera. A subsequent appearance at the 1948 convention of the Photographic Society of America stole the show, garnered reams of free publicity, and whetted the public's appetite. Finally, on November 26, 1948, the Polaroid Land Camera, Model 95, went on sale at the Jordan Marsh department store in Boston.

The first camera fell far short of Land's ideal of a compact, one-step, color picture machine. Large, heavy (five pounds), and relatively expensive ($89.95), it required manual setting of shutter speed and lens opening, needed considerable practice to get passable results, took a minute to develop its film, and turned out pictures printed in sepia tones reminiscent of a bygone era. The public, nevertheless, loved it; production took months to catch up with demand.

As Land had predicted, the new camera found its own unchallenged market niche. It catered to Americans' love of gadgetry, their craving for instant gratification, and their orientation toward things visual, a penchant long nurtured by movies, newsreels, picture magazines, and, in 1948, soon to include television. It also unleashed a whole new cottage industry, home pornography, permitting the libidinous to realize their fantasies without fear of exposure by prurient druggists or tale-bearing film developers. That sex sells, and sells so well, has long made it a market staple for capitalism; as recent studies by its friends, foes, and the (purportedly) objective have all shown, it has played a major role in expanding markets for new technologies. When, for example, 8mm home movie cameras and projectors entered the market, camera stores quickly followed by offering "blue" movies for rent. This development, said a government report on "obscenity," "served as a catalyst for the rental or purchase of movie projectors, screens, cameras, and other equipment." As for the video camcorder, in 1978, a business writer called it "an open secret" that sex constituted "the biggest market." Perhaps Land's comment that the instant camera would open "a domain . . . in which friends can share the deep satisfaction of creating together and in which strangers while photographing together can explore the pleasant periphery of friendship" spoke to a more complex market perception than evident at first glance.

Whatever the original perception, as the years passed Polaroid expanded its original market by cutting prices, which put the camera in reach of ever-larger segments of the public, and by improving quality, which rendered previous models obsolete. The two strategies were not always incorporated into a single camera model. Within 18 months, black-and-white film replaced the original sepia; in 1954, the Highlander model ($60) appeared; in 1960, 10-second developing film; in 1963, color film and the Automatic 100 to shoot it ($130–$160); in 1965, the Swinger ($14); in 1967, the Colorpack series ($50–$180); in 1968, the Big Swinger ($20) and the Colorpack II ($30). The firm thus roamed up and down the market, seeking customers among both serious photographers and the legions of artistically unwashed. The trick—getting the camera into people's hands—if accomplished would create an "installed base business" that would assure success, because the big profits, both in terms of volume and markup, lay in the sale of the film. Just as Gillette sells razors cheap and blades dear, and Hewlett-Packard sells printers at a pittance to sell cartridges priced to the point of pain, the lucrative film business justified Polaroid's selling the camera at cost (as Kodak had done in the past) and, in fact, might have justified giving it away.

Carrying on the simultaneous activities of research, manufacturing millions of cameras and hundreds of millions of film packets, and distributing the products into the mass consumer market entailed a burden of responsibilities that not even Land's energy could transcend. The combined operation, moreover, required vast masses of capital. Land, in the tradition of financially conservative manufacturers before him— Carnegie, Pierre du Pont, Ford—thought borrowed capital a shortcut to loss of control or ruin. Consequently, Polaroid in Land's time never borrowed a dime; it financed its growth with retained profits and the proceeds from the sale of additional stock.

Land surmounted the myriad problems by spinning off some to outside manufacturers and delegating other responsibilities within the company. He himself concentrated on research in physics, chemistry, and optics. The responsibility for creating a sales and distribution system went to J. Harold Booth, a former vice president at Bell and Howell, whom Land made executive vice president of Polaroid. Engineer William McCune had the job of making proposed products an engineering reality. "Land told us what we were going to make," one employee remembered. "Bill McCune showed us how to make everything." In other words, Land defined the requirements and the qualities that the market demanded, such as developing the pictures in less than a minute, leaving it to McCune's engineers to define the specifications, that is, the materials and processes that turned the requirements into products. Land always included price among the requirements, which had the effect of constraining the ingrained tendency among engineers to overengineer requirements into $pecification$.

The actual manufacture of the cameras Land subcontracted to Bell and Howell, a manufacturer of motion picture equipment, and U.S. Time, producer of Timex watches. Polaroid's arch competitor, Kodak, willingly made lenses and film to Polaroid specifications. By 1960, these arrangements ("outsourcing," but not "offshoring") had succeeded so well that Polaroid products sold in 45 countries around the world and penetrated new markets almost daily. The company's stock had a total market value of more than $1 billion; the share price of $250 or more equaled 90 times annual earnings, indicating what investors thought of future prospects. Through the 1960s, Land fueled this optimism by periodically dropping hints of better things to come, not only in photography, where his predictions generally came true sooner or later, but also in then-exotic areas such as photocopying and color television.

As prosperity replaced anxiety, Land acquired wealth and fame fit for the plots of Horatio Alger, collecting honorary degrees (14), medals and awards (37, including the Presidential Medal of Freedom), and prestigious appointments (to the faculties of Harvard and MIT, to the President's Science Advisory Committee, and to the President's Foreign Intelligence Advisory Board, among others). All this accumulated bijouterie of success vindicated Land's faith in his abilities as a technician and organizer, but eminently more gratifying, they validated his whole philosophy of life. Land always conceived of himself as a philosopher/scientist and thought the two roles intertwined and strengthened each other like the strands of a cable.

Land's creed had several distinct components. His faith in humankind's ability to solve its problems rationally underpinned all his work. "If you [can] state a problem—any problem—and if it is important enough," he declared categorically, "then the problem can be solved." At first glance, this proposition seems to expose Land as a humbug, a zealot, or a case of arrested development. American society, let alone the rest of the world, festers with important problems readily enough stated but stubbornly resistant to solutions. On reflection, however, Land's axiom emerges as one of the stars by which Americans have always steered. By and large, most Americans *have* believed society's ills susceptible of diagnosis and solution, an attitude enshrined in the Constitution, institutionalized in the public education system, transmogrified into the phalanxes of government agencies that send hither swarms of officers to harass our people, eat out their substance and vex them with standardized tests, and burlesqued by packs of social scientists roving the land, interviewing pimps and professors, and plugging wires into contract copulators.

For the rationally minded, no unknowables exist, only unknowns; nothing insoluble, only things unsolved. Failure proves only that the diagnosis, the prescription, or both went awry. Better luck next time. Certainly Land's philosophy took failure readily in stride. "Lots of companies put a great premium on avoiding . . . mistakes," he observed, but at Polaroid, they "put a great premium on being able to make mistakes" because "an essential aspect of creativity is not being afraid to fail. . . . By calling their activities hypotheses and experiments . . . scientists made it possible to fail repeatedly until in the end they got the results they wanted." Land thus functioned as a latter-day Edisonian and doubtless would have seen no paradox in the fact that Edison, who once said, "Results? I've gotten plenty of results. I know several thousand things that won't work," got more patents (1,093) than any other individual in history. Land, whose research team tried more than 5,000 compounds before coming up with one that worked as a dye-developer in instant color film, secured more 500 patents himself, second only to Edison.

Land saw the linked successes of his personal achievements, the scientific breakthroughs of his research teams, and the growth of the Polaroid Corporation as microcosms of the historical process at large. "There are two opposing theories of history," he declared:

> Either you believe that . . . individual greatness does exist and can be nurtured and developed, that such great individuals can be part of a cooperative community [Polaroid, America, the world] while they continue to be their happy, flourishing, contributing selves—or else you believe that there is some mystical, cyclical, overriding, predetermined, cultural law—a historical determinism.

Philosophers, historians, scientists, and people generally have pondered these options for centuries and debate them still. Land thought the choice between these historical philosophies "divides . . . the world . . . into two parties. They are not Democratic or Republican, or capitalist or communist," but one group that says that "Beethoven was a necessary, inevitable and predictable racial consequence of his predecessors," and another that argues that if Beethoven had never lived, "the history of music would have been entirely different." For Land, the choice seemed clear-cut. With Thomas Carlyle, he believed unequivocally that "Great Men make history" and do so not in thrall to ineluctable, predictable forces, but in interplay with chance and chaos: "For the most part there will be no change [in society] and there must be no change, but what real changes do occur are entirely the result of accidents called individuals."

Science, Land thought, confirmed his philosophy: "The great contribution of science is to say that [deterministic historical] theory is nonsense." "In retrospect," he observed, society *seems* to have been "continuous in its progress," thus giving the illusion of having followed a predetermined path. Deluded by these mirages in the past, a Karl Marx or a Herbert Spencer could articulate a philosophy that made the future inevitable and foreseeable. For Land, however, such false logic dead-ended in absurdity. Actually, "in prospect society is completely unpredictable." And there, in the very unpredictability and seeming disorder of society, lay its fascination and its challenge to the individual, and to individual scientists especially: "Science demonstrate[s] that a person can regard the world as chaos, but can find in himself a method of perceiving . . . small arrangements of order." If so, he can, by adding his own discovery to "the order that previous scientists have generated"—a process Sir Isaac Newton described as seeing far by "standing on the shoulders of giants"—"make things that are exciting and thrilling to make." And these sensations add up to something much more than the titillations of successful gadgeteering, because the scientist's creations can make "deeply spiritual contributions to himself and to his friends." Better yet, to all humankind: "The scientist comes to the world and says, 'I do not understand the divine source, but I know, in a way that I don't understand, that out of chaos, I can make order, out of loneliness I can make friendship, out of ugliness I can make beauty!'"

Land himself thought that he had accomplished all this, and his sense of having contributed to spirituality, order, friendship, and beauty bolstered his pride more than all the baubles, bangles, wampum, and glory he accumulated. Of course, what applied to him may not hold for everybody. (Okay, you're a bird, but suppose you're a worm?) His focus on the market, moreover, showed his awareness of wampum's contribution to his pursuit of more aesthetic rewards. He may have had a flawed understanding of history in thinking that "the factors . . . regarded as determinative [signified] only in a certain special case" while giving a misleading appearance of "accidental universality." Accidental universalities, however, may serve well enough to steer a course by. For centuries sailors navigated with pinpoint accuracy using the Ptolemaic system of the universe, for all that Ptolemy had it wrong. Certainly Land's philosophy sustained him through thick and thin, and he never needed it more than in the early 1970s, when the struggle to develop the SX-70, the ultimate in instant color cameras, turned into a struggle for Polaroid's survival.

The SX-70 represented the camera of Land's original dream, what came to be called a "point and shoot." Its electronic wizardry sensed light conditions and distance to the subject and then took care of adjusting the focus, lens opening, and shutter speed. Pushing the little red button activated a motor, powered by a battery contained in the film pack, that shoved out the picture, complete with protective plastic coating, which then developed in full color right before your eyes. No fuss, no muss, no garbage, no bother. No need to puzzle over a lot of complex instructions and then waste a lot of expensive film to find out that you didn't understand them. Just open the camera, shove in the film, close the camera, and blaze away. No wonder Land called the SX-70 "Aladdin."

And indeed the genie-like powers of the Polaroid SX-70 inspired new forms of artistic creativity in such as pop artist Andy Warhol, who incorporated thousands of Polaroid images into huge silk-screen prints, and the sleeve art for the1977 Rolling Stones album "Love You Live." David Byrne, presiding genius of the rock group Talking Heads, pieced together 529 SX-70 photos into a Cubist portrait of the band for the sleeve of the 1978 album "More Songs About Buildings and Food." In the 1980s, American photographer Sally Mann used Polaroid shots of aquatic still life in her book *Still Life*. The SX-70 thus proved an exciting creative tool in the hands of artists and a delight to the millions of people for whom "point and shoot" matched the limit of their photographic aspirations.

As a *fait accompli,* the camera seemed simple enough. In development, however, it inflicted a technological nightmare, demanding simultaneous path breaking in chemistry, optics, and electronics. In vintage Land fashion, he initiated the project by telling his staff what he wanted the camera to do, then complicated the whole business by demanding that Aladdin's genie fit in a very small bottle, to compete with Kodak's immensely successful pocket camera, the Instamatic. In a classic example of defining a requirement, "Land gave my boss a block of wood [the size of his jacket pocket]," one design engineer recalled, "and told him that's how large the camera could be. . . . So in a sense you could say that Dr. Land's tailor determined the size of the SX-70."

The project took eight years and carried Polaroid into areas it had previously avoided. Because, as Land said, "these cameras and film are technologically unique, involving new science at each point of manufacture," Polaroid decided that for the first time it must do its own manufacturing. Not only did this mean designing and building film and camera plants, but it also involved going into the chemical business to assure an adequate supply of film components. In the long run, this integration of design and manufacture might vastly increase Polaroid's profits, but first it demanded massive investment in plant and equipment. These expenses, added to a research budget that outran all expectations, put a massive strain on the company's finances. Altogether the SX-70 project gobbled up half a billion dollars before it returned a penny.

Finally, at the 1972 annual meeting, Land mounted the stage and announced, "Photography will never be the same." The new camera produced color pictures that he declared "astounding, having qualities for which we have no names." He thereupon pulled an SX-70 from his pocket and fired off five pictures in 10 seconds, to the tumultuous approval of the assembled faithful, who basked in the glow of riches certain to come. Land had done it again.

An auspicious beginning, surely, but big profits had to wait a while yet. Beset by production breakdowns, film spoilage, and a declining economy, Polaroid's sales and profits fell through 1973 and 1974. In January 1974, *Fortune* published an article called "Can Polaroid Win That Half-Billion Dollar Bet? How Polaroid Bet Its Future on the SX-70." A year later, things looked grim. Still learning how to run its new plants, Polaroid labored under the triple burden of high costs, low production, and erratic product quality. In November 1974, the firm took the unprecedented and embarrassing step of laying off a thousand employees; in January 1975, it deferred scheduled pay raises "to conserve [its] resources." Suppliers canceled contracts as Polaroid canceled orders. For a time, it looked as though 1975 might bring the company's first deficit year since 1948.

In addition to these woes, a new menace loomed on the horizon. In March 1974, Kodak announced development of its own instant camera. Given Kodak's resources (still 10 times greater than Polaroid's), its expertise, and its aggressive marketing techniques, it promised formidable competition that might win the field by the time Polaroid got its kinks worked out and demand revived. Through it all, while some of his executives confided to *Fortune's* reporter that the company's fate hung in the balance, Land himself radiated serenity and confidence. Asked by a *Forbes* reporter about Polaroid's troubles with the SX-70, Land retorted, "What problems? Those problems are largely problems in the press." In fact, he claimed, small troubles did good things for a big company. Take, for example, the obnoxious tendency of the SX-70's battery to leak onto the film: "I think the battery saved us," Land said, "because without the troubles with it, we would have been spoiled and . . . growing too fast. It was a happy accident, a cloud with a very silver lining."

By April 1976, when Kodak unveiled its own instant camera, Polaroid's clouds, silver-lined and otherwise, had thinned under the sunshine of resumed profits. Increased efficiency, revived consumer demand, and cheaper models of the camera all fed the surge, which continued through 1976, when Polaroid sold more than 6 million cameras, a new company record. In later years, although Kodak expanded its share of the instant camera market to one-third, it absorbed huge losses ($75 million in 1977), whereas Polaroid sold more cameras than ever and made money doing it. In the instant camera field, Kodak had met its match. Analyzing the crucial Christmas sales of 1977, when Polaroid's OneStep met Kodak's Handle head-on in competition for the low-priced market, *Fortune* trumpeted, "Polaroid's OneStep Is Stopping Kodak Cold."

By holding its share of the market, Polaroid justified William McCune's optimism, expressed in 1975, about Kodak's impending entry into the market: "We expect competition," he said, "and have been planning for it." In 1976, Polaroid sued Kodak for patent infringement; it won the case in 1985, effectively driving Kodak from the instant photography field.

Meanwhile, by Christmas 1977, Land, who thought "optimism is a moral duty," had introduced the Polavision instant movie system, thinking to seize yet another uncontested market niche. The magic had run its course, however, for the arrival of video camcorders brought a competition that Land had not anticipated and that Polavision could not meet.

As Land turned 70 in 1979, and the string of miraculous surprises obviously neared its end, speculation focused on Land's successor and the future of his company. Land had no sons, and no one person seemed adequate to replace him. Asked by *Fortune* about his successor, "Land launched into a description of such a paragon of talent, intelligence, and virtue that even he paused, laughed, and said, 'We're making him down in the laboratory.'" In fact, after Land retired in 1982, neither the laboratory nor the bureaucracy could meet the need. Polaroid after Land, like Kodak after George Eastman, passed from the ranks of the personal firms into the cadre of corporate bureaucratic giants. Nor did the resemblance end there. Both fell victim to a disruptive technology, as Polaroid, like Kodak, failed to foresee the digital camera and video recorder revolution, a damaging mistake for Kodak, but a near-fatal one for Polaroid, which went bankrupt in 2001 and again in 2008.

Polaroid pictures have nevertheless retained a cult following, as evidenced by computer software such as "Poladroid" that "vintagefies" digital images. When Polaroid discontinued production of film, a firm calling itself "The Impossible Project" bought an abandoned Polaroid factory in the Netherlands, hired some former Polaroid technicians, and filled the void. On July 28, 2010, the firm offered an "SX 70 Kit," consisting of a reconditioned camera and two packs of film for 299 Euros. The stock sold out "in two minutes."

As an industrialist, Land saw himself in the classic mold of the Schumpeterian entrepreneur, who functioned "to make a new kind of product." But industry had a further responsibility, "the production of a worthwhile, highly rewarding, highly creative, inspiring daily job for every one of a hundred million Americans." In 1945, in Polaroid's youth, Land declared his intention of creating "products that are genuinely unique and useful, excellent in quality, made well and efficiently, [to] present an attractive value to the public and an attractive profit to the Company." As a second goal, he hoped to provide "a worthwhile working life for each member of the Company—a working life that calls out the member's best talents and skills—in which he or she shares the responsibilities and the rewards."

The first task proved easier than the second, especially after Polaroid entered mass production. The assembly line presented problems of boredom and worker morale that not even Land's genius could resolve. Land, of course, thought someone would someday find an answer, perhaps some new actor emerging to play the lead role in what Land once called "high technological drama." He had it right, of course, as others have indeed followed in his footsteps, including Steve Jobs, whose career resembles Land's much as Land's resembled Edison's.

Like Land, Jobs dropped out of college, fascinated by the challenges and opportunities presented by the development of new technologies. A control freak like Land, Jobs rides herd on every aspect of Apple's operations: finance, product development, corporate message, and more. Like Land, he gives mesmerizing performances at stockholders' meetings and trade shows. As a "scientist," Land thought that "out of ugliness [he could] make beauty." Jobs sees technology as a vehicle for beauty as well as functionality, a view reflected in Apple's shimmering products and the glitzy stores that sell them. (Jobs did indeed solve the problem of assembly line alienation and ennui by outsourcing it to Taiwan and China.)

Land's innovations profitably restructured a small market—sunglasses—and a huge one—popular photography. Jobs has made a vast fortune by revolutionizing three: music, movies, and mobile telephones, and by finding a distinct niche at the top end of the personal computer market. Like Land, Jobs has resisted commoditization in his products, relying on proprietary technology protected by hundreds of patents and ferociously defended by lawsuits and threats of them.

Explaining his disdain for market research, Henry Ford reputedly said, "If I asked my customers what they wanted, they'd have said a faster horse." Land and Jobs similarly thought they knew what their customers wanted before the customers knew themselves, and results seem to have borne them out. Admiring biographers and journalists have made much of this prescience, indeed too much. Ford in effect gave his customers a faster horse. Land didn't invent sunglasses or affordable photography. Credit for creating movies goes to Edison, if anyone, and Walt Disney popularized animation; Sony's Walkman made portable music a popular obsession; the cellular telephone and efforts to develop it into a minicomputer predated the iPhone.

Moreover, both of these geniuses had commercial failures as well as successes: Land's Polavision instant movie camera flopped, as did Jobs's Lisa and Next computers. But none of this detracts from the accomplishments of Land or Jobs. They found profitable ways to exploit and expand existing markets by developing technologies that worked better and did things existing products couldn't do, thus fulfilling the classic innovator's role as defined by Schumpeter years before, infusing the economy with productive energy.

Edwin Land had it right; we do have a choice of historical philosophies. Some opted for determinism and said, as they said of Edison and others, we'd never see his like again. Others said maybe we won't, but who knows what human possibilities may lie ahead? Determinism offers only awaiting the outcome; possibility at least holds hope, and whatever else entrepreneurs have, hope surely tops the list. Perhaps that has kept them coming in America, and increasingly in places where hope may constitute the greatest need of all.

Chapter 11

And So It Goes . . . Burgers, Bargains, and Bytes

Arch of Triumph, American Style

Ａnd now, gentle reader, we enter the realm where wise historians tread warily: contemporary history, defined here as anything younger than the writer, which includes all three companies considered in this chapter—McDonald's, Walmart, and Dell. Their very success can trap anyone who tries to explain it, for the history of business contains no lesson starker than the perishable nature of power. Today's gifted analyst can look the dunce tomorrow. McDonald's, Walmart, and Dell have all topped various *Fortune* lists of companies "Most Admired" for this and that, but so too have some that later encountered a world of hurt. A partial list of past "Most Admired" includes Enron, soon after exposed as a case study in corporate misfeasance, nonfeasance, and malfeasance, run by thieves and mountebanks, and headed by a man whose subsequent defense consisted of the claim that he had no idea what went on in his company. Other list toppers fell on hard times: General Motors, whose future in 2005 looked perilous and, bankrupt, hung by a federal government thread in 2010; A.T.&T., which somehow mismanaged itself from the top of the telecom tree to a precarious perch on one of its former branches; Sears; IBM; Hewlett-Packard; and so on down the lugubrious list of past paragons, some of which have since managed to restore their fortunes.

McDonald's, Walmart, and Dell, in fact, figure in some of these stories. Once-mighty Sears, hammered by Walmart competition, merged with K-Mart, formerly "the Genghis Khan of discount firms," but ultimately just another antelope felled by the Walmart tiger; McDonald's passed Sears as holder of the world's most valuable collection of real estate; Dell drove IBM from the personal computer business and mounted an assault on Hewlett-Packard's cash cow, printers. For the reporters at *Fortune,* these developments provide fresh grist for the pulp mill, and never mind what they wrote yesterday. For the historian, however, they serve as reminders that all glory is fleeting. *Wall Street Journal* reporters, among others, call now and then to ask if I think Bill Gates the most powerful businessman ever. (No, not even close.) The owlish Mr. Gates's company, however powerful, has programmers scampering like gerbils in fear of competition from the Two Guys from Google who a few scant years ago, like Michael Dell, started a business in a college dorm room.

Those wont to scoff at the idea that Mighty Microsoft could flail competing with two guys named Sergey Brin and Larry Page might ponder these historical facts: when Ray Kroc went into the fast-food business in 1955, the only restaurant with national name recognition, Howard Johnson's, had 500 outlets (rising to a peak of 800) and called itself, with some merit, "Landmark for Hungry Americans." By 2005, only eight remained, dwindling to three in 2010, despite the fact that its trademark orange roofs, its "Simple Simon and the Pieman," signs, its fried clams, and its "Fearless Fido" kiddy hot dog once seemed as evocative and welcoming in the twentieth century as the Golden Arches, Ronald McDonald, the Big Mac, and Happy Meals do in the twenty-first. In a similar vein, when Sam Walton bought his first dime store in 1945, Sears straddled the retail industry like a colossus and had for decades; when Michael Dell's father asked him in 1983, "What do you want to do with your life?" Michael (then 18) replied, "I want to compete with IBM."

To think objectively about McDonald's, Walmart, and Dell—so large, so loud, so ubiquitous in the American physical and electronic landscapes—let alone assess them fairly in the context of business history, thus presents an impossible challenge.

So here goes: these three American firms flourish in the market created, served, and indulged by mass production and distribution, and they have seen the emergence of the "service" economy not as a handicap, but as an advantage. Indeed, each of them shows the unbreakable link between the manufacturing and service sectors; two of them, McDonald's and Dell, operate in both, whereas the third, Walmart, serves as the world's largest distributor of manufactured products.

In stark contrast to many floundering American firms, decimated or obliterated by overseas competitors in the latter part of the twentieth century, these companies more than survived the competition met in the increasingly globalized marketplace; they used it as a dynamic driver of growth in the United States and abroad. Their accomplishments bear out the wisdom of Henry Ford II's view "that we need competition the world over to keep us on our toes and sharpen our wits." In this and other ways, these three companies and their founders exemplified and validated many of the techniques described in earlier chapters here.

These companies, like the others, intersect the past and present of my own life. Flush with the prosperity brought by my father's job at Du Pont, we made occasional excursions to the then-dominant "fast-food" emporium, White Castle. There one found an aromatic heaven of little burgers (nicknamed "sliders" for the ease with which the tiny things traveled either down the throat or through the intestinal tract), cooked *en masse,* smothered in fried onions, dripping grease from their gooey little buns. All you could eat, 5¢ apiece. Heaven. White Castle's motto urged, "Buy 'Em by the Sack," and we did, for few members of a depression-scarred generation could resist 20 hamburgers for a dollar. For me, McDonald's always seemed a lame successor, but from my own memories, I could understand why my children badgered me to take them there.

While living and traveling in France, I made the startling discovery that McDonald's opened a window on France through which I could perceive the remarkable similarity of the two countries, proven rather than disproved by the occasional hissy fit. Though plenty of differences exist, many of them provoke no snarking: the French eat horse and snails, Americans don't, but neither cares. By contrast, from time to time some funk, expressed in a jejune congressional resolution calling for "freedom fries" instead of French fries, or the harebrained efforts of the Académie Française to purge "le weekend," "le drugstore," and "supercool" from its beloved tongue, shows a mutual penchant for pompous posturing.

The French and Americans in fact share a laundry list of opinions: both believe they live in the world's greatest country and think anyone who disagrees a fool on the face of it; both think they speak the world's best language and learn others reluctantly, while maintaining that everyone else should learn theirs; both love cars and superhighways and have masses of them; both think their country had the only revolution that mattered and dismiss the other's as overrated; both think they best comprehend the world's problems and could solve them if only the other would go along (although both ended baffled and defeated in Vietnam).

Most telling of all, except for the Japanese, no people outside the United States love McDonald's as much as the French. The Golden Arches pop up in literally a thousand locations in France (including soon the Louvre Museum!), and just about where Americans have learned to expect them at home. The French, it turns out, enjoy grease and starch and sugar and salt as much as Americans (in French the word *gourmand* implies not so much good taste as gluttony) and appreciate a cheap cup of coffee (better in France); clean restrooms; and a place that not only tolerates children, but actively seeks them as customers. Despite the supposed Gallic obsession with *haute cuisine*, the beloved "MacDo's" serve a million French a day and, as someone once observed, "Can a million Frenchmen be wrong?"

The French, despite their deserved reputation for revering artistic and intellectual creativity, also display a furious devotion to consumerism. The French economy caters to this hunger not only in famous department stores such as Printemps and Galeries Lafayette (provider of excellent, free Paris maps to generations of American tourists), but even more in gargantuan clusters of *hypermarchés* and *grands surfaces*, in which the average Walmart "Supercenter" would look like one kernel on a full cob. Carrefour, a French retailer, ranks as the world's second largest after Walmart. With a home market one-fifth the size of Walmart's and open only six days a week and few evenings, Carrefour's success shows that the French, like the Japanese (whose department stores make everyone else's look like rummage sales), comprise a consumer society as much developed and sustained by mass production and distribution as the Americans'.

Looking at the respective countries' stores, one can perhaps see the future as well as the past. Someday discounting will come to France, as it has to Britain and (marginally) to Germany; someday Walmart may emulate Carrefour and employ expert *fromagiers* and butchers to advise us on our choice of cheeses and meats. One can hope.

Walmart's popularity, when it arrived, came as no surprise to me. Long before Walmart, I had benefited from discount prices at the Tuesday night "Cowtown" flea market in the South Jersey boondocks. Better yet, a trip across the Delaware River took one to "Wilmington Dry Goods," a true forerunner to Walmart and its discounting ancestors such as Korvette's and K-Mart. In the bizarre warren of "Willy Dry," with its creaky wood floors and odd nooks and crannies, laced with overhead cables on which cartridges zinged to and from the cashier, you could find almost anything a low-brow might crave: clothes and compacts, pots and pans, pins and pencils, shirts and shorts, priced lower than anywhere else. As far as how these goods got to Cowtown or Wilmington Dry (discounting being then more or less illegal under the so-called "fair trade laws"), rumors and jokes abounded to the effect that they "had fallen off the back of a truck" or were "so hot you had to wear gloves to shop there." In fact, as long as the stuff came cheap, no one knew or cared how it got there, presaging later views on Walmart merchandise. Years before Walmart opened a "supercenter," I saw its forerunner in "Meijer's Thrifty Acres" in Ann Arbor, Michigan, where I, living like a sewer rat on an assistant professor's salary, walked the aisles on Sunday amid mobs of equally impoverished students and junior faculty enjoying free entertainment at one of the town's best shows—looking at each other looking at each other.

As for Mr. Dell and his magic machines (for such they are to me, and will always remain), the very act of typing on one connects me to the past as well as to the present and the future. I type with two fingers because the high school I attended barred boys from three courses: shorthand, typing, and "office machines." I have suffered ever since from the lack of the first two, though only occasionally until, having tired of working for a living, I decided to become a professor. This metamorphosis, I discovered, required taking a lot of notes that shorthand would have made duck soup and entailed a quantity of writing that multiplied as I passed from undergraduate to graduate school, then increased exponentially when I became a faculty member. During those years, most people wrote their first drafts by hand, often on yellow pads, and most men hired or bulldozed someone (usually female, and often a wife, for many women *could* type—see above) to transcribe the scribblings.

Among the many lucky things I have encountered along the road through Life's Great Pageant, none ranks higher than the advice I got before writing my first college paper: learn to compose on the typewriter. This I did, starting on a Smith-Corona electric and moving on to the wonder machine of its time, the IBM "Selectric," complete with lightning-fast type ball and breathtaking magical erasing tape. With these, I churned out hundreds of pages, including the first edition of this book. When the personal computer came within reach, I got one for the mechanical advantages it offered to a writer. Indeed, the computer was and has remained for me two things: a typewriter and a telegraph key, connecting me to anyone else in the world who has one. It took some time to realize that the computer can not only facilitate the writer's task, but also, like the diesel locomotive in railroading, make possible a revolution in technique that, once learned, multiplies efficiency. (I don't refer here to stealing or buying papers on the Internet.) I offer two examples: first, most of us hired an experienced "thesis typist" to prepare the final draft of our dissertations in the format prescribed by the university and savagely enforced by the "thesis clerk." Once typed, any change cost money because only clean copy (no erasures) would do; consequently, the inevitable revisions reflected not the writer's muse, but the need to fit changes onto single pages, thus avoiding expensive retyping of those that followed.

Second, the tools required to construct first drafts included not only typewriter, or pad and pencil according to individual taste, but also the following: pens of several colors, stapler, staple puller, scotch tape, and scissors. "Cut" and "Paste," now cuddly little commands in word processing, meant just that in days of yore. We typed; we scribbled; we scratched out; we cut and slashed; we pasted and stapled and taped, often assembling "pages" three feet long; we drew arrows and carets; we wrote insertions, put balloons around them, and drew lines to show where they went in the text. Periodically we spilled coffee on the whole mess.

In those circumstances, writers agonized over outlines, trying to figure out where to begin and where to go next, to minimize that scalpel and suture work. For me, it came as a great revelation that on the computer I could start anywhere, write sections in any order, move components—letters, words, sentences, paragraphs, chapters even—about at will and move them back if I disliked the result, all at the speed of light, more or less. How it works I can't imagine and don't care: I have the genie for that. I myself need the genie for those things; I'm happy for the little sprite to do other things for other folk: lighten their burdens, lower their costs, solve demonic math problems, help them find cures for disease, and in time do all sorts of things that we cannot yet imagine. At the outset, however, the computer meant to me what it meant to Michael Dell, what McDonald's meant to Ray Kroc, and what

Walmart meant to Sam Walton: a better way to do things already being done in an entrepreneur's dream market—one that already existed. Each of these men embodied the quintessential qualities of the entrepreneur: the ability to perceive a market and a better way to serve it, the skills necessary to create and manage a business, and the determination to make that business grow. In the hundreds of pages (thousands, counting electronic pages) written about Ray Kroc, the term "entrepreneur" appears repeatedly, often employed by people who think it interchangeable with "business-man." This imprecision pervades pro and con discussions of Kroc and McDonald's, producing a mountain of rubbish (not least Kroc's autobiography, *Grinding It Out*), ranging from slavish hagiography to savage hatcheting. This kind of trash makes contemporary history treacherous work, like digging lunch out of dumpsters, as "Freegans" are rumored to do.

All accounts agree, however, that Kroc's ultimate market perception came in 1954 in San Bernardino, California, at the hamburger stand of the McDonald brothers, Dick and Mack, where lines formed before the lunchtime opening and persisted late into the evening. Thousands of folks, including numbers of successful businesspeople, witnessed the same swarm every day. What differentiates an entrepreneur like Ray Kroc from the rank and file of us who see the world from the perspective of consumers and employees, lies in the contrasting nature of our reactions to the crowd. Most people—indeed history says all but one person—saw a reason to join the line or to drive past and find somewhere less crowded for lunch. Ray Kroc (or so he claimed, and events seem to bear him out) saw the future and said, "Some way I've got to become involved in this."

Having said that, we can define an entrepreneur in functional terms and thereby recognize one when we see one (all valid historical definitions being circular); historians have looked for other common traits—background and personality, to name two—in this uncommon breed. Ray Kroc exhibited many classical entrepreneurial characteristics in his career, including a reluctance to work for others and a sharp eye for opportunities he could exploit himself. In 1922, as a 20-year-old high school dropout, he took a job as paper cup salesman for Lily-Tulip Cup Company. For 17 years (minus a brief hiatus hustling Florida real estate), he lived the largely autonomous life of the hotshot traveling salesman. He prospered as a drummer because he found expanded markets for his products, persuading Walgreen Drugs, for example, to offer carryout food service in paper containers at their (now gone and mostly forgotten) lunch counters.

In creative minds, one insight tends to spawn another, and certainly Kroc had a creative mind. He sold paper cups to a dairy bar proprietor in Battle Creek, Michigan, who had devised a cheap formula for milk shakes that drew crowds and made money even in the Great Depression. Kroc hustled over to another of his customers, Earl Prince, who ran a chain of ice cream stands in Chicago, and persuaded Prince to add the milkshake to his stock in trade. The new treat sold so well that Kroc sold Prince 5 million paper cups a year. Ah, but it got better: swamped by milkshake customers, Prince sought a way to bring *Fordismus* to milkshake production, which led to his inventing a machine to mix five shakes at once: the "Multimixer." When Kroc saw this culinary machine tool, he had two reactions: first, if he could sell it to dairy bars, he could sell them a lot more cups; second, and better yet, he could build his own business selling the Multimixer itself. This he did, becoming its exclusive marketer.

Riding the Multimixer to prosperity, Kroc showed enormous energy and even greater adaptability; moreover, his market sense enabled him to shift his focus from individual lunch counters and dairy bars to chains such as Dairy Queen, Tastee-Freez, and to the expanding world of suburban drive-in restaurants such as those of the McDonald brothers, which attracted Kroc's attention by buying 10 Multimixers. What he "saw" there thus marked not the first flash of market insight, but the culmination of a series of them. Some of his ideas, like a folding table and bench set called "Fold-A-Nook," flopped but others had proved prescient enough to make him well off if not wealthy, with a home in a Chicago suburb and a country club membership.

Although Kroc later boasted that he had "put the hamburger on the assembly line," in fact the McDonald brothers, who had a cost consciousness to make Andrew Carnegie proud, had done that before Kroc came along. They had mechanized their hamburger factory right down to a "Lazy Susan" that spun two dozen buns at once past squirt guns dispensing precise doses of catsup and mustard, in a relentless drive to reduce costs and up volume. Kroc's market sense, not his knowledge of machinery, told him that he could take their concept nationwide. This vision reflected not only his salesman's sense of market, but also the cultural capital of someone who had spent three decades traveling coast-to-coast, acquiring a feel for the country, its people, and the restaurants that fed them. As one competitor observed, "Ray Kroc was always traveling, and when he thought of McDonald's, he thought big. He had seen cities all over the country and . . . could picture a McDonald's in every one of them." Kroc had encountered failure as well as success. The lessons of experience informed the unteachable instincts of the entrepreneur as he set out to turn his vision to reality by taking the entrepreneur's next step: assembling a strategy and a structure to embody it to reach the hordes of customers he *knew* waited all over America.

Between one hamburger stand in San Bernardino and a national, much less international, chain, there obviously lurked pitfalls aplenty. How many of these Kroc perceived at the outset will always remain a mystery, but he overcame them with a combination of logic, instinct, and a dash of good luck. He acted, moreover, as a man in a hurry, his hustling nature reinforced by an awareness that at age 52, he didn't have infinite amounts of time. This reality of course applies to people of any age, and the realization that time, not money, constitutes the scarcest resource often galvanizes entrepreneurial strategy. After all, running out of money ends in bankruptcy, for which the law offers remedies and American society absolution (like Henry Ford, most entrepreneurs have gone broke at one time or another); running out of time, however, ends in death, from which neither law nor society offers a reprieve.

As a peddler to restaurants, Kroc knew about franchising, the means by which most chain restaurants expanded quickly and widely. Dating back at least to the A&W Root Beer outlets of the 1920s, franchising powered the expansion of such stalwarts as Dairy Queen, Big Boy, Burger King, and Howard Johnson's. Franchising offered a lot of advantages: instant income from franchise fees; expansion using the franchisees' capital rather than that of the franchisors; and the prospect of long-term income from royalties on sales and markups on supplies. The method also exploited one of the principles dear to my father's generation: "People move fast with their own lumber." Because franchisees in effect worked for themselves, franchising provided the powerful capitalist incentive of personal gain and avoided the pitfalls of stifling bureaucracy that Pierre du Pont and Alfred Sloan had struggled to overcome. These benefits were moot, however, unless franchisees turned up, a development by no means assured in 1955, when Kroc made his deal with the McDonald brothers that gave him the right to run with the concept.

After the fact, Kroc's fans have cited his franchise agreements as evidence not only of his business acumen, but also of his fair, generous nature. Indeed, the agreements (the details of which we can leave to the legal historians) eschewed most of the usual devices whereby franchisors battened on the franchisees' lifeblood like ticks on a basset hound. Perhaps this restraint showed Kroc as a shrewd and generous fellow, but it may also have reflected a starker reality: when Kroc set out to expand McDonald's, he faced a major sales job. Few potential franchisees knew Kroc or the McDonald's concept. Alternative investment opportunities abounded in the restaurant business, itself notorious for a high failure rate among new entries. The thirst for capital always exceeds the supply, so investors can drive a hard bargain; to attract them Kroc offered generous terms, so generous, in fact, that by 1958 the firm's 38 franchises turned a profit while the McDonald's Corporation itself seemed headed for bankruptcy, having a limited income ($26,000 in 1957) and a net worth of $24,000, a pickle that Kroc himself knew no way to escape.

Kroc's refusal to grant more than one franchise at a time also lends itself to more than one interpretation. After the fact, it seemed astute because it enabled the parent company to control quality by declining, as it sometimes did, to grant a second franchise to an underperforming owner. On the other hand, people ready to take the risk of more than one unknown franchise, let alone several, proved so scarce that single-unit deals may simply have reflected a sellers' market for capital. It turned out that Kroc's "only hope of getting McDonald's off to a quick start" lay in his golfing buddies at the Rolling Green Country Club in Arlington Heights, Illinois. He recruited his first 18 franchisees from among these duffers, providing further proof (as though any were needed) of the wisdom of my advice to decades of first-year students: "Drop any business course you may have and add golf right away."

A similar duality applies to Kroc's lining up of suppliers. In the twenty-first century, suppliers hunger to serve McDonald's, the world's largest customer for beef, chicken, and potatoes. The company can afford to dispatch into outer darkness even such major providers as Kraft Foods, which refused to sharpen up the taste of its cheese, and Heinz, which—oh unforgivable trespass—failed to deliver catsup during a tomato shortage. But in the firm's early days, the shoe squeezed the other foot. When major producers such as Swift and Armour refused to extend credit to the fledgling firm, McDonald's had to seek smaller suppliers eager to take any business they could get and willing, if not eager, to accept McDonald's demands for credit and "quality" guidelines. (By "quality" I imply no endorsement of McDonald's food; you pays your money and you takes your choice. I mean only that McDonald's set certain standards for suppliers and dumped, or claimed to have dumped, those that didn't meet them.)

On the strength of such early connections, suppliers such as French-fry king J. R. Simplot and obscure Schreiber Cheese of Green Bay rode the McDonald's express to fortune if not fame. In business, such prosperity always comes at a price. Just as Henry Ford's notoriously parsimonious purchasing people showed up in Sloan's office at Hyatt Roller Bearing, demanding lower prices and showing him how to afford them, McDonald's demands for expanded volume at low prices drove food processors to develop new technologies and methods, such as Simplot's long-run search for a frozen French fry that would reduce the in-store cooking time while retaining enough flavor to keep customers buying it.

As originally structured, Kroc's McDonald's faced an uncertain fate, but salvation came by way of one of Kroc's genuine gifts, the ability to find talented subordinates, hire them, and let them work their wonders. This too constitutes one of the entrepreneur's most vital skills, as recognized by the venture capitalists' maxim that a second-rate idea in the hands of a first-rate team makes a far more promising investment than the reverse. Human expertise, like time, proves much harder to find than money. Kroc found just the help he needed in Harry J. Sonneborn, whom he hired in 1956. In four years, Sonneborn's strategy raised McDonald's net worth from $24,000 to more than $16 million and put the company firmly on the road to even greater growth.

Sonneborn's success stemmed from his dedication to and application of several basic principles of business, most of which Kroc himself either didn't know or didn't care about, something the founder acknowledged: "Harry alone put in the policy that salvaged this company . . . and really made McDonald's rich." Sonneborn shared Sloan's view that a business's first purpose was to make money; its products merely provided the means to that end. Sonneborn didn't give a damn about hamburgers per se, and frequently said so, much to the annoyance of Kroc, who genuinely seems to have thought of his company's products with affection. Kroc's franchise agreements precluded making much money from existing franchisees, but Sonneborn had answers to the questions all businesses should ask themselves regularly: "What business are we in? What business should we be in?" To Sonneborn, the answer seemed clear: the road to wealth lay not in the hamburger business, but in the real estate business.

To translate this realization into practice and profits, Sonneborn created a strategy that in effect converted the parent McDonald's Corporation into a landlord, amassing its revenues in the form of rent from franchisees, assessed at a rate that rose as a franchise's sales increased. Sonneborn himself said, "We are not basically in the food business. We are in the real estate business. The only reason we sell fifteen-cent hamburgers is because they are the greatest producers of revenue from which our tenants can pay us rent." Although Kroc deplored Sonneborn's characterization of his firm, the two men's talents powerfully reinforced each other, for Kroc proved to have a knack, bolstered by scouting from the air, for choosing locations, especially in or near the blossoming suburbs, and for hiring men with similar flair.

Despite more complex franchise agreements in later years that provide the company with a more diverse revenue stream, more than half of McDonald's profits come from its real estate operations, which now rest on the most valuable collection of real property in the world. American business history repeatedly shows the connection between real estate and other enterprises. Factories and stores don't float on air; they rest on the ground, which itself has a value at least partially determined by the fortunes of the businesses that occupy it. Andrew Carnegie cautioned his associates that the firm's own productivity would drive down the price of its products even as it carried the firm to prosperity. On the other hand, McDonald's, Walmart, and other firms with thousands of units may benefit from a reverse effect: their success can multiply the value of their own and adjacent properties, with a major impact on balance sheet assets as well as the fixed cost of property taxes.

All these realities Sonneborn understood, and he knew how to obtain the resources needed to get the burger chain into the landlord business. This task required persuading banks to supply some of the necessary capital, which meant overcoming a resistance grounded in the fact that bankers tend to understand debt, that is, an obligation secured by a mortgage on a real asset, but to have difficulty with the concept of equity, that is, ownership of something that will grow in value. Land the banks understood, but these parcels would have hamburger joints sitting on them. If the burgers didn't generate bucks, McDonald's would default on the mortgages. The banks could foreclose, but no bank wanted to own a slew of defunct fast-food emporia.

Sonneborn overcame the banks' resistance through a series of moves that lay beyond Kroc's ken. He hired a former IRS accountant and lawyer to give the McDonald's balance sheet a face-lift. With this in hand, Sonneborn persuaded State Mutual and Paul Revere insurance companies to take 22.5 percent of McDonald's stock in return for making a $3 million loan at 7 percent. The insurance companies' officers, unlike bank executives, understood equity, routinely did risk assessments, and thought McDonald's future promising, an opinion bolstered by several on-site visits including one to the then-most-successful franchise of all, located halfway between Boston and New York. One of the actuaries saw that future and it looked good: "I couldn't believe it," he said. "You could get a drink, fries, and a hamburger for less than fifty cents. *This was real value*" (italics added). And here lay the key to McDonald's coming success, for capitalism depends on investment, and investment depends upon expectations of *future* income.

To get the loan, McDonald's paid a steep price, but a bargain nevertheless given that it "bought" an unsecured loan 20 times the amount of the firm's real net worth at the time. Kroc saw this as an equity giveaway, which rubbed him the wrong way. "Ray was mad as hell," Sonneborn later reported, but he taught Kroc the basic lesson cited earlier about ownership and control: "You've got to remember, Ray, that seventy-eight percent of something is a lot better than one hundred percent of nothing." In the end, the loan turned out a bargain for everybody involved. The lenders got back their loan plus 7 percent interest and sold their stock, for which they had paid nothing, for $20 million. As for McDonald's, as one observer later declared, "This loan gave them credibility in the financial arena. They essentially built the company on it."

With the gussied-up balance sheet further adorned by the loans from two top-ranked financial institutions, Sonneborn went on to bigger and better things: a series of bank loans, followed by the proceeds from the sale of stock when the company went public in 1964, selling shares at $22.50 that by 2004 had a value of $24,000 each. Sonneborn parted ways with Ray Kroc in 1967, but by that time he had set the company on a solid financial footing and cleared the way for the growth of the following decades. Showing once again his talent-spotting abilities, Kroc promoted Fred Turner to head the company. Turner had started as a McDonald's counterman, moved up to franchisee, and made himself an operations specialist. With him in charge, McDonald's expanded rapidly, adding hundreds of units annually, many of them abroad.

The company's ongoing success demonstrated that Ray Kroc himself had an answer to the question "What business are you in?"; although his answer differed from Sonneborn's, it had a value of its own. McDonald's may or may not operate a food business, depending on one's definition of "food" (as opposed to, say, "fuel"), but a casual visit to a McDonald's anywhere in the world reveals its business of facilitating time management for young families. This market may embody Kroc's greatest perception: that in the late-twentieth-century world, more and more families needed two wage earners, but many had only one adult at home. Fewer and fewer people had the time or the energy to shop and cook. A competitor advertised, "Don't cook tonight. Call Chicken Delight." At McDonald's, this siren song became "You deserve a break today," and millions of people agreed. Kroc reinforced this strategy by pitching his place and his product line specifically to kids, with Ronald McDonald, Happy Meals, and playgrounds, confident that kids would bring their parents along (as mine certainly brought me), and that the lure would work on Canadians, Chinese, Japanese, Russians, indeed children the world round.

With this strategy, Kroc certainly caught a wave, for more and more families feel pressed for time. As evidence, we have jokes such as "How do the kids know it's dinner time?" Answer, "When the parents say 'Get your coats,'" and a 2005 statistic claiming that Americans swill 20 percent of their meals in cars, some major segment of these no doubt snarfed up at McDonald's "drive-through" troughs.

Kroc died in 1984, the year the company opened its 8,000th store. That statistic says many things about the power an entrepreneur can generate by combining a market perception with strategy and personnel able to weather the storms that inevitably beset a growing firm. As the global leader, McDonald's attracts a lot of flak, as it did in Kroc's day as well. He tended to dismiss detractors as cranks who wanted to undermine "our free enterprise system."

Kroc had a strategy, and he saw its success, as Carnegie saw his, as validation of both his own virtue and the beauties of the American system. That strategy also made the company a target for critics who attacked the diabolically uncomfortable seats and intense lighting that made it impossible to linger; the architecture that imprinted an identity at the cost of besmirching the landscape with thousands of eyesores; the labor practices that exploited and intimidated and regimented, resulting in a revolving-door turnover; the villainous food, saturated in grease and salt; the decimation of rainforests for the raising of cheap beef; the enormous quantity of waste flushed into the environment in the form of wrappers, cartons, and cups; the paranoiac fury with which the company unleashed its kennel of pit-bull lawyers on any who slandered or copied or imitated the Golden Arches and all they stood for; the Ronald McDonald Pied Piper and the "Happy Meal" jingles with which Ronald lured children to obese oblivion; and so on *ad nauseum*.

Kroc himself, rejecting criticism and eulogizing free enterprise, argued that the market would make the final judgments. His successors, fearing that despite market success, public complaints might perhaps bring government intervention—abroad, if not in America—faced the challenge of finding new ways to profit while soothing criticism. Thus motivated, the company came up with an answer, or at least a retort, for each complaint. Where once McDonald's prohibited pay telephones (remember those?) lest teenagers gabble endlessly while buying little, it now offers "free Wi-Fi" in 11,000 stores, including such remote locations as Greymouth, New Zealand. The company's once adamant stand on Golden Arches architecture has softened selectively to embrace designs more harmonious with store surroundings. The firm has reacted to critiques of its "McJobs" by publicizing success stories of workers, especially immigrants, who began at the bottom and became executives or franchisees.

McDonald's added a "dollar menu" and an assortment of premium coffees to entice consumers from a broader economic spectrum. It posted its nutritional information online and in its stores; it diversified its menu, adding salads, apple slices, and other less calorific options to its gallimaufry of burgers and deep-fried victuals; it uses Shrek and other cartoon characters on milk cartons and claims to have doubled milk sales; it has engaged in a widely publicized campaign to reduce waste by using 80 percent packaging made from renewable sources, including 30 percent from recycled materials. Altogether these stratagems have yielded impressive results. By 2009, McDonalds ranked #108 on the "Fortune 500," with $228 billion in sales. It operated 32,000 stores in 100 countries, including 12,000 in the United States and 3,000 in Japan. In the last quarter of 2009, its profits rose 23 percent over the last quarter of 2008.

Meanwhile, we have an impressive testimony to Kroc's theory of the universal appeal of the hamburger. *Economist* magazine (or "newspaper," as it foppishly insists on calling itself) annually publishes the "Big Mac Index," which uses a comparison of Big Mac prices around the world to assess the validity of international currency exchange rates. In the "basket of commodities," so essential to economists seeking to make such comparisons, the Big Mac may approximate the only constant in 119 countries.

In the United States itself, Walmart has emerged as an equally salient presence. In some ways it resembles McDonald's, and in fact it increasingly houses McDonald's restaurants on Walmart premises. Both firms, driven by the vision of an individual founder, sought, reached, and served mass markets at home and abroad so effectively that in the second half of the twentieth century, they rose from modest beginnings to the top of fiercely competitive retail trades. Both fall in the "service industry" category but sell manufactured products, primarily (entirely in McDonald's case) "low tech"; both have triggered fierce loyalty among customers and boiling geysers of vitriol among critics; both defend themselves belligerently against attack, deploying platoons of lawyers, lobbyists, publicists, spin doctors, and other shape-shifters to keep their escutcheons unbesmirched; both cite their commercial success as refutation of any indictments leveled against them. Detractors argue that success only proves the persuasive power of mass advertising, and that behind the façade of beneficence (Ronald McDonald Houses, Walmart & SAM'S CLUB Foundation), the ruthless competitive practices, the virulent hostility to unions, and the low wages generate a slagheap of consequences that outweigh any possible good.

Because these debates swirl around two iconic participants in the American business system, they effectively act as surrogates for the underlying debate about the nature of capitalism itself. The Krocs and the Waltons, much like classic economists, believe that the market provides all the mechanisms needed to assure proper distribution of goods and services, jobs and wages, dividends and fringe benefits. Customers can, as Walton pointed out, "vote with their feet," and in fact "voted" Howard Johnson's out of the food business and K-Mart into bankruptcy, while making McDonald's and Walmart rich, powerful, iconic. Sometimes pressure seems to yield some results, as when McDonald's posts nutritional data about its food, adds salads to its menu, and reduces its packaging; Walmart headlines its charitable contributions, the diversity of its workforce, and the benefits of working there.

In Walmart's case, the euphemistic company line masks some harsh realities. For example, Walmart claims to pay better than the average wage in its industry, but the company's own data reveal that the "average" full-time Walmart "associate" earns $20,134 a year, about enough below the federal poverty guideline income for a family of four ($22,050) to make the McDonald's "dollar menu" an expensive night on the town. Walmart exalts its "everyday low prices" and buyers flock to them, but the company doesn't say, and its customers may not realize, that not only cheap goods pour out of those containers from Guangzhou and Hanoi, but Chinese and Vietnamese wage scales as well. Sam Walton argued that his firm "saved" and "salvaged" small towns by bringing jobs to the residents and drawing customers into town from the hinterlands; critics say that Walmart's arrival "destroys" local businesses.

Amid the static of conflicting claims, this we know: people *must* buy to live, and not only the obvious necessities such as food, but over time most also crave the trappings that, thanks to the socialization process (catalyzed by advertising's drumfire), provide a sense of accomplishment, beauty, belonging, and status: television sets, face-lifts, the "right" athletic shoes, or BMWs. This proclivity leads to Thorstein Veblen's "conspicuous consumption" and underlies Alfred Sloan's insight that people wanted automobiles for something more than the utilitarian needs met by Ford's Model T. This too we know: all but a few must sell their labor for the best price it will command in the market. These transactions make lawyers rich and keep farm workers poor, an assessment of value that might seem a distorted reflection of their relative contributions to society. Americans certainly have the power to change the system if they wish, but thus far it seems to satisfy enough folks enough of the time to survive with its essential nature intact. Meanwhile, the Ray Krocs and Sam Waltons, like the Carnegies, Fords, Sloans, et al., accepted, yea verily embraced, these realities and found them good.

Sam Walton understood that people at all levels of income had similar motivations to buy, and that most people, especially in small towns, had to satisfy needs and wants on a limited income. Walton shared Henry Ford's perception about the market: the lower the price, the more people could and would buy. To this principle, he added the Carnegie strategy of maintaining low prices by relentlessly controlling costs. Everything he did followed from these axioms. Time bore out his belief in the compelling attraction of low prices, a no-brainer in the sense that stores had long had sales, including the famous ones at Filene's Basement in Boston that had customers lining up before dawn and Boston's mounted cops ready to ride in to restore order.

Walton, like other discounters, transformed the traditional "sale," limited to some items on special occasions, into a daily affair involving every item in the store, "all low prices all the time," in the Walmart vernacular. This principle succeeded from the outset, and it continues daily to draw millions of customers into the Walmart lairs in the United States and abroad. Plenty of other firms, however, embraced the same strategy;

Sam Walton exhorts his troops

in 1962, when Walton opened the first Walmart, Kresge opened the first K-Mart, Woolworth the first Woolco, and Dayton-Hudson the first Target. What distinguished Walton from his competitors was his ability to construct an organization that maintained the basic policy through the crises that attended an unremitting growth strategy.

Maintaining the Walmart discount "formula" involved judicious site selection, the care and feeding of employee enthusiasm, multiple cost-control strategies, and a massive investment in behind-the-scenes "high-tech" equipment that contrasted sharply with the low-tech stuff on the shelves. Walton himself played a major role. Learning to fly helped him, like Kroc, do aerial scouting for store sites; he also used his plane for years to flit around the growing Walmart empire, keeping an eye on things and whooping it up (literally) with the "associates," as he euphemistically called his myrmidons. Walton, like Henry Ford II, knew that a chance to talk to the owner made a lasting impression on rank-and-file toilers. He himself had a lifelong memory of meeting J. C. Penney. For Walton, who had a cheerleader's personality, the role came easily, and he reveled in it.

In addition to a flair for motivating minions by injecting them with the Walmart spirit, Walton also displayed that crucial faculty that, as the chapters here have shown, often determines success or failure: a gift for seeing and promoting management talent. In fact, Walton himself once described the manager's primary responsibility as "simply" that of getting "the right people in the right places . . . and then encourag[ing] them to use their own inventiveness to accomplish the job at hand." Some of the "right people" he found in odd places, including the first store manager he hired, Bob Bogle, the "town sanitarian" of Bentonville, Arkansas, whose work consisted of inspecting septic tanks and evaluating the hygienic conditions of dairy barns.

That Walmart began in, and has long been identified with small towns resulted naturally from Sam Walton's own background. Born in 1918, the son of a farmer turned farm-loan appraiser, Walton grew up in various Missouri towns, and much of his youth coincided with the Great Depression. Unlike Chicago city slicker Kroc, who dropped out of high school to try his luck as a piano player, small-town boy Walton graduated from high school in Columbia, Missouri, having distinguished himself as an athlete (quarterback of the state championship football team) and an assiduous if not a brilliant student, but especially as an engaging personality, voted president of his senior class and the school's "most versatile boy." Walton's family, like so many others in the Great Depression, lived in the ominous shadow of potential unemployment and practiced thrift accordingly: "My mother and dad shared completely . . . their approach to money: they just didn't spend it." They also shared a belief in the value of education, evidenced by Walton's matriculating at the nearby University of Missouri, where he built a reputation as a "hustler" (implying, in the vernacular of the time, a "go-getter," not a con man).

Walton graduated in 1940 with an undergraduate degree in economics, worth about as much then as in the early twenty-first century: it got him a job as a management trainee at J. C. Penney for $75 a month. (By way of comparison, my father started as a sheet metalworker at Du Pont the same year, making three times as much.) In 1942, he resigned and joined the army, where he spent the war supervising guards at defense plants and prisoner-of-war camps. Along the way he acquired a wife, a prosperous father-in-law, and a determination to work for himself in the only field he knew anything about, retailing. Once discharged from the military, Walton set out to fulfill his ambitions by acquiring a store. He had St. Louis in mind, but his wife wanted a town of no more than 10,000 people and her father had the money. In the fall of 1945, Walton bought a Ben Franklin variety store (a franchise of Butler Brothers, a national wholesaler) in Newport, Arkansas, population 5,000. Combining his natural talents as salesman, enthusiast, and all-around good fellow with the lessons he had learned at J. C. Penney, in the army, and from Butler Brothers training programs, he launched the career that made retailing history.

Walton soon discovered the magic of reduced prices and made it his basic stock in trade. Low prices fell even lower during frequent sales. Driven by the power of the elastic market for the simple household goods that Ben Franklin stores stocked and everyone needed, the store's sales rose from $105,000 in 1946 to $250,000 in five years. By 1951, he felt certain he had found a formula for success in any small town. His choice fell on Bentonville, Arkansas (population 3,000), where "Walton's 5 & 10" opened in 1950 (and where Walmart has had its headquarters since 1969). Success there led to a second store, in Fayetteville, Arkansas, followed in rapid succession by others in such way stations as Springdale, Siloam Springs, Neodesha, and Coffeyville. Walton found his managers by "nos[ing] around other people's stores searching . . . without any shame or embarrassment . . . for good talent." He also checked out other stores' prices, inventories, and store layouts to see what he could learn. In 1952, he rode a bus to Minnesota to see "self-service" (then virtually unknown) in two Ben Franklin stores. Impressed, he installed it in his Fayetteville store the following year, and it became standard throughout his growing empire, which by 1962 included 16 stores, many of them Ben Franklin franchises.

By 1962, however, Walton had seen the handwriting on the wall and didn't like what it said. The "discount revolution" had gotten underway in the 1950s, led by firms such as E. J. Korvette and "Two Guys From Harrison." By 1962, it had gathered momentum; average discount store sales doubled from $1.5 million per store in 1960 to $3 million in 1962. The traditional variety store, of which Walton owned 16, lay squarely in the path of this juggernaut. Although the discount store at the time remained primarily a feature of the United States north of the Ohio and east of the Mississippi Rivers, Walton, perhaps mindful of the success of his low prices, foresaw its inevitable expansion and went to see the phenomenon first hand. Traveling around the Northeast, passing himself off as a bumpkin from Arkansas, he found plenty of evidence to confirm his anxiety.

Soon enough the threat invaded Walton territory in the form of the Gibson's Discount Center chain, which operated with the motto "Buy it low, stack it high, sell it cheap." Gibson stores opened in Fort Smith and Fayetteville, prompting Walton to opt for the discount route himself. First he tried to persuade Ben Franklin's parent company to franchise him in a discount store; they'd have none of it. Then he tried to affiliate with Gibson, which also rejected him. This left him, he said, with "only two choices . . . stay in the variety store business" and "get hit hard by the discounting wave of the future, or open a discount store."

Walton spoke of the wave of "the future," but in fact he knew it had already arrived. Like Kroc and a handful of others, he saw the future in the now, the kind of market that entrepreneurs sense and exploit, the market that already exists. He knew the vigor that low prices injected into sales; he knew the statistics of discount store sales; he, like Sloan, stood ready to sink "everything he had in the world" in his business to turn his perception, his experience, and his resources into profits. And in fact, the venture took just that. Bankers rebuffed him, so Walton financed the new business himself, mortgaging "houses and property, everything we had." In July 1962, the first "Walmart" (the name suggested by Bob Bogle, erstwhile cesspool maven) opened in Rogers, Arkansas, with the slogans "We sell for less" and "Satisfaction guaranteed" emblazoned across the storefront. Store manager Don Whitaker advertised "everyday low prices in all departments." From the first day the store, and thus the concept, prospered.

Other stores soon followed in such places as Harrison, Springdale, Siloam Springs, Conway, Fayetteville, and Mountain Home in Arkansas; Sikeston, Missouri; and Tahlequah, Oklahoma—a total of 18 by the end of 1969. These stores exhibited two characteristics basic to the Walmart expansion strategy: locate in small towns and build out densely and gradually from the company center in Bentonville, rather than scatter widely. These principles reflected both the market and cost advantages that Walton saw inherent in small towns. As for the market, Walton, as a veteran operator of small-town variety stores, knew that in his chosen locales his firm would face little effective competition, giving him a monopoly likely to endure in places too small to support two such establishments. As late as the mid-1980s, more than a third of Walmart's 800 stores had no local competition, and more than half operated in towns with a population between 5,000 and 25,000.

Walton knew that in such small towns, the much-romanticized "small businesses" in fact often served customers poorly, the "personal touch" frequently overshadowed by mediocre service, limited choice, and high prices. Those high prices left room for Walton to maneuver—room he needed, for in the firm's early days it lacked the leverage it later acquired to drive merciless bargains with its suppliers. At the outset, some vendors would not sell to Walmart at all, or as Walton told it, exhibited "a good bit of arrogance." Vendors "wanted to dictate how much they would sell us and at what price. . . . They didn't need us, and they acted that way." (In time, the arrogance ran the other way; in the mid-1980s, one supplier called Walmart "the rudest account in America.")

Despite having an effective monopoly that in many cases endured for years, Walmart refrained from engaging in monopolistic pricing. Walton wanted to build customer loyalty and a reputation that would ensure a welcome for new Walmarts as they opened. In addition, while raising prices might have increased profits in the short run, such a price umbrella might also lure other discounters. In the early years, Walmart lacked the resources to confront K-Mart, Woolco, and Target, firms with "deep-pocket" corporate parents.

Small towns also offered many of the cost advantages Walton knew underpinned a low-price strategy. He understood this principle as well as Carnegie and Ford ever had, and like those firms before him, Walton insisted that Walmart management strategy must center on a relentless pursuit of cost reduction from the day the first door opened. Real estate cost less in small towns than in larger urban areas, an advantage whether the firm bought buildings or built them, owned them or leased them. Small-town labor came cheap as well, especially in the South with its long tradition of low-cost, nonunion workforces; the first Walmart paid its workers less than the minimum wage of the time. In most of the company's early locations, it quickly became the largest employer by far, with all the leverage attached to such power. Walton made no secret of his hostility to unions, openly threatening to fire or cancel the benefits of employees who flirted with unionization. He said he'd rather close a store than deal with a union, a threat later carried out by his successors.

Walton knew that labor presented him with a dilemma. On the one hand, like most discounters, he felt that he had to squeeze some profit from the workers by keeping labor costs—salaries, fringe benefits, number of employees per store—low. This policy meant not only paying low wages, but also limiting the number of full-time employees by hiring part-timers who got no benefits such as health insurance or paid vacations. On the other hand, unhappy employees cost money by offending customers, by venting their resentment in theft and sabotage—more common in American business than generally known—and above all by quitting. High employee turnover inflicts a high overhead cost, for even the most menial jobs require some degree of training, as well as the expense of hiring, processing paperwork, and so on. From the beginning, Walmart had a high turnover rate, and the problem metastasized as the company expanded into larger stores, many of them open seven days a week and 24 hours a day. The booming American economy further intensified competition for workers, especially good ones. Indeed, by the late 1990s, Walmart's annual turnover rates, long in the range of 30 percent to 40 percent, had risen to 70 percent.

Walton himself believed that success in the retail trade absolutely depended on employee morale that translated into good service to customers, and he saw himself as one of the keys to maintaining it. He wanted his "associates" to catch "Walmart fever," a hallucinogen inducing in employees the delusion that they had a great job working for a good company that cared about them as people despite paying them poverty-level wages, hiring as few as possible full-time workers, and threatening to dismiss the disloyal. Walton adopted a range of policies designed to spread and maintain this contagion, foremost among them the application of the folksy Walton personal touch.

This tactic Walton certainly didn't invent. Long before him, Carnegie had observed of his workers that they would "never [make] hopeless troubles . . . as long as they call me Andy." Henry Ford II, having inherited not just a crippled car company, but the most hostile labor force in the industry to boot, made a point of walking through Ford factories all over the world, starting at River Rouge in 1945. Walton, flying himself from town to town, showing up in his stores to mingle with the workers and managers, joined the ranks of these "charismatic bureaucrats" able to dazzle the rank and file into solidarity, preserving the image of a down-to-earth guy running a small-town variety store long after Walmart had dozens of stores and hundreds of millions of dollars in annual sales.

As part of the magic show, Walmart literature and industry journals over the years sported pictures of Sam amid his troops, often jaunty in a one-size-fits-all Walmart baseball cap, or in mid-gyration while leading the "Walmart Cheer," as in "Gimme a W, gimme an A, gimme . . . " well, never mind the rest. Occasionally the program included an adaptation of the Arkansas Razorbacks' battle cry, "Sooooooeeey Pig, Pig, Pig." (The delight this bunkum produced in the ranks testifies to the lifelong socializing impact of high school football games and evangelical Protestantism in the South.) That supposedly intelligent adult employees would see in this *opera bouffe* an adequate substitute for a living wage and health insurance speaks to both the mystery and the marvel of the American economy or, as explained in the musical *1776*, "most men with nothing would rather protect the possibility of becoming rich than face the reality of being poor."

Behind this hootenanny of hokum, Walmart adopted a more secular set of policies designed to secure employee continuity, morale, and good will. To its full-time workers, the firm gradually extended such fringe benefits as health insurance. Promotions often came from within the ranks, offering the faithful the chance to rise to management positions that paid better salaries and dangled the possibility of bonuses and profit sharing. In 1972, Walmart extended profit sharing, which Walton had offered his managers from the first day he hired one, down into the ranks and initiated a stock-purchase plan with shares paid for through payroll deductions boosted by a company contribution. Participants benefited from dividends and from the rising value of stock, which made a share that cost $16.50 in 1970 worth $26,000 when Walton died in 1991. For many workers who joined early, the returns from these plans often exceeded their incomes from wages or salaries. Walton himself gleefully told stories of employee enrichment, including a truck driver who collected $700,000 in 20 years of profit sharing, and another toiler who accumulated half a million dollars by age 40. That some of the profit "shared" came from the suppressed wages of all and the nonexistent benefit costs for part-timers didn't come up in Walton's homilies; moreover, one might ask how many reaped such bounties and how many it took to keep the myth vibrant enough to "string up the nerves" and "give tone and strength" to those trudging on the treadmill of poverty-level wages.

Walmart also provided incentives for employees to increase profits by sharing in cost savings that resulted from their efforts. By the late 1970s, for example, the firm had adopted a "shrink the shrink" program, the "shrink" being everything lost to employee theft (a common form of sabotage or an informal means of awarding oneself a pay raise), shoplifting, or breakage. By offering to share equally any store's shrinkage savings with its employees, Walmart reduced its shrinkage costs from 1.8 percent to 1.4 percent of sales in 1984. This amount might seem trivial, except that it occurred in an industry in which net profit margins run in the vicinity of 3 percent. In 1984, shrink shrinkage saved $6.5 million, which dropped straight to the bottom line, raising the net profit from 5.2 percent to 5.6 percent of sales, and adding to the firm's cost advantage over its competitors because the industry average for shrinkage loss almost doubled Walmart's.

As the firm grew from 38 stores in 1971 to 1,198 in 1988, when Walton retired as CEO, the most daunting cost-control problems involved inventory and distribution—having the right goods, bought at the right price, in the right stores at the right time, at the minimum cost of storing, shipping, labeling, and keeping track of them. Whatever variations on the original formula the firm introduced only intensified this challenge to cost minimization. Until the 1980s, the firm largely stuck to its small-town strategy, expanding in concentric circles around company "distribution centers" that served the function once performed by independent "jobbers": collecting merchandise from many suppliers and parceling it out in mixed batches to individual stores.

As the firm grew farther and farther beyond Bentonville, it developed a policy of building distribution centers first, then deploying stores around them, none at a distance greater than 400 miles. This system served well in the 1980s when Walton sought to diversify the company's format to accelerate growth. At his behest, Walmart reconfigured its strategy to serve markets in larger urban areas. This strategy had two parts: the first, based on Walton's perception, akin to Ray Kroc's, of the suburbs as "growth areas," involved surrounding cities with suburban stores bigger than those in small towns. By 1984, for example, Walmart had nine stores within a 30-mile radius of Springfield, Missouri, population 150,000, and average store size had risen from 47,000 square feet to 63,000.

The second part of the strategy took the form of "Sam's Wholesale Clubs." Designed to sell large quantities of a limited range of items (3,500, including packaged, canned, and frozen groceries, as opposed to 70,000 in a typical Walmart) at deep discounts in a bare-bones setting, the first Sam's Club opened in Oklahoma City in April 1983. Customers included not just individuals, but such small businesses as restaurants, convenience stores, mom-and-pop retailers, and gas stations as well. The advantage of selling groceries under the same roof as the traditional Walmart inventory led to the opening of the first "Supercenter" in Washington, Missouri, in March 1988.

In each store configuration, Sam Walton showed his acumen for improving an existing model to better serve an existing market. As K-Mart had provided a point of departure and comparison for Walmart, so Price Club, a West Coast firm, served as a template for Sam's Club, and Meijer's Thrifty Acres for the Walmart Supercenter. Walton's genius lay in the continuous adaptations that made Walmart more efficient and thus more profitable than its competitors. Some of these adaptations, like self-service, he implemented himself. Others demonstrated his ability to recognize good ideas that came from subordinates. Some, like the idea for the Walmart "greeter," rose from the employee rank and file. Others, for instance the 1977 introduction of computers to track and analyze sales and inventory data, came from executives such as David Glass, vice president of finance. "Sam never did like computers," Glass said, but he accepted the idea because he had self-confidence enough to bow to superior expertise. Walton had similar misgivings about the construction of a satellite network in 1987 to link all the company's units with multifaceted communications media to transmit voice and data. "It blows my mind," he said, "that we spent $20 million on a satellite outfit." He spent it nonetheless.

The wisdom of these strategies, including the melding of high-tech management and low-tech merchandise, appeared regularly in the company's cost data. By the late 1980s, for example, Walmart had reduced its distribution costs to 1.3 percent of sales, compared to 3.5 percent for K-Mart and 5 percent for Sears. In 1991, Walmart had overhead costs equal to 15 percent of sales, compared to K-Mart's 23 percent and Sears' 29 percent. These data foretold the grim future of Walton's erstwhile major competitors. The same data validated—at the bottom line and in the rising price of Walmart stock—Walmart's strategic blend of an unyielding focus on low costs and low prices with a supple outlook toward the stores themselves, that is, a willingness to match marts to markets by implementing a range of store locations, sizes, and inventories.

These policies made Sam Walton, at least for a while, the richest man in the world. Eventually, of course, Walmart confronted the succession crisis that comes to all successful firms when the time arrives for the founder to move along. For Walton, that time came in 1988, when he passed the job of CEO to David Glass. The continued meteoric rise of his company after Walton's retirement, followed by his death in 1991, shows that he passed with flying colors the ultimate test of a founding entrepreneur: knowing when to go and whom to put in charge. Under Glass and those who succeeded him, Walmart has prospered mightily, ranking #1 on the 2009 "Fortune 500" with $408 billion in sales—six times those of its closest retail rival, Target, and *11 times* those of the far flashier Apple.

Along the way, however, Walton's successors stumbled when they selectively abandoned the founder's cherished "Every Day Low Price" formula in favor of a smaller range of discounted items, interspersed with pricier (and thus more profitable) goods. Stung by this apostasy many customers skedaddled to dollar-store chains, a flight that hammered Walmart with seven consecutive quarters of declining sales beginning in 2009. "We tried to stretch the brand a little too far," admitted the Walmart factotum charged with reversing the decline.

Despite this stumble, Walmart in 2009 operated 8,446 stores in 15 countries in North America, Europe, Latin America, and Asia. Its unrelenting program of expansion translated into a Walmart within 15 miles of 90 percent of the U.S. population. Having added 500,000 employees in five years, it had 2.1 million workers, including 1.4 million in the United States (at an average full-time wage of $11.75 an hour), making it America's largest civilian employer. Its drug-marketing strategy ($4 for many prescriptions) forced competitors to go along and won the gratitude of millions, especially among the elderly. Its attempts to get into the banking business terrified the banking establishment into near hysteria at the thought of a competitor that might eliminate the piratical fees with which it bleeds its customers. As one observer said, "The banking community's opinion was that the world as [they] knew it would come to an end."

Walmart alone accounts for 10 percent of all U.S. imports from China, making it China's eighth largest customer, ahead of entire countries including Russia and India. It also buys more products from American suppliers such as Proctor and Gamble than any other client. It remains in the forefront of cost control and inventory management through technologies that connect the cash registers to warehouses and in some cases directly to suppliers. It has experimented with RFID (radio frequency identification tags) to replace bar codes.

Walmart remains under constant assault, in court and out, from many directions. These include a sex-discrimination class-action lawsuit; union attempts to organize the "associates," and union claims that Walmart's purchasing in China has cost 200,000 American manufacturing jobs; sundry accusations that Walmart pollutes, wastes energy, and uses excessive packaging; and a panoply of other indictments that fill the many websites dedicated to publicizing Walmart's warts. The company counterattacks energetically with its battalion of lawyers, its massive publicity engine, and its pep rallies for associates. Walmart claims to have adopted an ongoing program of waste reduction and energy conservation. It argues that it creates more jobs than it destroys, and that it treats all its employees fairly, promoting them on merit regardless of ethnicity or gender, and so on, and so on. Amidst these claims and counter claims, one certainty looms: these problems and others like them won't go away, and future managers will have to deal with them.

For Michael Dell, born in 1965, the succession challenge lies in the future. His demonstrated willingness to seek help outside the company and share power within it might bode well for a smooth transition when the time comes. On the other hand, some of his recruits, such as Kevin Rollins, named CEO in 2004 and deposed in 2007, have run aground on the Peter Principle, suggesting that Michael Dell may lack Sam Walton's knack for finding gifted subordinates. Meanwhile, Dell himself and the company he built have become the stuff of legends, particularly the American legend that individuals can achieve great things. Competitors have envied and emulated Dell Computer; business journalists have praised and pandered to it; business scholars have confected case studies explaining it; investors have adored and anointed it, especially the "Dellionaires" who tailed the company's comet into the growth galaxy. Founded in 1984, in 20 years the firm rose to or near the peak of its industry in terms of market share in the United States and abroad. Along the way, one share of Dell stock bought at $8.50 in 1988 had risen by April 2005 to $3,343.68 (though by 2010 the market price of Dell shares had fallen from $40 to $12).

The basic facts about the "Dell model" have become common currency. For much of its history, the firm sold through no intermediaries, only direct to customers by phone, by Internet, or in the case of large clients, through its own sales representatives. By assembling its products only when it had a customer order (and payment) in hand, it became the paradigmatic "build to order" (BTO) operation, reducing inventory of finished products to zero and of parts to four days, as opposed to 20 days at IBM and 28

Michael Dell atop the PC world

at Hewlett-Packard. The associated cost reductions translated into lower prices, thus greater sales, thus higher profits. Recognizing that in buying computers, customers choose as much or more on the basis of service as on price, Dell established a variety of service plans, including on-call, on-site support, throughout the 80 countries where it operated. (Validating Dell's theory: I bought a Dell to take to France for a year specifically because unlike its competitors, who made vague noises about "service centers where *you* can take it," Dell promised me that in case of trouble they'd come to me and fix it. They did, twice, and bilingually at that.)

Given Dell Computer's success and dominant position in its industry, journalists tended to perceive Michael Dell as a seer who peered into the welter of hardware and software, competition and strategy, and selected among them as one selects chocolates from a box—not this one, but that one. As so often happens with journalists, that version ignored the past and in the process did a disservice both to its subject and to its readers. Indeed, the Dell story proves that history can inform, in this case showing that the Dell model originally arose from necessity, not clairvoyance, and that Michael Dell's genius lay in adapting the method that served a dorm-room company of one to run a global company of 54,000. It also reveals that Dell, like Carnegie and so many other successful entrepreneurs, invented nothing in the classic sense—no gadgets, no machines, no better mousetraps. Instead, Dell epitomized Joseph Schumpeter's "entrepreneur," defined as an "innovator" who finds "a new way" to serve a market. Dell did this by making extensive use of existing components, both intangibles such as management techniques and tangibles such as computer chips and disc drives, thus minimizing the risks associated with the unknown and untried ("Pioneering don't pay," said Carnegie), risks that mow down startup companies like McCormick harvesters munching a wheat field. For Dell, innovation lay in finding new ways to use things readily at hand.

In fact, he could have done nothing else in the beginning. A teenager with few resources in terms of money and no formal management training, Dell started with a fund of cultural capital amassed during his youth in the 1970s by such things as family dinner table conversations "about what the chairman of the Federal Reserve was doing and how it affected the economy and the inflation rate; the oil crisis; which companies to invest in, and which stocks to buy." He also had displayed a knack for market exploitation, making $2000 on stamps, not as a collector, but as a middleman. Better yet, he made $18,000 selling subscriptions to the Houston *Post*. The newspaper's idea of market research consisted of handing Dell a list of newly activated telephone numbers to "cold call." This struck Dell as a "pretty random way of approaching new business." Instead, he "segmented" (a term much beloved of Alfred Sloan) the market through research and then focused on high-potential customers: "people who had just married and people who had just moved into new houses and apartments."

By the time he had finished high school, then, Dell had learned the profit potential of reselling commodities that others made and other others coveted, as well as the fact that the telephone could serve as a powerful sales tool, provided the pitch resonated with customers' needs. In both cases, he found ways to profit despite having little capital: the stamps belonged to people who consigned them to him; the telephone company provided at little cost the "infrastructure" needed to peddle his papers. He thus had discovered as a youth one of the two paths to wealth in American society (other than inheriting it): the brokerage function. The other, creating something like Dell Computer and then multiplying its value, also stemmed from an experience of his teens.

Through the generations of American history, machinery has fascinated children, a trait society traditionally channeled into tools for boys and domestic equipment for girls (though sense and necessity have lately, mercifully, eroded the gendered distinctions). For many boys, like my father the sheet metal worker, this interest led to a job; for others, like me, it faded into a hobby or into disuse. Some, however, it set on the path to wealth and power in careers that literally reshaped their worlds and ours. Eli Whitney, despite his Yale education, poured his life into machine tools; Thomas Edison and Henry Ford, to the dismay of their parents, took apart the first watches they ever got hold of to see how they worked.

For Michael Dell, as for so many children of his generation, the computer exerted the magnetism once associated with watches and for generations (including mine) with automobiles. The computer became his "new hobby." At 15, he bought his first one, an Apple II, took it home "and with great relish, promptly took [it] apart," infuriating his parents who thought he had "demolished it." Dell, however, like Edison and Ford, "just wanted to see how it worked." My mother had a similar reaction when I bought my first car and started to rebuild the carburetor. My father, more amused than annoyed, doubted I could put it back together, but I couldn't resist taking it apart and trying to make it work better and run faster, by "souping it up" in the lingo of the time.

Dell switched from an Apple to an IBM PC because he thought its superior "software and programs for business usage" made it the computer of the future. Not satisfied with its performance, he "bought . . . things that would enhance a PC, like more memory, disk drives, bigger monitors, and faster modems." These bits and pieces he bought off the shelf at Radio Shack, much as I bought kits to rebuild carburetors and fuel pumps at Pep Boys. "I would enhance a PC the way another guy would soup up a car," Dell remembered. Up to this point, his story doesn't differ much from my own, but now the difference emerges: when I got my car ready to rock and roll, I drove it far too fast on bald tires through the South Jersey swamps and pine barrens; when Dell got a computer powered up, "*I would sell it for a profit and do it again*" (italics added).

Word got around Houston that Dell understood computers and could make them work better, which brought him a stream of customers, a process that expanded when he arrived at the University of Texas in Austin in the fall of 1983. Soon his customer base expanded beyond students to include doctors and attorneys. Like many another entrepreneur, he benefited from government patronage, winning "a lot of bids" to sell computers to the state of Texas because he had little overhead and a low markup on parts bought cheaper and cheaper by buying more and more of them. Building a business through such a process seems improbable in the early twenty-first century, but in the 1980s, the computer seemed to most people as mysterious as voodoo and as risky to fool around with. I would no more have opened the case of one than I would have tried to defuse an unexploded bomb. Buying computers in stores meant dealing with sales people as ignorant as porcupines and often as prickly. Consequently, many people turned to someone like Michael Dell who seemed to understand the thing, promised to fix it if it broke, and in any case sold it for less than bigger competitors. Every college town had at least one such operation that served students and faculty.

With his expanding customer base, Dell soon found himself spending more time rebuilding computers than attending class. In this, he resembled hundreds of college dropouts all across the country (Bill Gates and Steve Jobs among them), but like Henry Ford and Ray Kroc, he saw something others didn't. "By December" of his first semester, Dell relates, "I knew my fascination with computers wasn't just a hobby or a passing phase. I knew in my heart [this] was a fabulous business opportunity that I could not let pass me by." The key to this "fabulous business opportunity" lay in Dell's perception of the future market, which much resembled Henry Ford's perception of the automobile market and Ray Kroc's of the market for fast food. At a time when most people saw the car as a bafflingly complex luxury for the few, Ford had seen it as a "blessing" for the "great multitude." Kroc saw a California hamburger stand and "felt like some latter-day Newton who'd just had an Idaho potato carom off his skull." In the computer, Dell saw "a device that . . . profoundly changed the way people worked . . . that if you took this tool, previously in the hands of a select few, and made it available to every big business, small business, individual, and student, it could become the most important device of this century." Moreover, one could do just that because "its cost was coming down." Dell thus echoed the same logic through which Ford had made the automobile "the most important device" of his century.

Confident of his vision, Dell took time off from school in 1984 to found "PCs Limited," soon changed to Dell Computer Corporation (shortened to simply "Dell" in 2003).

Marketing consisted of word-of-mouth and advertisements in the local newspaper. He "hired a few people to take orders over the telephone and a few more people to fulfill them." Manufacturing consisted of "three guys with screwdrivers sitting at six-foot tables upgrading machines." At the end of his first year, convinced he had a growing market ill supplied by existing manufacturers and their distributors, Dell left college for good. Certain he could buy all the parts he needed to build computers from scratch rather than upgrade other companies' products, he hired an engineer to design the first Dell computer and began assembling his wares. "Business," he said "was great," so great that Dell went from a 1,000-square-foot facility to a 30,000-square-foot one in a year.

Though a 1,000-square-foot building seems modest compared to the behemoth Dell Computer has become, in fact on the day the firm began assembling its own computers, as opposed to upgrading others', the essential Dell model, based on necessity informed by experience, had taken shape. Born "asset light," in Dell's words, and thus constrained by its limited capital resources, Dell Computer, barring an occasional painful apostasy, remained focused on those parts of the computer business that promised the highest rate of return on the assets it did have. Dell elected to use "industry standard" components (i.e., things any-one could buy, such as Intel chips and Microsoft operating systems) rather than develop "proprietary" technologies that only Dell could use (as IBM did with its "OS2" operating system and Apple with the Macintosh and its successors), a decision that paid off by carry-ing it to the top of the PC industry while Apple's devotees amounted to a niche market, albeit a profitable one. Dell's success illustrated the oft-demonstrated maxim that a com-petitive advantage based on control of technology rarely lasts long and often bankrupts those who stick with it.

In fact, Dell had at the outset no resources to pour into a technological treasure hunt even if he had wanted to. Later, when the company could afford any kind of R&D it cared to pursue, it behaved, like Pierre's Du Pont, as though it couldn't, limiting its research to areas that promised high return on investment and in which no one else seemed likely to do the work (and absorb the cost). In the early days, Dell learned from experience that while you couldn't buy all technologies, you could buy enough that worked well enough to satisfy customer needs. As the firm grew, of course, it benefited from the research done by its suppliers, often guided by Dell's telling them what its customers wanted. "Because we started the company with so little capital," Dell said, "we had to define our value-add very narrowly. Instead of trying to be excellent at making all the pieces and parts . . . we partnered for those capital-intensive services with suppliers and focused on customer-directed solutions." Since this method paid off in the firm's rise to the top of its industry, Dell's experience through 2005 validated Alfred Sloan's observation that "American industry has always drawn from a common pool of technology."

Outsourcing research to its suppliers enabled Dell to prosper with an R&D expense below that of the industry average, although it involved the gamble of push-ing "much of their intellectual property [i.e., patents and copyrights] away to the first tier of suppliers." Over time, Dell, General Electric, and other American firms moved research as well as production overseas to China, India, and elsewhere, in their own facilities and those of offshore firms. This shift enabled them both to get closer to emerging markets and to take advantage of lower labor costs, but involved the per-haps unintended consequence of nurturing overseas competitors in research and development, the "intellectually intensive" activities long thought a preserve of American business and government. Firms such as Huawei and Haier in China and HCL and Tata in India have diversified from production into product development and have the ominous potential to join ArcelorMittal and Lenovo as global research and development competitors in the twenty-first century.

Fundamental to Dell's development, the "direct sales" method yielded multiple benefits for the firm, but it too began in necessity. From his early days as a high school tinkerer, word-of-mouth brought Dell customers. In Austin, the same process, plus a few newspaper advertisements, sufficed to expand the customer base geometrically, as shown by the need for ever-greater space. In the beginning, Dell had nothing like the resources required to open a retail store and didn't need one. Dealing directly with customers not only cut out any intermediary's profit—something he had learned to appreciate while brokering stamps—but better yet, it brought him a flow of priceless information, telling him at no cost what other companies paid a lot of money to find out: what customers wanted and couldn't get to fill their needs.

As an "upgrader" of existing products in his early days, Dell served a market consisting almost entirely of people dissatisfied with the computer they had. He learned quickly that computer manufacturers concentrated on developing proprietary technology primarily to retain high profit margins, not to satisfy customer needs. This priority kept the focus on engineering specifications rather than customer requirements, which in turn led to the familiar trap into which technology companies often fall: producing solutions *looking for* problems rather than solutions *to* problems. According to Dell, ignoring customer needs meant that "Computer developers invented great new software and hardware because they could," resulting in new technologies "invented for the sake of being invented" with the costs passed onto customers. As an innovator with limited capital, not an inventor with a corporate research budget (Compaq, started two years before Dell, had an initial capitalization of $100 million compared to Dell's $1,000), Dell took the Edisonian attitude toward technology. Edison had said his people had no time to study "the fuzz on a bee" but had to "keep working up things of commercial value." Dell said, "We don't go searching for technology [like] some new compound on the element chart" but rather for products that will pass "the true test of [an] innovation: whether the customer [will] pay for it."

In the early years, Dell learned from his customers that he could meet their needs without spending a dime on research and development. In later years, with money to spend, he learned the hard way to ask customers what they wanted before spending any. In 1989, the firm tried to market a family of products it called "Olympic," created, Dell realized later, as "a product that was . . . technology for technology's sake." Though it hadn't consulted prospective buyers, the firm thought it had created a "boil the ocean" technology, the kind of thing that warms the cold cockles of venture capitalists' hearts when it works. Unhappily, in this case, the customers didn't want it. "If we had consulted our customers first," Dell lamented, "we could have saved ourselves a lot of time and aggravation." This lesson stuck. In 1991, for example, Dell declined to join a consortium to design products based on "MIPS" chips because the firm's customers asked, "Why would we want this?"

"We listen to our customers," said Dell. "That . . . tells us where we should go innovate." He might have added that they also tracked other firms' customers to find promising areas for expansion in existing markets, such as servers and printers, lush fields grazed by Hewlett-Packard, among others. Printers, a prototypical "installed-base business" bringing repeat sales in ink and toner cartridges, offered an irresistible target to Dell, not only because of the high markup, but also because Dell believed that H-P used its printer-cartridge profits to subsidize its PC competition with Dell.

Dealing directly with his customers, Dell avoided the distortion of information that always accompanies its passage through intervening layers such as retail dealers. Better yet, as a direct seller, he escaped the conflicting imperatives that arise when the needs of customers differ from those of end users. (Retailers, for example, want high markups, whereas end users want low prices.) Dell's customers *were* his end users. In addition, retail outlets, with their high prices, their "take it or leave it" inventory, their inadequate knowledge of the products, and their poor or nonexistent service facilities, did as much to bolster his business as to compete with it.

Indeed, customer complaints about retail dealers' poor service and high prices helped shape Dell's direct method as well as solidify his belief in it. Early on, he offered a 30-day money-back guarantee, built a faster machine than IBM's, and sold it for half the IBM price. The ongoing need for service, which naturally expanded along with sales, convinced Dell (as it had convinced Cyrus McCormick and successors who produced machines that customers could not fix themselves) that servicing the computers presented a challenge and profit opportunity as great as selling them, and that the ability to provide reliable service made a powerful selling point in itself. Tracking repair orders, moreover, enabled the firm to pinpoint problems in design, manufacture, and assembly. A corollary benefit, though one the company might prefer customers didn't notice, derived from buyers absorbing some of the costs of final product testing: "You can try out new ideas on them—ideas worth millions of R&D dollars and countless hours of your people's time—and they'll tell you whether you're on track or not."

Through direct contact with customers, Dell knew that many of them used the computer as a capital asset, a tool to generate income. For these customers, breakdowns inflicted not just inconvenience, but financial loss. Understanding this, knowing what businesses a firm's customers operated, and shaping your own business to serve them accordingly, had underpinned the success of such companies as Caterpillar Tractor and now honed Dell Computer's competitive edge. Dell argued that common sense dictated considering the customers' bottom line as well as your own, of thinking "strategically about your customers' businesses and find[ing] ways to help them cut costs and increase profits [by] improving how they can serve *their* customers." In the process of providing service to match customer needs, moreover, Dell often found "another whole business." Failure to understand such needs had undermined such long-forgotten firms as Commodore, the leading PC maker in Dell Computer's founding year, as well as any number of retail computer outlets. Retail outlets' notorious apathy in such matters made it all the less explicable to Dell that IBM, a company built as much on direct sales and the quality of its on-site service as on its products' performance, chose to market its PCs through retail stores. IBM's decision crippled its PC effort to the point of abandonment and made it vulnerable to Dell's marketing methods.

The value of all these direct sale benefits struck home at Dell Computer between 1991 and 1994, when, as part of an overall push to accelerate growth, the firm sold its products through five retail chains as well as directly. Not only did his firm lose the virtues of direct information flow, but Dell also discovered that "though we were successfully selling PCs via the retail channels, we weren't actually making any money." Unfortunately, this blunder came at a time when its overall growth strategy had driven Dell Computer into the kind of cash-flow crisis that sinks many a business when, despite making a profit on paper, it runs out of cash to pay the bills before it can collect the money owed to it. As Dell recalled,

> Like many companies we always focused on our profit and loss statement. But cash flow was not a regularly discussed topic. . . . In fact, we were running out of gas. . . . We were consuming huge amounts of cash, while our profitability began to deteriorate and both our inventory and accounts receivable were piling up

In other words, Dell turned into a textbook case of a cash-flow crisis. This revelation dictated a swift retreat from the dead zone of retail to the proven stronghold of direct sales.

Having built from scratch a company doing hundreds of millions of dollars in sales, and having successfully expanded overseas by opening for business in Great Britain in 1987, Dell took the firm public in 1988, selling 3.5 million shares of stock for $8.50 a share to acquire cash to finance even more rapid expansion. Despite this freshet of funds, the ensuing cash flow crisis soon taught Michael Dell multiple lessons about the perils of expansion. Whatever drove *him*—greed, ambition, the desire to "compete with IBM"—he drove his company from zero to $2 billion in annual sales in 10 years, more than doubling them between 1991 and 1992 alone, going from "a fairly simple business in one or two markets to a much broader business that featured many more product lines, channels, and geographies." This uncontrolled expansion brought nearly catastrophic results. "By the end of 1992," Dell said, "our growth initiative had gotten too strong. . . . We had outgrown our phone system, our basic financial system, our support system, and our parts numbering system." Worst of all, "we had outgrown some of our people." From all this, he drew the conclusion that saved the company: it had in fact outgrown him as well—not his visions, but his capacity to convert them into a viable enterprise. "I knew I needed help," he admitted.

At some point in its history, every growth-oriented firm confronts a crisis if, because of its very success, expansion overmatches the capacity of its managers. At that critical juncture, finding and empowering the right talent becomes a life-or-death matter. Locating people with such skills presents a difficult enough task; turning over the reins to them often proves psychologically impossible, especially for founding entrepreneurs such as Michael Dell. But because Pierre du Pont installed Sloan at General Motors, Henry Ford II anointed Ernest Breech, Kroc found Sonneborn, and Walton chose David Glass, their companies' stories appear here. Otherwise, they might have fallen into the category dubbed "CLOSE BUT NO CIGAR" by one business analyst.

At Dell, help came from people with relevant experience and expertise, such as Tom Meredith, brought from Sun Microsystems to become Dell's chief financial officer in December 1992; John Medica, who had developed the Apple Powerbook and arrived in April 1993 to sort out a mess in Dell Computer's notebook division; and most important of all, Kevin Rollins from Bain Consulting in August 1993. Although Dell himself had come to the nasty realization that Dell Computer had "areas . . . making money, and areas [that] weren't," he also confronted the fact that "we hadn't evolved enough to know exactly where, company-wide, nor did we know the magnitude of this disparity." Rollins and the others convinced Dell of some basic realities: Sloan's maxim that return on investment (ROI), not sales or gross profits, constituted the only legitimate measure of success; that adequate ROI demanded that each component in the company generate adequate profit, which in turn dictated the Du Pont principle that potential ROI determine investment decisions; that as Carnegie knew and preached, all these calculations depended upon knowing all costs, all the time.

At the start, Dell Computer had operated as a cost-conscious company out of the sheer necessity to get the most out of limited resources. Success and the headlong rush to expand, coupled to a lack of management structure and sophistication, caused the company to lose its way for a time. In effect, Rollins and the others put the company on Carnegie rails. Carnegie had insisted on a "system of weighing and accounting [so as] to know our cost . . . for each process" and thus know "what every department was doing . . . and compare one with another." At Dell Computer, this imperative hatched "a set of metrics that determined which business units were succeeding and which weren't. We could compare one group's metrics to another's" and decide which groups to reinforce as well as those in which to "cut our losses and close them down." The decision to operate as a "data-driven" company reflected Dell's acceptance of the ROI principle and its corollary that each unit within the company function and be judged on a "P&L" (profit and loss) basis. Neither Dell nor his associates invented any of this approach, of course; it traces back at least to Carnegie and the railroads and embodies the accumulated wisdom, at the core of which lies cost control, that forms the central theme of this book.

At or near the top of the list of cost-control opportunities, inventory reduction has preoccupied generations of managers, informing the strategies of Henry Ford, Alfred Sloan, Sam Walton, and others. Despite past efforts, the problem and opportunity presented by inventory costs remain. As one corporate manager recently observed, "American business is full of piles of inventory. I see it as an overhead conveyor belt with lots of $100 bills hanging from it. My job is to pull down those bills." In many businesses, it's pennies, not $100 bills, hanging around. For a company selling millions of units, like Dell Computer, pennies soon add up; saving them raises profits and permits lowering prices. In the best of all possible worlds, firms could eliminate finished product inventory altogether by operating on a strict BTO plan, producing nothing until a customer ordered and paid for it, and minimize parts inventories by forcing suppliers to deliver exactly the components needed, no more, no less, at just the time wanted, not sooner, not later. On the other hand, against the need to contain inventory costs, businesses had to balance the ability to supply customers promptly or see them go elsewhere.

When he began upgrading computers, Dell could combine BTO (since he did nothing until a customer ordered it) with the ideal inventory level of parts and products: none at all. A brief trip to Radio Shack, a quick installation, a call to the customer, added up to the "just-in-time" model of inventory management and production made famous by Toyota as the "Kan-Ban System." The challenge came when business increased, making it more efficient to have some stock of parts at hand than to make a separate trip for each order. When Dell started manufacturing his own machines, direct sales enabled him to stick to BTO production but required maintaining a component inventory that kept it going without interruption.

The very nature of the computer business added significantly to the traditional imperatives of inventory control, for as Gordon Moore, co-founder of Intel, had predicted, the ratio of processing power to unit cost did indeed double every two years or so, meaning that today's "cutting edge" chips could turn into bins of costly trash trash overnight. Dell painfully learned the consequences of "Moore's Law" in 1989 when, with sales "rising very, very quickly," the firm, foreseeing a need for quantities of memory chips, "bought as many of those suckers as we could get our hands on," whereupon the price collapsed as a more efficient chip appeared almost overnight. This experience taught Dell that "Inventory is the worst thing to own in an industry in which the value of materials or information declines quickly." This instructive episode added a further painful lesson to those of "Olympic," and the aborted strategy of retail sales, which perforce had involved a buildup of product inventory and a delay in payment.

Dell Computer further reinforced the cost savings of BTO by basing its product line on a restricted number of key hardware modules and components easily mixed and matched on "flexible assembly lines" that could put together a PC in four minutes. "Customization" of the product resulted primarily from the customers' choice of software. With these methods, any Dell plant could turn out a mix of products in a continuous stream determined not by market predictions but by orders in hand. This production system sustained Dell Computer's relentless policy of inventory cost minimization, breaking its suppliers' resistance to the just-in-time whip and beating down component prices. Like Walmart and McDonald's, Dell Computer's growth gave it increasing clout with suppliers, for none wanted to lose such a voracious customer. In addition, Dell further armed itself to bludgeon suppliers by learning their costs and profit-and-loss structure, a technique perfected (though again not invented) by Toyota and other Japanese firms, reimported, and widely adopted by Walmart and other American companies in the 1980s and 1990s with a ruthlessness that often drove suppliers into bankruptcy.

Once having embraced the cost-control regime and installed the "metrics" that made it work, Dell Computer found multiple ways to employ it, including, of course, the Carnegie method of "encouraging" managers to ever-greater thrift. In the 1990s, Dell Computer tried to promote the importance of ROI downward from the executive suite all the way to the shop floor, "explaining specifically how everyone could contribute: reducing cycle times, eliminating scrap and waste, selling more, forecasting accurately, scaling operating expenses, increasing inventory turns, [and] collecting accounts receivables efficiently." All this no doubt brought smiles in Managers' Valhalla among the likes of Carnegie, who had years in which all the profit came from recycled waste; Henry Ford, who observed that even a sweeper could earn his $5-a-day wage by picking up tools rather than throwing them away; and Sam Walton, who saw profit in "shrinking the shrinkage."

For many years, the program certainly seemed to pay dividends, literally and figuratively, at Dell Computer. It also fit well in a campaign designed to combat the "Schumpeterian Dilemma," described by Dell as "maintain[ing] the high energy culture of a startup" in a company many thousands strong, and the "energy of a focused team" as the company "expanded around the world." Dell's answer to this problem much resembled Sloan's, as Dell set out to "develop a company of owners . . . a culture in which every person in your organization at every level thinks and acts like an owner."

In this culture, contribution to meeting ROI goals affected compensation (pay scales) and incentives (profit sharing, stock options), a strategy Dell thought would serve to focus employees in all ranks upon the task at hand. That it might also create a culture of avarice, jealousy, and suspicion seems to have eluded Dell himself for some time, though rank-and-file employees certainly acknowledged it. Dell boasted of the effectiveness of this program, as Sloan boasted before him, but history tells a cautionary tale of such sweeteners turning into entitlements expected as a routine part of compensation, rather than rewards dependent upon performance. This change eroded efficiency at General Motors and has the potential to sap the vigor of any firm that employs a similar strategy. And in fact, Dell Computer's program set off what erstwhile CEO Kevin Rollins described as a corporate culture in which "everybody at Dell, down to the shop-floor person, followed the stock price." This rancid culture further soured when the shares tumbled in 2000. This poisonous atmosphere the firm undertook to reshape into a new "Soul of Dell" (somewhat akin to "Walmart Fever") that would engender a "Winning Culture." For its part, management struggled to combat its image as a chilly caste of "cold technocrats" (with Dell and Rollins topping the list of frozen chosen) by creating "Tell Dell," a system that permitted employees from top to bottom to submit (purportedly) anonymous evaluations of managers.

Dell's effort to maintain a unifying spirit in a growing, globalizing company, while at the same time squeezing costs and pitting managers against one another, has antecedents as far back as the nineteenth century. The separation of ownership from management, the bureaucratizing of operations, and the use of cost accounting both to dictate strategy and to judge performance—these themes waft through every triumphant tale of business, not just Dell Computer's. But they bear a whiff of irony as well as the sweet smell of success, a sense of something lost as well as so much gained, a feeling evident in Michael Dell's autobiography. In it, Dell descends from describing the days when he had the key to the Coke machine, hired "three guys with screwdrivers," looked for "people who had a great sense of adventure" and versatility, to stacking aphorisms such as "Swing for hits, not home runs," and "Be the hunter, not the hunted." Dull, trite, and shopworn stuff, certainly nothing new, and even a bit sad coming from such a creative mind.

Dell at his creative best, grasping the implications of technological change and injecting them into his company's operations, appeared in his application of the Internet to enhance the firm's already impressive efficiency. In the Internet, Dell saw "a logical extension of the direct model, creating even stronger relationships with our customers [by] augment[ing] conventional telephone, fax, and face-to-face encounters." At the outset, in 1994, dell.com provided technical information and an email link for customers with problems. In 1996, Dell Computer offered its products for sale with a link that enabled customers to configure and reconfigure the computer they wanted, checking the price as they went, then to place the order and track its progress. By 2000, customers ordered $50 million worth *a day* via the Internet at a transaction cost to the company that Dell himself calls "trivial."

The structure of the Dell website reflected Dell's enduring faith in the benefits of segmented markets served by direct sales. Steering the customer to enter geographic location, the website menu then offered links to products particularly suited to segments such as "Home and Home Office," "Small Business," and "Government, Education, and Healthcare," which contained subsets such as "K–12 Education" and "Higher Education." For customers, the products offered in most categories in fact looked much the same, because the firm had mastered the technique of competing by building on common platforms to serve market niches. Although catering to customer preferences, Dell constructed its website to elevate market analysis to new heights of sophistication and help fine-tune product offerings, all at essentially no additional administrative cost to the company.

Application of the Internet produced a "virtually integrated organization—an organization linked not by physical assets, but by information." With this, Michael Dell inserted, in classic entrepreneurial fashion, a new element into the process of serving a market. Many firms had integrated vertically: manufacturing firms such as Carnegie's and Henry Ford's had integrated forward to reach the customer; a few retail firms such as Sears had integrated backward into manufacturing; but Dell cannily used technology to implement a novel configuration—a manufacturing firm essentially integrated backward from its customers.

In the first few years of the twenty-first century, this dynamic structure produced impressive results. By 2005, Dell sold products—computers, workstations, printers, servers, storage devices, software and peripherals, networking equipment, as well as services—management, professional, deployment, support, training and certification—to the tune of more than $50 billion a year. In 2005, *Fortune* named Dell "America's Most Admired Company," as the Dell corporate web page "Dell at a Glance" bragged. The web page focused on the present, but Michael Dell himself knew some history, including his own, and observed wryly, "Being on the cover of *Fortune* doesn't guarantee anything."

The years following 2005 soon showed the wisdom of Dell's cautious reaction to fame and *Fortune*. As the decline of the stock price suggests, a series of crises beset the company, exposing it as rigid, its adherence to a structure no longer ideal in the changing market slowing its once-agile reactions. History has shown that most businesses react to change only when circumstances force a response, thus running the risk of waiting too long. Although Michael Dell had described "an industry in which the value of materials or information declines quickly," his firm seemed to have lost this awareness, its acuity perhaps dulled by the very strategies that had long served it well. By 2007, for example, the direct sales method no longer satisfied customers, more and more of whom wanted to see and touch before they bought. Meeting that demand forced Dell back into the retail market, selling through chains such as Best Buy, where competitors such as Hewlett-Packard had a long-established presence.

Dell's customer service, increasingly exiled offshore and performed by telephone (often poorly and after enraging hours wasted on hold), decayed from a source of customer satisfaction to a bane of customer existence, a target of blog and website fury. Correction came slowly, by which time many customers had gone elsewhere since commoditization meant that popular brands differed primarily on quality of service, not performance. Dell also proved slow to respond to the new waves of portable devices, including lightweight notebook computers, netbooks, and tablets, often making matters worse by arriving late with inferior products.

Despite these and other vicissitudes, Dell remains a significant force in the computer industry, ranking #38 in the 2010 "Fortune 500," and #2 in computers behind Hewlett-Packard. The company's 2010 sales and profits declined from 2009, 13 percent and 42 percent respectively, symptoms of past problems and future uncertainties. In the past decade, Dell's market value (shares of stock outstanding times share price) shrank from $130 billion to $24 billion, while Apple's (on iPod and iPhone wings) soared from $23 billion to $234 billion. Doubts about the future stem from the depressed state of the American and world economies, reservations about Michael Dell's managerial abilities, the lack of an obvious successor as CEO, and shaky prospects for PC sales in a world where, if Andy Grove of Intel and others are right, the Internet will increasingly *be* the computer, as "cloud computing" reduces the PC to a dumb terminal connected to vast banks of servers at the Googles and Amazon.coms anywhere in the world. Other companies have managed their way through worse predicaments, and so may Dell, if Michael Dell can find the strategy he needs and the people to make it work.

That people like Dell, Kroc, and Walton have continued to appear and pursue their visions has sustained American prosperity through a painful transition from a manufacturing-focused nation protected from foreign competition to an increasingly service-based economy integrated into and facing the competition surging into globalizing markets. As a result, although factory jobs have declined and individual firms have foundered, the American manufacturing sector as a whole has survived so well that, in terms of value added, it entered the twenty-first century as it entered the twentieth—on top of the world rankings.

The stories of Ray Kroc, Sam Walton, and Michael Dell, the companies they built and the competitors they vanquished, thus serve to illustrate the enduring relevance of past lessons in management, as well as the fragility that often lurks even in the most powerful of businesses. Perhaps the most compelling lesson lies in the explosive potential for the creation of wealth and jobs, goods and services ignited when an entrepreneur "sees" a market, finds a way to serve it, *and* survives the hazards, often fatal, that growing companies confront. It takes all three talents to produce the colossal results that Kroc, Walton, and Dell, like Carnegie, Ford, and Sloan before them, churned out. Few people have the particular gift of sight that detects the silhouette of a market in the obscurant glare of daily life. At best, most of us can say after the fact what physicist Rosalind Franklin supposedly said when she saw the Watson and Crick model of DNA: "I might have seen it, but I didn't."

Even among those who perceive the chance, few can make much of it. Obed Hussey saw the need for harvesters as clearly as Cyrus McCormick, but McCormick's name lives on while Hussey's has drifted into history's trivia bin. The few who take a big bite of the market often choke on it, as Billy Durant did at General Motors. In 1981, for example, Adam Osborne marketed the first true portable computer. An instant success, the Osborne Computer's sales soon reached 1,000 units a month, but Osborne's firm couldn't meet the demand it had itself done so much to unleash, and the company declared bankruptcy in 1983. Surviving the crisis of success requires finding the right help; Ford, McDonald's, Walmart, and Dell did; Osborne didn't. Even the survivors, moreover, live on borrowed time until the next predicament looms, as General Motors', Ford's, IBM's, and others' cycling fortunes have shown. Enduring, moreover, means not only outlasting competition from without, but also correcting mistakes from within. Dell blundered with "Olympic"; Ray Kroc flopped with pound cake, "Triple Ripple," and the "Hula Burger"; Sam Walton thought "dot Discount Drugs," "Helen's Arts and Crafts," and "Hypermart USA" would make stablemates for Walmart—all mistakes but none fatal, proving flexibility the cure for fallibility.

So the history of American business tells us this: no firm, no matter how powerful, enjoys immortality. Looking back, many would echo the fictional pitcher Henry Wiggin, who said in disbelief at the end of his career, "It seemed like forever." But we also know that as surely as titans waste away, newly born competitors grow and sometimes wax mighty. For every Howard Johnson, there someday comes a Ray Kroc, and for every IBM, a Michael Dell broods a dream of conquest. Pittsburgh once made steel like nowhere in the world but makes little now. Perhaps, then, even the mightiest might wonder "what rough beast, its hour come round at last, slouches toward [their particular] Bethlehem to be born?"

Chapter 12

Of Things Past and Things to Come

I once taught a course in American history to a class of United Auto Workers shop stewards. In terms of age and sex, and of religious, ethnic, and regional backgrounds, this group presented the most random sample of American workers I have ever encountered. A more contentious lot I never met; virtually every historical figure or topic I raised—Lincoln, F.D.R., John Kennedy, Lyndon Johnson, slavery, the New Deal, Vietnam, the "War on Poverty"—touched off a furious debate, with opinions crushed into venomous metaphors and delivered by voices accustomed to making themselves heard over assembly lines. Compared to these biweekly imbroglios, the class I taught at Jackson Penitentiary (technically the "Southern Michigan Correctional Facility") seemed like a Quaker meeting.

Only once, when I asked the shop stewards whether they agreed with "Engine Charlie" Wilson that "what's good for General Motors is good for the country," did the class declare a unanimous position. To these worthies, who spent a good part of their lives in a running battle with car company management, Wilson's statement rang so obviously true that talking about it would have wasted class time. When I said I could present a contrary opinion that some people, at least, firmly held, I first provoked open disbelief, then guffaws, and finally an accolade delivered by the senior member of the class: "For a professor, you're the damnedest agitator I ever saw, but you won't get us going with that one."

Finding a strong conservative element in such a group didn't exactly astonish me, for as I knew from my own experience, an optimist could be defined as someone who expects to uncover a genuine radical in the American trade union hierarchy. I must admit, however, that the unity of opinion and depth of sentiment *did* come as a surprise. No fools, these people; indeed, they labored (literally and figuratively) under far fewer illusions about American business than did most of my supposedly better-informed academic colleagues, including some considered experts in business and labor history.

The class disclosed the durable commonality of assumptions shared by American business and labor. From Eli Whitney through Henry Ford II to Kroc, Walton, Dell, and at all points between, American business owners generally believed that their individual efforts benefited their society as a whole and, by implication at least, humankind generally. Whereas this attitude sometimes served as an excuse for malevolent business conduct ranging from the outrageous to the criminally abusive, most entrepreneurs thought the progress of American society powered by the business system validated their rationale and justified their actions. Manufacturers, whose tangible products contributed visibly to the rising standard of living, particularly conceived of themselves as agents of progress. On the whole their fellow citizens, workers included, agreed and have continued to agree despite the squeeze that globalization has put on jobs and wages and the specter of anxiety that "outsourcing" and "offshoring" have cast on present and future employment. In May 2010, an *Economist* poll found that 76 percent of Americans agreed that America's strength mostly resulted from "the success of American business."

As American society grew more complex and more engaged with the rest of the world, American business owners and their organizations followed a parallel development. Tracing the route of American enterprise from Eli Whitney, who found the southern United States incomprehensible and felt at ease only in his New Haven water mill, surrounded by his fellow Yankees, to Henry Ford II, at home anywhere in the world, confidently guiding his global imperium, to the enterprises of Jobs, Kroc, Walton, and Dell, routinely buying and selling across once-impermeable national borders, one continually crosses the trail of all America's past and finds it converging with the track left by the broad caravan of world history. As once-isolated markets commingle, businesses expand to reach them, a process that inherently requires knowledge of multiple cultures, their attitudes and practices, as well as broadened expertise in languages and law.

As companies shift to meet the needs of globalization, the resulting structures might seem to diminish the potential impact of individual talents and efforts upon them. In fact, however, history shows that size can cut two ways: it may indeed cause the sclerosis and stagnation that beset General Motors, IBM, and others; conversely, the bigger the lever, the more an individual can move with it, as Henry Ford II and Michael Dell, among others, have repeatedly confirmed. Moreover, given that the most vibrant global businesses grow from firms nurtured by individuals, rather than from mergers among giants, the scope for individual talent in commerce seems broadened, not narrowed. It broadens, however, in the context of organizations that inevitably impose limits even as they empower.

Thus, as I have tried to show throughout this book, although an individual may supply the catalyst, the inspiration, the guiding force, the discipline to solve problems and get things done, and may indelibly stamp a personal flair into an organization or a product, success doesn't come from working alone. Each of my cast acted as a conductor, not as a soloist. Each showed an extraordinary ability to create and inspire an organization—at least for a time—with the joy of cooperative effort, a spirit on which corporate capitalism depends no less than any sort of socialism. Their charisma took many forms, from the exuberant Edison, flinging his top hat into a pan of oil, letting out a war whoop, and donning his greasy overalls, to the custom-tailored "Silent Sloan," who could ask a subordinate, "Have you ever heard me raise my voice about anything?" to Sam Walton, leading the Walmart cheer. The sheer variety of these characters' styles, as well as their disparate origins, typifies the American experience. Their businesses benefited from a characteristic American trait: the ability to apply effective leadership to a fractious rank and file, creating organizations that forge ahead with verve and efficiency despite an often informal mode.

Foreign observers, watching American soldiers in training, could never understand how they ever won battles. Similarly, an outsider who eavesdropped in an auto workers' bar on Eight Mile Road in Detroit, or read the diatribes in a union newspaper, or listened to Dell assembly workers in the watering holes of Round Rock, Texas, might well expect to hear at any moment that the toilers had arisen, slaughtered the bosses like swine, torn down the factories brick by brick, and smashed the machines. But it hasn't happened yet, and I doubt it ever will, for the same *Economist* poll found that *90 percent* of Americans still admire those who "get rich by working hard."

People must certainly work together, but unless the inspiration and guiding spirit flow from some individual, the result will rarely better the visions of the least common denominator and often turns out to be nothing at all. "Ten thousand committees," Eric Sevareid observed after a lifetime as an international news correspondent, "could never produce the Sistine ceiling. How many they prevent we shall never know." Sevareid, reflecting on many years as an eyewitness to some of history's most cataclysmic events, concluded that

> among the underpinnings of the world's interdependence, which we have desired, and which is unavoidable, the underpinning of business may be . . . the least offensive [because] business is flexible enough to take and to give, to advance and retreat. It does not want people's souls, as do the intellectuals; it does not want their obedience, as does the military; it only wants their money, the cheapest of all commodities.

In the United States, business and the people who ran it transformed from the hypothetical to the axiomatic what Sevareid called "our basic premise [which] has been, these many years, that peace, democracy and material gain are not only good each in itself, but interdependent."

Sevareid's contemporary, Theodore H. White, offered similar testimony, wound onto his "spool of inner rhetoric" by a career that put him at one nexus of history after another: "Most liberals [dislike] being linked historically with the traders because the driving force of trade is profit, a dirty word to moralists everywhere." Nevertheless, White admitted, "the values that liberals cherish . . . learning and religion, letters, poetry and science . . . flourish better in the trader's world than in the Pharaonic world." For White, the success of the Marshall Plan, by which the United States aided the post–World War II economic recovery in Western Europe to contain the spread of communism, furnished proof. The Marshall Plan, White argued, worked because

It had linked gain with freedom, had assumed that the movement of minds and the movement of peoples must go with the movement of goods and of merchants. In the noblest terms, it had enlisted the good will of free peoples against the discipline of orderly peoples. In the crudest terms, it had enlisted greed against terror.

No amount of optimism should loosen constraints against the abuses of greed, "hope of gain and selfish betterment." But history, as I have learned it in libraries, classrooms, and archives, experienced it in railroad yards, truck stops, steel mills, chemical plants, and the 82d Airborne Division, and as I have seen it in the streets of Germany and Russia, China and Japan, Mongolia and Tibet, Australia and New Zealand, Panama and Greece, tells me that Sevareid and White mostly got it right; things *have* worked that way in the past. Barring some sea change in human nature, they're likely to work that way in the future. Pursuing gain, power, and security in the elusive American marketplace, Whitney, McCormick, and the rest of my cast came forward to solve problems. Not all they wrought was good, but their labors eased, for most in America, the ancient yoke of cold, hunger, and want. A similar pursuit led Kroc, Walton, and Dell to push beyond the United States into the global economic arena, armed with Big Macs and PCs, not bombs and shells, to make sales, not war. Thereby, in time, we may hope for similar positive results in the lives abroad touched by these thrusting American enterprises, both for the moral reason that a people with so much should wish better lives for others, and the pragmatic reason that enriching others will enrich us all the more. Better yet, perhaps "the underpinning of business" may someday solidify the "world's interdependence" in ways that make war obsolete.

Gadfly author Thomas Friedman posited the "Golden Arches Theory of Conflict Resolution," pointing out that no two countries with McDonald's restaurants had ever gone to war. A world that sells to and buys from Walmart, filled with people webbed together on Dell computers and iPhones, may someday prove Friedman's notion something more than whimsy. I've seen some evidence along those lines myself. In my lifetime, my father and uncles fought in desperate wars against the formidable warriors of Germany and Japan; their descendants want to sell me a car or a camera. My generation lived in terror of what the communist hordes from Russia and China might inflict upon us; now they "attack" with Russian nested dolls "matrioshka" sporting Texas Aggie logos, and with cheap underwear.

Business has done reprehensible things: exploited labor, corrupted governments, degraded local dietary practices, polluted air and water, and so on down a long list of offences, some tacky, many brutalizing of body and mind, but nothing to match, say, the horrors of World War I. Businesses let loose overwhelmed the "communist menace" in Russia and China in a few decades without firing a shot. By contrast, politicians, by holding business in check, made Fidel Castro the longest-serving head of state in the twentieth century. In places such as the Balkans, where sacerdotal or tribal values prevail, hatred smolders for centuries, with no end in sight.

Whatever lies ahead, history will as always shape the future, and thus we should study it to see what we can see, bearing in mind that history is pentimento, both in its process, removing layers to see what lies below, and in its result, a picture revealed but still obscured. Carl Becker, a humanist as well as a historian, argued that in "our little world of endeavor we must be prepared for what is coming to us," which requires us not only "to recall certain past events, but [also] to anticipate (note I do not say predict) the future." "Though all our yesterdays grow dim . . . By deepening the sympathies, by fortifying the will," Becker said, "history may empower us to achieve something I have wished for myself, my children, and my students: to live well."

In my own lifetime, I have seen things long thought purely American penetrate distant corners of the globe, as people emerge from the wreckage of war and the shackles of poverty, ignorance, and bigotry. In time, perhaps Carl Becker's "us" who "live well" will include people everywhere.

A Note on Sources

This book owes as much to the 15 years I spent in railroad yards, steel mills, and truck stops as it does to the 40 subsequent years spent leafing through the papers of American businessmen and the articles and books written about them. I also owe a great debt to the late Jack Vitullo of the U.S. Department of Energy's Energy-Related Inventions Program, and to Marcia Rorke and her associates at Mohawk Research Corporation, with whom I spent 15 years grappling with the diabolically difficult task of commercializing new technologies. My own work as a historian, however, would have foundered without the labors of other historians and biographers.

Three works in particular persuaded me that a book like this one could say something worthwhile about America: Carl Degler's *Out of Our Past* (New York, 1972), then perhaps the best one-volume essay extant on American history, many of its interpretations now superseded, but still a shining example of how felicitous prose contributes to the power of history; Richard Hofstadter's *Age of Reform* (New York, 1948), many of its arguments now dated, but still a masterful demonstration of how individual lives can illuminate broader themes; and Robert Heilbroner's *Worldly Philosophers* (New York, 1972), in which biographical sketches elucidate complex minds and arcane theories comprehensibly and amusingly.

The literature of American history has reached intimidating dimensions, despite the fact that all of us who shuffle through the past are constantly re-impressed with how little we know about it. Every historical figure, every major theme, every peripheral comment in this book could be the subject of an extensive bibliography. One could, for example, while away many a shining hour exploring the debate about how much Eli Whitney actually contributed to the development of the American machine-tool industry. What follows here, then, is not a comprehensive list of the sources I used, but rather a starting point—a list of relevant works, widely available, many of them containing notes and bibliographies that will carry interested readers as deep into the past as they care to journey.

Finally, I emphasize that with the exception of brief updates, I have not tried to trace the history of these firms to the present day.

INTERNET SOURCES

Invaluable for researching recent events, including developments in the economy at large, particular industries, and individual firms, the galaxy of library-finding technologies and useful Internet sites has reached truly mind-boggling proportions, especially given that the Internet did not exist when this book first appeared, and had limited utility at the time of the second edition. By 2010, it had become a bottomless well into which one could dive and never resurface, dragged down by the endless array of fascinating details such as the fact that Steve Jobs holds a patent on a staircase and that in 2009 only three Howard Johnsons' restaurants survived. After a lot of thought, I decided not to list specific websites for fear that once started, I'd never stop. Readers can start anywhere by inserting any of my protagonists in a search engine. Students may find http://hcl.harvard.edu/ research/guides/google/ a useful aid in evaluating Internet sources. Surf's up.

NEWSPAPERS AND MAGAZINES

Following the fortunes of American firms in the domestic and global economies in the twenty-first century leads to newspapers and magazines as well as to the Internet. For broad trends, essays on particular countries, and assessments of technological change and its impact on particular industries and beyond, *The Economist,* despite its unbending faith in the benefits of free trade, has no equal in the world. *Fortune* supplies useful materials on American businesses but rarely probes beneath the surface of firms or industries. The *Wall Street Journal* and the *New York Times* head the list of newspapers, though they, like all newspapers, require close scrutiny. Online searches by subject render the vast world of periodic literature accessible to those who have mastered that aspect of computer literacy.

HISTORY OF THE AMERICAN ECONOMY

Economic history should attract more attention than it does. Its neglect by students and the general public owes something to the literature, much of it a swampland of abstruse and conflicting theory, mind-numbing jargon, and numerological magic shows, all obscuring the fact that the underlying processes are simple enough, however complex their manifestations. For a glowing exception, the uninitiated can begin with Robert Heilbroner's *Making of Economic Society* (Englewood Cliffs, N.J., 1975) (and many subsequent editions). Heilbroner conveys the reader from the ancient world of farmers and herdsmen armed with sticks and stones through to the modern world of multinational corporations equipped with computers and telecommunications, explaining and entertaining as he goes along. In general, however, economic historians have contributed little to the understanding of American business history.

Reading two classic works, however, would well serve anyone contemplating a career in the corporate world: Joseph Schumpeter's *Capitalism, Socialism and Democracy* (New York, 1942, 1948) raises the question of bureaucracy's stifling of entrepreneurial initiative; and Max Weber, "Bureaucracy," available in many collections such as Weber, et al., *Economy and Society* (Berkeley, 1978), dissects the beast and explains what makes it behave as it does.

HISTORY OF AMERICAN BUSINESS

Relatively young as specialized areas of history go, this subject remains the province of a small number of practitioners. Fortunately, two of them produced masterworks that cover a lot of ground and contain encyclopedic references. Thomas C. Cochran's *Business in American Life: A History* (New York, 1972) relates American business practice to the larger environment, something routinely done by European historians but rarely by American scholars. Alfred D. Chandler Jr.'s *Visible Hand* (Cambridge, Mass., 1977) traces the development of American business management from its inception to its zenith. His *Scale and Scope: The Dynamics of Industrial Capitalism* (Boston, 1994) extends the analysis (less persuasively) to Great Britain and Germany.

Mansel Blackford and K. Austin Kerr, *Business Enterprise in American History*, 3rd edition (Boston, 1994) is the best textbook on the subject, especially valuable for its emphasis on the role of government in the American economy throughout its history.

For the period it describes, Glenn Porter's *Rise of Big Business in the United States, 1860–1920,* 3rd edition (Wheeling, Ill., 2006), provides, with grace and humor, a summary of the facts and what historians have made of them, as well as an extremely useful bibliographic essay. The companion volume, Thomas K. McGraw's *American Business Since 1920: How It Worked,* 2nd edition (Wheeling, Ill., 2009) takes up the challenge of explaining events from 1920 into our own times and does it with remarkable clarity. The chapters on "The Financial System" and "Information Technology" have particular value. This work also has an extraordinarily useful "Bibliographical Essay." All these works embody analytical structures of elegant simplicity that bring order to, and establish causal relationships among, a welter of details.

Two volumes containing brief, more or less informative sketches of some of the characters appearing here are H. W. Brands, *Masters of Enterprise: Giants of American Business* (New York, 1999), and Harold Evans, et al., *They Made America* (New York, 2004), the latter focusing on inventors.

For an overview of the changing consumer society, consult Regina Lee Blaszczyk, *American Consumer Society, 1865–2005: From Hearth to HDTV* (Wheeling, Ill., 2009), which traces "seven major themes [that] have shaped the constant evolution of American consumer society," and contains a valuable bibliographic essay.

CHAPTER 2: ELI WHITNEY

Jeannette Mirsky and Alan Nevins, *The World of Eli Whitney* (New York, 1952) is a comprehensive biography containing a brief but useful summary of the history of machinery prior to Whitney. A shorter version is Constance Green, *Eli Whitney and the Birth of American Technology* (Boston, 1956). Much of the history of technology suffers from being written by and for technologists, but a helpful exception is Nathan Rosenberg, *Technology and American Economic Growth* (New York, 1972), which includes a discussion of the impact of patent laws on the rate of technological diffusion. H. J. Habbakuk, *British and American Technology in the Nineteenth Century* (Cambridge, 1962) examines the greater rapidity with which Americans adapted labor-saving machinery. Habbakuk also assesses whether Britain ultimately suffered from its early lead in technology, a question Americans might ponder with respect to their own fate in the twentieth and twenty-first centuries. Finally, an excellent essay on Whitney and his relevance to the American economy is in Jonathan Hughes's *Vital Few* (New York, 1973), which also contains chapters on Edison, Carnegie, and Ford.

CHAPTER 3: CYRUS HALL MCCORMICK

The definitive biography is William T. Hutchinson, *Cyrus Hall McCormick* (New York, 1930 and 1935), 2 vols. Useful, if sometimes self-serving, details can be found in Cyrus Hall McCormick III, *The Century of the Reaper* (New York, 1933). The emergence of International Harvester is examined in U.S. Bureau of Corporations, *International Harvester* (Washington, D.C., 1913), which contains extensive information on the pre-merger McCormick empire. The significance of McCormick's distribution methods is discussed in Chandler, *The Visible Hand*. Agriculture in the American breadbasket is the subject of Fred A. Shannon's *Farmer's Last Frontier: Agriculture, 1860–1897* (New York, 1957) and Gilbert C. Fite's *Farmer's Frontier, 1865–1900* (New York, 1966). Few history books, however, can match the evocative impact of novels such as Willa Cather, *My Ántonia* (New York, 1962), or Ole Rölvaag, *Giants in the Earth* (New York, 1956).

CHAPTER 4: ANDREW CARNEGIE

Carnegie is one of a handful of American manufacturers subjected to a full-scale biography by a modern scholar. Joseph F. Wall, *Andrew Carnegie* (New York, 1970), is painstaking and thorough and touches on all aspects of Carnegie's many-faceted life. Popular biographer Peter Krass's *Carnegie* (New York, 2002) adds some details and speculation about Carnegie's personality, but it doesn't add much to our understanding of Carnegie the businessman. David Nasaw, *Andrew Carnegie* (New York, 2007) supplies yet another scholar's extended treatment, but the riddle of Carnegie's success and all its paradoxes remains unbreached. Nasaw deprecates (unfairly in my view) previous biographers, especially Burton Hendrick, who mounted a less factually accurate but vividly reflective portrait of Carnegie's personality in *The Life of Andrew Carnegie* (New York, 1932). Harold C. Livesay, *Andrew Carnegie and the Rise of Big Business* (Boston, 1975), concentrates on Carnegie's development as a manager and his contribution to modern American manufacturing management methods.

The Homestead strike has drawn its share of attention as well. Paul Krause, *The Battle for Homestead, 1880–1992: Politics, Culture, and Steel* (Pittsburgh, 1992), presents a scholarly version. William Serrin's *Homestead: The Glory and Tragedy of an American Steel Town* (New York, 1993) gives a journalistic account of Homestead through the 1980s, when foreign competition brought an end to the mill and the workers' community attached to it.

An overview of America's economy in the time of Whitney, McCormick, and Carnegie can be found in George Rogers Taylor, *The Transportation Revolution, 1815–1860* (New York, 1968), and Edward C. Kirkland, *Industry Comes of Age* (New York, 1967). Alfred D. Chandler Jr., ed., *The Railroads: The Nation's First Big Business* (New York, 1965), documents the railroad's pioneering role in management. Edward C. Kirkland, *Dream and Thought in the Business Community, 1860–1900* (New York, 1964), highlights the self-image fancied by Carnegie and some of his mogul contemporaries. Carnegie himself held forth on his favorite theme in *The Autobiography of Andrew Carnegie* (Boston, 1920), a fascinating book, but one not over-wed to accuracy.

CHAPTER 5: THOMAS A. EDISON

Edison's striking life story sparked several biographies, and more of his life and works seems sure to appear now that Edison's papers are in one place and available. Matthew Josephson, long one of America's premier biographers, produced an entertaining volume in *Edison* (New York, 1959), one that benefited from Josephson's lifetime of study and writing about Edison's era, its knights and knaves. Less original, but brief and well written, is Ronald W. Clark, *Edison: The Man Who Made the Future* (New York, 1977). Better yet is Martin Melosi, *Thomas A. Edison and the Modernization of America*, 2nd edition (New York, 2007). One of the editors of the Edison papers, Paul Israel, produced *Edison: A Life of Invention* (New York, 2000). Edison's inventions, the extent of their originality, their relationship to the emerging world of commercial electricity and the machines it ran, make for a story as complex as the wiring for New York City. Thomas P. Hughes saw electricity as central to modern technological "systems" and situates Edison in this context in *American Genesis: A Century of Invention and Technological Enthusiasm, 1870–1970* (New York, 1989). Best for the non-masochist is to stick to Harold C. Passer, *The Electrical Manufacturers, 1875–1900* (Cambridge, Mass., 1953). A collection of original Edisonian observations is Dagobert D. Runes, ed., *The Diary and Sundry Observations of Thomas Alva Edison* (New York, 1948).

The process by which inventions reach (or mostly don't reach) the market has generated a massive literature, but the best explication remains Hugh Aitken's *Syntony and Spark: The Origins of Radio* (New York, 1970). A more recent dissection of technology commercialization appears in the masterful Tracy Kidder's *Soul of a New Machine* (New York, 1981). Kidder tells a now familiar story, but one filled with lessons as valid today as when he inscribed them.

In recent years, we have come to understand technology as a socially defined phenomenon. Ruth Schwartz Cowan's *A Social History of American Technology* (New York, 1997) makes the case forcefully. Also illuminating is Nina Lerman, et al., eds., *Gender and Technology: A Reader* (Baltimore, 2003).

CHAPTER 6: HENRY FORD

Ford ranks with the most-written-about Americans. Happily, Roger Burlingame, *Henry Ford* (New York, 1970), is one of the best brief biographies ever written about anyone. In addition, a massive, detailed opus includes the history of the company: Alan Nevins, et al., *Ford* (New York, 1954, 1957, and 1963), 3 vols. The Nevins team made extensive use of the Ford archives but may have been a bit too admiring in their analysis. No such accusation could be leveled at Keith Sward, whose *Legend of Henry Ford* (New York, 1948) remains the most acerbic interpretation. Many of Ford's contemporaries wrote their own observations, but the most valuable is Charles Sorenson, *My Forty Years with Ford* (London, 1957). Ford has also enjoyed the attentions of a psychological biographer, Anne Jardim. The result, *The First Henry Ford: A Study in Personality and Business Leadership* (Cambridge, Mass., 1970), is an interesting if inconclusive attempt to lasso a will-o'-the-wisp. The popular view of Ford is the subject of an essay in Sigmund Diamond, *The Reputation of American Businessmen* (New York, 1955), and rated two full-scale books in addition: David Lewis, *The Public Image of Henry Ford* (Ann Arbor, Mich., 1977), and Reynold M. Wik, *Henry Ford and Grass Roots America* (Ann Arbor, Mich., 1972). Both books contain rollicking good stories about Tin Lizzie and her creator. Lewis, in addition, furnishes a detailed, serious (if somewhat uncritical) account of the Ford public relations effort, including the disastrous anti-Semitic campaign.

Since the Nevins volumes, the continuing flow of books on Ford has often dealt with both Henry Fords and their company. Richard Bak, *Henry and Edsel: The Creation of the Ford Empire* (New York, 2003) tackles one of the least understood and most significant elements of the Ford Motor Company's history, but the lack of sources (Henry Ford II destroyed his father's papers) defeats him.

Douglas Brinkley, given the chance to update the Ford story post-Nevins, et al., with access to the Ford family and Ford Motor Company executives, unfortunately chose to revise Nevins's work, did it poorly, skimped on the rest of the story, and produced the disappointing *Wheels for the World: Henry Ford, His Company, and a Century of Progress* (New York, 2004). Steven Watts does better with *The People's Tycoon: Henry Ford and the American Century* (New York, 2006).

Most histories of the automobile industry are Gasoline Alley stuff, but Alfred D. Chandler Jr., ed., *Giant Enterprise: Ford, General Motors, and the Automobile Industry* (New York, 1964) summarizes major developments for the "Big Two" through 1941. The roller-coaster ride of the American automobile companies has attracted a lot of journalistic attention. Among many, many others, see Paul Ingrassia and Joseph B. White, *Comeback: Fall and Rise of the America Automobile Industry* (New York, 1995), updated by Ingrassia's *Crash Course: The American Automobile Industry's Road from Glory to Disaster* (New York, 2010).

CHAPTER 7: PIERRE S. DU PONT

The basic source for Pierre du Pont's career is Alfred D. Chandler Jr. and Stephen Salsbury, *Pierre S. du Pont and the Making of the Modern Corporation* (New York, 1971), an exhaustive work based on extensive research in the papers of Pierre and other du Ponts. The du Pont family squabbles and the career of one of the major combatants are in Marquis James, *Alfred I. du Pont, The Family Rebel* (Indianapolis, Ind., 1941). There are several histories of the Du Pont Company, none of them first class. Bessie G. du Pont, *E. I. du Pont de Nemours and Company: A History, 1802–1902* (Boston, 1920) features the personal viewpoint of its author, Alfred I. du Pont's first wife. William S. Dutton, *Du Pont: One Hundred and Forty Years* (New York, 1942) is better, but dated and pedestrian.

CHAPTER 8: ALFRED P. SLOAN

Details of Sloan's accession to the General Motors presidency, his reforms, and their impact on American industry are in Chandler, *Giant Enterprise,* and Chandler and Salsbury, *Pierre S. du Pont.* An intensive study of General Motors under Durant and its subsequent reorganization is in Alfred D. Chandler Jr., *Strategy and Structure* (Garden City, N.Y., 1966). Lawrence H. Seltzer, *A Financial History of the American Automobile Industry* (Boston, 1928), and Arthur Pound, *The Turning Wheel* (Garden City, N.Y., 1934) also contain useful information on the early days of GM. Sloan told his own story twice, in *Adventures of a White Collar Man* (New York, 1941) and *My Years with General Motors* (Garden City, N.Y., 1964). The latter, actually written by John McDonald, an editor at *Fortune,* not surprisingly proves the better of the two.

In it Sloan, in semiretirement, reflected on the meaning of his 50 years as an organization builder. Billy Durant deserves a better biography than he has gotten thus far in, for example, Axel Madsen, *The Deal Maker: How William C. Durant Made General Motors* (New York, 2000).

In the first decade of the twenty-first century, two volumes appeared that add little to our understanding of Sloan the manager, although they do depict him as an unattractive character. John McDonald's *A Ghost's Memoir: The Making of Alfred P. Sloan's "My Years with General Motors"* (Cambridge, Mass., 2002) portrays Sloan as "aloof and enigmatic," and GM's lawyers (who fought for five years to suppress publication of *My Years*) as sneaky and duplicitous. David Farber's *Sloan Rules: Alfred P. Sloan and the Triumph of General Motors* (Chicago, 2004) shows Sloan's increasingly dogmatic opposition to the New Deal and his hostile response to militant GM workers during the 1930s.

CHAPTER 9: HENRY FORD II

Volume III of Nevins, et al., *Ford: Decline and Rebirth,* discusses Henry Ford II's accession to power, his dismissal of Harry Bennett, and the early years of the company's reorganization. Ernest Breech, chief architect of the new structure, is the subject of Mel J. Hickerson, *Ernie Breech* (New York, 1969). Booton Herndon, *Ford: An Unconventional Biography of the Men and Their Times* (New York, 1969), is a journalistic but imaginative comparison of the two men and their companies, based on extensive interviews with Henry Ford II, some members of his family, and Ford executives.

After 1946, Henry II and his company were the subject of numerous articles in *Fortune* magazine, as well as other business journals. In addition, a perusal of the *New York Times Index* since World War II reveals how much, how often, and in how many contexts Henry II made news. Other members of the Ford hierarchy—Arjay Miller, Robert McNamara, Lee Iacocca, Bunkie Knudsen—also enjoyed their share of the journalistic limelight.

Mira Wilkins and Frank E. Hill, *American Business Abroad: Ford on Six Continents* (New York, 1964), tells the story of Ford overseas through the early 1960s; Wilkins, *The Emergence of Multinational Enterprise* and *The Maturing of Multinational Enterprise* (Cambridge, Mass., 1970 and 1974), put the Ford experience in the broader context of American overseas manufacturing operations. For the period since 1960, I have relied on my own research in company documents and interviews with Ford personnel in the United States and abroad, as well as on works listed for Chapter 6. Peter Collier and David Horowitz capture much of the essence of Ford II's compelling personality and provide a healthy debunking of the myth of Lee Iacocca as victim in *The Fords: An American Epic* (New York, 1987).

CHAPTER 10: EDWIN LAND

Mark Olshaker, *The Instant Image: Edwin Land and the Polaroid Experience* (New York, 1978), the only biography for many years, was followed by the more technically oriented Victor K. McElheny, *Insisting on the Invisible: The Life of Edwin Land*

(Reading, Mass, 1998). Land's career, like Henry Ford II's, can be followed in the pages of *Fortune,* the *New York Times,* and similar sources. The Polaroid Corporation *Annual Reports* also make worthwhile reading, as they record the company's success, speculate on its future, and include specimens of Land's unmistakable prose. Lately Polaroid cameras, film, and pictures have resurfaced as cult favorites in the market, as well as in magazine and newspaper stories.

The increasing centrality of the Internet has brought attention to the relationship between technology and pornography. See, for example, Frederick E. Allen, "When Sex Drives Technological Innovation," *American Heritage* (September, 2000): 19–20; Jonathan Coopersmith, "The Role of the Technology Industry in the Development of Videotape and the Internet," in *Women and Technology: Historical, Societal, and Professional* Perspectives (New Brunswick, N.J., 1990), and Coopersmith, "Pornography, Technology, and Progress," *ICON* 4 (1998): 94–125.

A career as spectacular as Steve Jobs's has naturally generated a lot of literature, in both articles and books. Among the 20-plus books, most paraphrase prior works extensively but tell surprisingly little about their notoriously prickly subject. Michael Moritz, *The Little Kingdom: The Private Story of Apple Computer* (New York, 1984) benefited from the author's access to Jobs in the early 1980s, after which the great man essentially shut the door to reporters. Nevertheless, Moritz published an update: *Return to the Little Kingdom: Steve Jobs and the Creation of Apple* (New York, 2009). Best of the rest include two from Steven Levy: *Insanely Great* (New York, 2000) about the Macintosh; and *The Perfect Thing* (New York, 2006) about the iPod. A better book than any of these, Frank Rose's *West of Eden* (New York, 1989), chronicles the troubled years when Jobs lost and regained his company.

CHAPTER 11: AND SO IT GOES . . . BURGERS, BARGAINS, AND BYTES

Here we enter the realm of "contemporary history," sparse in terms of scholarly works and thus requiring judicious use of sources reeking with one kind of bias and another. Articles on Kroc, Walton, Dell, and the businesses they founded appear in an unbroken stream in both traditional sources such as newspapers and magazines (*Wall Street Journal* and *Fortune,* to name only two salient examples) and in "modern" ones such as websites and blogs. Inserting any of the names, corporate or individual, into any search engine produces a multitude of sites, including those constructed by the corporations themselves, as well as by their critics. All these need applications of salt as generous as those McDonald's uses on its food. Moreover, each of these men had (or thought he had) plenty to say and could hire hacks to help him say it. The resulting autobiographical works fall in the American tradition of self-constructed tycoon hagiography that goes back at least as far as Carnegie and perhaps to Benjamin Franklin.

For franchising generally, see Thomas S. Dicke, *Franchising in America: The Development of a Business Method, 1840–1980* (Chapel Hill, N.C., 1992), and Peter M. Birkeland, *Franchising Dreams: The Lure of Entrepreneurship in America* (Chicago, Ill., 2002). On McDonald's specifically: Ray Kroc (with Robert Anderson) ginned out *Grinding It Out: The Making of McDonald's* (Chicago, Ill., 1977), a tome no more self-serving than most such and at least well written, with an occasional touch of humor. John Love, *McDonald's: Behind the Arches* (New York, 1986), slathers Kroc and McDonald's with admiration but does include some useful facts and chronologies. James L. Watson, ed., *Golden Arches East: McDonald's in East Asia* (Stansford, 2006) offers an anthropological analysis of McDonald's entry into Asian markets. Detractors abound, of course, including Joe L. Kincheloe, *The Sign of the Burger: McDonald's and the Culture of Power* (Philadelphia, Penn., 2002), and Jennifer Parker Talwar, *Fast Food, Fast Track: Immigrants, Big Business, and the American Dream* (Boulder, Colo., 2004).

On Walmart: Sam himself (with John Huey) gave us *Sam Walton, Made in America: My Story* (New York, 1992), as stuffed with self-righteous bombast, hooey, and dubious history as Kroc's tale, but lacking Kroc's welcome dabs of comic relief. Sandra S. Vance and Roy V. Scott's *Wal*Mart: A History of Sam Walton's Retail Phenomenon* (New York, 1994), presents an exception to the rule by providing a balanced, scholarly account through the early 1990s. Robert Slater's *The Wal-Mart Triumph* (New York, 2003) also appeared as *The Wal-Mart Decade* and offers little whatever the title.

What one might call the "Walmart effect" has generated growing interest among scholars. Thus we have Shane Hamilton, *Trucking Country: The Road to America's Wal-Mart Economy* (Princeton, N.J., 2008), a book not about Walmart, but about the cultural context in which it prospered; Bethany Moreton, *To Serve God and Wal-Mart: The Making of Christian Free Enterprise* (Cambridge, Mass., 2009) usefully connects various symbiotic phenomena to explain Walmart's success.

The vast corpus of literature on the computer and all that it entails grows apace. Good starting points include Kenneth Flamm, *Creating the Computer: Government, Industry, and High Technology* (Washington, D.C., 1988), which documents government's crucial role; James W. Cortada, *The Digital Hand,* 3 vols. (New York, 2003, 2005, 2007), details the computer's impact on business and government; Alfred D. Chandler Jr., *Inventing the Electronic Century: The Epic Story of the Consumer Electronics and Computer Industries* (New York, 2001), tells the story in the context of the interplay between American and Japanese electronics firms. A lively, highly readable account of the transpacific technological competition appears in Bob Johnstone, *We Were Burning: Japanese Entrepreneurs and the Forging of the Electronic Age* (New York, 1999).

On Dell: Michael Dell (with Catherine Fredman) explains his success in *Direct from Dell: Strategies That Revolutionized an Industry* (New York, 1992). Dell evinces more modesty and a greater willingness to credit others than either Kroc or Walton. As ongoing head of the firm, Michael Dell attracts constant journalistic attention. Among the most perceptive is Andy Serwer, "Dell's Midlife Crisis," *Fortune*, November 28, 2005, 147–52, which foresaw rough seas ahead.

CHAPTER 12: OF THINGS PAST AND THINGS TO COME

The White quotations are from Theodore H. White, *In Search of History* (New York, 1978); Eric Sevareid's from *Not So Wild a Dream* (New York, 1976).

Credits

Photo Credits

Chapter 1: *p.4:* Daniel J. Gelo; *p.5:* National Archives[557189]; Edward S. Curtis/Library of Congress Prints and Photographs Division[LC-USZ62-90821]; *p.6:* Roger Coulam/Alamy; *p.8:* David Hiser/Stone/Getty Images

Chapter 2: p.17: Bettman/Corbis

Chapter 3: p.39: Bettman/Corbis

Chapter 4: p.60: The Library of Congress

Chapter 5: p.86: Library of Congress; p.101: Library of Congress

Chapter 6: p.107: Ford Archives/Henry Ford Museum/Dearborn, MI; p.117: Ford Archives/Henry Ford Museum/Dearborn, MI

Chapter 7: p.123: Courtesy of Hagley Museum and Library

Chapter 8: p.142: Hulton-Deutsch Collection/CORBIS

Chapter 9: p.160: Ford Archives/Henry Ford Museum/Dearborn, MI; p.170: AP Photo

Chapter 10: p.176: Library of Congress

Chapter 11: p.192: Reuters/CORBIS; p.205: Eli Reichman//Time Life Pictures/Getty Images; p.213: Gianni Giansanti/Sygma/Corbis

Text Credits

Chapter 4: Lyrics; Mamas, don't let your babies grow up to be cowboys, by Ed & Patsy Bruce, Sony/ATV Music Publishing LLC.

Chapter 5: Poem by William B. Yeats; The Glassy Switch, Newsweek.

Chapter 7: Excerpt from Pierre S. Du Pont and the making of the Modern Corporation (NY: Harper and Row, 1971) by Alfred D. Chandler; Stephen Salsbury, Wolters Kluwer.

Chapter 8: Excerpt from Alfred P. Sloan, My years with General Motors. Edited by John McDonald, with Catharine Stevens. (Garden City, N.Y.: Doubleday, 1964 [c1963]), Harold Matson Company; GM Heritage Center biography of Delorean, by GM Heritage Center.

Chapter 9: Walt Kelly cartoon quote from Albert the Alligator, Okefenokee Glee and Perloo, Inc ; Pogo Possum cartoon quote, Okefenokee Glee and Perloo, Inc.; Henry Ford II quote by Alan Nevins, Simon & Schuster, Inc.; Ernest Breech quote by Mel J. Hickerson, Meredith Books; Henry Ford II quote by Alan Nevins, Simon & Schuster, Inc.; Henry Ford II by Allan Nevins, Columbia University Trust Administrator.

Chapter 10: Simon & Schuster, Inc. by Mark Olshakerv, Rowman & Littlefield Publishers, Inc.; New York Times quote by Mark Olshaker, Rowman & Littlefield Publishers, Inc.; New York Times quote by Mark Olshaker, Rowman &

Littlefield Publishers, Inc.; Edwin Land quotes by Mark Olshaker, Rowman & Littlefield Publishers, Inc.

Chapter 11: Henry Ford II quote by Mira Wilkins; Frank E. Hill, Cambridge University Press; Michael Dell/Catherine Friedman quotes by Michael Dell; Catherine Friedman, Wolters Kluwer; Poem: Wolters Kluwer by William B. Yeats.

Chapter 12: Eric Sevareid quote, Don Congdon Associates; Theodore H. White quote, Wolters Kluwer.

INDEX